Haven of Liberty

New York Jews in the
New World, 1654–1865

CITY OF PROMISES was made possible in part through the generosity of a number of individuals and foundations. Their thoughtful support will help ensure that this work is affordable to schools, libraries, and other not-for-profit institutions.

The Lucius N. Littauer Foundation made a leadership gift before a word of CITY OF PROMISES had been written, a gift that set this project on its way. Hugo Barreca, The Marian B. and Jacob K. Javits Foundation, Mr. and Mrs. Peter Malkin, David P. Solomon, and a donor who wishes to remain anonymous helped ensure that it never lost momentum. We are deeply grateful.

CITY OF PROMISES

A HISTORY OF THE JEWS OF NEW YORK

GENERAL EDITOR: DEBORAH DASH MOORE

VOLUME 1

Haven of Liberty

New York Jews in the
New World, 1654–1865

HOWARD B. ROCK

VOLUME 2

Emerging Metropolis

New York Jews in the
Age of Immigration, 1840–1920

ANNIE POLLAND AND

DANIEL SOYER

VOLUME 3

Jews in Gotham

New York Jews in a
Changing City, 1920–2010

JEFFREY S. GUROCK

CITY OF PROMISES

A HISTORY OF THE JEWS OF NEW YORK

HAVEN OF

LIBERTY

NEW YORK JEWS IN THE NEW WORLD, 1654–1865

HOWARD B. ROCK

WITH A FOREWORD BY

DEBORAH DASH MOORE

AND WITH A VISUAL ESSAY BY

DIANA L. LINDEN

NEW YORK UNIVERSITY PRESS ■ NEW YORK AND LONDON

NEW YORK UNIVERSITY PRESS
New York and London
www.nyupress.org

References to Internet websites (URLs) were accurate at the time of writing.
Neither the author nor New York University Press is responsible for URLs that
may have expired or changed since the manuscript was prepared.

Library of Congress Cataloging-in-Publication Data
City of promises : a history of the Jews of New York / general editor, Deborah Dash Moore.
v.   cm.
Includes bibliographical references and index.
Contents: v. 1. Haven of liberty: New York Jews in the New World, 1654–1865 / Howard B.
Rock — v. 2. Emerging metropolis: New York Jews in the age of immigration, 1840–1920 /
Annie Polland and Daniel Soyer — v. 3. Jews in Gotham: New York Jews in a changing city,
1920–2010.
ISBN 978-0-8147-7632-2 (cl : alk. paper) — ISBN 978-0-8147-4521-2 (ebook) —
ISBN 978-0-8147-7692-6 (ebook) — ISBN 978-0-8147-1731-8 (boxed set : alk. paper) —
ISBN 978-0-8147-2932-8 (e-set)
1. Jews—New York (State)—New York. 2. New York (N.Y.)—Ethnic relations.   I. Moore,
Deborah Dash, 1946– II. Rock, Howard B., 1944–
F128.9.J5C64 2012
305.892'40747—dc23   2012003246

New York University Press books are printed on acid-free paper,
and their binding materials are chosen for strength and durability.
We strive to use environmentally responsible suppliers and materials
to the greatest extent possible in publishing our books.

Manufactured in the United States of America

10   9   8   7   6   5   4   3   2   1

For my sisters, Elaine Gluck and Marcia Rock,
Who through the years have given me so much
    love and support
And for my grandson,
Caleb Joseph Rock,
May he find a life of peace and fulfillment

CONTENTS

"[O]f all the big cities," Sergeant Milton Lehman of the *Stars and Stripes* affirmed in 1945, "New York is still the promised land."[1] As a returning Jewish GI, Lehman compared New York with European cities. Other Jews also knew what New York offered that made it so desirable, even if they had not served overseas. First and foremost, security: Jews could live without fear in New York. Yes, they faced discrimination, but in this city of almost eight million residents, many members of its ethnic and religious groups encountered prejudice. Jews contended with anti-Semitism in the twentieth century more than German Protestants or Irish Catholics dealt with bias, perhaps; but the Irish had endured a lot in the nineteenth century, and Jews suffered less than African Americans, Latinos, and Asian New Yorkers. And New York provided more than security: Jews could live freely as Jews. The presence of a diverse population of close to two million New York Jews contributed to their sense that "everyone was Jewish."[2] New York Jews understood that there were many ways to be Jewish. The city welcomed Jews in all their variety. New York Jews saw the city as a place where they, too, could flourish and express themselves. As a result, they came to identify with the city, absorbing its ethos even as they helped to shape its urban characteristics. When World War II ended in Europe with victory over Nazi Germany, New York's promises glowed more brightly still.

New York's multiethnic diversity, shaped in vital dimensions by its large Jewish population, shimmered as a showplace of American democratic distinctiveness, especially vis-à-vis Europe. In contrast to a continent that had become a vast slaughterhouse, where millions of European Jews had been ruthlessly murdered with industrial efficiency, New York glistened as a city Jews could and did call their home in America. The famous skyline had defined urban cosmopolitanism in the years after World War I. Now the city's thriving ethnic neighborhoods—Jewish and Catholic, African American and Puerto Rican, Italian and Irish—came to represent modern urban culture. New York's economy responded robustly to demands of war production. By the end of hostilities, its per capita income exceeded the national average by 14 percent.

But as a poster city for immigration, with a majority population composed of immigrants and their children, the city had to contend with negative perceptions. Considered undesirable by many Americans, Jews and other foreigners in the city contributed to impressions that New York seemed less American than other cities with large percentages of native-born residents.[3]

As the city flourished during and after the war, it maintained its political commitments to generous social welfare benefits to help its poorest residents. Jews advocated for these policies, supporting efforts to establish a liberal urban legacy. In modeling a progressive and prosperous multiethnic twentieth-century American city, New York demonstrated what its Jews valued. Versions of Jewish urbanism played not just on the political stage but also on the streets of the city's neighborhoods. Its expressions could be found as well in New York's centers of cultural production.

By the middle of the twentieth century, no city offered Jews more than New York. It nourished both celebration and critique. New York gave Jews visibility as individuals and as a group. It provided employment and education, inspiration and freedom, fellowship and community. Jews reciprocated by falling in love with the city, its buildings' hard angles and perspectives, its grimy streets and harried pace. But by the 1960s and '70s, Jews' love affair with the city soured. For many of the second generation who grew up on New York's sidewalks, immersed in its babel of languages and cultural syncretism, prosperity dimmed their affection for the working-class urban world of their youth. Many of them aspired to suburban pleasures of home ownership, grass and trees that did not have to be shared with others in public parks. Yet New York City remained the wellspring of Jewish American culture for much of the century, a resource of Jewishness even for those living thousands of miles west of the Hudson River.

Jews had not always felt free to imagine the city as their special place. Indeed, not until mass immigration from Europe piled up their numbers, from the tens of thousands to the hundreds of thousands, had Jews laid claim to New York and influenced its politics and culture. Its Jewish population soared from five hundred thousand at the turn of the twentieth century to 1.1 million before the start of World War I. On the eve of World War II, Jews, over a quarter of New York's residents, ranked as the largest ethnic group.[4] Demography both encouraged many outsiders to perceive New York as a Jewish city and underwrote local cultural productions, such as a thriving theater scene, a flourishing popular music business, and extensive publishing in several languages. Jews were used to living as a minority in Europe and the Middle East. New York offered life without a majority population—without one single ethnic group dominating urban society. Now Jews could go about their business, much of it taking place within ethnic niches, as if they were the city's predominant group.

When and in what sense did New York become a city of promises for Jews? Certainly not in the colonial era. During that period, seeds for future promises were planted, most importantly political, economic, and religious rights. While New York's few hundred Jews lived in the shadow of far more prosperous Jewish communities in London and Amsterdam, New York Jewish men enjoyed citizenship rights and responsibilities that their peers in London could only envy. These rights gradually led New York Jews to emerge from a closed synagogue society and to participate with enthusiasm in revolutionary currents sweeping the colonies. Jews in New York absorbed formative ideas regarding human rights; they tasted freedom and put their lives on the line for it during the Revolution. In the decades that followed, they incorporated ideals of the American Enlightenment into their Jewish lives.

Sometime during the nineteenth century, these changes attracted increasing attention from European Jews. New York began to acquire a reputation as a destination in itself. Arriving from Europe at Castle Garden, increasing numbers of Jewish immigrants decided to stay. New York's bustling streets enticed them, so they put off riding west or south to peddle or settle. Sometimes, older brothers made that choice, as did Jonas and Louis Strauss, who sent their younger brother Levi to the West Coast via steamship in 1853 to open a branch of their New York City dry-goods firm. Levi Strauss did better, perhaps, than they expected when he went into manufacturing copper-riveted denim work pants after the Civil War.[5] But such a move into garment manufacturing from selling dry goods and, especially, used clothing had already taken root in New York prior to the war. It formed the basis of an industry that became the city's largest, and more than any other, it made New York the city of promises.

In 1962, the historian Moses Rischin published his pioneering book, *The Promised City: New York's Jews, 1870–1914*. Rischin aimed to "identify those currents of human and institutional vitality central to the American urban experience that converged on the Lower East Side in the era of the great Jewish migration just as New York emerged as the nation's and the world's most dynamic metropolis."[6] The interlocking themes of Jewish immigration from eastern Europe and the rise of New York as a "city of ambition" led Rischin to cast his account as a "revolutionary transformation" not only in American urban history but also in Jewish history.[7] Rischin saw a universal paradigm of modernization unfolding in the very particularistic experiences of New York Jews. His vision of democratic urban community remains relevant to contemporary scholars.

What did the city promise? First, a job. Close to half of all immigrants sewed clothing in hundreds of small-scale sweatshops that disguised an ever-burgeoning industry that soon became one of the nation's most important. Second, a place to live. True, the overcrowded Lower East Side bulged with residents, even its modern tenements straining to accommodate a density of Jewish population that rivaled Bombay. Yet by the early twentieth century, bridges to Brooklyn and rapid transit to Harlem and the Bronx promised improvements: fresh air, hot and cold running water, even a private toilet and bathroom. Third, food. Jewish immigrants had not starved in Europe, but New York's abundance changed their diets and attitudes toward food and its simple pleasures. In New York, a center of the nation's baking industry, Jews could enjoy a fresh roll and coffee each morning for pennies. Fourth, clothing. It did not take long, especially laboring in the garment industry, for Jews to trade their old-world clothes for the latest ready-made styles. Thus properly attired, they looked and felt like modern men and women, able and willing to make their way.[8]

Such promises might be quotidian, but they opened Jews' eyes to other more important ones. Young Jewish immigrants embraced the city's promise of free public education, from elementary school to secondary school, all the way through college. Only a handful of Jewish immigrants in the nineteenth century and years before World War I ever managed to take advantage of such a magnificent offer. Although a family economy that privileged sons over daughters when decisions about post-elementary education had to be made and costs of forgoing income from teenaged children often required Jews to go to work and not attend school, increasingly Jews flocked to the city's free schools. Some immigrants, especially women, thought the city promised freedom to choose a spouse, though matchmakers also migrated across the ocean. Still others rejoiced in what they imagined was a promise of uncensored language: written and spoken, published and on stage, in Yiddish, Hebrew,

German, Ladino, and English. Some conceived of the city's rough democracy as holding a promise of solidarity among working men and women, while a significant number demanded extension of civil and voting rights to women.

Then there were more ambiguous promises. Did New York offer Jews a chance to live without a formal, legally constituted Jewish community? Did it suggest that Jews no longer needed to practice Jewish rituals or observe the Sabbath? Some Jewish immigrants thought they could leave behind old-world ways of thinking and acting; they secularized their Jewish lives, often starting the process in Europe even before they emigrated. Others fashioned ways of being Jewish, both secular and religious, in tune with New York's evolving cultures. Both groups identified their own visions of what it meant to be Jewish in America with New York itself.

That New York City bloomed with such promises would have been hard to anticipate in 1654. Then the ragged seaport only reluctantly welcomed its first contingent of miserable Jewish migrants. In fact, not receiving permission to settle, Jews had to petition to stay, to live and work in the outpost. They agreed to practice their religion in private even as they participated in civic culture. When the British turned New Amsterdam into New York, they accepted these arrangements, giving Jews unprecedented legal rights. Here lay hints of future promises. Gradually the British increased opportunities for public religious expression and extended to Jewish men civil rights, including citizenship, the right to vote, and the right to hold office. When Jews founded their first congregation, they called it Shearith Israel (Remnant of Israel), an apt name for the handful living in a colonial town far from European centers of Jewish life. Yet during the eighteenth century, Jews integrated into the fabric of New York life. They faced challenges of identifying as Jews within a free society. As the first to enjoy such political freedoms, they struggled to balance assimilation with Jewish distinctiveness. By the time of the Revolution, many New York Jews felt deeply connected to their city and fellow American patriots, enough to flee the British occupation for Philadelphia. The end of the war marked a new democratic consciousness among New York Jews who returned to rebuild their city and community.

A democratic ethos pervaded Jewish urban life in the new republic, opening possibilities for individual and collective ambition as well as cooperation. This republicanism changed how Jews organized themselves religiously and how they imagined their opportunities. Shearith Israel incorporated and drafted its own constitution, modeled on the federal example. Republicanism animated women, inspiring them to establish charities to help succor the poor. Once Jewish immigration brought sufficient ethnic and economic diversity to New York in the 1830s and 1840s, Jews started to build a different type of community. They forged bonds based on intimacy, gender, shared backgrounds, common aspirations, and urgent necessities. Jewish religious life became increasingly diverse, competitive, and strident. Democracy without an established religion fostered creativity and experimentation. Congregations multiplied in the city, but most Jews chose not to join one, despite variety ranging from Orthodox to Reform. The city saw a fierce battle between proponents of orthodoxy and advocates of reform. These debates engaged Jews deeply but did not lead the majority to affiliate. Still, increasingly synagogue buildings formed part of the cityscape, an indication of Jewish presence. Democratic freedoms permitted a new type of urban Jewish life to emerge. Lacking formal communal structures, Jews innovated and turned to other forms of organization as alternatives. They established fraternal orders and literary societies, seeking a means to craft connections in a rapidly growing and bewildering city. Yet soon they multiplied these activities as well. Pleas for charity and education, hospitals and libraries, mobilized Jewish New Yorkers.

With the extension of the franchise, more Jewish men acquired the right to vote, irrespective of their economic situation, encouraging them to enter political debates with enthusiasm. They paid attention to events overseas affecting fellow Jews, especially examples of anti-Semitism, and tried to convince the president to help. New York Jews mastered the arts of petition and protest. They took sides as individuals in election cycles, first between Federalists and Jeffersonians, later between Democrats and Whigs, and finally between Democrats and Republicans. Domestic issues divided Jews; even the question of slavery found supporters and opponents. Rabbis debated the subject in pulpit and press until the Civil War ended their polemics and both sides rallied to the Union cause. Politics necessarily pushed Jews into public consciousness; non-Jews noticed them. Prejudice began to appear in social life, and stereotypes started to circulate in the press. Yet Jewish New Yorkers were hardly the retiring sort, and many gave as good as they got.

Jewish immigrants readily found employment, entering the city's expanding economic marketplace as they carefully tested its promises of personal fulfillment. Although the Panics of 1857 and 1873 threw thousands out of work, during normal times, Jews coped with capitalist volatilities. Many gravitated to small-scale commerce and craft production. Men and women both worked and drew on family resources, especially the labor of their children, to help make ends meet. Jews saved regularly to withstand seasonal swings in employment. Within the city's diversifying economy, they located ethnic niches that became occupational ladders of advancement for many. Some of the merchants trading in old clothes around Chatham Street initiated manufacturing of cheap goods. A garment industry took shape; it received a big boost with demand for uniforms in the Civil War. As the industry grew, its need for workers increased steadily, employing an ever-greater proportion of Jewish immigrants to the city. Small shops and a competitive contracting system continued to dominate the industry. Despite miserable conditions, the system tempted many workers with a promise of self-employment. Taking a risk, some immigrants borrowed money, often from relatives and fellow immigrants from the same European town, to supplement meager savings. Then they plunged into contracting, trying with a new design idea to secure prosperity. As often as not, they failed, falling back into the laboring class. But success stories trumped failures; they stood as reminders that the city had fulfilled its promise.

Merchants and peddlers, who occupied another popular Jewish economic niche, viewed the rise of department stores as an urban achievement. These commercial emporiums proffered a magical array of goods under one roof and represented the pinnacle of success for local hardware-store owners or dry-goods shopkeepers. Retail establishments proliferated around the city as it grew; Jewish entrepreneurship flourished on local shopping streets in the Bronx and Brooklyn. Pitkin Avenue in Brownsville and Fordham Road in the Bronx could not rival Manhattan's Fifth Avenue or even Fourteenth Street. But they provided a measure of prosperity and independence to Jewish merchants, enough so that they could enjoy some of the perquisites of middle-class living, such as sending one's sons and even one's daughters to high school and college. Mobility came in many forms, and often immigrant Jews achieved economic and social mobility first through business and then through education.

New York's explosive growth at the turn of the twentieth century produced radical social movements based on class struggle and politics. For many Jewish immigrants, becoming a small manufacturer paled beside a larger vision of a just society, one without workers living in overcrowded, filthy tenements, exposed to disease, and wracked by despair. Hedging their bets, they dreamed of becoming capitalists even as they sought in socialism better living conditions, fair wages, and reasonable working hours. Socialism as a utopian ideal promised equality, an economic system that took from each according to his or her ability and returned to everybody whatever he or she needed. Even some Jewish capitalists subscribed to such an ideal. But on a pragmatic level, socialism appealed to Jewish workers for its alternatives to unrestrained capitalist exploitation. Paths to socialism led through union organizing, the polling booth, fraternalism, and even cooperative housing. Jewish immigrants embraced them all. They forged vibrant garment-workers unions, as well as unions of bakers and plumbers, teachers and pharmacists. They voted for Socialist candidates, sending Meyer London in 1914 to represent the Lower East Side in Congress. They organized the Workmen's Circle, initially in 1892 as a mutual-aid society and then in 1900 as a multibranch fraternal order in which they could socialize with fellow workers and receive health and social welfare benefits not provided by a wealthy but stingy city government. And after World War I ended, New York Jews pushed for legislation that would allow them to build cooperative housing projects, so that they could enjoy living in decent apartments together with other Jewish workers. These examples of democratic community radically reshaped the city and contributed to its progressive commitments even as Jewish struggles for social justice empowered them both individually and as a group.

For several centuries, until the beginning of the twentieth, most New York Jews lived in Lower Manhattan, with smaller numbers residing in Williamsburg and Bedford, in the city of Brooklyn. The consolidation of New York with Brooklyn and the creation of a city of five boroughs, including the Bronx, Queens, and Staten Island, stimulated construction of subways and bridges which expanded opportunities for Jewish immigrants to leave the constricted quarters of the Lower East Side. Once they started to move, only the Great Depression, discrimination, and wartime constraints made Jews pause. New neighborhoods held out hopes of fresh beginnings. Adjusting to the strangeness of a neighborhood invited ways to reimagine one's relationship to New York City. Jews adopted different perspectives on themselves and their city as they exchanged views out kitchen windows. Modern tenements, with steam heat, hot and cold running water in the kitchen sink, and an icebox, proclaimed a sense of accomplishment worth the pain of dislocation produced by immigration. Modern apartment buildings with parquet floors, windows in every room, and the latest conveniences announced a form of success. It did not matter that these apartments were rented; home ownership did not rank high on Jewish New Yorkers' requirements for either the good life or economic security—better to be able to catch the express train and in ten minutes travel two stops on the subway to reach the Midtown garment district than to own a house in the suburbs with a commute of an hour to work each day. And renting let Jews move as their finances fluctuated, freeing funds for other purposes.

New York Jews committed themselves to a wide array of neighborhoods, reflecting different desires. Did one wish for a neighborhood filled with modern synagogues and kosher butcher shops, bakeries, and delicatessens? There was a range of choices based on how much rent one was willing to pay. Did one seek a lively center of radicalism where socialism was considered "right wing" in comparison to "left wing" communism, an area filled with union activities, cultural events, and places to debate politics? A slightly narrower number of neighborhoods fit the bill. Did one yearn to speak Yiddish or German or Ladino or Russian, to find traces of the old home in familiar styles of shopping and praying? Neighborhoods, not just a block or two but a cluster of them, catered to those who yearned for what they had left behind in Europe or the Middle East. Did one seek a yeshiva for sons and eventually for daughters, as well as intimate congregations for daily study and prayer? New York made room for these as well. In all of them, Jews had neighbors who were not Jewish, but that mattered less than the neighbors who were Jewish. Jews lived next door to other white ethnics, as well as to African Americans, and, after World War II, Puerto Ricans. While most Jews tolerated their non-Jewish neighbors, economic competition, national and international politics, and religious prejudice ignited conflict. An uneasy coexistence among neighbors characterized many New York neighborhoods. Despite this diversity of residential neighborhoods, Jews stayed in an area usually only for a generation. New neighborhoods beckoned constantly; children moved away from parents; parents lost money or made money. Primarily renters, unlike other groups, Jews did not remain committed for long to a neighborhood. They were ready to move elsewhere in the city, to try something different. Such was New York's promise of community for Jews.

New York Jews began to leave their city in the 1960s, a process that continued for the rest of the century. The largest decline in Jewish population occurred in the 1970s when the city's fiscal crisis arrived, just in time to welcome

Abe Beame, New York's first Jewish mayor. As Jews departed, African Americans and Puerto Ricans moved into the city in ever-greater numbers. By the mid-1950s, a million African Americans lived in New York. After liberalization of immigration laws in 1965, an increasingly diverse array of immigrants from Asia, especially China, and also from the Caribbean, Latin America, and Africa arrived in New York. Jewish immigrants figured among them, most prominently from the Soviet Union; these new immigrants brought some of the same drive and energy that had made New York a city of promises a hundred years earlier.

At the start of the twenty-first century, New York still lacked a majority population. In contemporary ethnic calculus, Jews made up a significant percentage of white New Yorkers. But whites constituted a minority in the city, hence Jews' overall percentage of the population declined. Most Jews were college educated; many had advanced degrees. Having overcome occupational discrimination that endured into the 1960s, Jews held jobs in real estate, finance, publishing, education, law, and medicine in this postindustrial city. They still congregated in neighborhoods, but Queens attracted more Jews than the Bronx did. They still worked in commerce, usually as managers of large stores rather than as owners of small ones. New York Jews still debated how to observe Jewish rituals and holidays. Most declined to join a congregation, yet many retained a consciousness of being Jewish. Often awareness of Jewish differences grew out of family bonds; for some, their sense of Jewishness flowed from work or neighborhood or culture or politics. A visible minority rigorously observed the strictures of Judaism, and their presence gave other Jews a kind of yardstick by which to judge themselves. Despite Jews' greatly reduced numbers, the city still honored Jewish holy days by adjusting its mundane rhythms. New York Jews knew they lived in American Jews' capital city; the cluster of national Jewish organizations announced this fact. These organizations, able to mobilize effective protests or to advocate for a cause, focused on problems facing Jews throughout the world. Jewish cultural creativity also endured along with effervescent, experimental, multiethnic commitments to new forms of democratic urban community.

City of Promises portrays the history of Jews in New York City from 1654 to the present. Its three volumes articulate perspectives of four historians. In the first volume, Howard Rock argues that the first two centuries of Jewish presence in the city proved critical to the development of New York Jews. He sees an influential template in communal structures created by colonial Jews and elaborated in the nineteenth century by Jewish immigrants from central Europe. Rock emphasizes the political freedom and economic strength of colonial and republican Jews in New York. He shows that democratic religious and ethnic community represented an unusual experiment for Jews. Using American political models, Jews in New York innovated. They developed an expansive role for an English-language Jewish press as a vehicle for collective consciousness; they introduced fraternal societies that secularized religious fellowship; they crafted independent philanthropic organizations along gendered lines; they discussed the pros and cons of reforming Judaism; and they passionately debated politics. They were the first American Jews to demonstrate how political and economic freedoms were integral to Jewish communal life. Although many of them arrived as immigrants themselves, they also pointed a path for future migrants who confronted the city's intoxicating and bewildering modern world. In so doing, these eighteenth- and early nineteenth-century Jews laid the foundations for the development of a robust American Jewish community in New York.

In the second volume, Annie Polland and Daniel Soyer describe the process by which New York emerged as a Jewish city, produced by a century of mass migration of Jews from central and eastern Europe as well as from the Middle East. Focusing on the urban Jewish built environment—its tenements and banks, its communal buildings and synagogues, its department stores and settlement houses—the authors convey the extraordinary complexity of Jewish immigrant society in New York. The theme of urban community runs like a thread through a century of mass migration beginning in 1840. Polland and Soyer revise classic accounts of immigration, paying attention to Jewish interactions in economic, social, religious, and cultural activities. Jews repeatedly seek to repair fissures in their individual and collective lives caused by dislocation. Their efforts to build connections through family and neighborhood networks across barriers of class and gender generated a staggering array of ethnic organizations, philanthropic initiatives, and political and religious movements. Despite enormous hardship and repeated failures, Jewish immigrants in New York developed sufficient institutional resilience to articulate a political vision of social solidarity and reform. New York Jews also stepped forward into national leadership positions by establishing organizations that effectively rallied American Jews on behalf of those still suffering in Europe.

New York City became the capital of American Jews in these years and the largest Jewish city in history.

In telling the story of twentieth-century New York Jews in the third volume of the series, Jeffrey S. Gurock looks to the neighborhood, the locale of community and the place where most Jews lived their lives. Jews liked their local community and appreciated its familiar warmth. But New York Jews also faced demands for political action on behalf of a transnational Jewish world. During the crucial decade from 1938 to 1948, New York Jews debated what course of action they should take. How should they balance domestic needs with those of European Jews? World War II and the Holocaust demonstrated the contrasts between Jews in New York and Jews in Europe. Gurock shows how Jewish neighborhoods spread across the boroughs. He describes Jewish settlement in Queens after World War II, illuminating processes of urban change. Ethnic-group conflict and racial antagonism left deep scars despite efforts to overcome prejudice and discrimination. New York Jews were found on both sides of the barricades; each decade produced a fresh conflagration. Yet Jewish New Yorkers never ceased to lead movements for social change, supporting women's rights as well as freedom for Soviet Jewry. New York City retained its preeminence as the capital of American Jews because of deep roots in local worlds. These urban neighborhoods, Gurock argues, nourish creative and unselfconscious forms of Jewishness.

Each volume contains a visual essay by art historian Diana L. Linden. These essays interpret Jewish experiences. Linden examines diverse objects, images, and artifacts. She suggests alternative narratives drawn from a record of cultural production. Artists and craftspeople, ordinary citizens and commercial firms provide multiple perspectives on the history of Jews in New York. Her view runs as a counterpoint and complement to the historical accounts. Each visual presentation can be read separately or in conjunction with the history. The combination of historical analysis and visual representation enriches the story of Jews in New York City. In the first essay, Linden emphasizes the foreignness and loneliness of being Jewish in the colonial and republican periods, even as Jews integrated themselves into Christian society. They were the first to create a new identity as "American Jews." The second visual essay chronicles the challenges of navigating a rapidly expanding city. It explores contrasts of rich and poor. Jews in immigrant New York fashioned new charitable, educational, and cultural institutions as they established the city as the capital of the

American Jewish world. The third visual essay takes as its theme New York Jews in popular American imagination. It presents many meanings and identities of "New York Jew" over the course of the twentieth century and the beginning years of the twenty-first century.

These different viewpoints on Jews in New York City situate their history within intersecting themes of urban growth, international migration, political change, economic mobility, religious innovation, organizational complexity, cultural creativity, and democratic community. Jews participated in building the Empire City by casting their lot with urbanism, even as they struggled to make New York a better place to live, work, and raise a family. Their aspirations changed New York and helped to transform it into a city of promises, some fulfilled, some pending, some beckoning new generations.

DEBORAH DASH MOORE

GENERAL EDITOR'S ACKNOWLEDGMENTS

All books are collaborative projects, but perhaps none more than this three-volume history of Jews in New York City. The eminent historians directly involved in the project, Jeffrey S. Gurock, Annie Polland, Howard Rock, Daniel Soyer, and art historian Diana L. Linden, have devoted their considerable skills not only to their own volumes but also to evaluating and enhancing each other's work. Editorial board members helped to guide the project and served as crucial resources. City of Promises began during my term as Chair of the Academic Council of the American Jewish Historical Society, and I owe a debt of gratitude to David P. Solomon for making a match between Jennifer Hammer of New York University Press and the Academic Council.

Good ideas have legs, but they require the devotion and support of influential men and women. City of Promises fortunately found both in William Frost z"l of the Lucius N. Littauer Foundation and Jennifer Hammer of NYU Press. Bill Frost generously underwrote the project when it was just an idea, and I think that he would have treasured this history of a city he loved. Jennifer Hammer worked prodigiously to turn vision into reality, never faltering in her critically engaged commitment despite inevitable obstacles. I am indebted to both of them for staying the course, and I greatly appreciate the opportunity to work with Jennifer, an excellent, flexible, and insightful editor.

City of Promises received additional important financial support from individuals and foundations. I want to thank the Malkin Fund, The Marian B. and Jacob K. Javits Foundation, Hugo Barreca, David P. Solomon, and an anonymous foundation donor for significant support, as well as several other individuals including Judd and Karen Aronowitz, David and Phyllis Grossman, Irving and Phyllis Levitt, Irwin and Debi Ungar, and Rabbi Marc Strauss-Cohen of Temple Emanuel, Winston-Salem, North Carolina. All recognized the importance of this project through timely contributions. I appreciate their generosity.

Several students at the University of Michigan provided assistance that helped to keep the volumes on track. Alexandra Maron and Katherine Rosenblatt did valuable research, and I am grateful for their aid.

These volumes are dedicated to my family of New York Jews. Without their steadfast encouragement, and especially that of my husband, MacDonald Moore, City of Promises would not have appeared.

Dedicated to my grandchildren,
Elijah Axt, Zoe Bella Moore, and Rose Alexa Moore,
authors of future chapters

DEBORAH DASH MOORE

AUTHOR'S ACKNOWLEDGMENTS

One of the pleasurable tasks of writing a book is the opportunity to acknowledge the many people who helped make this volume possible. The College of Arts and Sciences of Florida International University, where I am now Professor Emeritus, and the then chair of the History Department, Mark Szuchman, supported this project, giving me office space and financial assistance. The university's interlibrary loan department was a valuable resource. I wish to thank Clifton Hood, David Cobin, William Pencak, Jonathan Sarna, and Holly Snyder for making their work available to me. My research assistants, Jessica Barrella, Jill Strykowski, and Shoshana Olidort, provided important support and material. Hasia Diner discussed the project with me and read drafts of the first chapters, as did other anonymous readers to whom I am appreciative. Rabbi Emeritus Marc D. Angel most generously made available the invaluable collections of the venerable congregation Shearith Israel. The staff of the American Jewish Archives was very helpful, especially Dana Herman and Camille Servizzi. A few knowledgeable personal friends, notably David and Phyllis Grossman and Ruth Marks, read key chapters, offering useful analysis. I owe much gratitude to Leo Hershkowitz, the dean of early American Jewish history, who kindly read my chapters as they were completed and provided wise advice. Without his pioneering work, this book could not have been written. Deborah Dash Moore, the general editor of this series, also my Brandeis classmate and my coauthor of *Cityscapes*, went over the manuscript with enormous care, asking probing questions that were often difficult to answer but took me to the heart of each issue. Jennifer Hammer of NYU Press too examined every line with meticulous diligence and expertise. Together, Deborah and Jennifer added immeasurably to the merits of this book. Finally, I would like to thank my wife, Ellen, who stuck with me through the long hours I spent on this project, was always supportive, read the chapters with a critical eye, and was there for me when I needed her. Forever grateful.

HOWARD B. ROCK

Haven of Liberty

New York Jews in the
New World, 1654–1865

Introduction

   In the late summer and early fall of 1654, twenty-three Dutch Jews huddled together on the French ship *St. Catrina*, suffering the rolling waves of the North Atlantic while praying that they not fall victim to an early season hurricane. They were one of the last contingents of Dutch Jewish settlers to leave the Dutch colony of Recife, Brazil, following its fall to the Portuguese. But unlike their compatriots, who had chosen to return to the homeland, these souls had decided to venture what wealth they had to remain colonists in still another Dutch outpost, New Amsterdam. Why? Recife had been a good undertaking for Jews, who made up half the population, built two synagogues, and lived a harmonious communal life with their own rabbi. Perhaps New Amsterdam might be the same.

   Little did they know that the new Dutch West India Company outpost they were sailing toward, a small port on the tip of a rustic island filled with Indian trails, was a primitive, often violent colony, known for its tippling and bawdy houses, for its ugly street fights, and for an unstable mixture of men and women from all over Europe. They were unaware that the leader of the colony, the wooden-legged Peter Stuyvesant, was an ardent Dutch Reformed company veteran who, unlike the authorities in Amsterdam, held many traditional anti-Semitic prejudices and had no use for Jews in a colony already overrun with unwanted faiths. And they had no idea—nor, given the harsh welcome they received, would they have believed—that they were among the first Jews in a settlement that was to become America's largest city and to house the world's largest Jewish population. The quest for rights and recognition that their landing began ultimately helped create one of the great cultural and religious centers of Judaism. The story of the journey from these first poor settlers, wondering what kind of dilemma they had created for themselves by taking a different path, to the Jewish communities of twentieth- and twenty-first-century New York is long and diverse, filled with promise and disappointment, resulting in a community that became an important and sometimes a leading part of American society.

In 1945, at the end of World War II, the Jewish Publication Society released Hyman Grinstein's *The Rise of the Jewish Community of New York, 1654–1860*. This pathbreaking study, a volume that focused on the years 1825–1860, was to become a classic. Grinstein mined a dazzling array of sources, from synagogue and benevolent-society minutes written in English, Hebrew, German, and Portuguese to an abundance of printed primary documents, many of which are not available today, to offer the reader a journey into the depths of both synagogues' and communal societies' formation, accomplishments, and divisions.

The book's publication came just as American Jews were struggling to absorb the meaning of the Holocaust. With the tragic destruction of the centers of Jewish life and learning in Europe, the Jewish center of gravity and population shifted to America, and especially to New York City, a metropolis containing two million Jews, by far the largest concentration in the world. Now that America emerged as a focus of a devastated Jewish universe, it was important to study the history of American Judaism, beginning with its origins.

In the effort to recognize the importance of American Jewish history, Grinstein sought to demonstrate that the early decades of American society were critical seedbed years for the far more populous generations to follow. The hundreds of thousands of immigrants who set foot on Ellis Island arrived at a country whose Jewish population had already undergone generations of change—conflict and consensus that established traditions and associations that were part and parcel of American society. Those early transformations of American and Jewish society prepared a template of possibilities for the several million Jewish immigrants who were to make New York a city of promises.

What better place to demonstrate the importance of early American Jewry than New York? New York both as a British colony and as one of the original thirteen states was first to extend political citizenship to its Jewish residents. Its metropolis housed the country's first synagogue. While New York's original Jewish population numbered no more than thirty or forty families, never reaching more than five hundred individuals before 1825, by the 1830s more

Jews lived in New York than any in other American city, a standing New York never surrendered. Whether New York's Israelite community was a few hundred or at forty thousand in 1860, a quarter of all Jews in the republic, it stood at the forefront of every issue facing Jewish America. New York served as the pivotal point in the contest between Reform and Orthodox Jewry in the 1850s. The city's residents founded B'nai B'rith, the first secular Jewish fraternal organization, and built the nation's second Jewish hospital. As New York City became the nation's leading economic and cultural center, it was not surprising to find Jewish financial and industrial leaders or Jewish impresarios in the musical and theatrical life of the metropolis. Jews participated actively in Democratic, Whig, and Republican politics. New York, in sum, became the epicenter of American Jewry. New York Jews' triumphs and problems from the Dutch colonial years through the Civil War shaped what became the most prominent and most powerful Jewish community in the world.

Jews in the early days of New York were very much a part of the fabric of the general society at both a local and national level. They were knowledgeable and, depending on their circumstances, involved in American culture and affairs. Prior to 1870, it thus makes sense to view the Jews of any period through the currents of contemporary American institutions and conflicts. In the early republic, for example, Jews viewed their own lives and institutions through the lens of Jeffersonianism and Hamiltonianism, the two great ideologies competing to become the legacy of the American Revolution.

In antebellum New York, Jews lived in a dynamic society, one that offered both great opportunities and perplexing dilemmas. Achieving Americanization without the loss of a coherent Jewish community and individual Jewish identity, and even surviving in an environment largely void of European persecution and discrimination, posed a difficult problem. A society shaped on the one hand by the American version of the Enlightenment and on the other by potent strains of evangelical Protestantism unleashed by the Second Great Awakening sorely tested the viability of Jewish customs and religion. The emergence of Reform Jewry and the national fraternal society B'nai B'rith were important responses, but when these were placed alongside the Orthodox community and the growing numbers of unaffiliated Jews, a confusing scene emerged. The tension that grew between Sephardic (Jews of Spanish descent) and Ashkenazic (Jews of central and eastern European descent) ethnic groups, among German, Polish, English, and Russian Jewish immigrants and between them and native-born American Jews continually threatened communal fragmentation. Striving for unity amid these centrifugal forces was never an easy task.

As we will see, all of these dilemmas revolved around one overarching theme. What makes these first two centuries so momentous is the synthesis that New York's Jewish citizens achieved between the American republicanism that emerged and matured in the colonial, revolutionary, and early republican eras and flourished in the decades prior to the Civil War and their life as a community, both secular and religious. As perhaps never before in history, Jews engaged in republican movements, including the American Revolution, and then incorporated their ideas and ideals into their way of life. This could be seen in their synagogues' organization, in their enthusiastic participation in politics, in their integration into the life of the new nation, and in their expressions of intense patriotism. It was the republican revolutionary framework that allowed Reform Judaism to grow so quickly in New York in one decade and to flourish in the nation as a whole—unlike in a less hospitable, nonrepublican Europe. Republicanism presented challenges to Jews, particularly the dilemma of how to achieve integration without assimilation. But the republican moment makes these years particularly meaningful. In this era, New York's Jews incorporated American revolutionary ideology into the core of their individual and collective lives. Republicanism formed the seeds of the city of promises.

CHAPTER 1

A Dutch Beginning

Upon viewing Manhattan Island in the early seventeenth century, Dutch poet Jacob Steendam remarked, "This is Eden, where the land floweth with milk and honey." The "sweetness of the Air" transfixed the first explorers, astonished at the freshness and fragrance of the climate and by an island of "hilly, woody Country, full of Lakes and great Vallies." Visitors marveled at vast meadow grass, at fields flush with strawberries, at woods filled with towering trees of walnut, chestnut, maple, and oak, at abundant wildlife as beavers, wolves, and foxes roamed and doves, swans, and blackbirds took flight, and at waterways where whales and porpoises whirled freely while oysters and lobsters flourished. The trails of the Lenapes, a nomadic confederation of Indian tribes, crisscrossed the island, connecting their fields of maize, squash, melons, and tobacco. On the east side, a dangerous estuary flowed into the Atlantic, while on the west side, a wide stream emptied as well into the sea, a river that was to be named after the English explorer Henry Hudson, who sailed the Halve Maen (Half Moon) *into its waters in 1609. Three hundred years later, Steendam's "land of milk and honey" housed the world's largest and most prosperous Jewish urban population. The journey to this new world begins in fifteenth-century Spain and continues into Portugal, Holland, and Brazil before the landing on Manhattan Island in 1654.*[1]

▓ Sephardic Exile and Dutch Welcome

On a sultry early August morning in 1492 at the port of Huelva in southern Spain, Christopher Columbus sailed on the first of three epic voyages. On those same docks, a resident might have viewed hundreds of Spanish Jews, part of the 150,000 expelled from the kingdoms of Aragon and Castile by King

NIEUW AMSTERDAM ofte NUE NIEUW IORX opt TEYLANT MAN

The famed Prototype View of 1664 portrays New Amsterdam as a small Dutch village in 1655. Visible are the fort, church, and city hall (far right). Note the gabled Dutch homes. For the interior layout, see the Castello plan in the "Visual Essay." (Courtesy Museum of the City of New York, Print Archives)

Ferdinand and Queen Isabella. The conjunction of these world-shattering events proved pivotal in Jewish history. The Jews of Spain, known as Sephardic Jews, equipped with mercantile skills and close family networks from centuries of Iberian residency, became significant factors in the new world. As states that became the homes of the exiled Spanish Jews claimed possessions in the new world, the refugees joined colonists risking their fortunes and lives in America, opening a new era for the Jews of Europe.[2]

Jews flourished in Islamic Spain as essential aides to Islamic leadership and commerce. Following the "Reconquista," largely complete by the thirteenth century, Christian rulers welcomed them in similar roles. In Catholic Spain's reorganization and economic growth, they held important administrative positions in government and vigorously pursued international trade. Jewish support enabled the monarchy to grow at the expense of the aristocracy.[3]

Spanish Jewish society was largely autonomous before the expulsion. The Spanish government allowed the Jewish community to have its own councils enforce religious and even civil and criminal law, provided they did not interfere with affairs of state and church. While most Jews were not affluent, the well-educated economic and political elite dominated the councils. Many lived in Spain's grandest villas and produced a rich collection of Judaic law and literature. In the fifteenth century, however, the persecution of Jews, never absent despite their critical contribution to the state, increased, spurred by the inception of the Inquisition in 1478. Over one hundred thousand Jews became *conversos*, converts to Christianity. While a number of Jewish communities, including one in Barcelona, could no longer survive in the Christian world, a significant population persevered, often with the help of Ferdinand and Isabella, who looked to them for financial aid. The pressures of a militant Catholic Church, however, forced the monarchs to accede to papal pressure and order the expulsion of all practicing Jews in 1492.[4]

The Spanish exile expelled Jews with their household goods except for their gold and silver. The outcast Jews also carried years of mercantile practice with them, as well as family ties to *conversos* remaining in Spain, who while living as Christians did not sever their bonds of kinship. Spain's exiled Jewish population found refuge in many parts of the Mediterranean and Asia, including North Africa, Italy, and Ottoman Greece and Turkey. The great majority, however, perhaps 85 percent and numbering 85,000 to 115,000, traveled to Portugal, whose monarch, King Emmanuel I, welcomed this well-connected group. An Iberian nation, it offered Jews the greatest continuity with their former lives. In Portugal, Sephardic Jews continued to trade with Spain and strove to maintain a coherent community. However, in 1497, Emanuel I forcibly converted all Jews, while promising not to inquire into their religious beliefs for forty years. Not wishing to lose their valued commercial expertise and wealth, he forbade Jews, now unwilling *conversos*, to leave the country. A few managed to flee, but most remained. With the death of Emanuel in 1521 and the inception of the Portuguese Inquisition ten years later, however, emigration increased, not so much in the chaotic manner that marked the Spanish exodus but through planned departures. Some Jews left in fear of religious persecution and some for greater economic opportunity. As the Inquisition had not yet begun operation in Portuguese Brazil, a number of Portuguese *conversos* emigrated there as well as to France and Holland.[5]

The Portuguese Jews (as they were known) who chose to immigrate to Holland, a country that had never housed a sizable Jewish population, found a land in transition. They arrived during the long birth of the Dutch Republic, one of the great accomplishments of early modern Europe. Beginning in 1568, the United Provinces (the seven Dutch-speaking provinces of northern Netherlands, with Holland as the largest province and Amsterdam the largest city) waged an eighty-year war of independence against Spain, which had inherited the Netherlands in 1517. During these years of conflict, the Dutch people witnessed thousands of their brethren put to death and withstood long sieges. At the core of their endurance and final victory in the seventeenth century were the Netherlands' heritage of constitutional freedoms, representative government, and a strong Protestant faith founded in the Calvinist Dutch Reformed Church.[6]

The Netherlands, with vibrant stock and commodities exchanges, innovative banking and credit facilities, a strong army, heterogeneous population, and republican government, stood at the forefront of what historian David Israel terms the "Age of Mercantilism." In this world, commerce and the good of the state prevailed over religious conflict and dogma. The state determined to intervene in the economic life of the nation to ensure its continuing growth. The movement toward a mercantile Europe, neither a clear-cut nor simple transition, reflected a steady if uneven shift over two hundred years (1550–1770). By 1570–1600, a new religious skepticism and statecraft emerged that held the economic, political, and military health of the state primary.[7]

The Dutch Republic in the seventeenth century was "the most tolerant of European societies." Within this framework, the Jewish population grew and flourished, its numbers rising rapidly from 800 in 1610 to around 2,000 in the 1640s and 1650s to 3,350 by 1680. Most Jews were Sephardic, descendants of immigrants from Spain and Portugal; a smaller, separate, less influential Ashkenazi community was also present, immigrants from German states and eastern Europe. Portuguese Jews built on their legacy of internal governance, crafting a largely autonomous society. Its governing body, the Mahamad, whose membership included the city's most prominent Sephardic Jews, conducted schools (in Hebrew and Portuguese), supervised the morals of the city's Jews, monitored religious observance, took responsibility for social welfare, censored the increasing number of books published by the Sephardic population, and negotiated with Christian society. Its ultimate form of discipline was excommunication for those who violated community norms, and it wielded that discipline against rationalist philosopher Baruch Spinoza. The Mahamad also built the famed magnificent Esnoga synagogue, completed in 1675, which served the needs of the city's Jewish community for generations.[8]

Many occupations were either foreign to Jews or forbidden by the guilds of the city's craftsmen, but the Sephardic legacy of commercial expertise fit well within Amsterdam's economy. Leading Portuguese Jews of Amsterdam were merchants. While Jews constituted only 1.5 percent of the population, they composed between 4 and 6 percent of the major stockholders of the Dutch West India Company and more of the Bank of Exchange. They engaged in commerce with their former homelands, Spain and Portugal, particularly Portugal, a trade that reached its height during a twelve-year truce between these nations and the Dutch Republic from 1609 to 1621. With trade restrictions lifted, numerous Dutch ships entered Iberian harbors or Iberian colonial harbors; Sephardic merchants built fifteen ships a year for the Brazilian trade alone. The Dutch Republic understood the value of Jewish capital, commercial acumen, and mercantile connections.[9]

▪ Brazilian Community

In 1621, the Netherlands granted the Dutch West India Company, a joint stock company formed by Netherlands merchants and well capitalized at 7.5 million guilders, a state monopoly of trade in Africa and the Americas. The company had the power to maintain garrisons, to appoint directors, and to sign alliances with other nations. Under the supervision of the Estates General, the Netherlands legislature, it could procure troops and warships. Its most important initial objective was to seize control of Brazilian sugar production and its European markets from the Portuguese. In 1630, the company captured a sector in northeast Brazil; from Recife, the region's largest city, it maintained control there until the Portuguese recaptured it in 1654.[10]

Dutch Recife was the prelude to Jewish immigration to New Amsterdam. The Dutch West India Company, not having adequate resources, relied on Jewish wealth and expertise. Dutch Jews possessed manpower, capital, and important connections with Portuguese merchants and the Brazilian trade. Recife and its environs attracted Amsterdam's Jews; as many as a third of the city's Jewish population emigrated. At the outpost's height, it housed between 850 and 1,000 Jewish residents, nearly half the colony. Recife tempted Jewish artisans precluded from their craft in Amsterdam as well as wealthy traders; prominent Portuguese Jews purchased sugar plantations. While the Jews of Brazil did not achieve full religious or political equality, and while their prominence produced resentment among non-Jewish immigrants, they attained considerable autonomy and protection amid financial opportunity. When Christian merchants complained that "every contact with a Jew ends in bankruptcy," the governor reported that Jews were "reliable political allies."[11]

Recife's Jewish community mirrored Amsterdam's. Control of Jewish life lay with the Mahamad, five leading members of the community. The Mahamad protected synagogue property, provided regular services, supervised religious observance, maintained a cemetery, established schools for Jewish children, and provided poor relief. The colony housed two major synagogues, Zur Israel in Recife and Magen Abraham in the outlying town of Mauricia. The Recife synagogue, built of stone and caulk, boasted two stories. Its spiritual leader, the first rabbi in the new world, was Isaac Aboab da Fonseca, a grammarian, mystic, and popular preacher.[12]

■ The First "Twenty-Three"

When Henry Hudson arrived in North America, he sailed under a Dutch flag. Commissioned by the Dutch East India Company, Hudson's reports of abundant furs aroused the interest of the merchants of the sister West India Company walking the docks of Amsterdam. In quest of these skins, the company founded the colony of New Netherland. In 1623–1624 settlers were sent to Fort Orange (later the site of Albany) and along the Delaware and Connecticut Rivers to harvest furs. When the first ships returned brimming with pelts, more settlers were sent, and the tip of the island named Manhattan ("Island of Hills" based on Indian language) was chosen as the site of a fort to protect the company's possessions throughout the province. (Governor Peter Minuit purchased the island from the Indians for the famous sixty guilders [$24] of trade items.) Because of intense warfare for furs among Indian tribes, and the shifting alliances of Iroquois and Mahicans near Fort Orange, the West India Company focused its settlement on Manhattan, its immediate surroundings, and the Hudson River valley.[13]

Poet Steendam's vision notwithstanding, early New Amsterdam was largely a horror story. The company's directors—most notoriously, Willem Kieft, who arrived in 1638—mismanaged the settlements. While Kieft provided settlers the opportunity to acquire private property, repaired a number of the buildings on the island, and fostered the settlement of nearby outposts, he was personally corrupt while cruel to the Lenape native peoples. The colony, meanwhile, soon housed a collection of various nationalities, from Danish to French, speaking eighteen different languages and known for drunkenness, promiscuity, and disrespect for law and order. Kieft's downfall followed a war that killed sixteen hundred Indians and a few hundred colonists, destroying new settlements. Kieft was recalled, and the fate of New Netherland hung in the balance. Unlike Recife, which produced valuable goods and a clear profit for the company, New Amsterdam was less productive, had fewer valuable foodstuffs, was constantly under English threat, and never became the focus of the company's directors.[14]

In a final effort to salvage the outpost, the company appointed Peter Stuyvesant director general, a position he held from 1647 until the British conquest in 1664. Stuyvesant fought for the West India Company in the Caribbean and in a battle in St. Martin lost his right leg, which was replaced by his famous wooden limb. The son and son-in-law of Reformed Dutch clergymen and a strict Dutch Calvinist, he brought order and growth to New Amsterdam, requiring landowners to replace the run-down dwellings that littered the island with sturdy buildings. New immigrants arrived, a municipal government system similar to that in Amsterdam matured, and Stuyvesant refurbished the fort. Houses rose in the Dutch gabled style as the population grew slowly to fifteen hundred by 1660. The company remained powerful but no longer controlled daily life. The city's burghers wrested increasing power from Stuyvesant as they instituted laws for the price of bread, regulation of markets, and provision of orphans. The transition of a tavern into the noted Stadt Huys (city hall) signaled that New Amsterdam was a seaport dominated, like its namesake, by a prominent merchant class, whose efforts produced an entrepôt for furs, tobacco, and foodstuffs.[15]

Such was the site of the first North American Jewish settlement. Nearly every community has a mythic founding. So it was with the Jews of America. The original myth, based on a 1784 article written in Hebrew by Dutch poet David Franco Mendes, tells of a group of twenty-three Jews fleeing Recife who were captured by a Spanish ship and recaptured by a French warship. In Mendes's words, "God caused a Savior to arise unto them, the captain of a French Ship, . . . and he conducted them until they reached the end of the inhabited earth

called New Holland." Contemporary research questions this tale. In the exodus of Jews from Brazil following Dutch capitulation to the Portuguese, Jews
received the same right as other Dutch residents to leave freely within three
months and to take all their "movable property." Almost all returned safely to
the Dutch Republic. One group, however, planning to sail to Martinique and
from there to New England or New Amsterdam on the *Valck*, encountered
adverse winds, forcing them to land in Spanish Jamaica (rendered "Gamon-
ike" by Dutch officials of New Amsterdam). Obtaining permission to depart
from Spanish authorities, this band, which historian Jacob Marcus estimates
consisted of "four married males, six adult married and widowed women and
thirteen children of various ages," traveled to Cape St. Anthony, Cuba. There
they hired the French vessel *St. Catrina* to take them to New Amsterdam with
their goods, at the high cost of 2,500 guilders, likely more than the worth of
their possessions.[16]

The choice of New Amsterdam by these refugees fit within the vision of
Amsterdam's Jewish elders that the vast lands of New Netherland replace Brazil as a haven for Portuguese Jews. An enticement may have been the description of New Netherland published in Holland by Adriaen Van der Donck:
"a very beautiful, pleasant, healthy, and delightful land, where all manner of
men can more easily earn a good living . . . than in the Netherlands or any
other part of the globe that I know." The elders' scout and emissary was likely
merchant Jacob Barsimon, who, preceding the twenty-three, arrived on the
Peartree from Amsterdam in mid-August 1654. He entered the outpost legally
with a passport issued by the West India Company at the same time that another Amsterdam Jew, Menasseh ben Israel, was successfully entreating Oliver
Cromwell to allow Jews to reenter England in a similar quest to locate new
areas of settlement for Dutch Jews.[17]

The *St. Catrina* sailed into New Amsterdam in early September. Aboard it,
according to Solomon Pietersen, another Dutch Jew who traveled to New Amsterdam legally on the *Peartree* and who acted as attorney for the immigrants,
were "twenty-three souls, big and little." These twenty-three, whose number
comes from only this one statement, and who have become legendary, disembarked just before the Jewish New Year. They were the first Jews to celebrate
Rosh Hashanah in what was to become the United States. Clearly they were
not the first Jews in New Amsterdam, as Pietersen, Barsimon, and a third man,
Asser Levy of Vilna, all merchant traders, disembarked from the *Peartree*.[18]

On arrival, the twenty-three Jews found themselves in peril. At Cape St. Anthony, Master Jacques de la Motthe of the *St. Catrina* signed an agreement with the Jewish passengers "in solidum," making them collectively responsible for the cost of passage. When their resources proved insufficient, he went before the Dutch court in New Amsterdam; it gave the Jews forty-eight hours to pay. Three days later, the court concluded that the required amount (1,567 florins) had not been remitted, "though they have property sufficient to defray the debt," and authorized Master de la Motthe to seize the property of "the greatest debtors" and vend them at auction. When that sale proved insufficient, the master returned to court and asked that Israel and Moses Ambrosius be held in custody until the debt was satisfied. The court granted the request, providing de la Motthe pay the cost of confinement. Significantly, in accord with Dutch policy of religious toleration, a delay in the proceedings was granted for the two days of the Jewish New Year. It is likely that a number of Christian citizens aided the Jews by buying their goods at nominal prices and returning them to their owners. In addition, minister Johannes Megapolensis helped the refugees as an act of Christian charity. He did so, however, in anger over the behavior of the Jewish merchants who had come over on the *Peartree*. These local Jewish merchants, who "would not even lend . . . a few stivers" to the refugees, had "no other God than the unrighteous Mammon" and were of "no benefit to the country, but look at everything for their own profit." The twenty-three appealed to their counterparts in Holland "by the ships sailing for Patria." Their Dutch brethren ended the saga by providing funds to discharge the debts.[19]

Only a few of the twenty-three are found in the records of New Amsterdam. Historian Leo Hershkowitz, who wrote the most recent analysis of these immigrants, can only identify five Jews who arrived on the *St. Catrina* as living in New Amsterdam: Abraham and David Israel, Judicq (Judith) de Mereda, Moses Ambrosius, and likely Ricke Nunes. He identifies seven other Jews in New Amsterdam in 1655 who had been in Brazil but may not have arrived on the *St Catrina* but on the *Peartree* or another ship. Other Jewish names appear in various records from 1656, 1661, 1662, and 1666. What are we, then, to make of Pietersen's account of the twenty-three Jews? As there is no apparent reason why Pietersen would have lied, the most likely explanation is that a significant number of refugees arrived on the *St. Catrina* entwined in debt, with no Jewish community to assist them and no means of support or income. Encountering a small seaport governed by a strict Calvinist more invested with religious zeal than were the company's directors, whose concern was to maintain New Amsterdam as a profitable Dutch Reformed outpost of the company, they likely departed within the next few years.[20]

Stuyvesant believed that "diversity and toleration would undermine social harmony." Alarmed by the poverty of the Recife Jews and the possibility that they might either demand poor relief or become "fly-by-night" traders like the itinerant Christians who paid little in taxes, he petitioned the West India Company's directors for permission to deport the refugees. Stuyvesant wrote that "the Jews who have arrived would nearly all like to remain here," an important indication of the refugees' original intent. Stuyvesant echoed Dominie Megapolensis, who had called the Jews an "obstinate and immovable" people, whose settlement would cause even more confusion by adding their practices to those of Catholics, Quakers, and Lutherans. Invoking traditional anti-Semitic attitudes, the director first decried Jews' economic practices, their selfishness and "customary usury and deceitful trading with the Christians," and he belittled their religion as poison to a community: a "deceitful race,— such hateful enemies and blasphemers of the name of Christ." On practical grounds, he warned that the Jews, "owing to their present indigence, . . . might become a charge in the coming winter." Thus, he concluded, "for the benefit of this weak and newly developing place and the land in general," it was "useful to require them in a friendly way to depart." Five months later, the inferior magistrates and leading burgomasters (merchants) affirmed Stuyvesant's request and included mercantile itinerants such as Pietersen, Barsimon, and Levy, Jewish merchants who might become competitors, resolving that "the Jews who came last year from the West Indies and now from Fatherland, must prepare to depart therewith."[21]

■ Seeking Rights in New Netherland

In response to the Stuyvesant's deportation request, the Jewish elders (*parnassim*) of Amsterdam wrote to their city fathers, the "Right Honorable Mayors and Councillors of the City of Amsterdam," that "many and various persons and households of . . . [the Jewish] nation" were "well disposed" to set out for New Netherland "on the same footing and condition extended to all," there to "enjoy freedom to exercise their religion as they were permitted in Brazil." If these conditions were met, "many of their Nation" would settle in the new world and "contribute considerably" to peopling the new colony. Despite the trauma of Brazil, these Jewish pioneers were "willing again to try their fortunes and settle over there provided that they [were] given the opportunity to practice their religion in full freedom (but quietly and with due obedience), and provided that they [were] given the same protection as are the other inhabitants, and were admitted to the same rights of housing, commerce, trade and liberty."[22]

A second petition was sent to the directors of the West India Company by "the merchants of the Portuguese Nation residing in [the] city." These burghers, noting that "many of the Jewish nation [were] principal shareholders," argued that closing New Amsterdam to Jews would "result to the great disadvantage of the Jewish nation." All of the exiles from Brazil could not return to Amsterdam "because of the lack of opportunity" and could not return to Spain or Portugal "because of the Inquisition." Too, the merchants declared, the "Honorable Lords, the Burgomasters of the City" and the "Honorable, High Illustrious Mighty Lords, the States General" had "in political matters always protected and considered the Jewish nation as upon the same footing as all the inhabitants and burghers." As foreign nations with less liberty allowed Jews to "live and trade in their territories," they asked that the "Jewish nation" be allowed, like other inhabitants, to "travel, live and traffic there, and . . . enjoy liberty on condition of contributing like others."[23]

Given the weight afforded economic reasoning in this era, the influence and wealth of Amsterdam's Jews, and their presence in the company, it is not surprising that, in one of the founding documents of American Jewish history, the company rebuked Stuyvesant. While it agreed in principle that "the new territories should no more be allowed to be infected by people of the Jewish Nation," mercantile interests took precedence over Calvinist doctrine. Noting the sacrifice of the Jewish nation in the taking of Recife and the "large amount of capital they still ha[d] invested in the shares of the company," the directors, "after many deliberations," declared, "these people may travel and trade to and in New Netherland and live and remain there, provided the poor among them shall not become a burden to the company or to the community, but be supported by their own nation. You will now govern yourself accordingly." Without the aid of the Jewish community of Amsterdam, Jews in New Netherland would have had no opportunity to contend for the rights of Dutch citizenship. Those in New Amsterdam could now carry on the struggle. The company's directive gave them the opportunity to pursue this quest in a hostile climate.[24]

The next two years, 1655–1656, proved critical. Jews of considerably greater stature than the Recife immigrants, who came to New Amsterdam after the twenty-three, led the mission. The most prominent were five Sephardic merchants, Abraham de Lucena, Salvador D'Andrada, Jacob Cohen Henriques, Joseph D'Acosta, and David Ferera. Of these, the most important were the merchants D'Acosta and Cohen Henriques, both West India Company shareholders and past members of Recife's Mahamad. D'Acosta was a "principal shareholder," while Cohen Henriques was the son of principal investor Abraham Cohen. D'Acosta, who leased a house on Pearl Street in 1656, came with a four-year contract as agent for a company formed in Amsterdam to trade with New Netherland. These merchants, with other Jewish residents, including members of the twenty-three who had not yet departed, created a critical mass that included men with leadership skills and standing. That, in turn, allowed the Jews of New Amsterdam to effectively seek the rights that their Dutch brethren possessed.[25]

Jewish settlers sought first to acquire the religious privileges held by the Jews of Amsterdam and Recife. By 1614, the Jewish community of Amsterdam had gained the right to build and worship in their own meeting place, and Amsterdam housed a number of synagogues. Evidence that New Amsterdam's Jews sought similar standing can be found in the concern of the religious governing body, or classis, of Amsterdam's statement in 1655 that "even the Jews have made request of the Honorable Governor and have also attempted in that country to erect a synagogue for the exercise of their blasphemous religion." Stuyvesant confirmed this application of New Amsterdam's Jews, writing that though Jews were no longer hindered "with regard to trade," they yet sought other rights and "have many times requested of us the free and public exercise of their abominable religion, but this can not yet be accorded to them." Stuyvesant resisted, fearing that "to give liberty to the Jews will be very detrimental there, because the Christians there will not be able at the same time to do business. Giving them liberty, we cannot refuse the Lutherans and the Papists." Dominie Megapolensis also wrote Holland that if immigration of Jews were permitted, "a great lot would follow and build here their synagogue," a good reason that "these godless rascals . . . may be sent away from here."

Given the alarm of Dutch officials, it is likely that Jewish colonists sought the right of public worship in the first years of their settlement, as they had done in Recife.[26]

The West India Company, in its initial response to Stuyvesant, only granted Jews the right to practice their faith within their homes. The directors considered Stuyvesant's concern about the spread of organized Judaism "premature," instructing him, if and when it did occur, "you will do well to refer the matter to us in order to await upon the necessary orders." A later communication noted that Jews "exercise in all quietness their religion within their house" and advised them to live close to each other as they did in Amsterdam. The company directors envisioned New Amsterdam with a group of Jews living in a tightly knit community—but without public worship.[27]

Little evidence remains of the religious practices of the Jewish community. However, it is suggestive that in 1655 Abraham de Lucena, on behalf of the Jewish elders of Amsterdam, provided the Jews of New Amsterdam "a Sephfer Thora of parchment with its green veil and cloak and band of India damask of dark purple." Another sign of Jewish religious activity was Jacob Barsimon's unwillingness to appear in court in 1658 on a Saturday to answer a summons; default judgment was not entered against him, "as he was summoned on his Sabbath." Too, the Jewish citizens, "being we ar all mortall men," requested land for a burying ground from the burgomasters in 1665. In February 1666, they received permission to "purchase a burying ground," in particular, "a little hook of land" outside the city. This was the origin of the Chatham Street cemetery. It is also noteworthy that the outpost's two Jewish butchers were excused from slaughtering hogs; they supplied kosher meat to the community. The only Jew to remain through the decade was Asser Levy, a butcher and trader, whose will inventory included instruments for kosher slaughter.[28]

Thus, the evidence, though limited, indicates that Jews remained ritually observant—to what degree is unknown. Did they, now in possession of a Torah, conduct regular religious services inside their homes? It seems likely that they did, but the unfriendly environment helped persuade most Jewish settlers to return to Amsterdam's public synagogues and well-placed community. An alternative path to civil acceptance was conversion to the Dutch Reformed Church. Solomon Pietersen made that choice, but he appears the exception; most Jews maintained allegiance to their faith.[29]

A second critical right sought by New Amsterdam's Jews was free access to the marketplace and public square. Though ordered by the directors of the West India Company to give the Jews full "civil and political" rights, Stuyvesant and the burgomasters resisted. In 1655, Asser Levy and Jacob Barsimon requested permission to stand guard with other citizens rather than pay a tax for a substitute. They were denied that privilege: "first in the disinclination and unwillingness of these trainbands [guards] to be fellow-soldiers with the aforesaid [Jewish] nation" and second because "the said nation was not admitted or counted among the citizens, as regards trainbands or common citizens' guards neither in the illustrious city of Amsterdam nor (to our knowledge) in any city in Netherland." When Levy and Barsimon complained of the tax burdens, the municipality instructed them to "depart whenever and whither it pleases them." Levy persisted, however, and won the right to do guard duty in 1657. Also in 1655, New Amsterdam's burghers implemented a second form of discrimination. Imposing a special assessment on city residents to guard against Indian attack, the city fathers assessed the seaport's prominent Jewish merchants, who made up only 5 out of the 210 citizens with ratable assets, the sum of 100 guilders each. These merchants, composing one-thirtieth of the taxable population, had to pay one-twelfth the required amount.[30]

Jews gained the right to trade freely and purchase real estate, privileges long common to their Dutch counterparts, but only through persistent efforts. In 1655, merchants de Lucena, D'Andrada, and Cohen Henriques, requested permission to trade on the South River (Delaware) and at Fort Orange (the Hudson River valley and northward). They reasoned that "as the Jewish residents received consent from the West India Company to trade and travel freely," to "enjoy the same liberties," they must receive consent to travel and trade to all places "within the jurisdiction of the Government." The director general and council declined the request for "weighty reasons." A councilor declared that it "would be injurious to the community and the population of the said places to grant the petitions of the Jews," though he allowed goods already bought to be sold. In addition, despite company orders to the contrary, Jews were unable to purchase real estate. In December 1655, Salvador D'Andrada, a "Jewish merchant . . . in the city," petitioned to ratify the sale of the house he was leasing. As the lawful proprietor of the dwelling that he had purchased "at a public sale," he wished to "enjoy the rights and privileges" of ownership. The council declined the petition "for pregnant reasons."[31]

The following March, the Jewish merchants renewed their requests, quoting the directive of the West India Company that they be permitted "to live and traffic and to enjoy the same liberty" as in Holland. As they were paying more than their share of taxes, they must be given "the same liberty allowed to other burghers as well in trading to all places within the jurisdiction of this Government as in the purchase of real estate," a privilege granted by the West India Company. The council replied that Jews had the same rights as other merchants and refused to reconsider the issue of real property ownership. However, in June 1656, the company directors, fearful that they would lose Jewish trade to Jamaica and England, again rebuked Stuyvesant, stating that they wished that the director and council "had obeyed [the company's] orders," which they "must thereafter execute punctually and with more respect." After this rebuff, Jews were allowed to trade and to maintain retail shops.[32]

The right of full citizenship remained to be won. In April 1657, Jewish merchants D'Andrada, Cohen Henriques, De Lucena, and D'Acosta, noting that in 1655 they had petitioned for a Jewish citizen to become a burgher, to be treated "as other inhabitants of New Netherland," on the grounds that Jews enjoyed the privileges of burgher standing in Amsterdam and that, they claimed, "as long as they have been here, have, with others, borne and paid, and still bear, all Burgher burdens." They again asked "to enjoy the Burger right" in conformity with the directives of the West India Company. Responding, the city fathers agreed to admit Asser Levy to burgher standing, stating, "The Burgomasters of this City are hereby authorized and at the same time charged to admit the petitioners herein and their Nation to the Burghership, in due form." The Jewish merchants prevailed, but not without initial defeats, numerous slights, appeals, and the support of Amsterdam's Jewish community and the directors of the West India Company. Jews also won the right to purchase property; in 1660, Asser Levy purchased a house on Stone Street, later the site of the Mill Street synagogue. He became the first Jewish citizen to possess real estate in what was to become New York City. In 1678, after the English took over the colony, he bought property north of Wall Street for use as a "public slaughter house."[33]

With mercantile freedom, Jewish merchants traded throughout New Netherland, including the Hudson and Delaware River valleys, and with the West Indies, Europe, Virginia, and Maryland. Although the most common and valuable commodities were fur, tobacco, and liquor, they also traded in foodstuffs. They shipped goods and liquor to settlers and Indians in exchange for furs and tobacco. Much of the exchange was done through barter, including leasing homes for beaver and brandy. Jewish merchants both imported and distilled liquor, which was ubiquitous in New Amsterdam.[34]

Legal disputes constantly troubled the merchants' business careers. Joseph D'Acosta defended a number of suits, some over damages to his ships' cargo. In one instance, merchant Johannes Vervelen told D'Acosta, "You are a Jew, you are all cheats together." D'Acosta left for Holland in 1660 at the end of his four-year contract. Lawsuits entwined Jacob Cohen Henriques, a trader with Curaçao, importing "Venetian pearls, Venetian pendants, thimbles, scissors, knives and bells." Authorities charged him with smuggling tobacco, fined him for baking bread with the door open—perhaps an attempt to break the monopoly of the city's bakers—and accused him of engaging in a fight in a canoe over the vessel's ownership. He departed soon after this complaint. Dutch prosecutors arrested and fined Abraham de Lucena for selling at retail and for keeping his store open during the weekly Sunday sermon, demanding an unusually steep fine of 600 guilders. With Salvador D'Andrada, de Lucena became entangled in a suit over tobacco ownership. In another case, the court required him, David Ferera, and D'Andrada to pay freight for a shipment of goods on the *Great Christopher* despite de Lucena's claim that pipes of brandy were missing. In 1660, he and his wife appeared before the magistrates over charges and countercharges of slander. That same year, rather than pay three beavers for his burgher right, de Lucena took leave of the city. In 1656, Jacob Barsimon faced charges of striking Isaac Israel, a Jewish trader, on the Delaware River. Barsimon left New Amsterdam in 1660.

A bitter dispute embroiled David Ferera, agent for Amsterdam merchant Moses de Silva. The City accused him of stealing a chest of clothes, which he contended was his own, from Bailiff Dirck van Schelluyne's home. He then allegedly seized beaver skins put up as bond. For showing disrespect to a public official, the court ordered Ferera whipped and banished. D'Acosta managed to rescue Ferera from the humiliation of a public lashing—a penalty possibly imposed because of anti-Semitic prejudice—by paying a steep fine of 170 guilders. Ferera departed for Maryland, where he continued to trade until at least 1659. D'Andrada appeared in court over a charge that he had stolen a small silver cup. He, too, soon quit New Amsterdam.[35]

These incidents indicate that the early Jewish merchants could be, in Jacob Marcus's words, "a rude and conglomerate lot." Or perhaps this aggressiveness stemmed in part from the inordinate stress of leading the struggle for civil rights in New Amsterdam, a struggle likely requiring a contentious nature.[36]

▪ A Jewish Pioneer

One Jewish resident, Asser Levy, remained in New Amsterdam the full ten years to Britain's seizure in 1664 and then lived under English rule. He was one of the two Jewish male citizens who took the oath of allegiance to the British Crown. He and his wife, Miriam, both died in New Amsterdam/New York, he in 1682, she in 1685. Levy was not a member of the Portuguese Jewish community but an Ashkenazi Jew who immigrated from Vilna to Amsterdam perhaps because of the Chmielnicki pogroms of 1648–1649. From there, he came to New Amsterdam in 1654, likely on the *Peartree*, arriving as an obscure immigrant who had not achieved burgher standing in Amsterdam. As noted, Levy petitioned to do guard duty rather than pay a tax, and, with the help of prominent Sephardic merchants, he obtained burgher standing. From then on, he became increasingly wealthy. A butcher by trade, Levy left his heirs a full stock of butcher's implements. As he prospered, he ventured into the fur trade, buying beaver at Fort Orange (Albany) in 1660. He also invested in real estate, accepting a mortgage for land near Fort Orange in 1660 in exchange for a loan he had made, and in 1661 he purchased "a house and a lot lying in the Village of Beverwyck," possibly to establish trading rights. That same year, he bought his historic home on Stone Street. When he died, Levy ranked among the top third of the New York's population. His will inventory reveals that he owned an assortment of fine ware including "two bedds," "twelf Cussons," "two looking glasses," a "Sabbath lamb," a gold "bodkine," silver cups and "sawsers," and a "spice box." He and his wife dressed well: he wore a "black velvet jacket and broadcloth black coat and breeches" with a "silver banded sword" and a black hat; Miriam treasured a Dutch gown adorned with the gold bodkin, gold pendants, scarlet petticoat, and a lace cap. They owned a "Negro boy." The couple had no children, only relatives in Amsterdam. The presence of religious objects, including multiple sets of dishes, suggests that Asser and Miriam, despite the absence of many Jews in the seaport, remained to some degree observant. They were the first "Jewish pilgrims" of New Amsterdam and New York.[37]

▪ The Dutch Years

What can be said of the Jews' ten years in New Amsterdam? They were never truly welcome. Traditional anti-Semitism lay at the root of the hostility: witness the condemnation by devout Calvinist director Stuyvesant that Jews practiced an "Abominable religion." Dutch merchants also resisted Jewish competition. Jewish residents had to overcome ongoing opposition to their right to trade and faced constant legal harassment. Finally, the commercial connections developed by Dutch Jewry, specializing in the sugar trade and as brokers, did not help in a colony whose chief commodity was furs, a staple unfamiliar in Sephardic Atlantic networks. So few Jews settled in New Amsterdam. Prominent merchants, men who might have become the core of a vital Dutch Jewish community, departed by 1660. A few additional Jewish traders ventured to America and returned to Amsterdam in the years before the Dutch residents capitulated to a British fleet in 1664, but no Jewish mercantile community emerged. Only a handful of Jewish residents lived in the city in the 1660s. If there was greater freedom and opportunity in Amsterdam and larger Jewish communities in Suriname and Curaçao, why stay in New Amsterdam? If the Dutch West India Company, already in dire financial straits, did not foresee New Netherland as a major trading post, economic opportunities were not going to improve. The vision of the Jewish elders of Amsterdam, that New Netherland would be home to a large Jewish community and play a significant role in the Atlantic trading network, foundered. No Jewish births were recorded. In 1663, only a year before the British conquest, de Lucena's Torah returned to Amsterdam, the final signal of the failure to establish a Jewish community.[38]

Yet the relentless effort of Jewish merchants, inspired by the Dutch legacy of toleration and entrepreneurial freedom and aided by fellow Jews in Amsterdam, gained them the right of trade, burghership, citizenship, and land ownership. Even if few Jews remained, these rights endured, and, when the British took possession of New Amsterdam, they recognized them. This is the critical legacy of the Jewish experience in New Netherland: religious toleration, economic opportunity, and equal citizenship.

The terms of capitulation that guaranteed the Dutch their traditional rights included the Jewish population. The Dutch decade was prelude to a long era of colonial British rule that was far more welcoming to Jews. The Jewish community that matured in newly named New York achieved far greater standing.

Though the community was small in number, its leaders developed important positions in British Atlantic commerce, valuable political connections, unmatched religious toleration, and widespread social acceptance, laying a cornerstone for future generations of American Jews. A commercial acumen, following in the footsteps of these first Jewish merchants, came to define much of the New York Jewish community in its first 175 years. The British colonial experience produced a solid Jewish community, led by a strong mercantile elite, with a political and economic clout well beyond its numbers. The story of the Jews of early New York in this volume highlights these political and economic strengths, which played a key role in shaping the rest of Jewish life and culture as it developed in this new world. These strengths also brought into play the difficulties of balancing efforts at commercial success in a Christian world with the requirements of religious observance, a theme that resonated for generations to come. Too, the winning of rights in New Amsterdam laid the foundations for Jewish entry into American republican traditions, an auspicious beginning which has shaped American Jewry in New York and beyond to the present day.

The Merchant's Exchange opened on Broad Street in 1751. Financed by local merchants and the Common Council, the ground level contained an open-air marketplace for street sales, while the upper floors housed elegant meeting rooms for dinners and concerts. It represented the commercial side of this thriving British port. (Courtesy Eno Collection, New York Public Library)

CHAPTER 2

A Merchant Community

In 1708, twenty-year-old Jacob Franks, son of Abraham Franks, one of London's twelve Jewish stockbrokers, arrived on the docks of New York City, a small colonial seaport in the far-flung British Empire. What motivated Franks to leave Britain? He sought a chance to make his fortune. The same impetus spurred other Jewish emigrants. Many young single men of middling status from the Ashkenazi population thought of America as a final destination, and those who intended to return often remained. Relatives proved critical, as a successful New Yorker would commonly persuade a cousin, uncle, brother or sister to join him. This was the age of the "Port Jews," mercantile entrepreneurs who dominated the Jewish community.[1]

New Amsterdam Becomes New York

During the seventeenth century, the British and Dutch, so close in religious leaning, parliamentary maturity, commercial entrepreneurship, and imperial ambition, entered into wars over dominion of the Americas, particularly the Caribbean. The American coastline from Massachusetts to South Carolina housed a series of British colonies differing in government, culture, and religion but all professing allegiance to the Crown. The one gap was New Netherland, a key English rival. An isolated enemy colony could not stand, and in 1664 the Duke of York, brother of Charles II, sent an expedition to New Amsterdam, whose residents, seeing a British fleet in the harbor, quickly capitulated.

Colonel Richard Nicholls, the commander of the British fleet and first governor of the newly named New York (after the king's brother), while demanding "full and absolute power and authority," gave Dutch inhabitants significant concessions. He declared that "all people shall still continue free denizens and enjoy their lands, houses, goods, ships wheresoever they are within this country, and dispose of them as they please. . . . The Dutch here shall enjoy the liberty of their consciences in divine worship and church discipline." This liberty was central to British mercantilism. Commercial regulation assumed more importance than religious orthodoxy. Thus, in 1674 Governor Andros received the following orders: "permit all persons of what Religion so ever, quietly to inhabit within ye precincts of your jurisdiccion without giving ym any disturbance or disquiet whatsoever, for or by reason of their differing opinion in matter of Religion," with a critical proviso that they "give noe disturbance to ye publique peace nor doe molest or disquiet others in ye free exercise of their religion."[2]

Discriminatory rules against Jews selling by retail were allowed to lapse, permitting Jews to enter the handicrafts. While either citizenship or endenization was required to engage in trade within the British Empire, neither was difficult to acquire. A few Jews became denizens, resident aliens admitted to commercial rights within English territories, but after 1715, when the New York Assembly passed legislation allowing naturalization to any foreigner in the colony who either owned real estate or was present in New York prior to November 1, 1683, most sought citizenship. In 1740, Parliament, viewing citizenship as a tool to populate its colonies, naturalized all residents of the colonies who had lived there for seven continuous years (13 George II, 1740). The act included a clause allowing the exclusion of the phrase "upon the true faith of a Christian" in oaths required of voters and holders of government positions. Colonial (but not English) Jews could hold office and vote. Between 1688 and 1770, fifty-seven Jewish residents of New York were admitted to freemanship, which carried the right to engage in a retail trade, to vote in municipal and colonial elections, and to hold public office, with or without real property. The rights won by the Jews of New Amsterdam with difficulty against Calvinist Stuyvesant were part and parcel of the English governing outlook in New York. The free environment proved pivotal in New York Jewish history, as it allowed for the growth of a strong synagogue community and a wealthy, influential elite.[3]

■ Colonial New York

Early in the British colonial era, Dutch and increasingly dominant English interests clashed in New York, leading to Leisler's Rebellion in 1689, an attempt to restore Dutch Calvinist governance. After this unsuccessful uprising, Anglicization proceeded unhindered; all succeeding factions were British. Politically, New York Colony included commercial interests revolving around New York City, where sugar refining and artisan manufactures thrived together with commerce with the motherland and the West Indies, a fur-trading faction centered in Albany, and an agricultural combination on Long Island and the large Hudson River estates. These rival interest groups dominated the political scene, producing closely fought elections for the colony's Provincial Assembly and the city's Common Council, contests that included Jewish voters.[4]

During this era, the population of New York City increased from about 1,500 at the close of the Dutch era to 3,000 in 1680, 11,000 by 1743, and 21,000 in 1770. From the mid-1770s on, this included a large black population of 11–15 percent, including the largest number of slaves in the northern colonies. The number of Jews in New York City remained fairly constant, with about 100 souls in the 1680s, 200 in 1730, and 250 in 1750 and prior to the Revolution. Until the mid-eighteenth century, New York City housed the only organized Jewish community in mainland North America, though it was far smaller than settlements in Dutch Curaçao and Suriname and British Jamaica.[5]

■ Moving to America

Jacob Franks left an English community whose modern origins date to the arrival of Dutch immigrants in the mid-seventeenth century. By 1700, five hundred largely Sephardic Jews lived in England with a limited degree of autonomy and self-government. In the 1700s, the influx of poor Ashkenazi immigrants outnumbered the Sephardim, causing the population to increase to six thousand by the mid-eighteenth century. Jews held mercantile positions on the high end and were street peddlers and small retailers on the low end. Other than not having the right to hold office and vote, disabilities all nonmembers of the Anglican Church endured, Britain offered considerable freedom. Jews adapted well to English life, dressing in current English fashion. Few English Jews maintained strict ritual observance, nor did many achieve a high level of Jewish education. Few rabbis lived in England. Despite Britain's tradition of toleration, anti-Semitism remained common.[6]

The Jewish community that developed in eighteenth-century New York built on both the Dutch and English models. As in Britain, the first immigrants were largely Sephardic, and their traditions held sway at the city's only synagogue, Shearith Israel, constructed in 1730 on Mill Street. As in Amsterdam, by the early eighteenth century, Ashkenazi immigrants outnumbered Sephardic Jews, but both worshiped and accepted the supervision of this one synagogue. Yet, as in Britain, New York's synagogue elders possessed less legal authority than did the leaders of the large Esnoga sanctuary in Amsterdam. What influence and control the Jewish community exerted over its members came through moral suasion and, if necessary, social ostracism, not legal authority. The city's small Jewish community enjoyed a stronger sense of common identity than London's. Finally, since New York's Jews did not depend on their European brethren as had the Jews of New Amsterdam, commercial rather than paternal ties developed between London and New York. Elite American traders had relatives in London as agents, and British mercantile families had similar connections in New York.

■ Jewish Merchants of New York: The Early Colonial Era

Understanding the Jewish world of colonial New York begins with a portrait of their leaders, the merchant elite, and the Atlantic network in which they lived. Not all Jews were wealthy. But a good number were, and those who were not sought to become so. As historian Eli Faber notes, "Whether Sephardic or Ashkenazi, Jews who settled in colonial America . . . aspired to become merchants participating in transatlantic commerce." Even if one began as a shopkeeper, he wanted to die as a merchant. Of the twenty-three Jewish wills probated in New York between 1704 and 1774, nineteen of the deceased identified themselves as merchants.[7]

Among the more interesting Sephardic Jewish merchants was Joseph Bueno de Mesquita, whose life spanned nearly a century. Born in the early seventeenth century near the Spanish-French border, he moved first to Amsterdam, where he married in 1641, and finally to New York around 1680. Until his death in 1708, he traded with London and the Caribbean. Records of his shipments include textiles from London on the *Helena*, sugar and rum from Barbados on his sloop *Mary*, cargoes of dry goods and rum from London on three different ships in 1703 and 1704, and a 1705 transport of a large consignment of furs (including 1,064 pounds of elk and eighty-six fox skins). During King William's War (1689–1697), fought between Britain and France both in Europe and in America, he supplied gunpowder to Albany. A man of prominence, he participated in provincial matters. He was likely the same Joseph Bueno who, though no pirate, sailed with Captain Kidd and was asked by Governor Bellomont in 1698 to value the spoils of the notorious buccaneer. In 1704, Governor Edward Cornbury accused him of bribing a government official over an attempt to sequester cocoa (he was never charged). The incident revealed another of his connections, namely, with the chief customs official in New York. At his death in 1708, Bueno, one of the wealthiest New Yorkers, left his wife £600. His estate included five slaves and the furniture of a well-to-do home ("Striped Satin," "leather Couch," "Blew Linon," kitchen and dining-room accessories). His Jewish possessions included both a Hebrew Bible and a Torah scroll with a silver bell. A Torah, an expensive item, speaks to the centrality of Judaism to the fabric of his life.[8]

Luis Gomez, scion of a great mercantile family, followed a slightly different path to prosperity. Born Moses Gomez in Madrid, he changed his name to honor the French king who gave his family asylum. After living in England, he moved to New York, becoming one of the two wealthiest merchants on Queen Street. A West Indian trader, many of his children were born in Jamaica, as was his first wife. It was not uncommon for Jewish merchants to live periodically in the different ports of their mercantile network. The importation of fine goods (Persian silk, calico) from London and trade in wheat added to his fortune. In 1710, as the first merchant to export wheat to the Madeira Islands, he imported the island's coveted wines. He supplied a military expedition in Canada with flour and butter. Gomez speculated in real estate, buying hundreds of acres in Orange and Ulster counties. In the fifty years prior to the Revolution, seven of his descendants served as *parnas* (president) of the community's synagogue.[9]

Ashkenazi Jews also figured among the first generation of Jewish merchants. In addition to Asser Levy, the most prominent Ashkenazi merchant of the early generations was Moses Levy, father of Jacob Frank's wife, Abigaill. Born in Germany in 1665, he immigrated first to London and then to New York. Like the others, he traded with the West Indies. One typical shipment sent axes to St. Thomas in exchange for cocoa. He distilled rum, provoking a municipal regulation outlawing distilleries within a mile of city hall. Levy traveled frequently; on one trip to London, he placed son-in-law Jacob as his representative in New York. In 1711, he supplied British forces in Canada with corn and butter. He speculated in real estate in Westchester and Manhattan. Respected by the entire community, he died in 1728 worth about £6,000.[10]

These early Jewish merchants made their presence felt in the life of the city's political economy. Governor Bellomont complained to the Board of Trade that he was ill treated by most of the city's merchants, and, he said, "were it not for one Dutch merchant and two or three Jews that have let me have money, I should have been undone." Governor Robert Hunter relied on Ashkenazi merchant Nathan Simson for loans to pay soldiers during Queen Anne's war early in the eighteenth century. Simson, an English émigré who returned to Britain for the final years of his life with a fortune of £60,000, became so prominent that New Yorker Francis Harison wrote him two letters asking him to intervene in Parliament on his behalf for the position of comptroller of the Port of Boston. Powerful political figures regularly turned to wealthy Jewish merchants for assistance.[11]

■ Jewish Merchants of New York: The Later Colonial Era

In the second half of the colonial era, Prime Minister William Pitt inundated New York with British military funds to prosecute the French and Indian War, a conflict that saw England incorporate Canada and Florida to become the dominant imperial power in North America. In this period, a new generation of Jewish merchants emerged as the community's leaders. The Gomez family produced prominent sons including Moses and Daniel. Daniel, perhaps the most successful, exemplifies a prosperous mid-eighteenth-century Sephardic merchant. Born in New York on 23 June 1695 and naturalized a British citizen in 1740, he early partnered with his father and brother in the West Indian trade, making frequent visits to the island of Jamaica. There he met and married his first wife, Rebecca de Torres, who bore him a son, Moses, before her death after five years of marriage. His second wife, Esther Levy from Curaçao, died childless in 1753. Gomez became a major English importer, advertising in one of America's earliest newspapers, the *New-York Gazette*, announcing a typical shipment from Liverpool: "earthenware in casks and crates, Cheshire cheese, loaf sugar, cutlery ware, pewter, grindstones, coals, and sundry other goods too tedious to mention." Fluent in Spanish, he traded with leading West Indian merchants, specializing in sugar, and with merchants along the mainland. Like many Jewish merchants, he partnered and traded both with fellow Jewish traders and with such eminent Christian New York families as the Beekmans, Van Cortlandts, and Van Wycks, as well as with New York's governor, George Clinton. His ships could be sighted in ports as diverse as Barbados, Curaçao, London, Dublin, Boston, Charleston, Newport, and Philadelphia.[12]

Daniel Gomez speculated in real estate and by his twenties had bought land in Ulster and Westchester Counties and New Jersey. Likely in concert with his father, he purchased twenty-two hundred acres in Newburgh on the western bank of the Hudson River. He aimed to control a rocky point of land that jutted into the river, a site where Algonquin Indians gathered for ceremonial dances, preparing for hunting expeditions or warfare. Gomez built a blockhouse as a trading station, six miles from Newburgh, the closest nonnative habitation. Constructed of stone, lime, and mortar, it was known as "the Jew's house." There Gomez and his associates spent weeks in isolation, trading hatchets, knives, and trinkets for furs. Prominence as a merchant meant leadership in the Jewish community. Gomez fulfilled these expectations, participating actively in the building and life of congregation Shearith Israel, which elected him parnas eight separate years. An ardent American patriot during the Revolution, he fled to Philadelphia, where he died in 1780.[13]

The other leading Jewish figure in mid-eighteenth-century New York was Ashkenazi Jacob Franks, "New York's most successful Jewish merchant in the colonial era." Like so many Jewish colonial American merchants, he married within the group of Jewish merchants, wedding Abigaill Levy, daughter of Moses Levy. Franks stood at the center of a network that included his son David in Philadelphia and his sons Moses and Naphtali in London (both of whom became wealthy Englishman). He traded numerous commodities with London and the West Indies. An advertisement in the *New-York Gazette* of April 16, 1739, for example, included items ranging from nails, spades, and frying pans to bohea tea. Rum, wine, rice, and skins filled the holds of his ships.[14]

Details of Franks's business appear in a 1743 message to his partner/son Naphtali in London, a letter that described the interests of a prosperous New York Jewish merchant. Franks expressed concern with invoices and bills for the loading of tea sold on three months' credit, commented that he was in the process of loading five "wessels" for London, noted that a ship of his had left for Jamaica with building materials, and mentioned that he recently spent £3,000 "our currency" for another craft and £1,500 for a shipment of "bread." The letter also referred to difficulties with insurance and debt collection, problems with notes owed him ranging from £30 to £100, the state of the tea trade

This engraving of the south prospect of New York Harbor from 1760, during the French and Indian War, includes captured French ships. The city has a prosperous, mercantile look, as the war brought increased British expenditures that arrived through prominent merchants, including Jacob Franks. (Courtesy Collections of the New-York Historical Society)

with Boston, and a desire for a shipment of guns and cannon. He relied on his uncle in London for collateral for some shipments.[15]

Franks, like many of his earlier Jewish merchant counterparts, was an army purveyor, an agent for the king in New York and other northern colonies. During King George's War against the French and Spanish, he dispatched foodstuffs and building materials to Jamaica and outfitted General James Oglethorpe of Georgia for an attack on Florida. Franks received sugar in exchange. During the French and Indian War, son Moses was the Frankses' British liaison. Moses played an integral part of a syndicate of highly placed London merchants who became the largest purveyor of goods to British forces. Working through subagencies in New York and Philadelphia, the Franks family made commissions of greater than 10 percent on their provisions. In Philadelphia, son David was a partner in army supply. Government contracts from the 1740s through the 1780s were worth more than a million pounds sterling, allowing the Frankses to amass far more wealth than any other colonial Jewish family.[16]

Yet Jacob Franks was not only a rich man but also a Jewish scholar, parnas of his synagogue, and head of one of the leading families of New York. At home in the midst of fellow Jews of every standing, he also felt comfortable in the homes of New York's Christian elite. He lived in the Dock ward on Duke Street near the residences of Robert Livingston, Abraham DePeyster, and Stephen Bayard, all wealthy merchants. Like them, he owned a country house in Flatt Bush on Long Island. His family was keenly aware of and involved in local, national, and international politics. Franks dressed as a gentleman of the English upper class. His household contained slaves and servants. He held the deferential expectations of a member of the eighteenth-century gentry. One of the leading women in the city, his wife, Abigaill, was as educated and informed as a European woman of means, though she acquired her education in the colony.[17]

The Franks and Gomez transactions reveal common traits of an eighteenth-century Jewish merchant. Unlike New Amsterdam, a port that was not critical to the Dutch commercial empire and did not deal with goods with which Jews were familiar, New York occupied an important place as a site of legal trade with the English Atlantic network and surreptitious exchange with Dutch, French, and Spanish Caribbean partners. A Jewish merchant traded many goods, often in his own ships, importing manufactured wares to America, West Indian staples to Britain, and whatever the market demanded from America to the West Indies. Jewish merchants possessed a vast network of connections, often negotiating temporary partnerships or agent agreements with relatives as well as non-Jewish business partners.[18]

Shipping involved risks, given storms, piracy, and war; the price and demand for goods could change markedly in the time it took for a ship to cross the Atlantic. For example, after Queen Caroline's death in 1737, merchant Rodrigo Pacheco gambled that mourning cloth would be in high demand and dispatched a large shipment to New York, hoping to be first to deliver the garments. He was second but still profited. On the other hand, Nathan Simson found himself with one thousand barrels of onions in Jamaica and no buyers. Any shipment meant considerable risks. Consider Pacheco's 1732 ship, outfitted in New York with "choice flour, pork, peasee. Tarr, staves . . . ," that sailed to Jamaica, where it sold the cargo for "sugar, Rum, Limes, Negros and Cash," after which it proceeded to South Carolina to trade for rice and then to Lisbon, the end of the voyage. Would it travel safely? Would the goods be in demand at arrival? Would they be able to sell and barter them (both were common) to local shopkeepers and country merchants? Would a hurricane destroy their ship, as happened to Simson in 1722 when he lost 110 barrels of flour? Would a war suddenly be declared? A conflict between the Dutch and Spanish prevented Simson from collecting a debt in Amsterdam. Jewish merchants tried to reduce their risks with international and local connections. Speaking Spanish, Portuguese, Yiddish, German, and Hebrew, they relied on counterparts from thriving Jewish communities in Curaçao, Suriname, Jamaica, and Barbados. Together, they knew the markets and were as up-to-date as possible on supply and demand. With so many unknowns in the Atlantic trade, bonds of consanguinity proved invaluable.[19]

Jewish merchants actively pursued related enterprises. As early as the 1670s, Asser Levy was an incipient banker, with four hundred outstanding loans at his death in 1682. The New York firm of Levy and Marache ventured into insurance brokerage. The Gomez family and Judah Hays loaned money and issued and accepted bills of exchange. A Jewish supplier in Pennsylvania, for example, sent a London bill of exchange to Hays for credit. Merchants also engaged in manufacturing. David Hays owned a vinegar manufactory in the city, and the Gomez family produced snuff as well as pickling beef and pork for export. And, with other merchants, the Gomezes prepared and exported kosher meat to the Caribbean. Moses Levy manufactured soap, and others produced candles and chocolate. Jewish entrepreneurs operated as many as seventeen distilleries in New York.[20]

Early in the colony's history, Jewish merchants played a role in the Atlantic trade far greater than their numbers would suggest. Customs records indicate that in the early eighteenth century Jewish commerce constituted 12 percent of port entries. However, trade patterns changed as the colony matured. Moreover, the Jewish population remained static as the colony's grew. In turn, the proportion of enterprise handled by Jewish merchants diminished. The average dropped to 7 percent by 1725, to 3 percent in 1735, and to 2 percent by midcentury. While early exchange was largely with the Caribbean and London, by the 1730s the majority of trade occurred within the British Empire. At midcentury, Madeira became an additional major port. By then, many Jewish merchants had non-Jewish as well as Jewish partners.[21]

Colonial New York was a litigious society, and Jewish merchants, like their Christian counterparts, were often in court. A few examples are illustrative.

Moses Levy initiated a five-year case in chancery court in 1722 against Nathan Simson and Jacob Franks, executors of his brother Samuel Levy's estate. Moses, accusing Samuel of throwing salt in a shipment of cocoa and then selling it to him, won the suit. In another case, a mariner sued Moses over nonpayment of salary. Moses lost that case in a jury trial but won a similar case against Thomas Rollins, also a sailor, whom, Moses argued, was paid in London. The most famous case, over rights to a Spanish ship captured as a war prize, lasted fifteen years, ending in the Privy Council (royal cabinet). The Jewish merchants who bought the ship claimed the cargo as rightfully theirs, defeating the British owners of the privateer and the Crown, which claimed part of the merchandise as contraband. While not professional lawyers, merchants became well versed in pertinent aspects of the law and competently represented themselves and fellow traders.[22]

■ A Colonial Silversmith of Consummate Skill

A number of Jewish residents desirous of merchant standing began as tradesmen/artisans. Craftsmen were generally of middling status, trained in the traditions or "mysteries" of their crafts through a seven-year apprenticeship and years as journeymen, working for skilled master craftsmen. They manufactured products ranging from rough garments, shoes, and loaf bread to intricate woodwork and silver and gold objects treasured today.

The most celebrated colonial Jewish artisan was Ashkenazi Myer Myers. Son of shopkeeper Solomon Myers, an immigrant perhaps from Amsterdam, he became New York's most noted silversmith. Myers served a seven-year apprenticeship, becoming a freeman of New York. He found success from his formidable talent and from his marriage to Elkalel Cohen, daughter of wealthy merchant Samuel Myers Cohen, with connections to the prominent Jewish Philadelphia Gratz family. Myers's commercial and professional achievement allowed him to purchase a large double house on King Street, thirty-four feet by seventy-eight feet, twice the size of an average English silversmith's household. His home included a residence, a store, and a workshop. Myers employed his silversmith brother to purchase goods in London for retail sale in his shop and entered into a partnership with Benjamin Halsted, a silversmith with lesser skill but valuable capital. Myers's patrons included the first president of Kings College, William Samuel Johnson, the Livingston family, and the Brick Presbyterian Church. His physician, Peter Middleton, introduced him to the Duane and Morris clans. Perhaps his greatest honor came upon his election as president of New York's Gold and Silver Smith's Society in 1786.[23]

Myers stayed abreast of European trends by learning readily from immigrants. His style progressed first to the rococo, stressing curvilinear elegance in the natural beauty of shells and flowers, and then to neoclassicism, centering on the restraint, balance, and proportion of geometric forms. His preference for the neoclassical lasted beyond the Revolutionary era. He employed European-trained engravers, chasers, and piercers. Myers crafted decorative pieces of hollow silver, such as coffee pots, work that was done only by the finest silversmiths and was always "bespoken" or preordered by his patrons. Myers also imported gold and silver jewelry. He attracted a middling clientele with silver flatware and tankards and with repair work.[24]

Mercantile aspirations led Myers to invest in the Spruce Hill Lead Mine in Connecticut, a failure that cost him a considerable part of his wealth, led to suits for debt, and forced him to sell his residence on King Street. Fortunately, his skill returned him to solvency.[25]

Despite intimate business ties to the city's prominent Christian families, Myers strongly identified with the Jewish community. A leading member of Shearith Israel, he served three terms as parnas. He crafted silver for religious occasions including weddings and funerals, often modest items such as spoons whose simplicity bespoke a Jewish intention of maintaining a low profile. Few Jewish families bought expensive hollow ware. The silversmith best expressed his Jewish commitment by producing five pairs of Torah finials (decorative holders). Myers followed Maimonides's decree for "silver and golden pomegranates," visible in the finials' bells (likely imported from Holland) and in the finely wrought engraving. He produced finials for Shearith Israel and for the Jews of Newport and Philadelphia. They remain "unique examples of eighteenth-century American Jewish religious silver."[26]

Myers was the most famous Jewish artisan in colonial America, but he was but one of many Jewish craftsmen. The need for kosher meat, which New York exported throughout the Caribbean, guaranteed a livelihood for butchers. Jewish shoemakers, soap makers, watchmakers, tailors, and wig makers also found sustenance in New York. Benjamin Seixas, advertising his wares, declared that he "makes and sells all sort of saddles, chairs, chaises and harnesses." Jacob De Acosta announced that anyone who had broken glasses or china could have them fixed "in the neatest MANNER ever seen in this city" and that the work would not be "botched up for half price." Levy Simons, an "Embroiderer from LONDON," announced that he could embellish gold and silver, silks, aprons, shoes, and other items "in the neatest and newest fashion." London "taylor" Michael Hyams wished to "acquaint gentlemen and ladies" of his "peculiar method" of making dresses as well as officers' uniforms and ladies' riding garments. Simon Franks, a wig maker from London, announced his knowledge of the "best and neatest Fashion," and that he cut and dressed "Lady's Wigs and Towers" in a mode "better than is pretended to be done by some others." Free of restrictive guilds, Jews entered the artisan classes, the heart of eighteenth-century seaports' populations.[27]

Jewish grocers, retailers, and physicians, similar in standing to artisans, also lived in colonial New York. One shopkeeper, Moses Jacobs, "lately from Germany," announced that, among his wares, was an "IRON MOULD PODER" to remove stains and a "Venetian TOOTH-POWDER" to whiten good teeth and prevent teeth "that are rotten from growing worse." He also sold "an excellent WORM-POWDER" that produced "an effectual cure in a fortnight." Jewish physician Dr. Elias Woolin of Bohemia, advertised in 1740 that he had served in his "Imperial Majesties Army" as "Chirurgeon" for four years. In 1752, Jacob Isaacs, also from Germany, stated that he treated venereal diseases, promising "wonderful cures." Andrew Judah informed the public in the *New-York Gazette* that "a medicinal doctor" had "lately arrived in the city." Judah was Shearith Israel's physician, treating the poor; the congregation paid bills up to sixteen pounds. Abraham Abrahams, the first Jewish graduate from King's College, became a physician.[28]

Silversmith Myers and most fellow artisans and physicians occupied the middling class of New Yorkers. Historian Jacob Rader Marcus's analysis of New York colonial tax records reveals that most Jews were in the upper-middle ranks of society during colonial wars and in other years in either the middle or lower-middle orders. They paid taxes and usually owned their own homes. Jews were also present at the bottom of the economic ladder.

Given the uncertainties of the colonial markets, it is not surprising that a number of Jewish merchants failed. Some, such as Isaac Levy, Moses Hart, and Hayman Levy, went bankrupt. Levy, who supplied the British during the French and Indian War, became insolvent in 1765, asking Newport merchant Aaron Lopez for aid. (Lopez could only send him a few candles to sell, as he had a New York agent.) A few merchants and tradesmen landed in debtor's prison. In 1773, shopkeeper Michael Jacobs sent a letter (with his mark, since he could not write English) to prominent merchant Solomon Simson seeking assistance, pleading that he had languished in debtor's jail for "upwards of twenty-six weeks, . . . which has so reduced him that he . . . cannot afford himself the common necessary's of life." Still others absconded. Gerardus Beekman, a prominent merchant landowner, tried to find the whereabouts of debtor Ralph Isaacs. Moses Franks of London eventually informed him that Isaacs was last seen in Holland, the location of "new scenes of villainy." A last, uncommon resort was crime. Moses Susman, indicted for stealing "Gold Silver money bag rings &c." from fellow Jew Moses Levy, was hanged on the City Common in August 1727.[29]

■ Slavery in New York

A resident of New York standing outside the Mill Street synagogue in the 1730s could not have missed the arrival of Lewis Gomez, one of the city's wealthiest Jewish merchants. The family marched in procession, led by the elder Gomez. Following them were his personal slaves carrying the family's prayer books and prayer shawls. In a ceremony symbolic of the deferential nature of colonial American society, upon reaching the synagogue the slaves entered, placed the books and shawls on the proper chairs, and left as the family took their seats.[30]

Slavery was a major part of New York's colonial life from the Dutch era on. During the second and third decades of the eighteenth century, with Caribbean trade flourishing, the city's slave population increased to over 15 percent of the population. By the end of the era, New York housed more slaves than any colony north of Maryland. Men of both middling and genteel standing might own slaves. Slaves worked on the docks, as assistants to craftsmen, and, most commonly, as household servants for the city's elite. Wealthy slave owners leased slaves to tradesmen in need of temporary labor.[31]

Extant wills and the 1703 census indicate the common ownership of slaves among wealthy Jews. In 1703, four out of the six Jewish families listed owned slaves. Thirteen of the twenty-three extant wills written prior to the Revolutionary era (1765) bequeathed slaves. In 1740, Uriah Hyam, a little-known member of Shearith Israel, left his son Andrew Israel in Jamaica: "my Negro boy named CAVANDRO." Joseph Bueno de Mesquita willed his "Loving wife RACHELL . . . & to her heires forever" most of his fortune, his household goods, and, the will states, "all the slaves now belonging to mee." Samuel Myers Cohen bestowed on his spouse: "all those negroes Slaves I have which I shall die possessed of." Merchant Isaac Gomez provided his ailing wife his home and "as many of [his] Slaves as are necessary to attend her." Isaac Pinheiro bequeathed his son Jacob £250 and "A Negro Boy Named ANDOVER," and his son Moses £100, "together with one Negro boy, named SHARLOW." He left both sons, "to share and share alike," fifteen "Negros" in Nevis. Silversmith Myers owned slaves and a "servant man." In 1763, he offered a reward for the return of his "Negro Wench," Daphne, who was "tall and not very black."[32]

A few Jewish merchants manumitted slaves. Moses Michal, who lived both in New York and Curaçao and who wrote his will in Dutch, on the one hand left his children two slaves, THAM and PRINS, and on the other gave his "Negro PIRO freedom and discharge of all Slavish service." Similarly, Benjamin Gomez, parnas for three terms, bequeathed his wife two slaves and gave his married daughter Rachel his household furniture, plate, jewels, linen, and his "two slaves ISHMAEL & JENNEY to her & her heirs forever." Yet he also directed that his "Mustie Wench KATTEY" be "made free from the Yoke of Slavery" in gratitude for her "fidelity & faithfull Services" to his daughter Rachel, by then deceased. Gomez also freed another slave.[33]

Beyond ownership of slaves, a number of Jewish merchants participated in the slave trade, though their consignments represented a small fraction of these enterprises. Jewish shipowners participated in 8.3 percent of the New York slave trade, importing 377 slaves of the 4,363 known to have arrived in the seaport between 1715 and 1765. A quarter of these came directly from Africa on 14 slave ships; 140 vessels originated in the Caribbean. Jews partnered in two African voyages: Nathan Simson was a colleague in the importation of 100 slaves in 1717 with two non-Jewish partners, and in 1721 Simson joined Isaac Levy (then in London but later a resident of New York) and Richard Janeway and William Walton to import 240 slaves on the *Crown Galley*, from Madagascar through Brazil and Barbados. The latter voyage was horrific, as only 117 Africans survived the diseases on board. Of those who made it to New York, 106 were sold at auction to ninety-five different New Yorkers; the other 11 were too sick for sale. Other Jews, while not owning ships, participated in the trade. Mordecai Gomez and two of his brothers imported 61 slaves: 55 in partnership with non-Jews, 6 on their own. Moses Levy and brother-in-law Jacob Franks imported 71 slaves: 52 in partnership with Gentile merchants, 19 on their own. Robert Pacheco imported 21 slaves in tandem with non-Jewish partners. The widow Simja da Silva De Torres imported 3 slaves in 1728 via the *Duke of Portland* and 4 in 1742, one of whom was, she said, "for my person." Jewish merchants took part in New York's slave trade, a trade that provided income for a few leading families.[34]

Colonial New York witnessed two slave revolts, the first in 1712 and the second in 1741. Jews were involved in the second revolt, a plot that historians have debated as a possible political fabrication. The outbreak allegedly began with ten separate fires (including one in Fort George) within a few weeks. Fear spread of a Spanish/Catholic conspiracy. Over a hundred blacks were arrested and held in the city hall dungeon. Thirteen were burned at the stake; seventeen were hanged, as were four whites suspected as ringleaders. Jews owned five of the arrested blacks. Transcripts—Mordecai Gomez served as the Spanish translator during legal proceedings—indicated that Samuel Myers Cohen's house was a target, and he testified against two slaves for stealing goods worth five pounds. When Hereford, one of his own slaves, was implicated, Cohen insisted on personally interrogating Jack, the accuser. Under cross-examination, Jack recanted his testimony, and Hereford was discharged. Cuffee, Luis Gomez's slave, went to the stake, condemned as a ringleader. The court transported Cajoe, Mordecai Gomez's slave, and Windsor, another of Myers Cohen's slaves, to the West Indies. Diana, slave of David Machado; Jack, the slave of Judah Hays; and Lucena, slave of Jacob Franks were arrested but never tried.[35]

Well-to-do Jewish merchants, dressed in the stylish English waistcoats and linen of their Christian counterparts, shared a common attitude to slavery. They accepted it as part of daily life. On average, they owned no more and no fewer slaves than their non-Jewish peers. At Passover, they did not relate the story of their exodus from Egyptian bondage to African-American slavery. Colonial Jews sought standing in a society in which slave owning was the norm. Like their neighbors, they accepted this institution as part of the accepted social hierarchy and organization.

The merchant princes of New York were the undisputed leaders of the city's small but coherent Jewish community. Clothed in fashionable eighteenth-century English attire, Ashkenazi and Sephardic merchants worked and mixed easily with each other and with their Christian counterparts while yet retaining their Jewish identity and allegiance. They took advantage of the political freedom and economic openness of New York Colony to make the city an ever welcoming haven for Jews and a fertile ground for the growth of Jewish republican ideals.

A Chanukah menorah from the seventeenth or early eighteenth century, probably made in Holland. (Courtesy Congregation Shearith Israel)

CHAPTER 3

A Synagogue Community

Abraham Rodriguez de Rivera was born on the Iberian Peninsula late in the seventeenth century. There he married and fathered a son. After the death of his wife, he remarried and later immigrated to New York with that son, his new wife, and their two children. Upon arrival in the new world, he adopted the name Abraham. (His original name is not known.) His wife took the name of Sarah. His children were named Isaac, Jacob, Rebecca, and Rachel. In coming to the new world, they believed that they were following the example of their biblical patriarchs and matriarchs as they journeyed to the Promised Land. In 1730, during Abraham's residency in New York, the city's Jews consecrated the first synagogue built on the North American mainland; Abraham contributed the substantial sum of eight pounds. The community named it Shearith Israel (Remnant of Israel), indicating that they saw themselves as refugees. Would New York be a new homeland, a permanent haven, or would it be a harbor of exile, looking to a future Zion? The divergent meanings expressed in these symbolic name echoed through New York City's Jewish history for generations.[1]

New York's First Synagogue

In 1682, under English rule, New York's Jews began to gather for private religious services. (The mayor and Common Council banned public worship until 1691.) The return of British rule in 1691 following Leisler's Rebellion opened public worship to the Jewish community. Tradition places a religious meetinghouse in the mid-1690s at a home on Beaver Street. The first evidence of a synagogue is a house on Mill Street on the site of a horse mill. Tax rolls indicate that the Jewish community leased it as a place of worship in 1703, using it continuously from 1709. Assessment rolls term the dwelling the "Jew synagogue" and the house next door as rented to "the Jew Rabby [teacher]." Rent was eight pounds. This early congregation named itself Shearith Jacob, the remnant of Jacob, referring to Micah's promise that Jews would prosper in the midst of other nations. While its bylaws are lost, records from 1720 to 1722 reveal a congregation with thirty-seven active members. Unlike its successor, it owned no building.[2]

In 1728, the Jewish community, headed by prominent merchants including Sephardi Luis Gomez and Ashkenazi Jacob Franks, formed a new congregation; in 1730 its members raised funds needed to purchase a lot and construct a new building, the first home of Shearith Israel. While New York's Jews provided the major backing, contributions arrived from many Jewish communities including Boston, Barbados, Jamaica, Curaçao, and London. A third of the £600 collected came from outside New York. Unlike the wooden-frame rented house, the synagogue was constructed of brick with a floor of Bristol stone covered with sand. Its interior followed the Sephardic architectural style of London and Amsterdam, with the ark at the east end, separated by banisters. The ark held the congregation's Torah scrolls, the Pentateuch, decorated with silver finials. Benches ran north and south; women's benches were in a separate gallery/balcony that extended over three-quarters of the room and had its own entrance. The president (parnas) and vice president had their own seats (banco) near the ark. Space was reserved for standees and processions. Seven candles, each "as large as a man's arm," illuminated the elevated reading desk in the center, three feet above the floor. Five candelabras lit the sanctuary; the centerpiece featured thirty-two candles. Along with tablets depicting the Ten Commandments, a perpetual lamp hung in front of the ark. Most visitors noticed the ark. The synagogue's exterior, standing thirty-five feet square and twenty-one feet high, was not ornate. The lot included a courtyard large enough to accommodate a mikveh (ritual bath) using water from the spring that fed the original mill. In 1731, with the help of a London merchant, the congregation erected a two-story building to house a school and administrative offices. In 1758, Shearith Israel purchased a third building as a home for the shamash, or caretaker. The synagogue's cemetery, acquired by the Jewish community in 1682, was located on New Bowery near Chatham Square.[3]

The Jews of New York, following the model of Amsterdam and London, formed a "synagogue community." Living in a Christian society, numbering less than 1 percent of the city's population, they made the synagogue their spiritual center of gravity and the focus of the community's ethnic identity. The rules and rituals for which it stood governed much of the nonbusiness lives of its members. Since riding on the Sabbath was forbidden, most Jews resided within close walking distance in the South, East, and especially the Dock Ward, the site of Shearith Israel. Following Jewish dietary laws, most members ate only at their own or each other's kosher homes, enhancing the sense of community. As the only synagogue in the thirteen colonies from 1730 to 1763, the sanctuary drew crowds during autumn High Holy Days as Jews traveled to New York from Philadelphia and as far as Halifax in Canada. Wills indicate devotion to the synagogue; many members left it part of their fortune. Rachel Luis in 1737 ordered her "houshold furnitur" sold, including all "potts and pans," to buy a "Shefer Tora [Torah] for the use of Kall Kados [Holy Congregation] of Sherith Ysraell." Joshua Isaacs bequeathed fifty pounds "to teach poor Children the Hebrew tongue." Widow Simja De Torres left five pounds, Mordecai Gomez twenty-five pounds, and Solomon Simson twenty pounds. Material gifts included rams' horns, wine goblets, pointers for reading the Torah, decorative hangings, and tablecloths.[4]

■ Synagogue Governance

Authority at Shearith Israel reflected the deference common to colonial America and to the traditions of the Sephardic communities of Amsterdam and London. That the synagogue never sought a rabbi before the 1840s in part reflected the desire of its lay leaders to be at the helm of the Jewish community. Shearith Israel employed three officials. The hazan, the spiritual leader of the congregation, circumcised male newborns, prepared male youth for bar mitzvah, and, when a teacher was not employed, ran the school. He conducted services twice a day during the week and three times on the Sabbath. Though not ordained, he was fluent in Hebrew and could respond to religious questions not demanding intensive Talmudic inquiry. Assisting him was the shamash, who kept the sanctuary clean and supplied with wood, water, and candles. The *bodeck/ shochet* provided certified kosher meat for the community and beyond.[5]

The most important synagogue official, the parnas, or president of the congregation, was not an employee. As the lay chief officer, he oversaw the three paid officials, distributed funds to the poor (or secured their exit from the city), supervised the congregation's finances, and maintained order in the synagogue, including mediation of disputes, religious and otherwise. The position was time-consuming, and many of the men most in demand, the leading married merchants of the city, given the requirements of their trade, often declined to serve more than once or twice and preferred to pay a fine for their refusal. In 1751, the congregation split the position into six-month segments to attract candidates. Members of the Gomez and Franks families, the congregation's most prominent families, served most often, though many men of standing held this honored position. A small governing board, known in Amsterdam as the *Mahamad* and in New York as the *adjuntos* or elders, assisted the parnas. Composed of the city's distinguished Jewish citizens, the board elected the next parnas, advising him on synagogue issues. Jews who supported the synagogue by paying seat assessments were the members (*yehidim*). Those who did not pay could stand at religious services.[6]

While London and Amsterdam had both Ashkenazi and Sephardic synagogues, New York, with its small Jewish population, supported only Shearith Israel from 1730 to 1824. Though Ashkenazim outnumbered Sephardim after 1720, the synagogue followed Sephardic traditions. It incorporated the practice of European Sephardic synagogues of placing authority in the hands of the parnas and the elders who made most decisions; yehidim participated in governance for the election of the hazan, shamash, and shochet and at times of crisis. Shearith Israel adopted the Sephardic practice of positioning the hazan in the center of the synagogue when leading prayers; Hebrew pronunciation followed the Sephardic manner; morning blessings took place in the synagogue rather than at home. The early minutes of the synagogue were in Portuguese, and, until the Revolution, the prayer for the king was offered in Spanish. Despite Sephardic ritual, Ashkenazim regularly served as *parnassim*. Shearith Israel ignored the advice of the rabbi of the Curaçao congregation to get the Ashkenazim to "signe an agreement" to limit their authority. When internal dissension endangered the congregation, as in 1746 when "something must immediately be done," the elders turned to Jacob Franks, an Ashkenazi, and Mordecai Gomez, a Sephardi, for resolution. Still, intermarriage between Ashkenazim and Sephardim could occasion tension within the small community.[7]

Since New York had no public education until the 1820s, the congregation maintained a school, offered gratis to poor members. The first academy, founded in 1730 and named Yeshivat Minchat Arav, taught Hebrew for three hours a day; secular subjects were quickly added. Wealthier Jewish New Yorkers employed the school for part of their children's education. Jacob Franks sent his sons and daughters to the synagogue school in the morning for instruction in "french, Spanish hebrew and writing"; in the afternoon, George Brownell taught them "Reading Writing Cyphering, Merchant Accoumpts, Latin, Greek, etc." At Shearith Israel's school, the teacher was either a "ribbi," an instructor whose duty was to teach and accompany the children to Sabbath services, or the hazan, who taught for an additional fee. In 1775, for example, the elders contracted with the hazan, for an additional twenty pounds salary, to keep daily school at his home, "Fryday afternoons Holy Days and Fast days Excepted," for six hours in summer and four hours otherwise. He taught "Hebrew, Spanish, English, writting & Arithmetick." The elders visited monthly. Minutes reveal that schools held sessions only periodically. Even so, the congregation increased Jewish and secular literacy, allowing the next generation to surpass their parents' education and fit more comfortably into British-American society.[8]

The congregation accepted responsibility for poor relief, seeing it as a begrudging, discretionary obligation. The congregation was charged to assist the poor "with as much as the Parnaz and his assistants shall think fitt." One of the largest expenses of Shearith Israel, relief strained synagogue resources. In 1728–1729, the elders allocated thirty pounds for *obras pias* (work of the poor), an expense second only to the hazan's salary. The next year the amount (fifty-three pounds) exceeded his salary, and it increased to seventy-eight pounds by 1748. The congregation availed itself of one solution: it shipped the indigent out of the city. If a poor Jew, incapable of maintaining him- or herself "should happen to come to this place," he or she would be entitled to eight shillings a week for twelve weeks. After that, the parnas was to "despatch them to sum othere place," assisting them in "their Voyage." For example, on September 18, 1755, the elders resolved "that the widow Abrams and her family shall be shipt off & her passage paid," and on July 7, 1756, they ordered that "Mrs. Hannah Louzada should be dispatched to Lancaster." In 1765, the congregation gave Aaron Pinto "three Corse Shirts," as he was "almost naked." He was then "to be dispatchd by first oppty" to Newport "to take passage to Surinam." If he refused to leave, he must remain "at his own Expence."[9]

■ Ritual Observance

Ritual observance was central to eighteenth-century Jewish identity in colonial New York. Tradition dictated life-cycle events. Circumcision, the foremost requirement, took place eight days after the birth of a male child, provided a *mohel* (ritual circumciser) could be found in time. Male children celebrated bar mitzvah at thirteen. Celebrations began immediately after the service and ran for two days, at which "anybody who was anybody" began to "blow their heads off." Saturday night was for dancing, and Sunday an open house. When children sought a marriage partner, the father of a prospective groom asked the future bride's family for consent to proceed. If the couple wished to wed, the groom requested permission from the congregation. The two families prepared a carefully written contract according to ancient custom, including sections ensuring the bride's financial security if she became a widow. Weddings occurred on Sundays in the bride's home, outside if weather permitted. For funerals, the coffin of the deceased would be carried "on the shoulders of the members of the congregation" in procession to the sacred burying ground.[10]

Sabbath, from Friday evening to Saturday evening, anchored the week. Jewish law and custom permitted no work, no writing, no transaction of business. It was a day of profound rest. Jacob Franks's wife, Abigaill, noted its importance to an observant family: "I never knew the benifit of the Sabath before," she wrote to her son in London, "but Now I am Glad when it comes for his [Jacob's] Sake that he may have a Little reLaxation from t[ha]t Continuall Hurry he is in." Swedish botanist Peter Kalm, visiting America in 1747, was impressed with Sabbath observance. He noted that New York's Jews "never cook any food for themselves on Saturday but that it is done on the day before; they keep a fire in their houses on Saturday in the winter." Jacob Franks, because he could not handle money on the Sabbath or a holiday, asked his merchant friend Isaac Watts to temporarily pay an account when funds were due on a High Holy Day. The congregation conducted weekly Sabbath prayer services at the synagogue; Jewish holidays were celebrated similarly.[11]

A critical area of ritual observance, *kashrut*, included the supply and inspection of kosher meat. The ritual slaughterer (shochet), one of the three paid officials of the synagogue, was carefully supervised. In 1771, for example, the board inquired whether malpractice of its bodek/shochet caused a number of kitchens to become *traif*, or nonkosher, preventing Jewish residents from

The Omer Counter used by Congregation Shearith Israel in the eighteenth century. The Omer represents the commandment to count forty-nine days beginning from the day on which the Omer, a sacrifice conaining an omer, a measure of barley, was offered in the Temple in Jerusalem, to the day before an offering of wheat was brought to the Temple on Shavuot. "H" stands for *Homer* (Omer), "S" stands for *semana* (week), and "D" stands for *dia* (day). (Courtesy Congregation Shearith Israel)

using their dining facilities. As members supplied kosher meat to coastal and Caribbean communities, the synagogue determined to ensure its beef met requirements of Jewish law. Elders spent hours dealing with the inspection and labeling of beef. When Jamaican Jews accused the New York congregation of laxity, parnas Sampson Simson responded that "every quarter [of beef] is seal'd with Led. [lead] & the persons who put up Beef take care to see it cut up & properly sent to their Houses." The elders, he declared, "have the principles of our Holy Religion truly at Heart and that we shall not knowingly permit any thing in our power to be done Contrary thereto." When scarcity threatened, the community limited the exportation of beef to ensure ample meat for the congregation, levying a forty-shilling fine on anyone who "takes any beef or fatt on any fryday or Hereb Yomtob [holiday eve] for Exportation or Sale."[12]

Shearith Israel viewed itself as the guardian of Jewish tradition in New

York's hinterlands. In 1757, the congregation's elders, concerned that too many people "that reside in the Country . . . do dayly violate the principles [of their] holy religion such as Trading On the Sabath, Eating of forbidden Meats & other Henious Crimes," warned country brethren either to return to strict religious behavior or to lose the "Mitztote [privileges] of the Sinagoge." The following year, believing that their decree had "in some measure succeeded," the elders reconsidered "the admonition read last Kippur" and invited "whosoever may thinck that they are quallified, but wrongfully debard" to participate in synagogue rituals. The elders saw themselves as "fiatful Sheepherds [who] call into the fold the wandring sheep"; their concern was "establishing & supporting [their] holy religion." Expressing the same unease, merchant Uriah Hendricks rejected a suitor for his Aunt Hava, though the young man had sufficient money, because he "continually Break Shabbat & Eat trefat & have no Regard to Religion."[13]

How observant were New York's Jews? Kalm noted that Jews "commonly eat no pork" but that those traveling on business did not hesitate to break the dietary laws, "even though they were in company of Christians." Such laxity likely triggered the congregation's concern with country Jews. It is not possible to go into the homes of the Livingstons, Morisses, Gomezes, and Frankses to see how the Jewish mercantile elite behaved when they dined with their Christian counterparts. Some may have compromised. Yet Jacob Franks's wife, Abigaill, instructed son Naphtali not to eat anything but "bread & butter" at her brother Asher's home in London or anywhere where "there is the Least doubt of things not done after [their own] Strict Judaicall method." She cautioned, "wathever my thoughts may be Concerning Some Fables, . . . I look Opon the Observence Conscientioussly and therefore with my blessing I Strictly injoyn it to your care."[14]

Not only did ritual observance inform New York Jewish social and religious life, but it also linked New Yorkers to Jewish communities in the Caribbean, Europe, and North Africa. Although it served as a strong bond within the community, how strictly the city's Jews observed religious ritual is impossible to determine.

∎ Conflict in the Synagogue

Maintaining peace in the synagogue and community proved the elders' most difficult and time-consuming task. Synagogue minutes reveal periodic congregational conflict, often so intense that it threatened not only the comity but the very existence of the synagogue. There were two basic themes: the difficulty that the dues-paying members had with those not paying their fair share, and the difficulty in mediating between highly sensitive members.

Shearith Israel's income came chiefly from seat assessments, gifts, legacies, fines, and offerings. The problem of fiscal accountability surfaced in 1737 when the synagogue's board decreed that "every family or private person that carries on trade in the country" must pay yearly dues of forty shillings. Those who refused would receive "no benifit nor *Mitzvah*" from the congregation, including the right of burial in the synagogue's cemetery. In 1747, at a general meeting to discuss Jews who did not support the synagogue, the "the Mejorety of the Jehidim here present" levied a tax to cover synagogue costs. Anyone who paid timely would "be intiteled to a Siat in the Sinagog," be listed in the book of "Jehidim," and could become parnas or an *adjunto* provided he "behaves with decency quiatly and peasefuly." Any member refusing to pay his assessment for four successive quarters would have his name "Rased out of the Book of offerings," would not be given the honor of being called to the Torah, and would no longer be "Loock't upon as a Member of [the] Congregation."[15]

Five years later, financial pressures produced "all manner of discord & Division amongst the Members," many of whom resented fellow Jews who received benefits without supporting the synagogue. Addressing unacceptable acts of protest, the elders declared that a member called to the "Sepher" (Torah) had to follow the parnas's request or pay a fine of twenty shillings. Responding to members' outrage, they decreed that a Jew who "in his lifetime" had "absented himself from the Sinagogue" or was "no ways a benefactor to the Congregation" would not have his "corps" interred "within the walls of [the congregation's] Burrying Ground," absent a special exemption.[16]

The most common source of turmoil was the issue of authority. Although deference was part of the social fabric of colonial America and the Sephardic tradition, many members were educated, prominent figures who had difficulty respecting any power other than themselves. Recognizing the problem, the earliest minutes of the synagogue delegated "authority to the Gentm That shall be elected yearly [the elders or *adjuntos*] . . . that with the fear of God they may act as their Conscience shall dictate them for well Governing" of the congregation. If "any persons or persons whatsoever shall offer to give any affront or abuse, Either by words or action to any person or persons within the said Sinagog," they were to pay the parnas a fine of twenty shillings. If they refused, "the whole Congregation" would "assist" in its collection, suggesting ostracism. Three years later, the elders issued a regulation "for the peace and harmony of the Kahal [community] and of the holy synagogue," stating that a member called to the "Sepher Torah," the central act of the Sabbath service, had to offer blessings for the health of the parnas and the congregation. Refusal incurred a fine of thirty shillings. The parnas represented the congregation; disrespect undermined the entire community.[17]

In 1746, conflict ignited beyond the elders' capacity for control and conciliation. Calling a special meeting, the yehidim charged the parnas, two elders, and the two of the city's most eminent Jews, Jacob Franks and Mordecai Gomez, with the task of preparing "good and wholesome Laws." In the meantime, the yehidim, "finding it necessary for the peace of our said congregation that something must immediately be done," decreed that any member disturbing "the devotion and quiet of our holy worship," would be ordered out of the synagogue by the parnas, not to return until he paid a fine of up to five pounds. Fifty members signed the decree.[18]

Despite the work of Franks and Gomez, disputes continued. In 1748, the conduct of Judah Hays, a dealer in wholesale and retail goods and a synagogue founder who served twice as parnas, became a serious issue. Hays was outspoken in synagogue, insulting authority. Responding to his behavior, the elders stipulated a twenty-shilling fine for any member causing a disturbance or speaking without the parnas's consent, other than "in their proper turn or place." In addition, the elders excused Hays, "for sufficient reasons" and "at his request," from attending meetings of the congregation. The following year, "frequent disturbances" disrupted New Year's services when the parnas refused to carry out his duties. As a result, synagogue notables, including Daniel Gomez and Jacob Franks, agreed to accept the position of parnas in set order.[19]

In 1755, the most troubling controversy during the colonial era erupted. On the evening of Kol Nidre 1755, a warm night, Gitlah, wife of Solomon Hays, sat in a packed women's gallery with an invited guest. (Solomon, brother of Judah, was a shochet and a merchant.) The sash on the window had been removed because of the day's heat. Unexpectedly a storm drenched Mrs. Hays. Without consulting the elders, Solomon went to the women's gallery and replaced the sash, only to have it removed, with permission of the elders, by ladies in the gallery. Mrs. Hays then closed the window, but women in the gallery, uncomfortable in the stifling sanctuary, again reopened it. Ensuring it would not again be shut, Moses Gomez, son of Daniel Gomez, went upstairs and removed the window entirely. This encounter concluded in the courtyard with the physical ejection of Hays, who continued to vociferously protest, from the synagogue. The elders fined Hays twenty shillings. Hays responded by filing assault charges against the parnas and a number of elders. Shearith Israel reacted to this public, legal attack with its first and only excommunication, issuing an edict, read in February, May, and October of 1756, stating that no member of the congregation was to have "Conversation Correspondance or Commasty With him [Hays] because he has Candellise [Scandalized] us amonst the Christens."[20]

The trial of the assault charges against Moses Gomez and the elders lasted nineteen days, with nine witnesses for the Crown and forty-five for the elders. The prosecutor, using Solomon Hays's testimony, argued that when Hays reproved Gomez, stating, "So you show your Authority that you are an Elder," Gomez struck Hays in the face "so that Blood flew from his Mouth." Then the elders forcefully removed Hays from synagogue grounds. Members of the synagogue, the prosecutor reasoned, were angry at Hays for charging that Daniel Gomez practiced usury in his business; for exposing two Jewish residents of Albany as noncitizens, causing them to lose trading privileges; and for alleging that the congregation attempted to cause the Christian wife of Isaac Isaacs "to renounce her Savior, and become a proselite to the Jewish Religion." These incidents led to an "inveterate Hatred" toward "Informer" Hays. The jury found the elders innocent and ordered Hays to pay the costs of the defense attorney.[21]

The dispute simmered for five more years. Seeking revenge, Hays began writing a book detailing sins of the synagogue. But the pains of ostracism took their toll. In January 1760, at a meeting of the elders, Hays made "proper submission for the Injuries done the Congregation," paid a hefty twenty-pound fine, gave bond for good behavior, and pledged to "deliver up a certain book in his possession wrote against [the Shearith Israel] Society." The elders then readmitted him as "a member of this Kaal," adding the words "Salom hal Israel" (peace upon Israel).[22]

But trouble in the women's gallery had not ended. In 1760, what seemed more like a comic opera roiled the synagogue again. This time Judah Hays's wife, Josse, was "turned" out of her seat by Judah Mears, who wanted it for his

A stone from Sheaerith Israel's first cemetery. The position of the hands indicates that the man buried was a Cohen, a descendant of the priestly tribe. Maintenance of the cemetery was one of the synagogue's most important responsibilities. (Courtesy Congregation Shearith Israel)

daughter. The congregation tried to make peace by widening the seat so both could be accommodated, but to no avail. Judah Hays, refusing to settle, was fined and threatened with excommunication. He refused to pay. Three years later, after Josse's death, Jacob Franks paid the fine, and Judah was readmitted to the "Rights and Ceremonies of the Synagogue," though his name no longer appeared in congregational minutes. In 1796, the synagogue removed the offending *banca*, "the cause of much dissatisfaction."[23]

Jews valued deference and decorum as part of their European tradition and as a means to win acceptance within the Christian community. However, the importance of status and standing within the small community and congregation could overcome the forces of comity and restraint. Too, the resentment of members against Jews not paying dues or attending services indicated the synagogue's belief in its centrality. Members expected Jews to give the congregation allegiance and took umbrage at some Jews' willingness to remain outside of synagogue governance. Unlike Amsterdam, the American synagogue possessed no legal authority to maintain order and discipline. That Shearith Israel, serving a population of 200 to 250 Jews, Ashkenazi and Sephardic, many proud and difficult, held together despite serious stress and disorder represented a significant accomplishment. The congregation proved its centrality to the maintenance of Jewish identity and society in colonial New York City.

■ The State of Religious Belief

The state of religious belief beyond ritual observance of the colonial community is difficult to evaluate. Extant wills offer evidence of core beliefs. In the earliest known Jewish New York will (1704), merchant Joseph Tores Nunez stated in the opening paragraph, "I do recommend my Soule to God that gave it me & my body to the Earth there to be decently buried in hopes of a glorious resurrecion at the last day." Four years later, Joseph Bueno used the same phrase in his will. In 1716, the second hazan of the congregation and a merchant, Abraham Haim De Lucena, wrote, "I bequeath my Immortal Soul into the hands of the Almighty God of Israel My Creator Trusting in his Mercy for pardon of All my sines, and hoping for A Joyful resurr[ection] to Life Eternal." Although most colonial Jews "never doubted that there was life after death," the word *resurrection*, was used only in the first decades of the eighteenth century. Those who inserted it in their wills lived most of their lives in the seventeenth century. Its use may reflect the legacy of medieval Catholicism on Jews who had lived in Catholic Europe, as well as the messianic belief in resurrection of medieval Judaism. More common in the mid- and later eighteenth century was Samuel Myers Cohen's statement, "I bequeath my soul unto God that gave it trusting and alone depending on his mercy for my Eternal Salvation," or Mordecai Gomez's assertion in 1750, "I committ my

Precious and immortal Soul into The hands of God who gave it To me and my body to The Earth to be buried in the Jews Burying Ground according To the Jewish Custom." In both cases, they expressed belief in an external soul as separate from the body.[24]

If the concept of resurrection receded, piety did not. Within Daniel Gomez's ledger book, in the midst of ordinary business entries in the mid-eighteenth century, a prayer is suddenly interjected;

> Be mercyfull to me, O Lord, forgive my Eniquettys. I am morning for my transgretions, they Compres me with tearror of Your Wroth, being sensible, of my sin I begg for forgivnes, and as Your, goodnes, is great, I rely on your mercey and beseach your blesing that I maye be preservd under the Shado of your wings; not for aney wourdenes in me but for your goodnes Sake maye my souel Cleave to the they Comandments and maye I walke in uprightnes, that I maye be one of your belovd Chosen Israelite amen.

The mixture of business entries and soulful prayer is an indication of how "Jewish merchants in eighteenth-century British America expressed, defined and were defined by their religiosity." Prominent Jewish merchant Aaron Lopez of Newport advised bankrupt New Yorker Hayman Levy that, given the "instability of human affairs," it must be "consolation" to know that such events "are the decrees of a just [and] wise Ruler, who directs all events for our own good." The words of these prominent Jewish merchants provide evidence of a strong faith. A religious perspective could bring solace and meaning to businessmen dealing with the vicissitudes of fortune. There was little space between the counting house and the synagogue.[25]

The hazans of the synagogue give further insight into Jewish piety. The most distinguished colonial figure was Joseph Jeshurun Pinto, hazan from 1758 to 1766, hired from London (though born in Amsterdam) following a lengthy search. Pinto, who earned the title of "Learned Scholar" at the Ets Haim Rabbinical Seminary in Amsterdam, possessed an "introspective spiritual personality," questioning his fate and seeking to know God's purpose.[26]

For Pinto, a Hebraic scholar, though he taught languages on the side, the role of hazan was a full-time rather than a part-time position. He prepared time tables for the Sabbath and compiled a book of the particular "traditions, customs and ceremonies of the New York congregation." For example, on the seventh night of Passover, the anniversary of the consecration of the synagogue, the ark would be open throughout the service. Or during Tisha B'Av, the fast commemorating the destruction of the Temples in Jerusalem, the hazan would interject Spanish paraphrases for each verse when chanting from the Book of Lamentations.[27]

Pinto was the first to publish an English translation of Jewish liturgy in America, *The Form of Prayer*, a special 1760 prayer service of thanksgiving for the British victory in the French and Indian War. That service invokes a traditional deity, the "Most gracious Lord of the Universe, GOD above all Gods, and exalted beyond the highest Powers, the Great, the Mighty, and the Omnipotent, who alone can perform Wonders, and in whose Hand is the Salvation of Kings and who directs the whole Power of Earthly Princes."[28]

In 1766, Isaac Pinto, a scholarly merchant, teacher, and translator unrelated to the hazan, published a translation of both the Sabbath and High Holy Day services. His preface noted that services were conducted in Hebrew in "Veneration" of the "*sacred*" language in which God first revealed himself and to preserve it in the "firm Persuasion that it will again be re-established in Israel." However, as Hebrew was "imperfectly understood by many, by some, not at all," a translation was in order. The book began with an exhortation to "MORTAL Man" to "Consider that thou art going to present thyself before the Eternal Omnipotent and Omniscient Being . . . ; Consider . . . that he beholds and observes thee." If "thou adorest him as thou oughtest, and as is thy duty, thou obtainest Salvation." Failure to act "bringst Condemnation on thyself." (The emphasis on salvation may reflect Dutch Calvinist influence, though the piety is in harmony with the language of Jewish wills.) The service would be recognizable at a contemporary Jewish gathering. It began with opening prayers and psalms; included the "Barchu," "Ahavat Olam," the "Shema," the "Kedusha," the reading of the Torah with prayers in use today; and ended with a "Musaph" service, the "Kaddish," and the hymns "En Kelohenu" and "Adon Olam."[29]

Peter Kalm and physician Alexander Hamilton visited the synagogue in the mid-eighteenth century. Kalm was impressed with the modernity of the service, noting that both men and women dressed in the English fashion and that men kept their hats on during the service. During prayers, men "spread a white cloth over their heads," with the wealthier sporting a "much richer cloth than the poorer ones." He noticed that the men had Hebrew books for prayer and song and that the hazan, whom visitors mistook for a rabbi, read prayers while elevated in the center of the room. Hamilton observed "an assembly of about fifty of the seed of Abraham chanting and singing their doleful hymns round the sanctuary" while dressed in "robes of white silk." He could not get the "lugubrious songs" out of his head for a day. The "seven golden candlesticks transformed into silver gilt" in front of the hazan captured his attention. Hamilton compared the women's gallery to a "hen coop" in which females either prayed "or talked about business." Kalm saw an educated modern congregation, Hamilton a scene from the Middle Ages. New York's Jews were modern in the street, but in their sanctuary they held fast to venerable traditions.[30]

Did the Enlightenment, with its critical view of traditional religion, hold any sway within the Jewish community? While it is difficult to measure its impact, skepticism was present in the letters of Abigaill Franks. The wife of New York's most prominent Jewish citizen, Abigaill socialized with the best families of New York. A highly educated, well-read woman, she expressed impatience with eighteenth-century Judaism. Writing to her son, she remarked that the author of a recent book on religion was unlikely to be Jewish, for the writer "thought too reasonable." Critical of the Judaism practiced in New York, she stated, "I cant help Condemning the many Supersti[ti]ons wee are Clog'd with & heartly wish a Calvin or Luther would rise amongst Us, . . . for I don't think religeon Consist in Idle Cerimonies & works of Supperoregations Wich if they send people to heaven wee & the papist have the Greatest title too." Abigaill, whose thoughts were often contradictory, was referring to traditional Jewish rituals. While advising her son to strictly observe the dietary laws and noting the Sabbath's beneficial impact on her husband, she nevertheless could think of Jewish customs as outdated superstition.[31]

Abigaill Franks, unlike her seventeenth-century progenitors, had little use for the traditional concept of resurrection. In comforting her son over the death of his father-in-law, she wrote that "all the difference after deaths is a mans works here on Earth for that never dyes" and that he or she who has "Left soe Great and Good a name may be Said to have Livd full of days and dyed in a Good Ould Age." Those who have the "happyness" to be his "relations" will, she trusted, "fallow his Steps in dischageing theire duty to God an man" in the "Severall Stages of Life" that the "Allmighty" yet allows them.[32]

But Abigaill's Jewish identity also had a pious aspect. In 1740, she wrote Naphtali that, as she and her husband were well, "I bless god this Leaves Us praying the Allmighty to preserve you in the Same and All other Felicity." Learning of the death of her son's infant child, she counseled that it was "the

Will of that Divine Power to wich all must submit and say with Aaron it's the Lords doeing and Wee must be Silent." An age of skepticism influenced Jewish religiosity. However, in the case of Abigaill Franks, when it came to dietary advice to her son, tradition prevailed, And, in times of crisis, such as the death of a child, traditional Judaic piety also triumphed. This was likely true for much of the community.[33]

■ Abigaill Franks: Faith, Reason, Intermarriage, and Women's Place in the Community

Abigaill Franks wrote about far more than religious beliefs. Her remarkable letters to her son Naphtali, in London as a partner of his father and to seek his fortune, provide a unique window into the life of New York's Jewish community, its ties to the outside world, and the place of men and women in that world. Abigaill came to New York from London as the daughter of Moses Levy and his first wife, Rycha. At sixteen, she married Franks, also a London émigré, in part to be rid of her stepmother, Grace Mears, whom she intensely disliked. The Franks lived well in New York and Long Island. Abigaill bore eight children, four of whom survived to adulthood. She devoted herself both to their education and to her own. A highly educated woman, she would have been comfortable in a contemporary Berlin salon.

Abigaill diligently sought reading material, following the *Gentleman's Magazine*, "the *New Yorker* of the eighteenth century." She casually quoted Joseph Addison on conscience and commented that while Smollett's *The Adventures of Roderick Random*, "pleassed Me Much," Fielding's *Joseph Andrews* "Exceeds him." She admired Pope's poetry: "I read him with Some Sort of adoration." She asked her son for a multivolume history of Poland (in French) and for new books in history, literature, or philosophy. Her wit and erudition are apparent when in telling her son of the death of Bilah Hart, wife of her brother-in-law, she quotes a proverb in Spanish ("A pain in the elbow and the pain for a [lost] spouse hurt a great deal but lasts a short time."). She follows this quip with a quote from Genesis on the comforting of Judah following his wife's death. She mused, "I could with Vast Pleassure Imploy three hours of the 24 from my Family Affairs to be diping in a good Author: And relinquish Every other Gaity Commonly Called the pleassure of Life."[34]

Abigaill was politically well connected and well informed. During the 1730s, when a serious dispute broke out between, on the one side, Governor

Cosby and the Delancey family (the family representing the British court party, favoring a strong executive, either monarch or governor) and, on the other side, William Morris and the Livingston clan (representing the country party, favoring a stronger role for Parliament or Assembly), the Franks sought good relations with both. Abigaill stated that she and her husband chose not to take sides; a successful merchant needed allies with both factions. She mixed easily in the homes of notable neighbors including Robert Livingston, perhaps the most esteemed New Yorker, as well as Stephen Bayard and Jacobus Van Cortlandt. It gave her "a Secret pleasure," she confided, to "Observe the faire Charecter" her family held "in the place by Jews & Christians."[35]

As for Abigaill's Jewish female compatriots, she preferred the cosmopolitan world. "I don't offten See . . . any of our Ladys but at Synagogue for they are a Stupid Set of People." Abigaill had little respect for women's synagogue talk, with its "Variety of News & Tatle," about which, she said, "I Never am Concerned [and] I dont Care to trouble my Self." She had limited tolerance for Sephardic pretension. She told her son that the "Portugueze there are in A Violent Uproar" about the coming marriage of Sephardi Isaac Mendes Seixas and Ashkenazi Rachel Levy. She found the controversy trivial, and she wrote merely "to fill a space." In addition, as a woman of reason, she had little patience for Jewish miscreants, male and female, who were "soe stupid to think all Villiany is to be forgiven Provided they can call themselves good Jews."[36]

Abigaill was an ardent British patriot. Aware that her husband was a supplier of the British military in North America, she freely commented on foreign policy. In 1740, at the beginning of King George's War, a conflict that pitted the British against the Spanish, she supported the Duke of Argyle's belligerent policy toward Spain, as "Very agreeable to Our Politicians," viewing him with "A Mixture of Pride as Well As Patriotism." She regretted that the British did not give greater support to Admiral Vernon's campaign in the Caribbean, for if he "had bin Assisted [in] a Just manner the Spanish West Indias would by this have bin Very much demolished [if] not the best part in the possession of the English." When the war ended status quo antebellum in 1748, she remarked that her "Paciffic dispossition" ought to be grateful, but she still wished that "for the honor of Brittian Our Ennimies had bin a little more humble."[37]

Abigaill offered advice on proper social conduct. Early in her correspondence, she urged Naphtali, "[Do] not be So free in y[ou]r Discourse on religeon be more Circumspect in the Observence of some things Especialy y[ou]r morning Dev[otio]ns." She likely worried that the laying of tephelin (phylacteries) could be misinterpreted by non-Jews. Displeased by his argumentativeness, she warned him, "[You are] Soe Intent by your Disputes to think Anyone will follow you. It shows in one of your Age" a certain "Self-Opinion," which, if not "Nipt in the bud," will "grow opon you." Two years later, she advised him, as he was "Now Launcht out Amongst Strangers," to be "Exceeding Circumspect": "In Your Conduct be Affable to All men." Naphtali must not be fooled by "fair Speeches of friendship" but rather must be "a Very Just Observer" of his "word, in all Respects," lest "Ill Habits" become "Customs." As Naphtali prepared to marry first cousin Phila, Abigaill wrote about the "marri'd state":

> without the Ingredient of good Sence & good Nature it Must be Very Insiped for I think there is required the Same Maxims & Reasson to Make a Friendship in Mariage as in any other Article of Life And As you Say you are now blessed with the Utmost of your wishes I dare Say You will Endeavour to Live Up to the Charector You have allways Injoye'd of being Guided by Reasson and Lett that charming Guide be your Director in Every Minutt Circumstance.

Abigaill advised her son to seek moderation and to make his wife a friend. Never make an issue of religion or self-worth; always strive for reason. In that, she was a child of the eighteenth century.[38]

Abigaill never reconciled her Enlightenment values, including a critique of Jewish religion and its practices, with her piety or her dedication to ritual. Moreover, despite her intellectual cast and her contempt for the superficial lives of the women of Shearith Israel, she often gossiped. Her letters are replete with the problems of her relations, marriages—troubled and otherwise—and of anger and contempt toward her despised stepmother. Moreover, though she denigrated the pettiness of the Sephardic community, when David Gomez, son of prominent Sephardic merchant Luis Gomez, sought the hand of her daughter Richa, she condemned him as a "stupid Wretch" who would never have her consent and, she trusted, would never get her daughter's.[39]

The greatest test of Abigaill's belief in reason, moderation, and circumspection came with her daughter Phila's elopement. A few years before, Abigaill had criticized her daughters for aiming too high, asking her son, "doe you Expect Your Sisters to be Nuns for Unless they can Meet with a Person that Can keep them a Coach & Six I suppose they must not think of Changeing there Condition?" Would "chance," she wondered, "Pres[en]t a Worthy Person?"

Indeed, not in the eyes of Abigaill, for Phila, who had told her mother "that noe Consideration in Life should Ever Induce her to Disoblige Such good Parents," deceived Abigaill by clandestinely marrying out of her religion, living at home six months without divulging her espousal, then sneaking out one night to join her husband, Oliver Delancey. Oliver, the younger brother of the leader of a politically privileged family, James Delancey, was known as a rake, prone to violence and profanity.[40]

Devastated, Abigaill retreated to her Long Island home, nursing a festering sense of betrayal. It was of no consolation that the Christian community did not criticize Phila for marrying "a man of worth and Charector." Rather, she said she had been "Soe Depresst that it was a pain to [her] to Speak or See Any one." She wrote Naphtali (already informed by his brother), lamenting, "[I can never regain] that Serenitty nor Peace within I have Soe happyly had hittherto." She refused to leave home: "My house has bin my prisson." Though Oliver asked to see her, she refused. However, if she met him on the street, she said she would "be Civill." As for her errant daughter, she said, "I am determined I never will See nor Lett none of ye Family Goe Near her." Jacob Franks acted more propitiously. A businessman who wanted good relations with the Delancey family and a father who wished to protect his daughter, he determined not to interfere with Phila's £1,000 inheritance for fear that she be "Ill Used by her husband or Relations which at present is other ways." Understanding that she "heartily Repents" her behavior, he was "Inclined" to give her "Liberty to Come to See us [her parents] but can Not Bring y[ou]r mother to It." After settlement of the legacy, neither of Phila's parents spoke to her again.[41]

One intermarriage followed another. Abigaill's son David, after moving to Philadelphia, married Margaret Evans, daughter of the recorder of Pennsylvania. David, who at his bar mitzvah read the entire weekly portion from the Torah in a virtuoso performance, did not convert to Christianity, but his children were baptized. Abigaill reacted as she did with Phila: "If I cant throw him from My heart I Will by my Conduct have the Appearance of it." Once again, she endured a "Firey Tryall" and determined she would have no contact with two children whom she raised and cherished ever so closely.[42]

In the contest between reason and faith, ties of religion and ethnicity won out in Abigaill's heart, as she unconditionally broke off relations with her children. They, on the other hand, grew up in a cosmopolitan community. The

Franks family is reminiscent of the fate of the children of Jewish philosopher Moses Mendelssohn, who worked to reconcile faith and reason, Christian and Jew. Like Abigaill Franks, Mendelssohn remained an Orthodox Jew his entire life. And, like Abigaill Franks, some of his children and all of his grandchildren converted to or were born into Christianity. All of David Franks's children were raised as Christians, as were Phila's. Abigaill's son Naphtali remained Jewish, but his children converted, as did the children of her other London son, Moses. David Franks's family in Philadelphia became members of the "Christian establishment," and Oliver and Phila Delancey moved to England as loyalists and entered Christian society there. So, despite Abigaill's intense loyalty to her Judaic roots, she, like many of her German Jewish counterparts, had children who, raised in the spirit of the Enlightenment, found little value in the rituals and tenets of Judaism, given the opportunities that awaited in the Christian world.[43]

■ A Woman's Place

Was Abigaill a typical Jewish woman of eighteenth-century colonial America? Clearly not. Born into a prominent family, she socialized with the province's elite. She was extremely well read; most women were not. She was politically well informed. She found her fellow women of Shearith Israel "a Stupid Set of people" and chose not to socialize with them outside the synagogue. What of these women? Colonial American women who were not among the elite generally lived monotonous lives dominated by domestic chores, marriage, childbirth, and child rearing. Jewish women were part of that society, though there were some differences. First, European Jewish tradition sanctioned women's entering the marketplace to allow their spouses time to study. Second, many Jews in New York did not marry, and a number of these women likely worked in market trades open to females, such as teaching, retailing, or the needle trades. Third, rabbinic law and tradition "gave a sense of authority to Jewish women in marriage that their Gentile counterparts did not always find," including considerate treatment of the wife, the sacredness of household peace, the option of divorce, and provision for a wife who became a widow. Nor did Judaism accept the concept of original sin, of man's fall from grace due to the cunning of a woman.[44]

Women most commonly entered the mercantile world after the death of a well-to-do spouse; eighteenth-century society deemed it acceptable for a woman to take on her husband's trade. Esther (Hester) Brown Pardo, wife of Saul Pardo, the first hazan in New York, continued his commerce with the West Indies. In 1708, she imported twenty-five gallons of rum from St. Thomas on the sloop *Flying Horse*. Widow Rachel Levy imported rum from Boston and Rhode Island. Simja De Torres, whose husband, as noted in chapter 2, died twenty-two years before her death, traded in slaves for at least fourteen years. When synagogue charity proved inadequate, Hetty Hays opened a kosher boarding house, perhaps to serve the community of Jewish single men, and Grace Levy and Rebecca Gomez opened retail and grocery stores.[45]

Most Jewish women devoted the majority of their hours to raising their children in a traditional Jewish home. Maintaining a kosher home required an extensive commitment of time. A member of Shearith Israel reminisced that the "women of the congregation were real actors in [the] kitchen business." Women cooked and baked for themselves; servants could not work in the kitchen without the immediate supervision of the woman of the home; otherwise the dwelling would be "*treifa*" (unclean). If a woman suspected that the rules of kashrut, including separate dishes for meat and dairy products, were not followed, she was obliged to report it to the synagogue. One woman, so concerned about the kashrut of her home that she climbed a ladder to inspect the dishes in detail, slipped and fell, losing her life. Most homes produced a specialty food such as a unique pound cake or "stickies, . . . dough with sugar and stuff over them," or "sopes peridoes," a type of French toast eaten at Purim. If the burdens of maintaining a kosher kitchen gave special meaning to life, it also meant added work.[46]

Jewish women attended synagogue, though they had a lesser role than Christian women did in church. Unlike the men, attendance for women was optional, except on Purim and High Holy Days. With the women sitting in the balcony's sixty-five seats behind a latticed "breast work as high as their chins," few could see clearly, and none participated in the service's rituals. Yet due to the presence of Jewish schools and Judaism's stress on literacy, many Jewish women could follow the service. Two of the three Jewish women leaving eighteenth-century wills signed their name.[47]

Historian Holly Snyder argues that the book of Esther and the holiday of Purim strongly influenced Jewish women in colonial America. Esther's courage in risking her life to save the Jews of Persia inspired descendants of Jewish Marranos, who secretly practiced Judaism while in danger of the Inquisition.

Esther maintained her humility after becoming queen to King Ahasueras, deferring to her husband and to her cousin Mordecai. A Jewish woman, while praised as valiant at the Sabbath table, was expected to assume the "traditional models of humility, obedience and modesty" of eighteenth-century British society.[48]

If women's position in the home and synagogue was submissive, they were also heirs to a tradition of piety expressed in *tkhines*, female petitional devotions on matters such as pregnancy and childbirth, as well as visits to the cemetery and special prayers for the Sabbath, festivals, and High Holy Days. If women were not allowed a ritual role in Jewish services, those who sought deeper religious solace could gain some comfort and spiritual life from a tradition of private prayer.[49]

▪ Conversion, Assimilation, and Anti-Semitism: The Place of Jews in Gentile Society

The entire Jewish community faced the dilemma of the Franks family. Would a small society of less than 1 percent of the population survive as an identifiable community? Would the children of the community marry within? If not, assimilation threatened its existence. Historian Robert Cohen discovered that Jewish families tended to have about five children, though not all lived to adulthood. Women married around the age of twenty, men at twenty-seven, and marriages lasted close to thirty years. Most surprising in the demographic evidence is the number of young Jewish men and women who remained single. In New York, 45 percent of men and 41 percent of women did not marry. Possibly the paucity of eligible compatible mates, the transience of men seeking fortunes in the West Indies, or the sense of common identity and shame of marrying outside the religion kept many young Jews from marrying. The rate of intermarriage was only between 10 and 15 percent. Low marriage rates enhanced the importance of new Jewish immigrants in ensuring a population adequate to maintain a community, however small.[50]

The synagogue did not sanction conversion as a solution to the problem of intermarriage. There were rare exceptions, such as Frances, wife of Parnas Isaac Isaacs, who became part of the 1755 controversy when Solomon Hays accused the congregation of persuading her to renounce Christianity. In 1763, the elders passed a resolution prohibiting any member from assisting "in making proselytes, or performing the marriage of any jew to a proselyte."

Consequently, when Benjamin Jacobs petitioned the congregation to marry a Christian who was "desirous to live as a jewess" and to be "married according to the manners and custom of the Jews, as it is her desire to live in the strict observance of all [Jewish] Laws and customs," the elders denied the request. Opposition stemmed from lack of a rabbi to perform the conversion ceremony and fear of angering the Christian community. There were, of course, intermarriages, the majority being Jewish men wedding Christian women. Some were performed in civil ceremonies, after which the couple might maintain a presence in the Jewish community, while others took place in a Christian church, with the couple separating from the community.[51]

New York's Jews were patriotic Britons who participated in the political life of New York Colony to a greater extent than did Jews of the other colonies. To make this transition easier, they occasionally Anglicized their names. The Bueno family took the name of Bones, Rachel Luiza changed her name to Rachel Lewis, Rodrigo Pacheco became Benjamin Mendes Pacheco, and Luis Gomez became Lewis Moses Gomez or Moses Gomez. Many served the Crown. Mordecai and Daniel Gomez were named Spanish interpreters to the Admiralty and Supreme Courts. In 1731, Rodrigo Pacheco attained the most prestigious office, the colony's agent to Parliament. Jewish citizens, if freemen or property owners, could vote and run for office. The highest elective positions they held were constable, assessor, and collector of taxes. Jews served in the militia; in 1738, eleven members of Shearith Israel were enrolled. The congregation prayed weekly for the health of their king in Spanish. At a special service following the French and Indian War, they offered "Thanksgiving to Almighty GOD," that he had given the king's generals "such Power, Strength, and Wisdom, to conquer all the Country of *Canada* and reduce the same to the happy Dominion of his Sacred Majesty, King GEORGE the Second, whose Name be exalted, as a Banner to be displayed for Glory and Renown."[52]

As Jews strove for acceptance as loyal British patriots with the right to lead their lives and work in the marketplace in harmony with the majority Christian society, they encountered anti-Semitism, long a Western tradition. Recorded references to Jewish citizens note a separate identity. Luis and Daniel Gomez's trading house in upstate New York was known as "the Jew house." Governor Cornbury in 1704, discussing a dispute in the cocoa trade, labeled one of the merchants involved as "one Joseph Bueno, a Jew." In 1765, the Board of Trade charged that "a Jew," Hyam Myers, "seduced" two Mohawk Indians into coming to London to be exhibited for profit and ordered them back to America. Christians also used the word *Jew* as a term of opprobrium. Merchant Gerardus Beekman, commenting on the problems of selling his "Muscavado Sugar," wrote, "I have almost turned jew in running from merchant to merchant to offer them."[53]

Overt anti-Semitic acts occasionally occurred. In 1668, the excuse of a Christian trader charged with cheating a Jewish merchant was that his poor flour was only "for a devilish Jew." In 1743, during a Jewish funeral, "a Rabble was got together," led by "one whom by his dress would have thought to be a Gentleman." As the coffin was lowered, he waved "an image," likely a crucifix, and uttered a Latin paternoster, insulting the "dead, in such a vile manner, that, to mention all would Shock a human ear." The reporter lamented that these "liege citizens" have "too often felt the heavy hand of their Outrageous and principled Neighbors." Historian William Pencak identifies the leader of the mob as Oliver Delancey, bitter over the Franks family's reaction to his marriage. Oliver was also indicted in 1740 for attacking the home of a "poor Jew and his wife who had lately come from Holland." Delancey's crowd broke the couple's windows, "tore everything to pieces and then swore they would lie with the woman."[54]

In politics, it is noteworthy that merchants as wealthy and prominent as Luis and Daniel Gomez or Jacob Franks were never elected to either the Assembly or the Common Council. Had figures of this stature been Christian, they would have served on one or both of these bodies. In 1737, strong anti-Semitic statements were expressed in the Assembly following a close race between Cornelis Van Horne and Adolph Philipse, representing the followers of Lewis Morris and Governor William Cosby, two bitter political factions struggling for control of the Assembly. As part of the Assembly's investigation of the contest, it stated that, as Jews did not vote for Parliament in England, "It is the unanimous Opinion of this House that they ought not to be admitted to vote for Representatives in this Colony." William Smith, Sr., a proponent of disallowance, invoked the "bloody tragedy [crucifixion] at Mount Calvary," stating that as Jews had been fortunate "to escape with their lives," they should not object to the mere loss of their votes. Pencak asserts that this was the rhetorical height of anti-Semitism in colonial British North America. Exacerbating some of these problems, the closeness of the synagogue community could give the appearance of clannishness, eliciting common prejudice.

In 1765, Major Rodgers of the British military published a *Concise History of North America* in which he wrote disparagingly that the Jews "who have been tolerated to settle here . . . sustain no very good character, being many of them selfish and knavish (and where they have the opportunity) an oppressive and cruel people."[55]

Yet these incidents were exceptional, not the rule. Three years after William Smith's angry tirade, the naturalization law of 1740 affirmed Jews' right to vote in New York. Jews and Christians more often than not cooperated with each other. Nearly every major Jewish merchant partnered with non-Jewish merchants. Jews and Christians joined the same Masonic lodges and served together in the militia. British forces in America welcomed Jews as military suppliers. The elite of the Jewish community in New York socialized with the Christian elite. Five prominent New York Jews contributed to the construction of the Anglican Trinity Church in 1711, including merchants Luis Gomez and Moses Levy. During a smallpox epidemic, Mordecai Gomez housed the New York Assembly at his estate in Greenwich Village. Moreover, artisans such as Myer Myers worked with non-Jewish partners and journeymen as well as with a largely Christian clientele, who bought his silver because it was the best in town. As Peter Kalm remarked, the Jews of New York "possess great privileges; . . . they enjoy all the privileges common to the other inhabitants of this town and province." When Mordecai Gomez died, the *New-York Gazette* eulogized him as an "esteemed fair trader, and charitable to the poor, . . . with an unblemish'd character, [who] left a large family, by who he is deservedly lamented, as he is by all his acquaintances."[56]

Unlike the Jews of New Amsterdam, the Jews of British colonial New York did not have to struggle with British authorities and British merchants for political and economic rights. They possessed nearly the same political and religious freedom as their Christian neighbors did. Their leading merchants ranked among the wealthiest New Yorkers. An accepted part of the colony's life, though they were small in number, they played a significant role in its economy. Their struggle was not, as in New Amsterdam, for the right to live in the city, to practice their religion, and to seek their fortunes. They strove, instead, to maintain a cohesive ethnic and religious society, to overcome pressures of assimilation that inevitably pushed at so tiny a sector of the population, and to practice and preserve ancient rituals in a world ever more part of the Enlightenment. In this they succeeded. Though their population did not grow, as did the city's, with the help of immigration and an active synagogue they sustained their community, passing on their traditions and standing to future generations. If we return to our original question at the outset of this chapter—whether New York was to be a permanent home or a harbor of exile—the Jews of colonial New York looked to America more and more as a haven than as a refuge. They identified with British-American culture, an affiliation that caused many to cast their lots with the Americans in the ensuing Revolution.

A carefully executed painting by Howard Pyle titled *The Continental Army Marching Down the Old Bowery New York*, as the army entered the city after the British evacuated on November 25, 1783. (Courtesy Collections of the New-York Historical Society)

CHAPTER 4

The Jewish Community and the American Revolution

In 1782, near the end of the War for Independence, Hazan Gershom Seixas, in exile in Philadelphia, studied the calculations of a German rabbi whose numerical analysis of the words of the book of Daniel concluded that the messiah would appear in 1783. At the same time, Seixas was working for reform of Pennsylvania's constitution to allow full political participation by Jewish citizens. Was the American Revolution a millennial sign of the return of Jews to Zion, or was it a sign of a new republican order and a new era in American Jewish history? The war, Seixas declared, was "a wonderful display of . . . divine providence," an act of God whose ultimate meaning was yet to unfold.[1]

In 1760, the 250 Jews in New York City were, like most colonists, patriotic citizens of the British Empire and proud of the recent military conquest of Canada in the French and Indian War. Yet between 1765 and 1775, the majority of the Jewish community, like their Christian counterparts, turned from loyal Britons to rebellious Americans. In a long encounter that deeply altered the outlook and way of life of America's foremost Jewish community, many of the city's Jews endured exile and took to arms against their once-beloved mother country.

Most New York Jews prospered during the late 1750s and early 1760s. Merchants gained fortunes on an unprecedented scale supplying his majesty's forces in the struggle against the French and Spanish. However, the war's end with the 1763 Treaty of Paris, the departure of troops, and the cessation of expenditures triggered a severe recession in the American colonies. Strained by a large national debt, the British determined to tighten supervision of its

widening empire. Accordingly, it introduced measures that hit the econo-
mies of the colonies' major seaports, including New York, which, by 1775, had
grown to a population of twenty-five thousand, second only to Philadelphia's
forty thousand inhabitants.[2]

■ The Coming of Revolution

The 1764 Sugar Act, which not only increased the price of foreign molasses but
also cracked down on smuggling, imposing onerous bonding procedures on
coastal and Atlantic commercial shipping, came into effect as the economic
slowdown began. The notorious Stamp Act followed in 1765, imposing duties
on domestic wares such as newspapers and playing cards as well as on shipping documents. The impost hurt both the New York City's commercial elite
and ordinary citizens. Violating the colonists' understanding that the mother
county was a source of nurturance, it initiated a growing sense of alienation
as British Americans saw their interests as distinct from those of Britons not
residing in the colonies. These perceptions led to an intense constitutional
examination, in the newspapers and colonial legislatures, of the rights of
colonists. The Stamp Act also unleashed social friction among the lower and
lower-middling classes. Taken aback by the militant reaction as Americans
took to the streets and began a boycott of British shipping, the British repealed
the Stamp Act. Unwisely they followed it with the Townshend Acts in 1767, a
tax applying only to imports. This, too, triggered a strong reaction, a policy of
nonimportation by merchants and artisans.[3]

As incident upon incident played out, the city's Jewish mercantile elite,
the leaders of their community, joined other merchants and artisans ponder-
ing how to respond to British policies. After passage of the Stamp Act, Jewish merchants were likely signers of a nonimportation resolution, though no
lists are extant. After the Townshend Acts became law, ten prominent Jewish
merchants, including Uriah Hendricks (later a loyalist), Hayman Levy, Jonas
Phillips, and Manuel Josephson, joined 190 New York traders who pledged not
to import "articles as are or may hereafter be subject to duty, for the purpose
of raising revenue in America." Sampson Simson served as one of the city's
mercantile spokesmen. Appealing to resistance to British measures, Jewish
merchant Isaac Adolphus advertised his hosiery as "equal in price and superior in goodness to British goods, . . . which, if the Patriotic Americans should
approve, large quantities can readily be furnished."[4]

These Jewish merchants were part of the conservative wing of the growing revolutionary movement. They did not go as far as artisan radicals, who advocated total nonimportation, instead resolving not to import articles subject to the Townshend taxes. Two Jewish merchants, Isaac Pinto and Isaac Solomon, weary of conflicting demands from merchants wanting to continue trade and from artisans demanding strict nonimportation, and exhausted by the "frequent applications made to them to sign papers," publicly announced that their initial agreement was sufficient. Another moderate merchant, Jacob Abrahams, found himself "ducked in the creek" in New Jersey for his more conservative stance.[5]

Despite these tensions, however, until 1773 life for the Jewish population continued with some degree of normalcy. The city's papers published numerous ads of ambitious Jewish merchants. Jonas Phillips, insolvent in 1764, regained his footing and advertised in 1770 as an auctioneer and broker who "buys and sells all sorts of goods on commission" for home or abroad, selling objects ranging from Irish linens to toothpick cases. Benjamin Seixas, saddler, told the public that at his shop "nearly opposite to his Excellency [British commander] General Gage," a buyer might find saddles, chairs, harnesses, and combs, "which he will sell cheap for cash." Manuel Josephson advertised children's toys, silks, and refined English sugar.[6]

Noncommercial life also proceeded with a sense of normality. The death of noted merchant Sampson Simson in 1773 elicited notices in the city's newspapers describing "An Israelite, indeed, in whom unfeigned reverence for the Supreme Being, Integrity of heart and Humanity were Characteristick," a man "always upright in his dealings," a " real Friend to the Liberties of his country." The *New-York Gazette* advertised a sermon of Rabbi Haim Isaac Karigal, a visitor from the Holy Land, and Jacob Moses sought the return of a "runaway negro" who spoke English but "has a slow way in his speech."[7]

■ Pre-Revolutionary Synagogue Tensions

Congregation Shearith Israel, center of the Jewish community of New York, experienced periods of both normalcy and serious tension. The elders continued to handle routine issues such as an ongoing debate over the hazan's salary. However, given the agitation embroiling the city, it is not surprising that the congregation suffered internal conflict so severe that it reached beyond the synagogue into the courts. It is not known if the quarrels were related to differences about imperial politics, but given the volatile political climate, tempers were short. The synagogue took to keeping secret minutes to record its worst quarrels. In 1767, Isaac Pinto was fined for "abusing" the parnas; a shamash was suspended for insubordination. In 1771, a general meeting had to be called because of "disorder" in the synagogue when parnas-elect Moses Gomez refused to assume his position. Congregants complained that the shochet was not doing his duties.[8]

As the legitimacy of governance was questioned in the streets, so too was it at issue in the synagogue, magnifying internal struggles. Two disputes ended with public civil trials. In 1770, Manuel Josephson disparaged eighty-four-year-old Joseph Simson, father of merchants Solomon and Sampson Simson, because the elder Simson's prayer shawl was unkempt and because of his flawed speech and unseemly gestures. Sampson labeled Josephson a "dirty hog" for teasing a man "old enough to be [his] grandfather." He also claimed that Josephson had been a dishonest merchant both in Pensacola and in New York and belittled his lowly origins as a "shoeblack." At the ensuing trial, Josephson, responding through witness Solomon Hays, claimed that the elders, "all of one Family," were deadly plotters who "if it was not for the Christian Law . . . would kill many." The court found for the synagogue and against Josephson.[9]

A dispute in 1772 involved a charge of assault against Solomon Simson and Benjamin Seixas. The problem began with an internal quarrel within the Hays family. Judah Hays disinherited his son Michael and Michael's daughter Rachel. When Michael brought his newborn daughter to the synagogue to be named, Barak, Michael's brother, called his brother a "bastard" and shouted, "Father, what can you expect from a parcel of Scoundrels?" When Parnas Hayman Levy attempted to expel him, Barak unbuttoned his waistcoat and prepared "to fight any scoundrel that should dare to touch him." After he was physically removed from the sanctuary, Barak filed charges against Solomon Simson and Benjamin Seixas, the two elders who ejected him. Judge Robert Livingston ruled against Barak, who with brother Solomon was expelled from the congregation. That year the elders also suspended Manuel Josephson for insulting the parnas ("if you are Parnass over the Bog House, you are not Parnass here").[10]

Historian William Pencak terms these confrontations a generational feud between families who ran the synagogue and those who felt neglected, a struggle in which "elite Christian magistrates . . . supported... elite Jews" in a challenge to authority. The American Revolution too can be thought of as a generational struggle, a conflict among elites, and a challenge to authority. Tensions inflamed the city and shook the comity of the synagogue.[11]

■ 1776

The Boston Tea Party of 1773 and the punitive Coercive Acts that followed proved to be the tipping points of the American Revolution. Positions hardened; reconciliation became nearly impossible. Fierce ideological debates filled pages of the city's newspapers. Hostility heightened in 1770 when a British soldier in New York killed a seaman with a bayonet as soldiers attempted to remove a liberty pole. As British control weakened, merchants, preferring conciliatory resistance, and artisans, desiring radical measures, strove for political supremacy, ultimately forming a joint governing committee. After the Battle of Lexington and Concord in April 1775, British authority collapsed. The remaining troops were removed.[12]

On April 19, New Yorkers quickly learned that eight minutemen, members of the local militia, had been killed by British soldiers on a bridge at Lexington. They carefully followed the proceedings of the Continental Congress in Philadelphia; the courage displayed at Bunker Hill cheered them, as did the appointment of George Washington as commander in chief. Even so, New York, with the exception of its artisan community and a few upstart merchants, remained a conservative province, reluctant to advocate independence. When the British arrived on Staten Island in the summer of 1776 with the largest forces yet seen in North America, New Yorkers could no longer avoid a decision. Commanded by Admiral Richard Howe and General William Howe, the flotilla contained thirty thousand British soldiers and Hessian mercenaries. They confronted Washington's Continental army, recently arrived from Cambridge.

With invasion imminent, the Declaration of Independence, signed on July 4, was read with great ceremony to the Continental Army. The city's Jewish community had to choose either to join the American patriot cause and likely leave the city or to remain loyal to George III. It was not an easy decision for many. Some argued that to leave New York would mean the end of Shearith Israel, the oldest synagogue in the thirteen colonies, the fruits of the work of so many families over many years. Jonas Phillips, who moved to New York from Albany, emerging as a prominent merchant and member of the synagogue, "worked energetically among the other members of the Congregation in which his influence was beginning to be felt, to range them upon the side of liberty, notwithstanding a determination upon the part of many to remain in New York, and continue the Synagogue under Tory supervision, of which faction there was a large and important clique in New York." When members argued that leaving would mean the end of the synagogue, Philips rejoined "that it were better that the Congregation should die in the cause of liberty than to live and submit to the impositions of an arrogant government," and the "position was finally decided upon favorably."[13]

Phillips's courage derived in part from his analysis that the Americans would prevail. In Philadelphia in 1776, he wrote Gumpel Samson, a merchant in Amsterdam, predicting the Revolution's outcome, but not without misgivings: "The war will make all England bankrupt. The Americans have an army of 100,000 fellows and the English only 25,000 and some ships. The Americans have already made themselves like the States of Holland. The enclosed [Declaration of Independence] is a declaration of the whole country. How it will end, the blessed God knows. The war does me no damage, thank God!"[14]

By contrast, a year earlier, Oliver Delancey, Phila Franks's spouse, who became a loyalist and British general when put to the final test, wrote to brother-in-law Moses Franks in London (after Abigaill's death, there was a reconciliation within the family) hoping the well-connected Moses could use his influence within the British government. Delancey declared that the provinces were "in a ferment," and, if "violent Councils prevail in England," then "adieu to Peace of Government for the People of this country have more firmness than any of their Neighbors." The consequence would be "desolation Bloodshed and an Eternal Warr," ruin for both sides. He still held "faint glimpses of the Hope of Peace and the Enjoyment of Former Happiness." It was not in the interest "of the Child to Affront Parent or the Parent to use Cruel Chastisement on its Ignorant Offspring." The Franks family, whose leadership in America now focused on David in Philadelphia, vacillated between its loyalty and connection to the British government and its American roots. David Franks became a reluctant loyalist: after the war he went into exile in Britain and then returned to the United States, a broken man who lost most of his wealth.[15]

During the pre-Revolutionary years, Hazan Gershom Seixas, a young man who had been an eager and ambitious student of Hazan Pinto and who so impressed the congregation with his quick grasp of Jewish learning that it appointed him hazan in 1768 when he was only twenty-three, saw the British

The British attempted to capture Fort Lee in New Jersey by crossing the Hudson River and climbing the Palisades. Engraving probably by British captain Thomas Davies. (Courtesy Prints Department, New York Public Library)

as oppressors and American colonists as defenders of liberty. A few months before the British invasion, Seixas, recently turned thirty, spoke to his congregants, beseeching God to prevent the horrors of civil war. Like many New England ministers, Seixas saw divine meaning in revolutionary events. He likened British tyranny to Pharaoh and the colonists to the children of Israel. With the British flotilla weeks away from New York Harbor, Seixas pleaded to God, "put in the heart of our Sovereign Lord, George the third, and in the hearts of his Councellors, Princes and Servants, to turn away their fierce Wrath from our North America. . . . [May] there may no more blood be shed in these Countries, . . . That thou mayest once more plant an everlasting peace between Great Britain and Her Colonies as in former times." After the British arrival, with invasion imminent, Seixas "personally addressed . . . every member of the synagogue on the question of closing it rather than let it be a Tory congregation," an issue that was "fiercely contested, even families being split as a result." In August, days before the battle, he gave a sermon lamenting that this might be the last service at Shearith Israel. He carried most of the synagogue's Torahs and valuables in a locked box north to Stratford, Connecticut, and then to Philadelphia.[16]

Most Jewish citizens who went into exile did so before the Battle of New York. Perhaps they understood the military situation better than Washington, who placed part of his army in Brooklyn, anticipating that the British would attempt to scale Brooklyn Heights, only to suffer horrendous casualties as at Bunker Hill. But General Howe outmaneuvered Washington, sending troops behind his forces in Brooklyn, forcing American recruits to retreat toward the East River, where they were rescued at the last minute by fog and Marblehead fishermen who ferried the soldiers to the mainland at night. Still, the situation remained perilous. The city had to be abandoned; otherwise the British would trap the army at the tip of Manhattan Island. During the hasty retreat that followed, merchant Jonas Phillips slipped out of the city with his fifteen children. Amid the noise of cannon and musket fire, merchant Isaac Moses began to walk northward, refusing to ride on the Sabbath. Reaching the present Twenty-Third Street, he found a farm that would shelter him. Saturday night he and his family boarded a wagon and followed the army into Westchester. He later found his way to Philadelphia, where most exiled New York Jews gathered.[17]

What motivated Jews to abandon their beloved synagogue and a city that had safely housed Jews for over a hundred years? First, they were part of the community and with their fellow Americans shared in the growing alienation from the British. Second, the freedom, respect, and economic opportunity they found in New York put many in alliance with rebel leaders of the colony, their partners and compatriots. Third, they may have felt conflicted allegiance to an English government that treated its Jewish citizens as "second class," whose royal privileges were given but to favorites, including only a few Jews, most notably the loyalist Franks family.[18] Finally, they lived in a colony, now a state, that offered Jews full rights of citizenship, including the right to vote. There was no question that the state's constitutional convention would continue the province's egalitarian heritage and grant Jews "full political equality." Indeed, "New York in 1777 was the first state in the western world to confer total citizenship upon the Jews." At that convention, during a moment of wartime peril, John Jay, later chief justice of the U.S. Supreme Court, told fellow New Yorkers that they were born "equally free with the Jews," a people notable for their resistance to tyranny. Tyrants attempting to persecute the Israelites "receive[d] the rewards justly due for their violation of the sacred rights of mankind." If America, like the Jews, turned away from its "sins," then its "arms will be crowned with success, and the pride and power of [its] enemies, like the arrogance and pride of Nebuchadnezzar, will vanish away." For Jay, the Jews were an exemplary people for a new nation. In this political climate, most Jews chose to support the Revolution.[19]

■ Jewish Loyalists and Jewish Life in Occupied New York

Following Washington's departure, New York became British military headquarters until Evacuation Day in November 1783. Loyalists seeking refuge under British military protection replaced New Yorkers who fled. The city's population swelled to twelve thousand in 1777 and then to thirty-three thousand two years later, taxing its resources. Blacks seeking freedom crowded the outskirts of the seaport. A great fire destroyed a third of the housing stock on the city's west (Hudson River) side in September 1776, making shelter scarce and costly. The military commandeered most public buildings and churches, including the Presbyterian and Dutch Reform churches and the French and Quaker meeting places. Many residents lived in "canvastown," a makeshift camp of tents in the ruins of the fire. Inflation drove the price of food up 800 percent. The city remained under martial law throughout its occupation, governed by a commandant who used arbitrary power in issuing passes, permits, and regulations. Despite the war, British military officers did not refrain from gaiety, including theater productions and parties. They attended races "at the Flatlands [Long Island]" that, according to Rebecca Franks, "swarmed with beaus and some very smart ones," and they celebrated the queen's birthday in 1780 with transparent paintings and illuminated lamps.[20]

When the British arrived, a number of prominent Jews who remained loyal to the Crown decided to stay, including Barak Hays, Uriah Hendricks, and two Gomez bothers, Abraham and Moses Jr. There was no correlation between synagogue infighting and decisions on loyalism, as both Manuel Josephson and the Simsons fled into exile, while Barak Hays did not. Sixteen Jews joined 932 New Yorkers who signed an Address of Loyalty to General Howe, expressing gratefulness for "his Majesty's paternal Goodness" and pledging "true allegiance" to their "Rightful Sovereign George the Third." The signers affirmed that the "constitutional Supremacy of Great Britain, over these Colonies" was "Essential to the Union, Security, and Welfare, of the whole Empire." Occupied

New York housed perhaps thirty Jewish loyalists. Despite the declaration of loyalty, only Barak Hays was known as a fervent British patriot, moving to Montreal after the war. More typical were merchants Uriah Hendricks and Samuel Lazarus, loyalists who continued to reside in the city after the war—with little difficulty.[21]

The preservation of Shearith Israel was clearly on the mind of the remaining Jewish inhabitants. The elders left Torah scrolls for use by Jewish loyalists. The British army considered using the sanctuary for a hospital, but the influence of Barak Hays, furrier Lyon Jonas, and Alexander Zuntz, a Jewish sutler (army supplier) who accompanied the Hessian troops, persuaded military authorities to spare the synagogue. Jonas was the synagogue's titular head, but Zuntz became its leader. That two soldiers who vandalized the synagogue were punished severely indicates that the British valued Jewish loyalty and support. Abraham Abrahams likely served as hazan during British occupation, along with two professionals. Isaac Touro, formerly hazan in Newport, moved to New York in 1780 before settling in Jamaica. North African Jacob Raphael Cohen landed in New York from Montreal in 1782 and served until Seixas returned after the war. Services were held irregularly, when a *minyan* could be gathered.[22]

Life in occupied New York was difficult for all except nearby farmers, privateers, and select merchants. No fewer than five hundred ships crowded the city's docks. Newspaper ads provide evidence that a number of the remaining Jewish merchants earned a living supplying the town's refugees, soldiers, and locals. Uriah Hendricks bought space in the *New-York Gazette* and Rivington's *Royal Gazette* from 1777 through 1782, placing ads that offered spermaceti candles from Rhode Island and imports from London, including bohea tea, striped blankets, silk waistcoats, Irish beef, and, strangely, in 1781, "Superfine Philadelphia table flour fit for the nicest pantry." Barak Hays purchased even more ads, as he auctioned "rum, sugar, etc, a negro, dry goods," as well as linens, indigo, feather beds, and ironware. In 1782, with the war ending, he wrote that, "intending to go to Europe," he desired "all those that are indebted to him since his Majesty's troops took possession of this place, pay off the same," to prevent further sale "at prime cost."[23]

Alexander Zuntz opened a store on King Street by 1780 advertising that "ALEXANDER ZUNTZ from Hesse Cassel" sold imports from London and Germany, including "millinery ribbons in the latest London fashion." In 1781, he offered for sale "a true Steiner Violin," a variety of sheet music, and the "newest fashion" of men's and women's shoes "by the trunk." Other ambitious Jewish entrepreneurs included Jacob Abrahams, who bartered oil; Mrs. Moses, who promised to "cure permanently anybody of fever and ague"; Jacob De Costa, who sold textiles, coffee, and mahogany furniture; Abraham Abrahams, who vended hog tails and cut tobacco; Rebecca Gomez, who traded "Vinegar spices, Pepper Mustard," and other foodstuffs; and Samuel Levy, who carried "all kinds of English and other soal and upper Leather." On Nassau Street, Rebecca and Moses Gomez Jr. offered "Chocolate manufactured in the best manner and warranted pure." Rebecca also sold tea, sugar, pickles, and indigo. Haym Salomon, a newcomer to New York, traded "Ship bread and fresh Rice" at 222 Broad Street, prior to his flight to Philadelphia in 1778.[24]

A visiting German mercenary, Johann Conrad Dohla, wrote that the Jews of occupied New York were unlike "the ones we have in Europe." Rather, they "dressed like other citizens, get shaved regularly; and also eat pork, although that is forbidden in their Law." Jewish women sported "curled hair" and dressed in "French finery such as are worn by the ladies of the other religions." Jews and Christians "intermarry without scruple." Given the small number of Jews remaining in the city, lack of a significant synagogue community profoundly diminished religious observance and identity.[25]

While most Jewish New Yorkers living in occupied New York concerned themselves with getting by day to day in the midst of military occupation, there were exceptions. Abraham Wagg, a former aide to Prime Minister Robert Walpole during the South Sea Bubble, a speculation that cost many a fortune, lived in New York in 1770 as a grocer and chocolate maker. An observant Jew, at age forty-nine he married twenty-nine-year-old Rachel Gomez of the elite Gomez family. Fate was unkind to him. He lost a young son and suffered a disabling accident while on fire patrol. Unable to work, he returned to Britain in 1779 with his wife and three children, living in Bristol, where five more children were born. Losing his American property, he spent the rest of his life in penury. While Wagg's attachment to the Crown never faltered—he joined the civic militia in 1777—he took a hard analytical view of the Crown's dilemma. In 1778, he wrote a treatise arguing that conquering America, a task requiring 117,000 men, was not worth the cost. Because "English blood flows in the viens [*sic*] of Americans," America was a natural ally of Britain. He advised the British to use its troops to protect Canada and its West Indian possessions. In 1782, he sent a letter to prominent British merchant Solomon Henry urging the British, in making peace with America, to destroy the Franco-American alliance. Wagg possessed a global perspective wider than most loyalists embroiled in the heat of conflict.[26]

The foremost representative of Jewish loyalist aristocracy, the family of David Franks, moved to New York. Daughter Rebecca's letters give a sense of her society. In words that might have gladdened grandmother Abigaill's heart, if Rebecca had not been raised a Christian, Rebecca scorned New York's women, who knew how to entertain only by opening "the card tables" and could not "chat more than a half hour," and then only "on the form of a cap, the colour of a ribbon, or the set of a hoop stay or *jupon* [petticoat]." Gotham's ladies were solely interested in impressing men, none more than a British officer: "I sincerely believe the lowest ensign thinks 'tis but ask and have; a red coat and smart epaulet is sufficient to secure a female heart." Despite these words, Rebecca too succumbed to a redcoat. The *New-York Gazette* of January 28, 1782, announced that she wed Sir Henry Johnson, a British officer. Despite her Christian upbringing, she was known as a Jew. After the British evacuated New York, the couple made their home in England, with her descendants prominent in *Burke's Peerage*. Even so, late in life, Rebecca reminisced, "I have glorified in my rebel countrymen! Would to God I, too, had been a patriot!" —a late conversion to the American cause.[27]

At the other end of the spectrum were Jewish loyalists in need of aid. Hazan Touro in 1781 wrote Sir Guy Carleton, commander in chief, pleading that "the distresses" that he had "sufferd from Persecution for his attachment to [His Majesty's] government" had so "reduced" his circumstance that he had to ask for funds to move to Jamaica. This was but one of various petitions. Except for established merchants and the elite such as the Franks family, life was not easy for Jews in occupied New York, most of whom left no record of their lives.[28]

▪ Military Service

Most Jewish New Yorkers who served in the military chose the state militias. Prior to the war, in September 1775, saddler Benjamin Seixas, brother of Reverend Gershom Seixas, was a third lieutenant in the Fusiliers Company of the First Battalion of the New York State Militia and a signer of a "petition of New York Officers" from New York City to the "Committee of Safety for the Province of New York." With his fellow officers, Seixas urged New Yorkers "capable of bearing arms" to prepare themselves by training at "least once a week," as "the safety of the nation may be longer preserved by every citizen being a soldier than by particular persons solicited for that purpose." In 1776, Benjamin fled to Connecticut to stay with relatives. Another member of the New York militia, Hart Jacobs, petitioned the Provincial Council in January 1776 for exemption from watch duty, stating that "it is inconsistent with his religious profession to perform military duty on Friday nights, being part of the Jewish Sabbath." Permission was granted. Much had changed since Asser Levy's struggle to enroll in the New Amsterdam militia.[29]

Fifty-five-year-old Jacob Mordecai enlisted as a private in the Fourth Battalion of the Pennsylvania militia, as did his son-in law Isaac Moses. Hayman Levy and son Eleazar served as militia privates. (Levy complained for years about the destructive use of his property at West Point by Washington's army and his failure to receive compensation.) Eighty-four-year-old Daniel Gomez left New York stating that he could "stop a bullet as well as a younger man," but he did not serve. His grandson Daniel, however, joined the Philadelphia militia, as did Abraham Judah and Jonas Phillips. Manuel Josephson escaped occupied New York in 1776 in a "leaky boat" with information about the British. Other New York Israelites served in Connecticut militias.[30]

One Jewish New Yorker served with the Continental army. Isaac Franks, son of a nephew of Jacob Franks, seventeen years old at the outbreak of war, enlisted in Colonel John Lasher's "six month regiment" and fought with Washington at the Battle of New York in 1776, only to be captured and imprisoned. Franks escaped, crossing the Hudson "in a small leaky skiff with one single paddle to the Jersey shore," where he reconnected with Washington's army and served as the forage master at West Point. From 1780 to 1782, he was an ensign with the Seventh Massachusetts Regiment of the Line. After the war, he moved to Philadelphia.[31]

New York's Jewish community made its most important military contribution in finance. Jews had gained valuable experience in privateering in the French and Indian War and knew how to prepare a merchant vessel to raid British shipping. Privateering significantly assisted American strategy and finances. In 1776, Americans outfitted 136 vessels with 1,360 guns; in 1782, 323 ships with 4,854 guns sailed the Atlantic. Americans captured over six hundred British ships worth $18 million.[32]

The foremost Jewish privateer, Isaac Moses, immigrated from Germany to

New York in 1764, becoming a British citizen four years later. A prosperous merchant in New York, he became the wealthiest Jewish citizen in Philadelphia, worth £115,000 in 1780. He outfitted eight ships, from the *Chance* in 1779, a schooner with six guns, to the *Marbois* in 1780, a brig that held sixteen guns and a crew of eighty-five. Moses was joined by many partners, including financier Richard Morris and New Yorkers Benjamin Seixas and Solomon Marache. In addition, in 1780, Moses participated with other merchants to raise bonds of up to £260,000 "in gold and silver" to provision the army. Moses personally pledged £3,000. He also supplied capital for a bank "for furnishing a supply of provisions for the Armies of the United States." His goal was, he said, "our own freedom and that of our posterity, and the freedom and independence of the United States." After the war, Moses and several fellow merchants petitioned the New York legislature for land seized from former loyalists, particularly the Delancey family. Because the war caused interruption of trade, they argued, they remained indebted to British merchants "for considerable sums." "Nearly ruined" by their patriotism, they asked that loyalist estates be converted into a fund to reimburse them "for their many and good sacrifices." Alternatives proposed included the sale of "immense tracts of unappropriated lands" or that their losses "be funded as a state debt." Estates were confiscated and sold, but proceeds did not compensate the merchants.[33]

Reverend Seixas contributed spiritual support to the war. In a 1782 consecration sermon for Philadelphia's first constructed synagogue, Mikveh Israel, he blessed the efforts of the Continental army. Appealing to the "high & Exalted King of Israel, Lord of Hosts," who was "near to all those that call upon him . . . in time of their distress," Seixas asked the "King of Kings" to protect General Washington and the Continental Congress and to "save and prosper the Men of these United States, who are gone forth to War. . . . May thy Angels have them in Charge, and save them from Death," implanting "Amity, brotherly Love, peace and Sociableness." He evoked a millennial end of this great struggle, a "Covenant of Peace, until time shall be no more, so that Nation shall not lift up their sword against nation, neither shall they combat or make war any more, Amen."[34]

■ Exile and the Quest for Equality

The Jews of New York made significant nonmilitary contributions to Philadelphia's Jewish community. Prior to the war, Philadelphia had a tiny Jewish population of perhaps twenty-five families. During the war, many Jewish refugees fled there, to the capital of the new republic. For many New Yorkers, it became their home away from home. They established themselves in trade and devoted themselves to remaking the city in the ways of their former life. Isaac Moses, Benjamin Seixas, Jonas Phillips, Hayman Levy, and Matthew Josephson became major figures in the community. Reverend Seixas arrived from Connecticut in 1780. New York's Jews inspired Philadelphians to erect the synagogue Mikveh Israel (services had been in rental quarters). Isaac Moses headed the committee to build the synagogue, a red-brick building similar to Shearith Israel and dedicated in September 1782. Mikveh Israel hired Gershom Seixas as hazan, and former New York elders wrote its bylaws. New Yorkers supporting the new synagogue wondered if they would ever leave their adopted city. A few, including Jonas Phillips and Manuel Josephson, remained in Philadelphia. Most, however, returned to New York.[35]

Gotham's Jews possessed political equality and wanted the same rights for Jews throughout the new American nation. They started where they lived, in Pennsylvania. The commonwealth's new constitution contained a "test oath" requiring members of the General Assembly to affirm that the Old and the New Testaments were the result of "divine inspiration." Jews could not take such an oath. Gershom Seixas, along with Mikveh Israel's president, Asher Myers, Bernard Gratz, and Haym Salomon, wrote the Council of Censors, charged with reviewing Pennsylvania's constitution. The act, they declared, placed a "stigma upon their nation and the commonwealth," inconsistent with the Pennsylvania constitution, which stated that "no man who acknowledges the being of a God" could be deprived of his civil rights. Jews, "allied with the great design of the revolution," had proven that they were "as fond of liberty as other religious societies can be." They served in the Continental Army and paid taxes. They "stand unimpeached of any matter whatsoever against the safety and happiness of the people." The Jewish people, Seixas argued, would thrive in Pennsylvania if the Test Act were eliminated, adding to the prosperity of the commonwealth. If not, they would go elsewhere. The petition was tabled, but the constitution written in 1790 dropped the offending clause.[36]

In 1787, Jonas Phillips sought similar relief from the Constitutional Convention meeting in Philadelphia. Condemning the Pennsylvania constitution's Test Act, Phillips declared that "all men have a natural & unalienable Right to worship almighty God according to the dictates of their own Conscience and understanding" and that no man could be compelled to attend religious services "against his own free will and Consent," or deprived of a "Civil Right" because of his "Religious sentiments or peculiar mode of Religious worship." Noting Jews' patriotic service as "faithful whigs" during the war, a conflict in which they offered "their lifes & fortunes," Philips asked the convention to eliminate the offending words. Phillips, however, was confused over the purpose of the Philadelphia gathering. The convention's mandate did not include state bylaws. Delegates did unanimously approve a clause providing "that no religious test shall ever be required as a qualification to any office of public trust under the United States." Philips's letter became part of the legacy of political equality that New York's Jewish leaders left to Jews of the new republic.[37]

■ A New Beginning

On November 25, 1783, General Guy Carleton loaded the last of the British troops and departing American loyalists on British frigates and sailed for England. On a day that would be celebrated as a major Gotham holiday for the next hundred years, George Washington triumphantly entered the battered city of New York. Many residences stood in shambles, public buildings and churches in need of repair. But 1783 ushered in a time of great hope. Once in possession of the city, New Yorkers organized quickly, electing new aldermen. The state appointed James Duane mayor and confiscated loyalist estates including the Delancey's vast urban holdings. Thousands returned, and in two years New York grew from twelve to twenty-four thousand inhabitants, among them Alexander Hamilton and Governor George Clinton.[38]

Jews rejoined those who had lived in occupied New York. Despite anger at loyalists, the two groups reintegrated without significant resentment. Newspapers of the mid-1780s reveal a revival of Jewish commerce by both merchants who stayed and those who returned. Uriah Hendricks continued to advertise imported goods from London, including leather, pewter, and china, and Abraham Abrahams manufactured and sold snuff. Hayman Levy offered wine, tea, and an assortment of European imports. Benjamin Judah announced that he had beaver hats and "Scotch snuff in bladders" for sale. Haym Salomon, while yet residing in Philadelphia, opened a brokerage office in New York, noting his position as "Broker to the Office of Finance," his connections with "French Merchants," and the "affection of merchants of the United Provinces." Benjamin Seixas resumed business, not as a saddler but as proprietor of an "auction store," where buyers could find "Bohea tea in chests, Gin in cases." He stood "ready to receive all kinds of Dry Goods, for public or private sale."[39]

A declining economy tempered early optimism. The British opened the mother country to American trade but prohibited American ships from critical trading venues in the West Indies. In addition, the British influx of manufactured goods that poured into the country drained needed specie. By flooding the New York market with manufactures, the British made it difficult for local artisans to compete. In addition, imposts levied by the New York State Assembly threatened trade wars with nearby states. The city and nation fell into a severe recession. Jews were not immune. Alexander Zuntz, Jacob Mordecai, Lion Hart, Moses Franks, and Ephraim Hart all posted notices of insolvency. Even Isaac Moses's firm failed in 1785.[40]

The delegates in Philadelphia in 1787, responding to the nation's fiscal crisis, crafted a constitution intended to reestablish credit, to set up a national market, and to launch a strong federal government. In comparison to the state-centered Confederation established during the war, the federal Constitution was a revolution in itself. Most urban dwellers, almost certainly including the city's Jewish community, strongly favored ratification. In New York's famous July 1788 parade urging the state's delegates in Poughkeepsie to approve the federal charter, Jewish artisan Asher Myers led the city's coppersmiths.[41]

▪ The Revival of Shearith Israel

In this atmosphere, Shearith Israel resumed operations. Unlike in Pennsylvania, the political and religious freedom of Jews in New York was never in doubt. New York's constitution of 1777 declared that "Free Toleration be forever allowed in the state." The synagogue's minutes, picking up in 1783, note the appointment of a temporary parnas. Among its first issues, the synagogue faced a request of Benjamin I. Jacobs: "to admit his being married to a Woman not belonging to our society, with intent to make her a Proselite." The congregation denied his petition, continuing its prewar policy against conversions. Certain doctrines did not change, even with the Revolution. But this was an internal affair. Determined to demonstrate Shearith Israel's compatibility within a republic, the elders, "Members of the Antient Congregation of Israelites, lately returned from Exile," welcomed the arrival of Governor Clinton. Though they might be "small when Compared with other Religious Societies," they declared, no other congregation "has Manifested a more Zealous

Attachment to the Sacred Cause of America." The Jews of New York City looked forward to living "under a Constitution, wisely framed to preserve the inestimable Blessings of Civil, and Religious Liberty." They said that both the teachings of "our Divine Legislator to Obey our Rulers" and the "Dictates of our own reason" led members to pledge to discharge "the duties of Good Citizens." They would, they trusted, receive "an equal share of [the governor's] patronage." They prayed that "the Supreme Governor of the Universe" would take the governor "under his Holy Protection."[42]

That same year, the congregation offered a prayer in Hebrew, praising the Revolution's achievements and the blessings of peace, but also proposing that the war and its outcome perhaps foreshadowed the promised return to Zion: "as Thou has granted to these thirteen states everlasting freedom," so it may be that God will "bring us forth once again from bondage to freedom," and the "dispersed . . . shall come and bow down to the Lord on the holy mount of Jerusalem."[43]

The congregation sought to regain its former leader, Gershom Seixas, then hazan at Mikveh Israel. In November 1783, while Seixas was negotiating a contract with the Philadelphia congregation, Shearith Israel wrote, asking him to return. In reply, Seixas wondered if he would be able to render the New York congregation the "degree of general satisfaction, which is absolutely requisite for any person who serves in that Vocation." He expressed concern that he was "unacquainted with the Spanish & Portugueze languages." He also remarked that he had been informed that the synagogue was again in turmoil, with "many parties . . . form'd (and forming) to create divisions among the reputable members of the congregation," resulting in a "general disunion." Finally, Seixas noted that as he had "a family to provide for," he could only leave Philadelphia on certain conditions: "some encouragement from you that my salary will be made equivalent to what I receive here." However, if he could conduct decorous services, if "some regular form of government be adopted so as to have a proper subordination in the society," and if Shearith Israel afforded him "a comfortable maintenance," he would be "very willing" to rejoin the congregation.[44]

Negotiations concluded with the synagogue offering Seixas £200 a year, a salary placing him among the city's upper-middle class, along with six cords of wood, matzos, and travel expenses from Philadelphia. Upon arrival in New York, he gave a welcoming sermon in which he thanked "Almighty Providence" that the congregation was "again restor'd to [its] former place of

Residence in Peace." As "just Tribute due to Omnipotence," Seixas requested, in the name of the parnas, that "stricter attention may be paid to the Rules of Decency & Decorum," which tend to "excite Devotion especially in Time of divine Service." Services must command "Respect" instead of "Contempt." The "Evil Practices," namely, the behavior "of a few weak & inconsiderate set of men" who left the Synagogue during prayers, talking and laughing with each other, must cease. Men and women should consider "in whose Presence they are & to Whom they address themselves." Seixas stated that he did not intend "to arrogate to himself any power which is not legally entitled to by the Nature of his Office." His motivations were only his zeal for holy worship and an "innate Principle of Benevolence." Aware "of the Difficulties attending those who govern," he called on members to join him, "Heart & Hand." Seixas, an ardent revolutionary, sought to create in the synagogue a dignified republican order, the kind of order envisioned by the Constitution of the United States.[45]

In 1784, the New York legislature passed an act allowing for the incorporation of religious societies. On May 24, 1784, the congregation of Shearith Israel crafted articles of incorporation, establishing a governing Board of Trustees. Six trustees were elected: Myer Myers, Hayman Levy, Solomon Simson, Isaac Moses, Solomon Myers Cohen, and Benjamin Seixas, men from families that composed the leadership of pre-Revolutionary Shearith Israel. In August, a meeting of the congregation—with thirty-two members attending—decided to write a new charter. However, delays occurred, and the first constitution was not promulgated until after the federal Constitution was ratified in 1789.[46]

Under incorporation, a dual system of government prevailed. The Board of Trustees assumed authority above the elders (*adjuntos*). At times elders and trustees worked together, and at times they were in conflict. A dispute erupted in 1785 over the right of the charitable society Gemilut Hasidim, responsible for the care and burial of the dead, to collect money at the synagogue. (The society wished to supplement its dues with synagogue collections.) The parnas and elders agreed to the society's request with conditions, but the trustees rejected this decision. Asking the trustees to reconsider and "rescind the same," the elders declared that they were "of the Opinion that the Parnassim & Adjuntas have a right to grant Indulgences to any useful & religious Institution in this Congregation," provided it not interfere with the congregation's funds. The trustees replied that they had consulted counsel and "that the right of granting Liberty to the Hebra Gemiluth Hazedim, is vested in the Trustees only." The elders, "wishing to unite with the Trustees," conceded. Although they hoped the trustees might consider the "Advantage" to the congregation of allowing them the "Liberty" that they, the *parnassim* and *adjuntos*, thought justified. But they understood where authority lay. In 1791, the trustees took on all fiscal and religious supervision. The parnas became the presiding officer of the trustees.[47]

The right to negotiate with the hazan shifted to the Board of Trustees. In charge of finances, the board assumed responsibility to hold the synagogue together when funds were short. In the mid-1780s, with a number of leading Jewish merchants bankrupt, the congregation could not collect funds to pay its officers. Consequently, in the winter of 1785, because of the congregation's "distressed Situation," the board decided that Seixas, along with the shamash, shochet, and clerk, were "discharged in Tammuz next ensuing." Fortunately, funds were found to avoid this action, though the shochet departed for Philadelphia. That year, Seixas wrote the trustees of his need to have "some certain assurance" in his salary's "being punctually paid when due"; otherwise he would have to find "a different manner to obtain a Livelihood." Unfortunately, economic conditions remained perilous, and in 1787 Hazan Seixas resigned. Instead of leaving, however, he accepted a reduction in his salary, first to £170 and then to £120 a year plus firewood, "upon the assurance given [him] by the Board of Trustees that whenever the funds of the Synagogue were adequate they would be ready to fix [his] Salary equal if not Superior to what it had always been." After ratification of the Constitution in 1789, the economy strengthened; Seixas's salary improved, and he went on to a distinguished career, becoming one of New York's most prominent clergy.[48]

The board took charge of the sale of seats in the sanctuary, its most important source of revenue. Front seats in the women's gallery cost fifteen pounds, and were given to married ladies and family representatives. Back seats were valued at three pounds each. In 1785, the elders requested a conference with the board to agree on "some decisive plan for the immediate regulation of said seats." The problem involved three young sisters, Abigail, Becky, and Sally Judah, who refused the seats assigned them and occupied others. The trustees, following unsuccessful negotiations with the head of the family, troublesome brother Benjamin Judah, announced a fine of three pounds, four shillings ($25) each time a member took a seat without permission of the trustees. The young women still refused their assigned seats, declaring, "when the gentlemen trustees can convince us that we are subject to any laws they choose to make which is to hinder us from attending Divine Worship, they may endeavor to exercise their authority." Reverend Seixas wrote the board that the mother of the three sisters "is willing to pay for her own and her Daughters Seats the same price that the ladies of [the] Society did." While he hoped his intervention to promote "Peace and concord in [the] Holy Congregation" might prevent legal measures, it brought only a rebuke from the board and an apology from Seixas for interfering. The trustees took the case to Mayor's Court, which, after testimony of ten congregants, found the girls guilty of trespass. Their mother vowed she "would have nothing further to do with the congregation." Eventually Becky and Sally were forgiven "for the sake of peace." Abigail rejoined as well and two years later unsuccessfully applied to become the first female shamash. Through such actions, the board established its authority to oversee "good order and decency in the Holy place of Worship" and to be the final arbiter with the congregation's charity societies, its elders, and individual congregants.[49]

With the rise of the Board of Trustees, the "synagogue community" yielded to a corporate model. The old system saw the Jews as an inward-looking community living within a Gentile world, keeping to themselves as much as possible. In the new republic, Jews were part and parcel of the commonwealth, and their synagogue was a chartered institution of the state.

■ A Revolutionary Legacy

Revolutionary experience gave New York's Jews a heightened sense of common citizenship. Longstanding Jewish preference for restraint receded. While living in Philadelphia, mixing with Jews from different colonies, they became more cosmopolitan. A new generation of merchants replaced the Frankses and Gomezes. Even in New York, where Jews had always had political rights, these rights were now those of any American citizen, not a privilege granted by a Christian elite to a quiescent minority. The Revolution marked a new beginning for New York's Jewish community. Patriotism, unrestricted citizenships as founders of the new republic, and a spirit of egalitarianism replaced a sense of separateness. The promise of the new nation to the hundreds of thousands of Americans who lived through the hard years of war was as much a promise for the city's Jewish community. They were now adept, politically aware, loyal republican citizens. But living in a revolutionary republican society presented New York's Jews with both momentous opportunities and momentous challenges in the first decades of the early American republic.[50]

This lithograph from *Valentine's Manual*, from a painting by George Catlin, portrays Five Points in 1828, before it became notorious for vice and poverty. In the late twenties it was a vibrant mixed neighborhood symbolic of the high economic ambitions of the new republic. Many Jews sold garments and other wares along the five streets that gave the site its name. (Courtesy Collections of the New-York Historical Society)

CHAPTER 5

The Jewish Community of Republican New York

On a spring day at the end of April 1789, George Washington took the oath of office as the first president of the United States on the balcony of Federal Hall, New York's city hall. For the next year, New York served as the capital of the United States. While the nature of republicanism continued to be the subject of fierce debate, the early republic inaugurated a new era for the Jews of New York. An open egalitarian society signaled the beginning of the integration of Jews into the mainstream of American life. The impact of republicanism deeply influenced the emerging Jewish community.

When Washington took his oath, six years after British troops evacuated the city, New York's population had reached 33,000, of whom around 350 were Jews, slightly more than 1 percent. By 1810, the city's population had grown to over 96,000, but the Jewish population, at 450, had declined in proportion to 0.5 percent. Fifteen years later, a mere 500 Jews lived in a city of 166,000 inhabitants, about 0.3 percent. Jews were becoming an even smaller minority, their immigration limited by continuous wars in Europe.

In 1790, the city still centered on today's Lower Manhattan, stretching only a few miles north of Wall Street. By 1810, it had progressed north as far as Houston Street, and by the 1830s, it had passed Fourteenth Street. The lower part of the city, the site of Shearith Israel, became increasingly commercial. Pearl Street, the area's main thoroughfare, was known for its large warehouses. While a few of the wealthier citizens stayed in the vicinity of the Battery, the park at the tip of Manhattan Island, most moved near the new city hall, built in 1815 a mile further north up Broadway. The city's neighborhoods were mixed, although the more opulent residents tended to live in the center and west side of the island, and poorer artisans and laborers toward the East River, with a few remaining in Lower Manhattan.[1]

Home to the first Congress, New York directly witnessed the nation begin to implement its republican revolution. Two visions emerged, each with appeal to the Jewish community. On the one hand, the liberal Jeffersonian understanding stressed egalitarianism, promising greater opportunities for all classes in the nation's political, cultural, and social life. On the other hand, Hamiltonian republicanism emphasized deference, reasoning that even in a republic those who had less education, wealth, and breeding ought to willingly defer to those who had greater wisdom, usually the wealthy and better educated.[2]

■ Entrepreneurial Horizons

The American Revolution unleashed far more than a political movement. Republicanism increased the entrepreneurial expectations of New Yorkers, who had previously worked under the restraints of British mercantilism and a paternalist society. The prospect of an open market widened the horizon of economic enterprise for newly aspiring artisans, merchants, and manufacturers. Jews as well could freely venture into all areas of the marketplace.

Soon after the Revolution, New York emerged as the nation's financial center. Its merchants, such as Elisha Peck, Anson G. Phelps, John Jacob Astor, and Nicholas Low, cornered the cotton trade, became expert at speculation and insurance, and launched ambitious economic adventures, including clipper ships to China. In 1825, with the opening of the Erie Canal, New York began its journey to a world-class metropolis. It became the entry point for immigrants and the choice entrepôt for all imports and for exports from the West. In 1821, only 38 percent of the nation's imports arrived in New York; by 1838, that figure rose to 62 percent. No city could match its merchants, artisans, or manufacturers. Growth brought increased economic stratification: by 1800, 20 percent of the population owned 80 percent of the city's wealth, while the bottom half owned less than 5 percent. This inequality grew greater as the age progressed.[3]

New York's Jewish population most commonly fell within the middle or lower-middle classes. A study of the New York directories from 1789 to 1830, incorporating most men and a few working women, revealed that the most common Jewish entry was "merchant," with 127 of the 306 probable Jewish entries, or about 41 percent. The next highest categories (aside from the sixty-four "unlisted") were "auctioneer" and "broker," related professions, with eighteen each. The three together composed over half the listed occupations.[4]

With a Jewish population of less than 1 percent, New York's wealthy Jews no longer possessed the economic standing of earlier years, but prominent figures existed. These included the wealthiest Israelite, Harmon Hendricks, second son of Uriah Hendricks. His father imported metals among many items. Harmon, partnering with agents in England, Jamaica, and major American seaports, expanded his father's wholesale trade, moving from plates and glasses to kettles and pianos, iron and tinplate. Working out of a store on Pearl Street, he advertised the sale of "British copper, riverts, pewter ware" and "tons of pig iron." Hendricks's most important accomplishments were as a copper manufacturer. In 1812, he opened a copper-rolling mill in New Jersey that built boilers for Robert Fulton's early steamboats. He and his brother-in-law Solomon Isaacs acted as agents for Paul Revere, to whom they sold copper and saltpeter, often on credit. In April 1805, Hendricks wrote Revere that he not been able to sell copper for some time, as it was "so extremely scarce & high in Europe" that he had no "surplus." Recently, however, he had obtained seven tons of "India Block Tin," which he offered at a discount of twenty-six and a half cents per pound on three- to six-months' credit. At one time, he considered a plan in which he and Revere would corner the American copper market, though the scheme never materialized. He remained one of Revere's most trusted associates. Hendricks became wealthy, purchasing thirty acres of real estate along Broadway and loaning the government $60,000 to help finance the War of 1812. At his death in 1838, he was worth over $3 million. Like many prominent Jews, he played an active role at Shearith Israel, where he served as parnas.[5]

Four Jewish businessmen joined twenty Christian New Yorkers to found the New York Stock Exchange in 1793. They included investor and real estate speculator Ephraim Hart, partner of John Jacob Astor, as well as Alexander Zuntz, Benjamin Seixas, and Isaac Gomez. Auctioneer Isaac Moses, who owned sixteen separate real estate lots at his death in 1816, was known for his collection of European paintings. Simon Nathan was one of four Jewish merchants active in building the Park Theater. Eminent merchant Solomon Simson gained renown for the use of swift clipper ships that sailed to the Far East. Simson used his vessels to learn more about Jews in these remote venues. In 1787, he exchanged letters with Jews in Malabar, India, learning that there were two groups of Jews there, white Jews who had emigrated from Palestine and black Jews who were descendants of converts. A letter to China in 1794, inquiring whether Jewish descendants of the ten lost tribes lived in the East and declaring that thirty to forty Jewish families lived in peace in New York, never reached its destination.[6]

Most Jewish merchants worked on a smaller level. Many bought goods at auction and sold them in retail stores, sometimes advertising their goods. Jacques Ruden, a small-scale merchant, supplied lumber toward the building of the new city hall until his death in 1806. He learned to work with wood in Dutch Suriname, a colony he left in 1800. For every Harmon Hendricks, there were many small retailers and grocers earning a meager livelihood.[7]

While craftsmen constituted the majority of the working population in early republican New York, relatively few Jews labored in these trades. Jewish craftsmen ranged from the highly successful David Seixas, son of Hazan Gershom Seixas, a manufacturer of sealing wax, ink, and crockery, to shoemaker Isaac Moses, so poor he was given a synagogue seat at no charge. From 1786 to 1830, two bakers, two chair makers, and three butchers were listed in city directories, along with a single clock maker, shoemaker, carpenter, and sailmaker. The largest craft, tailoring, numbered six men in thirty years. Nine Jewish smiths worked in the city, including goldsmiths, silversmiths, coppersmiths, and blacksmiths. Among them was Asher Myers, younger brother of the famous silversmith Myer Myers, a brazier who soldered the copper roof of the old city hall and sold two bells to the city for its new city hall and jail.[8]

Jewish artisans displayed their enterprise in the city's newspapers. Solomon Emmanuel told customers he carried "a general assortment of Gold, Silver Metal and Tortoiseshell Watches." Silversmith Daniel Coen set up a lottery for the "Encouragement of literature," entitling the winner to an "Elegant Tea Sett of Silver Plate," which could be seen at his "lucky Lottery Office" on Maiden Lane. Solomon Hays, "well acquainted with the Indian and French languages," sold furs on Chatham Street. He welcomed a partner who could "advance [him] from 8 to 10 thousand dollars."[9]

Printers achieved the most prominence. Benjamin Gomez, the city's first Jewish publisher, produced more than twenty books either singly or with Naphtali Judah. He published deist John Priestley as well as *Robinson Crusoe* and *Tom Jones*. Judah, who printed the radical tracts of Thomas Paine, advertised his imports, including forty "boxes of playing cards" as well as "an assortment of books, writing, wrapping and bonnet papers, . . . gold leaf, ink powder, quills." He gave "the highest prices" for "clean linen and Cotton Rags, old Sail Cloth and Junk" and sold "Lottery tickets in the Third Class for encouragement of Literature," with a top prize of $25,000. Publisher Naphtali Phillips owned the *National Advocate*, hiring Mordecai M. Noah as editor. Solomon Jackson edited the first American Jewish periodical and, in the 1830s, published the first Haggadah printed in America.[10]

Jews readily entered the professions. Sampson Simson, son of Solomon Simson, graduated from Columbia College and then studied law under Aaron Burr. He practiced briefly before retiring to the life of a philanthropist. Six Jewish physicians are listed either in the *New-York City Directory* or in the records of Shearith Israel, including Dr. Saul Israel, who specialized in treating deafness. The first American-born Jewish physician to attend medical school was Walter Jonas Judah, grandson of Polish immigrants. Walter attended Columbia College in the early 1790s and then the college's medical school from 1795 to 1798. In 1798, a yellow-fever epidemic devastated the city, killing 2,806 inhabitants, nearly 4 percent of the population. Refusing to leave the city, as so many residents of means did, Judah treated patients daily. Unfortunately the fever struck him, and he died as one of its victims, worn down, his epitaph states, by "his exertions to alleviate the sufferings of his fellow citizens." Judah pioneered what was to become a common Jewish profession in New York.[11]

The number of slaves in New York increased markedly in the decade following the Revolution, and as Jews continued to own slaves as commonly as their non-Jewish peers did, many Jewish merchants and craftsmen owned them in the 1790s as well. The 1790 census lists seventeen Jews owning slaves; one, Isaac Gomez Jr., a founder of the New York Stock Exchange, possessed seven. Three Jews owned three slaves, six held title to two, and the rest to one. Most slaves were household servants. The Gradual Manumission Law of 1799 rapidly reduced the number of slaves in New York, as slaves bought their freedom. (The 1820 census listed only four Jews owning slaves.) For example, in 1818, Jacob Levy Jr. pledged freedom to his bondsman in three years: "upon the express condition that the said George Roper shall during that term well & faithfully serve me & my family as a Slave, & dutifully obey all my lawful commands." The Manumission Society listed one Jew, Moses Judah, among its 340 members between 1785 and 1815.[12]

While the number and proportion of poor Jews is unknown, the minutes of

Shearith Israel indicate a few of these individuals, such as shoemaker Moses. In 1805, Eleazar Levy pleaded that he was old, infirm, and destitute; with winter in sight, he needed provisions. He received $150 over the year. Simeon Levy requested aid—"for my sake and the sake of my young and suffering family" —lest he be "committed to the Common Jail." Indentured servant L. E. Miller asked the congregation to redeem him from his "deplorable situation" among the "goyim," stating he would serve any "*Yehida*" (Jew). The congregation declined to intervene. Catherine Abrahams, who wrote that she was in a "Destitute" situation with a blind son, weak sight of her own, and an ill husband, received $2 a week. During the severe Panic of 1819, caused by a sharp drop in the price of cotton and the near total halt of bank credit, Abraham Barnet, confined in jail, appealed for aid. A member of the congregation for eighteen years, he received $25.[13]

Disability, mental illness, and crime also existed among the city's Jews. Of the few recorded cases, Shearith Israel's clerk, Isaac Gomez, was a "Cripple," and Isaac Abraham's son was blind. In 1824, brothers John and Raphael Hart, aged thirty and twenty-four, each took his own life with a pistol in their Nassau Street lodgings. These suicides likely stemmed from mental illness. In one instance of criminal behavior, one of the city's Jewish merchants was arrested in 1816 for scuttling his ship and attempting to collect insurance while he hid the cargo. Also disturbing the community's harmony were bitter intrafamily disputes that resulted in litigation over finances.[14]

The presence of poverty, disability, and crime did not diminish the entrepreneurial enthusiasm of New York's Jews as they embraced the republican spirit of enterprise. Whether it was Asher Myers crafting bells for city hall, Harmon Hendricks constructing a copper-rolling mill, or Solomon Simson launching clipper ships, Jews took advantage of the new marketplace. Success was uncertain, as ambitions were often higher than a man's reach, but a venturesome spirit penetrated the Jewish community. Less tight-knit, and still largely mercantile, it branched into more trades, working with non-Jewish and Jewish partners, competitors, and clientele.

■ Republican Fraternalism

Early national New York nourished numerous fraternal societies. Many included both Jews and non-Jews, an important sign of Jewish emergence into the broader world. Naphtali Judah, Mordecai M. Noah, and Emmanuel Hart were grand sachem and sachems (leaders) of the venerable Tammany Society, an elite fraternal/political organization. With Benjamin Seixas, they were also members of the prestigious Mechanics Society. Benjamin Hart belonged to the St. George Society, one of the New York's oldest organizations. Myer Myers assumed the presidency of the New York Gold and Silver Smiths Society after the Revolution. Solomon Simson was a member of the Chamber of Commerce and the Mineralogical Society. Joel Hart helped found the New York Medical Society in 1806. Daniel Peixotto, the son of Moses Peixotto, the hazan who succeeded Gershom Seixas in 1816, edited the *New York Medical and Physical Journal*, later serving as president of the Medical Society. Moses Judah, as noted, belonged to the Manumission Society.[15]

While no Jews served on the Common Council or as mayor, a number won election as tax assessor, and two achieved high political office. Mordecai M. Noah served as consul to Tunis and sheriff of New York; Ephraim Hart, father of Joel, was consul in Scotland. In the military, Dr. Jacob La Motta was surgeon of the Third Brigade of the 51st Regiment of the New York State Militia. Haym Salomon, Aaron Levy, and Eleazer Philips were officers in the militia, and Bernard Hart was brigade quarter master. Captain Mordecai Myers fought in the War of 1812.[16]

By far the most popular fraternal organization for Jews of middling standing and above was the Masonic Order. Despite its medieval origins, the Masons accepted all who believed in a "supreme being" and were pledged to good deeds and the pursuit of knowledge. Masons acquired reputations as supporters of progressive causes; their ornate buildings often hosted antislavery gatherings. Jewish Masons included leading figures in the community such as Mordecai Myers, Sampson Simson (Solomon's son), Seixas Nathan, and Moses Peixotto. A number attained high rank: Joel Hart was a Grand Orator and Keeper of the Seals and later Deputy Grand High Priest of the Grand Chapter, Royal Arch Masons. Peixotto was Captain of the Life Guard, Simson a Lieutenant Grand Commander. Historian Samuel Oppenheim finds at least fifty New York Israelite members in Masonic records of the early republic.

Jewish Masons established a Jerusalem chapter within the different lodges. Participating at events such as the interring of the dead from the *Jersey* prison ship, a vessel notorious for holding American Revolutionary prisoners in sickly conditions, causing most to die, the chapter's members crafted a prayer for Jewish Masons. Their entreaty beseeched the Lord, "excellent thou art in thy truth, Enlighten us . . . in the true knowledge of Masonry." Jewish Masons pleaded not to be numbered "among those that know not thy statutes, nor the divine mysteries of thy secret Cabala," and that the "ruler of this Lodge may be endued with knowledge and wisdom" to explain secret mysteries, as Moses did "in his Lodge to *Aaron* to *Eleazar* and *Ithamar* [the sons of *Aaron*] and the several elders of Israel." That so many of the city's leading Jews were Masons, joining with Christian Masons in a fraternity of science and ritual, speaks to their integration into elite society in republican New York.[17]

∎ Republican Politics

New York's Jewish population joined the rest of the growing seaport community in one of the greatest contests in American political history: the battle over the legacy of the American Revolution. With the new nation deeply divided over the meaning of 1776, the 1790s became one of the most passionate political decades in American history. The Hamiltonians, soon to become the Federalist Party, sought a strong central government. They passed legislation creating a potent national bank, similar to the Bank of England; encouraged the growth of manufacturing, including factory production; and became staunch supporters of Britain and fierce opponents of the French Revolution. Federalist ideology embraced deference. Centered in the North, with limited southern support, Federalism was generally uncomfortable with slavery. Its backers supported the Constitution in 1788 and were likely to be orthodox Christians.

Jeffersonians, when confronted with Hamilton's economic plan, formed the Democratic-Republican Party, the nation's first political party and ancestor of today's Democratic Party. Supporters of an agriculturally based society with weak central and stronger state governments, they were hostile to financial speculation, regarding banks, and particularly a national bank, with fear and suspicion; they preferred that factories remain in England. Many followers initially opposed the Constitution. They supported the French Revolution from its inception through the Days of Terror and continued to see Britain as a foe of American independence. Advocates of political egalitarianism, they argued that a shoemaker could make as wise a choice regarding government policies as a learned attorney could. Defenders of civil liberties and a free press, some tended to deist theology. Centered in the South, the party sympathized with slave owners.

New Yorkers could not have been closer to the dispute, as Hamilton formulated his controversial economic program, including federalizing state debts and chartering a national bank, in New York. Even after the city lost its standing as capital in 1791, it remained a key factor in the partisan struggle. The outcome of the 1800 Assembly elections in the city was central to Jefferson's election as president. In contest after contest, whether for the Common Council or State Assembly, citizens debated the fate of the nation. Federalists accused Republicans of standing for godlessness and anarchy, while Democratic-Republicans argued that the Federalists stood for the British aristocracy that they defeated in '76. Nothing less than the definition of American republicanism was at stake.[18]

Jews entered the political fray, an important sign of their integration into the political heart of the new republic. In the tumultuous 1790s, though Jews aligned with both parties, the majority were Jeffersonians. Federalists savagely attacked the Democratic Society, an association that backed both Jefferson and the French Revolution. Jewish members of New York's Democratic Society included Isaac Gomez, Isaac Seixas, Naphtali Judah, and Solomon Simson; Simson became the organization's vice president. (He was also elected assessor in 1794 and 1795.) In 1798, an ad in both the *Commercial Advertiser* and the *Argus* announced that Jeffersonians gathered at Martling's Tavern, in a meeting chaired by Solomon Simson, agreed to draft a "respectful address" to Congress, calling on it "to take effectual measures to prevent further depredations upon American commerce by the British Government, or any other nation." At a time when most people in the nation regarded the French as the major enemy of America, the Democratic-Republicans continued to single out the British.[19]

The year 1798 occasioned one of the most notable sermons of Shearith Israel's spiritual leader, Hazan Gershom Seixas. He delivered this discourse at a time of fear and frenzy. Hostilities with France seemed inevitable because of French seizures of American ships in the midst of its war with Britain, and Federalists were using the charged national atmosphere to implement their recently passed Alien and Sedition Acts, closing newspapers and jailing opponents. Protestant ministers were not reluctant to condemn the French and their anticlerical revolution. Seixas, however, while criticizing France as "a conquering nation" that threatened conflict, yet recalled it as a nation that but "a few years past" was America's ally: "when we were oppressed by the ravages and devastations of an enraged enemy." Resisting Federalist attempts to destroy its opposition, Seixas argued that when "various opinions" were at play, the solution was "strictly adhering to the grand principles of benevolence towards all our fellow creatures." Americans ought to follow God's commandment to "love thy neighbor as thyself." A year later, Seixas beseeched the Lord to remove the "spirit of envy and jealousy" from the nation's leaders, producing "peace and harmony" in the branches of government and a society united "in the bonds of brotherly and social love." Naphtali Judah printed the 1798 sermon and advertised it for sale from May 30 through June 18. In 1803, with the Jeffersonians in power, Seixas expressed hope that the "evil spirit of disunion" would remain far from the "Rulers and Administrators of the government." His call for unity reflected the republicanism of the founders in Philadelphia: that political parties were unnecessary; and that the United States could unite under nonpartisan leadership. But when he had to make a choice, Seixas sided with the Jeffersonians.[20]

Taking a different position, Jewish merchant Benjamin Judah, a Federalist supporter, wrote Alexander Hamilton from London in 1798 that he might be able to procure arms in Europe "on the lowest Terms." Judah, "roused to a just sense of dignity," wished his country to defend its claims against "an insidious foe." He regretted that war with France portended, but as it was a "cause on which depends . . . [the] independent existence" of the United States, "every American must feel the ardour of aiding his country to justify her rights." The battle for America's future even divided Jewish households: real estate entrepreneur Aaron Levy supported the Federalists, while his wife championed the Jeffersonians.[21]

The memoir of Mordecai Myers, a New Yorker politically active in the 1790s who later became a captain in the state militia, reveals the opportunity for Jewish grass-roots political enterprise. In the election of 1800, when he was twenty-four, Myers described Aaron Burr telling fellow Democratic-Republicans, "we must, at the next election, put a period to the [Federalist] 'reign of terror.' " Burr constructed a winning ticket by sponsoring "inspiring speeches" by some of the "most active and patriotic Democrats, young and old" in each ward. Burr chose Myers as one these ward spokesmen, and the Democratic-Republicans carried New York, providing the electoral votes that made Jefferson president. Myers's republicanism endured. In 1812, he wrote publisher Phillips for copies of the *National Advocate*. Pleased "with the Mater it contains," he declared that "the time has arrived when the nation requirs

John Wesley Jarvis's 1820 portrait of Mordecai M. Noah, New York's most prominent Jewish citizen. (Courtesy Congregation Shearith Israel)

all its advocats"; a "republican paper" was a "grate Treate." After leaving the armed forces, Myers served in the New York Assembly. Though he intermarried, he identified as a Jew.[22]

▪ Mordecai M. Noah

After 1800, Jefferson and the Democratic-Republicans controlled New York politics. Federalists put up serious opposition only in times of crisis such as the Embargo of 1807–1808, which closed all ports to both French and British ships and shipping, and the War of 1812. Otherwise the party could only support one of the Democratic-Republican factions that emerged in the wake of Federalist powerlessness. The key political Jewish figure in this era was Mordecai M. Noah, who moved to New York in 1817.

Prior to Noah's arrival in New York, he had achieved a reputation as a playwright, diplomat, editor, and politician. Born in Philadelphia in 1785, his father, a German immigrant, abandoned his family in bankruptcy, shortly before the death of his mother, leaving Noah in the hands of his grandparents Jonas and Rebecca Phillips. Jonas Phillips, a prosperous Philadelphia merchant formerly of New York, stood at the forefront of the movement for full Jewish citizenship. Noah spent his childhood in Philadelphia and New York.

Though apprenticed as a teenager to a carver and gilder, the theater proved more attractive than woodwork. As a youth, Mordecai hung out at the John Street Theater in New York. At twenty-three years old, he published his first drama, a tale of a wife who dressed as a man to save her spouse. With his grandfather's training, Noah entered politics as an ardent Jeffersonian. In his twenties, reminding President Madison of the "strong attachment" of Jews to the nation, he lobbied for a diplomatic appointment. When this proved unsuccessful, Noah began his career in journalism in Charleston, South Carolina. A supporter of Madison and the War of 1812, he depicted Madison's foe, Dewitt Clinton, as a would-be "Roman Dictator."[23]

In 1813, Noah won appointment as consul in Tunis, only to be abruptly recalled in 1816. His ambition unshaken by this setback, he accepted an invitation from his uncle to become editor of the *National Advocate*. The *Advocate*, the partisan newspaper of Tammany Hall, the Democratic-Republican Party's headquarters, supported the Madison and Monroe administrations against the "forbiddingly aristocratic" Clinton. As editor, he opposed all Clintonian projects, even the Erie Canal, a position he later regretted. In 1824, upon the retirement of President Monroe, he supported Treasury Secretary Crawford for president, accusing rival Andrew Jackson of attempting to establish "MILITARY DESPOTISM." Though of middle-class means, Noah became the most significant Jewish citizen in the city, New York's foremost representative of Jeffersonian republicanism.[24]

Noah championed patriotic, secular Jeffersonian republicanism, a position he articulated in orations before the Tammany and Mechanics Societies. He colorfully described the hardships of Revolutionary patriots, exposed in "rags and tatters" to the "chilling blasts of winter." Soldiers of '76, though "weak in numbers," understood that they were endowing "millions yet unborn" with the treasure of "rational liberty." Revolutionary veterans could rest assured that the cause of liberty yet burned in American hearts. With the help of immigrants, coming to a land where "establishing merit is the only passport to power," and of artisan citizens, exchanging "cramped and uncultivated" minds for "study and reflection," America would prove false the "maxim of tyrants," that "man cannot govern himself."[25]

Noah's plays elaborated republican themes. The preface to *The Grecian Captive*, paying homage to the source of republican thought, declared, "we, citizens of a free country, cannot observe with indifference the present struggle for liberty in Greece." *She Would Be a Soldier*, taking place during the War of 1812, attacked paternalism and extolled the republican virtue of American women. Noah depicted an independent lady, "a stranger to falsehood and dissimulation," spurning a father's order to marry a man of means and—like the real Deborah Sampson, who fought in the American Revolution while impersonating a man—joining the army in male disguise. Noah lauded the American Indian, symbol of Tammany and the American spirit, who told his British patron, "We fight for freedom, and in that cause, the great king and poor Indian start on equal terms." With egalitarian sentiment, he scorned the English as aristocratic, condescending dandies.[26]

Noah's journalism also espoused secular republican thought. Noah promoted universal (male) suffrage for New York's newly drafted 1820 constitution and championed an improved water supply, a modern police force, reform of the penal code, and manual-labor classes for youths. His reflections on daily life, published in essays in the *Advocate*, reveal Jeffersonian values. Noah criticized luxury. "Dress is exorbitantly extravagant—simplicity is unknown," he lamented. Dressing up a three-year-old with a "cambric dress . . . [with] wreaths of embroidered flowers, pantalets, silk stockings, and pink kid slippers" wasted money. The expense of dinner parties, $500 a table, serving only to weaken "the organs of digestion," could clothe and school "for the winter, *nearly sixty poor children.*" Men, "toiling in the sun," only a step from ruin, paid rents of over a thousand dollars a year to satisfy the demands of "amiable" wives. The "extravagance" expected by women caused too many men to remain single.[27]

In Jeffersonian spirit, Noah declared, "no occupation is more useful, more valuable to a country, than that of agriculture," and he welcomed immigrants to farm America's vast lands. He advocated public support for female education. A woman could be "accomplished" without being a "pedant," be "learned, yet amiable," possess both a "strong mind" and "soft manners." The institution of slavery troubled Noah in 1820. Owners of an illegal slave ship (the importation of slaves was outlawed by Congress in 1808) deserved "solitary confinement." Nothing justified this practice among "men whose birthright is *liberty*, whose eminent peculiarity is *freedom.*" Acknowledging "repeated instances that the intellect of the blacks is capable of high cultivation," he yet distinguished between the slave trade and the traffic of domestic slavery. While the latter might be "deplored" as a "domestic evil," the trade must be "cursed."[28]

Noah also assumed position as the most prominent leader of the city's Jewish community. In 1818, a year after moving to the city, he delivered the consecration address at the newly rebuilt Shearith Israel. His oration enunciated
a Jewish persuasion of Jeffersonian republicanism. Noah began with a survey
of Jewish history, noting Jewish gifts to civilization through the "laws of Moses" and the many centuries when "Jews have been the objects of hatred and
persecution." Only in "OUR COUNTRY, the bright example of universal tolerance, of liberality, true religion and good faith," did Jews find acceptance. In a
nation where justice is administered "impartially," where "dignity is blended
with equality," and where "merit alone has a fixed value," this troubled people
found peace and safety. Noah's oration contained no references to revelation,
salvation, punishment of sin, and repentance. Rather, it asserted that Judaism,
"the religion of nature—the religion of reason and philosophy," would flourish
in a republican society.[29]

Noah's closing words expressed the conservative republicanism of the synagogue's leaders. Though not rigorously observant, he declared it the duty of
Jews to maintain "strict observance of the Sabbath day" and the "religious tenets which make [Jews] a distinct people." To those who found it difficult to
reconcile ancient laws and customs with the modern age, Noah asked, "who is
he that can amend them?" For "once innovate upon their principles and who
can say where it will end; what dangers may not arise, what destruction may not
be anticipated!" Jews, even in an enlightened world, must follow tradition.[30]

Noah sent Thomas Jefferson, whose ideals inspired his republicanism, including its Jewish strain, a copy of his 1818 dedicatory speech at Shearith Israel.
Jefferson replied that Noah's historical summary offered "remarkable proof"
that every religious sect "in power" practiced intolerance, in opposition to "the
moral basis, on which all our religions rest." Jefferson also endorsed Noah's
hope that the Jews of America would place "its members on the equal and
commanding benches of science."[31]

Jefferson's letter to Noah might also have spurred a movement based on
reason and universality of morals, but Noah was more the politician than the
philosopher. While he personally shunned some traditional practices, he remained loyal to the traditions of Shearith Israel. When Canadian Moses Hart
published a pamphlet "in a classical deistic tradition" emphasizing a unitarian God and reward and punishment in this life, it found little favor in New

York's Jewish community. No Jewish leader in the 1820s used republicanism to found a reform synagogue in New York. That came in the next generation. Noah's thoughts led him in a different direction.[32]

■ Ararat

For Mordecai M. Noah, America was the Jews' "chosen country." As a former diplomat who had served in the Middle East, Noah believed that Jews would not immigrate to Palestine "if they recovered it tomorrow." Too, he doubted that "animal sacrifices would ever be restored." Thus, a return to Jerusalem to build the Temple was no longer central to Jewish civilization. Jeffersonian America represented the future. The homeland of the Jewish people should be there, not in a backward corner of the world where Jews lived as second-class citizens. The "restoration of the Jewish nation to their ancient rights and dominion more brilliant than they are at present" ought to be in the United States, where the most enlightened country of an enlightened age would provide Jewish immigrants from throughout the world with equality and opportunity.[33]

In 1820, Noah asked the New York State legislature to put Grand Island in the Niagara River on the market as a colony for world Jewry. As title to that land was not yet secure, the petition died. In 1824, however, the legislature sold Grand Island. Speculators purchased the land. Noah bought a few acres. His movement would have to negotiate with these investors.[34]

In Buffalo on September 25, 1825, Noah donned ceremonial robes "of crimson silk, trimmed with ermine" borrowed from a production of *Richard III*, and, to the music of Handel's *Judas Maccabeus* and accompanied by Seneca Chief Red Jacket, led a procession to St. Paul's Episcopal Church, where the new colony's cornerstone, inscribed with the Shema, lay on the communion table. There Noah, "under the auspices and protection of the Constitution and laws of the United States of America" and "by the Grace of God, Governor and Judge of Israel," did "revive, renew and *reestablish* the government of the Jewish Nation." All Jews would find "asylum" in this "free and powerful country," where they would live in peace in the colony of Ararat (the resting place of the biblical Noah's ark), with the tools of "learning and civilization" and relearn how to till the soil. They would also learn the "science of government," in harmony with American republican ideals. Although Noah was to be a appointed judge to begin the colony, all further judges would be elected. Noah believed that the "Mosaic constitution he advocated conformed to the U.S. Constitution and the laws of the land."[35]

Although no Jew would be forced to immigrate to the new colony, Noah urged all Jewish people to go to Ararat: "that thou mayest prosper in all thou doest." "Caraites and Samaritan" Jews, who, with Indians, were believed to be descendants of the ten lost tribes, would "unite with their brethren, the chosen people." Polygamy would be forbidden. All prayer would be in Hebrew, though sermons could be "in the language of the country." He proposed to pay the colony's expenses through a tax on world Jewry.[36]

Noah received encouragement. The *Commercial Advertiser* wrote that, in these "enlightened times," Jewish immigrants, with the benefit of their "wealth and enterprise," would have "every inducement to become valuable members of society." In Germany, Eduard Gans and Leopold Zunz, leaders of a society devoted to the "advancement of science and knowledge among the Jews," made Noah an "Extraordinary Member" of their *Verein* (society), assuring him that "the better part of the European Jews are looking with the eager countenance of hope to the United States . . . to exchange the miseries of their native soil for public freedom."[37]

Once Noah announced his specific plan, he also met ridicule. Newspapers charged that "the corner-stone" was a ruse to "fill the pockets of Mr. Noah and his associates." American Jews attacked his project as "profane" and "contrary to scriptural authority." European Jews judged Noah a "crazy man." Ararat became "a source of amusement" for Noah's political foes. Today only the corner-stone remains. Noah likely did not comprehend the difficulties of assimilating Jews into American culture while also maintaining a separate ethnic identity. Simultaneous "integration and segregation" would be difficult, if not impossible, to achieve.[38]

It is best to see Noah's project less as a forerunner of Zionism and more as a vision of a Jeffersonian New York Jew. Noah saw America as a tolerant, enlightened society. There, in "pursuit of happiness," Jews could find fulfillment—at least until a distant messianic future. If the Jews of America could no longer identify with a closed synagogue community, they could still maintain communal identity in a republican nation. Other religious groups, such as the Mormons and the Moravians, successfully sought a religious haven in the American West. Why could it not work for Jews as well?

■ Anti-Semitism

Acceptance of Jews into the mainstream of American life did not go unchallenged. The partisan battles of the 1790s ignited anti-Semitic charges. In 1790, a Democratic-Republican newspaper printed a letter from a "Citizen" accusing (Hamiltonian) speculators of descending to the level of Jews. Though these people were uncircumcised, "their minds are far gone in *Israelitish* avarice." Those who were made rich by Hamilton were "brokers, speculators, Jews, M[embers] of C[ongress] and foreigners." As Jews migrated to the Jeffersonians, anti-Semitism became the province of the Federalists. Printer James Rivington published a preface to a novel singling out Solomon Simson as a leader of men who "will easily be known by their physiognomy; they all seem to be, like their Vice-President [of the Democratic Society], of the tribe of Shylock; they have that leering underlook, and malicious grin that seem to say to the honest man—*approach me not.*" Rivington linked Jews with blacks and the Haitian Revolution. Jeffersonians responded that "it is a good maxim not to ridicule religion." Alexander Hamilton represented Jews in his law practice and wrote of the "*progress of the Jews*" as "entirely out of the *ordinary course* of human affairs," the result of "some great providential Plan." Yet, at the height of reaction in 1798, he compared his political enemies to "Shylock the Jew." During the 1790s, "a wide and fetid stream of antisemitism" ran through "Federalist thought."[39]

Twenty years later, Mordecai M. Noah ran for sheriff. Appointed to this position in 1820, the highest political office yet achieved by New York's Jews, he acquitted himself well, working for debtor reform. When the office became elective in 1821, anti-Semitism emerged as a major issue in the contest. The *Evening Post* reminded voters that Noah's opponent was "an old member of the church." The *Commercial Advertiser* expressed alarm that on the second day of the election "the Jews prevailed against the Gentiles." A leader of the Protestant missionary American Society for Meliorating the Condition of the Jews claimed that a recent outbreak of yellow fever was God's "judgement" for prominent citizens "publically abetting the election of an infidel in preference to a Christian." Noah wrote that on the eve of election "Churchmen, Sextons, Bell-ringers [and] Deacons . . . of the Church Militant scoured the wards to oppose what they called the unbeliever.'" Lamenting that the election had become a religious war that could threaten members of other sects, he lost, attracting 41 percent of the vote.[40]

Historian Jacob Marcus argues that most Americans believed that, as the new nation was Christian, Jews were not entitled to political rights. Leading writers vented anti-Semitic remarks. For example, while a young politico, Washington Irving smeared a Clintonian Democratic-Republican as a "little ugly Jew." In America, as in Europe, "the word 'Jew' was a synonym for a cheat." However, given New York's political heritage, the impact of anti-Semitism should not be exaggerated. Jews made significant strides in the marketplace, mainstream culture, and politics. For example, *The Merchant of Venice* played to large audiences in 1810–1812; Shylock was depicted as "diabolic, enraged and vengeful." In another production in 1820–1821, Shylock was portrayed as a "person of mixed and justifiable emotions." And then in a later production, he was depicted as a "guardian of Hebrew law and grandeur," to equally appreciative audiences. American republicanism's better angels flew more freely in New York City.[41]

Although American missionaries saw themselves as anything but anti-Semitic, when they attempted to convert Jews, they aroused antagonism in the Jewish community. This movement began in the United States with the Second Great Awakening and the formation of such organizations as the American Tract Society and the American Bible Society. Intensity increased with the arrival in 1816 of Joseph Frey, a converted Jew knowledgeable in Greek, Latin, and Hebrew. With local clergy, he formed the American Society for Evangelizing the Jews, whose name was changed to the American Society for Meliorating the Condition of the Jews to secure incorporation. The society, drawing the support of John Quincy Adams and the president of Yale, published a magazine in 1823, *Israel's Advocate*. Many of the city's ministers joined Frey's effort at a "large meeting." In his autobiography, Frey termed the Jews a fainthearted people, as "the mere idea of going among Christians excites in [them] a timidity indescribable."[42]

In 1822, a converted Polish Jew, Bernard Jadownicky, with European success converting Jews, traveled to America. Spurning old methods of handing out Bibles and sending missionaries to debate, he advocated a colony. Frey's society also endorsed colonization, claiming the moment of mass conversion was at hand. In 1824, however, the society, reporting its effort to purchase thousands of acres of upstate New York land unfeasible, recommended a "plan *of amalgamation*" in which Jewish immigrants would be met on arrival and given instruction in agriculture and the Gospels, becoming a new Christian "band of brethren."[43]

New York Jewry responded. An anonymously written pamphlet, *Israel Vindicated*, warned that there was no excuse for Jews not defending themselves from "base and unfounded charges." Missionary societies' descriptions of Jews in a "degraded and uncultivated state" made it more difficult for Jews to attain greater standing. Deficiencies in Jewish occupational structure resulted from anti-Semitism. Those who opposed toleration, an integral part of a republican society, did the work of "tyrants." Printer Samuel Jackson's periodical, *The Jew*, published in 1823, targeted missionaries. Noting that twenty Christians expressed an interest in conversion to Judaism, Jackson saw the emissaries as cowards, unable to defend their own faith. As a result, "disbelief of the gospels has increased."[44]

Republican America offered those who wished to convert the Jews the liberty to organize and disseminate their literature. But it also gave the Jewish community a free hand and a free pen. Missionaries encountered little success in New York, a state in which Jews found much opportunity. More important, the Jewish community claimed its voice and learned how to use it, both to defend itself against missionaries and to fully participate in the republican life of the new nation.

In 1818, the congregation of Shearith Israel decided to remodel its original building rather than to construct a synagogue uptown. The new sanctuary was 60 percent larger than the original Mill Street synagogue and seated three hundred. (Courtesy Congregation Shearith Israel)

CHAPTER 6

A Republican Faith

*In 1790, the congregation of Shearith Israel drafted a new con-
stitution. It included a bill of rights, which opened with a ringing statement:
"Whereas in free states all power originates and is derived from the people who
always retain every right necessary for their well being individually, . . . therefore
we the profession [professors] of the Divine laws . . . conceive it our duty to make
this declaration of our rights and privileges." The first right, entitling "every free
person professing the Jewish religion, and who lives according to its holy precepts"
to a seat in the synagogue "as a brother" and as a "subject of every fraternal
duty," hinted at a worldwide brotherhood of Jews, perhaps reflecting the French
Revolution's idea of* fraternité. *While most rights were traditional, such as a
member's prerogative to have the hazan officiate at a wedding, these compelling
words marked a new era in the practice of Judaism in New York. As republicanism reshaped the Jewish community's secular world, it also dramatically changed
the world of Jewish spirituality.*[1]

■ Republicanism and Shearith Israel

Shearith Israel resumed services immediately after the British evacuation, but
its future course was in doubt. The concept of the synagogue-community was
incompatible with a republican society in which Jews no longer had to seclude
themselves around a plainly constructed sanctuary. Could their synagogue re-
define itself to remain central to the community? The congregation's new constitution, completed under the leadership of Jeffersonian Solomon Simson a
year after the U.S. Constitution was ratified, attempted to combine both synagogue traditions and republican ideals.

By the end of the eighteenth century, New York had grown northward toward the present Houston Street. While all neighborhoods were mixed, the wealthy tended to move
from their downtown residences to new brownstones in the center of the island above
Chatham Park and, after 1812, the new city hall. The working classes tended to reside in
the wards adjoining the East and Hudson Rivers. (Courtesy Prints Division, New York
Public Library)

The charter's preamble, similar to the opening lines of the Bill of Rights, declared that the congregation had authority, "in the presence of the Almighty"
and in "a state happily constituted upon the principles of equal liberty civil and
religious," to formulate a "compact" containing "rules, and regulations" for the
"general good." The "congregation of *yehudim*," fulfilling their duty "to themselves and posterity," pledged to "perform all acts" required for the support of
their "religious and holy divine service."[2]

The constitution offered membership to every Jewish male at least twenty-
one years old (except indentured or hired servants), not married "contrary to
the rules of [the Jewish] religion," and "conforming hereunto." It enumerated
the duties of the president or parnas and the council of elders, the *maamad*.
The new compact allowed all members to vote for members of the board. (The

transfer and settlement of power from the elders to the trustees was still in progress, and the constitution was unclear about the relationship of the two.) The constitution directed that arbitration would end the internal controversies that had so often divided the congregation.[3]

The congregation's bylaws detailed duties of the hazan, shochet, and shamash; the right of three members to call a synagogue meeting; and the means to secure revenue. They included a clause forbidding any Jew who violated Jewish "religious laws by eating trafa, breakeing the Sabath, or any other sacred day" from being called to the Torah or running for congregational office. On July 11, 1790, the Board of Trustees ratified the charter, repealing all prior congregational laws, and reminded the congregation that the "temporalities" of the congregation were vested in its hands.[4]

The writing of the 1790 constitution coincided with a second expression of the congregation's republicanism. Following the example of the Newport congregation, they penned a joint letter (with congregations in Richmond, Charleston, and Philadelphia) to President Washington. The congregations declared that they would "yield to no class of their fellow-citizens . . . in affection" for the nation's glorious leader. The "wonders . . . the Lord of Hosts had worked" in ancient Israel were visible in the "late glorious revolution" and in the federal Constitution, a compact that sealed "in peace what [Washington] had achieved in war." The Jewish community prayed that God would protect Washington in his remaining days and assured him, "when full of years, thou shalt be gathered unto thy people," that his name and virtues "will remain an indelible memorial on our minds." Washington responded that the affection of America's Jews was a "treasure beyond the reach of calculation." In the new republic, "the liberality of sentiment toward each other, which marks every political and religious denomination of men in this country, stands unparalleled in the history of Nations." Agreeing that "the power and goodness of the Almighty" were visible in "our late glorious revolution . . . and in the establishment of our present equal government," he wished America's Jewish congregations "the same temporal and eternal blessings" that they "implore" for him. The Jewish community was a partner in the republican experiment.[5]

■ A Republican Synagogue Community

Shearith Israel remained the only synagogue in New York throughout the first thirty-five years of the early republic. While critical to the perseverance of Judaism in Gotham, it no longer served as the cornerstone of Jewish existence. The population of Jews in New York rose, but the congregation's membership did not. There were more choices. Jews could choose to affiliate with the Masonic Order or the Mechanics Society. However, most seats at High Holy Days were filled. For example, in 1815, the congregation sold all but 25 of its 132 men's seats and nearly all of the 72 seats in the women's gallery. Yet only about fifty of those purchasing seats were members; the others just bought seats for the holidays. For many Jews, the synagogue assumed relevance for only part of their lives: primarily life-cycle ceremonies and the High Holy Days. Thus, New York's Jews initiated a practice that became increasingly common.[6]

The early republican era was difficult for Shearith Israel. The physical condition of the synagogue continued to deteriorate. Services, lasting as long as four to five hours, were often conducted in a cacophonous manner, as congregants, when they were not gossiping, prayed at their own rates. Attendance was another problem. It was more and more difficult to gather a minyan of ten adult males; at times, only three men turned up at the daily service. In 1814, the trustees declared that diminished Sabbath attendance made the required two shillings per offering (*aliyah*, or call to the Torah) burdensome for conscientious attendees. Haym Salomon wrote in 1825 that the present generation had "fallen on evil times"; some Friday evenings, only "three heads of families" and the "reader" were present. Attendance waxed and waned but remained problematic throughout the era.[7]

Shearith Israel's financial crises offered further evidence of its weakened standing in the Jewish community. Minutes of the Board of Trustees focus on the synagogue's dire circumstances. The sale of seats and members' dues and contributions were not adequate; as a result, synagogue employees came under stress. In 1805, the shamash requested a raise from a fifty-dollar salary that "will scarcely find bread." Though aware that "the funds of the society will not afford him" what his family needs, he sought some increase in compensation. Clerk Isaac Gomez in 1807 stated that he had "waited for a long period previous to this application in order that the funds might be in a better state." In 1813, the clerk again asked for a raise, stating that he received "only a pittance" because of the "deranged state of the funds of the Congregation." That year, the board failed to pay the Mechanics Bank $300 due on a note until a trustee loaned it the funds. An 1815 report found "the finances of the Congregation in a very deranged state," with the "dignity of the Board" harmed by its inability to pay debts.[8]

The trustees pursued debtors. In 1812, declaring that the "immoral" neglect of financial responsibilities could "destroy the well being of the Congregation," the board ruled that members in arrears would lose their vote and other "rights privileges and immunities" until they paid their debts. The board also turned outstanding debts, including those of members, over to a "trusty and vigilant marshall," attorney John Ackerman. Economic conditions improved after the War of 1812, allowing Jewish leaders to collect funds to refurbish the synagogue. The Panic of 1819, however, caused "retrenchments." While internal quarrels and market conditions were factors, limited allegiance and identity also caused problems, as income remained insufficient for many years.[9]

Though there were yet no independent Jewish welfare societies, a few semi-autonomous organizations emerged in the early republic, loosely affiliated with Shearith Israel. The first society, Hebra Gemiluth Hasidim (Society for Dispensing Acts of Kindness), began its work in 1785 with fifty-five members. Members paid a four-shilling initiation fee and dues. For five years, this organization dispensed medicine, fuel, and money to those in need; visited the sick; and prepared the dead for burial. In 1802, Hebra Hased Vaamet (Society of Kindness and Truth), with its own constitution, took over the duties to the dead and dying, and it remains an ongoing institution. Shearith Israel provided the society its hearse and keys to the cemetery. In 1827, Hased Vaamet published a "Compendium of the Order of the Burial Service." Rules prohibited moving a dying person from his or her residence unless directed by a physician; no noise was permitted to disturb the dying. With death near, the members of the society gathered in a circle. After the last breath, they recited the Shema and then the word "one" seven times. In 1798, the charitable society Kalpe Mattan Basether emerged with the help of Reverend Seixas. It sought to give charity in secret, one of Judaism's highest forms of alms. Directors were "in no case" to "divulge the names of persons receiving aid" or how the directors spent their grants. The Hebrew Benevolent Society began in 1820, focusing on English and Polish Jews. In 1825, it aligned with a new congregation, B'nai Jeshurun.[10]

■ A Hamiltonian Synagogue

American republicanism possessed two outlooks vying to become the nation's creed. The Hamiltonian version that stressed deference and tradition found a home in Shearith Israel at the same time that the egalitarian Jeffersonian strain was defeating Hamilton's conservative republicanism at the polls. As the city fathers attempted to establish order within a republican framework by laying out the rectangular grid that was to define Manhattan Island, so, too, the prominent Jews who led Shearith Israel attempted to establish an ordered structure.[11]

This quest appears in the constitution that the congregation ratified in 1805. The new charter contained neither a bill of rights nor a statement proclaiming the right to enact compacts. It named only a single governing body, the Board of Trustees; the president of the board was parnas. The corporate structure was fully in place. The compact stressed order and decorum. The board could levy a fine of up to $250 for disruptive behavior, a much larger sum than was permitted in 1790. To "promote Solemnity and Order" during worship and make members' prayers "acceptable to ALMIGHTY GOD," article 8 of the bylaws required members not to chant a psalm until the hazan "shall signify the tone or key, in which the [psalm] is to be sung." Members could pray "with an equal voice but neither higher nor louder than the [hazan]." Members were to exit "in a quiet and orderly manner." Jews living within "the corporation of the city of New York" who were not members had to pay ten dollars if they wished any of "the rights, benefits or immunities" of members. The congregation expected all Jews to support the synagogue. This charter reflected an increase in the influence of conservative republicanism, as the need of making a living and raising families replaced the initial wave of republican enthusiasm.[12]

The Board of Trustees, legal head of a chartered corporation, exercised tight control over the hazan, shochet, and shamash; disbursed charity; and oversaw the school. Though the hazan was the religious leader, the board governed. It demonstrated no reluctance in disciplining Hazan Peixotto when he acted in an "unbecoming manner" by showing discourtesy to the acting parnas. The trustees expected obedience.[13]

The board feared innovation. Traditional Sephardic ritual (even though most members were Ashkenazi) and order of prayers continued. In 1818, when a group of young congregants proposed forming a choir to beautify the service, the trustees extended the "thanks and approbation of the . . . congregation for their good intention" to "give the service that solemnity that [the] prayers and psalms should have." But, they warned, "innovations" must be approached "with great cautions and defference" so as not to create a greater "evil." Too often, factions, "from private pique," attempted to control the service, causing older members to cease attending. The board encouraged the youths to continue their rehearsals and to create a new, acceptable "harmony in singing." There is no evidence that this movement went forward.[14]

In 1820, the board deplored "attempts to introduce a mode of offering," unknown to the congregation, which could "subvert the usages and customs . . . established by [the congregation's] fathers." A member who dared "interrupt the solemnity of . . . holy worship" incurred "the displeasure of the great Creator of the Universe." The requirement to wear tallit (prayer shawls) at services was another issue of contention. A number of members chose not to wear the shawls, claiming that doing so was not required by Jewish law. The committee investigating this question found no "imperative religious obligation." However, as the custom had been "strictly observed," any "departure," they declared, would be an "innovation," which could lead to further "deviations" and, finally, to the "subversion of all the venerable & established usages of this Congregation." Consequently, only men wearing tallit would be called to the Torah. These conservative trustees stressed tradition over experiment.[15]

Dr. John Pierce of Brookline, Massachusetts, a minister who understood Hebrew, visited the synagogue in 1812 and reported favorably on its Sabbath prayers. The gathering was decorous, as men wearing "white sashes" (prayer shawls) went "with great ceremony" to the altar to take out the Torah. The service, "consisting of prayers and singing from the Psalms and recitations from the law, was performed by young and old, and altogether in the Hebrew language." New England ministers demanded decorum, and Pierce saw little of the cacophony common to services at the time. Perhaps the trustees achieved a measure of success in their quest for order, or perhaps the presence of a visiting Christian divine had a quieting impact.[16]

The congregation's decision to replace the crumbling, demoralizing, and "deplorable" 1730 structure proved to be its most important accomplishment in the early republic. Fewer and fewer congregants trekked downtown to attend services in a cramped, unattractive setting. During the window of opportunity that the more prosperous years of 1817 and 1818 provided, a number of leading members raised the funds for and oversaw the construction of a new sanctuary. Harmon Hendricks gave $250 and an interest-free loan of $1,000 (later increased to $2,000). Jews from beyond New York contributed, including the congregation of Curaçao (600 pieces of eight).[17]

The decision to rebuild rather than to relocate exemplified conservative members exerting control. It would have been wiser to move where the well-to-do Jewish population was living, north of city hall, in the tree-lined neighborhood of upper Greenwich, Laight, Charlton, and Wooster Streets, but devotion to Mill Street prevailed. The new brick and stone building, thirty-five feet by fifty-eight feet, was 60 percent larger than the original structure and nine feet higher, with 167 seats for men and 133 in the women's gallery. The candelabra remained, illuminating the Roman cement floor. Naphtali Judah donated a white marble tablet chiseled with the Ten Commandments. The synagogue made a few nods toward egalitarianism. All men's seats were priced at four pounds. A "plane turned mahogany banister" allowed women a better view than the previous breastwork had. Despite these reforms, the decision exacted a price. Attractive as the new sanctuary was, it filled its seats only in the first years. In 1822, only 102 of the men's seats were sold and only 108 of the women's.[18]

Deferential republicanism emerged in disciplinary cases before the board. In 1796, a congregant landed in jail for disturbing the service. The board received a letter from his wife, "G. Philips," pleading for release. She acknowledged that "he deserved some punishment" but promised that, if he was released "from confinement," she would "keep him from going to Synagoge any more." In 1806, the trustees summoned a congregant for refusing to stand on Yom Kippur. Learning that he was ill, they revoked his fine. The shamash was brought before the board for refusing to open a window when ordered by the parnas. After a suitable apology and a "promise of good behavior," he was allowed to keep his position. The board called congregant Solomon Levy before it for refusing to accept the honor of the *sepher* (being called to the Torah, requiring a two-shilling offering). Levy was acquitted on the grounds that he intended no insult. In 1809, the board tried E. N. Carvalho for "eating Trephah."

While the 1805 constitution no longer required observance of ritual, and it was not uncommon for members to violate dietary laws, this was not permitted for applicants for office, in this case, acting hazan. Jacob Hart testified that Carvalho ate lobster at the house of a man named Nunes. Carvalho replied that when he ate with Nunes, the food was always "Casher" and that he had his "Negroe boy" superintend its preparation. He vowed that he was "as cautious eating at Mr. Nunes' House, as he would be at the house of a Goye." Carvalho was acquitted.[19]

In 1818, the board summoned a constable to remove the wife of David Levy from a seat in the women's gallery that was not assigned to her. (After her ejection, she took a seat in the back.) In 1820, the trustees confronted "Rabi Pique," their learned Belgian teacher, accusing him of alcoholism and meddling "in the arranging of the service," causing "a scene highly disgraceful in itself." The board instructed Pique not to "interfere with any service or order of prayers" and to obey the hazan, the "officer of the congregation." Unable to reform, Pique was terminated.[20]

Those who were summoned before the board struck a deferential attitude. With Jeffersonian ideals prominent in the republic, the congregation's acceptance of deferential Hamiltonian republicanism was at issue with any break in decorum or any innovation.

■ A Jeffersonian Synagogue

The Jeffersonian republicanism that propelled Jefferson and Madison into the presidency also played a major role in synagogue affairs. One tenet of Jeffersonianism, the right to challenge authority, confounded the Board of Trustees from 1811 to 1814 over election of new trustees, amid allegations that "presiding trustees" refused to appoint legal inspectors. For reasons not spelled out in the minutes, the congregation voted out two long-serving members. Three resignations followed immediately. Isaac Moses, noting that he had been a trustee for years, abandoned his post with "great pain and anxiety" because of a "combination tending to destroy the peace and happiness of the Congregation" by driving away men "who have unremittingly and honestly laboured to promote their prosperity" and selecting individuals who "have been steadily hostile to the present constitution," a charter "drafted and ratified by the congregation." M. L. Moses vacated his seat because that same "Combination" threatened to undermine "the Harmony and prosperity of the Congregation." Seixas Nathan stepped down because of "the late Election of a Gentleman to the Trusteeship who has uniformly refused to subscribe to either [the constitution or bylaws]." The synagogue's eminent treasurer, Solomon Simson, resigned, and book-keeper Solomon Seixas left his position in July 1813, "in consequence of the election of the two late elected members, . . . who disgrace the station of the Trustees." Seixas also resigned his seat in the sanctuary, as he was "no longer coming to Synagogue." He pledged to return when "respectable members" re-placed these trustees.[21]

None of the 1811 trustees remained a member of the 1812 board. The new body included Hayam Solomon, son the of the famed revolutionary of the same name, representing Ashkenazim critical of laxity in religious observance, and Benjamin Judah, a synagogue gadfly, who resigned in 1824 after being ex-pelled on Yom Kippur eve for defying the parnas regarding an open door.

Strife continued in 1814 when Judah declared himself president by virtue of seniority. Judah also became parnas, a position that normally accompanied the presidency, by voting twice (once as president) to break a three-three tie. A contentious period ensued: the board had difficulty reaching a quorum, the synagogue failed to pay its notes, and Judah peremptorily postponed the sale of seats. Rebuked by fellow trustees for actions contrary to the constitu-tion, Judah, together with Isaac Gomez Jr., resigned the following April. Haym Salomon had already left. The intrigues within the synagogue leadership and the bitterly contested elections reveal the presence of the more egalitarian strain of republicanism, as members shunned deference in order to oust tra-ditional leadership. Generational conflict and friction between Ashkenazi and Sephardi members also contributed to the conflict.[22]

Jeffersonian republican appeals surfaced during these schisms over the election of the shochet. Whatever members did outside their homes, the availability of kosher meat remained of great importance to the community. In 1813, there were no Jewish butchers; non-Jewish meat handlers under the Common Council's supervision supplied kosher meat. (In 1805, the council's Market Committee revoked the license of a butcher who deceptively offered nonkosher meat as kosher.) These butchers slaughtered from their stock under the watch of the shochet. The shochet's contract required him to have meat available on a daily basis. He received a salary for his services ($400 in 1813) and kept beef tongues as a perk.[23]

An election took place in January 1813, shortly after the overthrow of the former Board of Trustees. Thirty-five members voted for one of two candidates. The first, current shochet Abraham Abrahams, faced criticism for laxity and self-serving interpretations of his contract. Opposing him was Mark Solomon of Charleston, South Carolina, a former New York shochet. The new board was likely looking for a change since, though the vote favored Abrahams 25–18, it was unable to reach agreement with him over salary demands and working conditions. Consequently, the board gave the contract to Solomon and ordered Abrahams to return the congregation's knives and pincers.[24]

Though Abrahams did not win appointment, a number of members of the congregation continued to employ him. In response, the board wrote the Common Council requesting an ordinance prohibiting the sale of "meats sealed after the customs of their Society" by anyone not under contract with the synagogue. Under Jewish law, they wrote, it was unlawful for a Jew to eat "flesh" unless "killed, inspected & sealed" by *shochetim* "duly authorized by the Mahamad or Trustees of the Synagogue & by them pronounced to be sound." Unfortunately, "certain persons" not employed by Shearith Israel had "killed & sealed meat."[25]

On February 1, the Common Council complied, forbidding sale of "meat known as Jews meat" by those not "engaged" by Shearith Israel, with a penalty of twenty-five dollars per offense. The synagogue now possessed a legal monopoly. Members employing Abrahams petitioned the council to repeal the measure as an "encroachment on our religious rites and a restriction of those general privileges to which we are entitled." They were certain that the council "did not intend to impair the civil rights, or wound the religious feelings of [their] sect." The trustees, in other words, had misled the council. The council repealed the act. Among the opponents of the trustees were former board members Nathan and Moses, former treasurer Simson, and industrialist Harmon Hendricks.[26]

Furious at the repeal, the board termed the rebellious petitioners, their congregants, "wicked and irreligious, . . . tending to destroy the respectability of the Congregation." Moreover, the trustees said they objected to fellow members making public "an unfortunate Schism in our society." This was critical, as the council's decision turned on its intent not to "interfere in [the] controversy." Aware of republican disdain of monopoly, the board retreated, stating that as it did not aim to prevent other *shochetim* from working, "far be it from

The expression depicted on the seal of congregation Shearith Israel, that the world stands on justice, truth, and charity, is a republican Americanized translation of a saying from *Pirke Avot* (*Ethics of the Fathers*), which is in harmony with the republican ideals of the early republic. (Courtesy Congregation Shearith Israel)

the Trustees to impose shackles upon any man's conscience." If members "opposed to the Shohet employed by the Trustees" chose not to eat of the meat he supervised, "let them employ a Shohet of their own and designate it by a particular mark of their own." The trustees intended to safeguard congregants who looked to them "for direction in all their religious concerns." Their petition for reconsideration was unsuccessful, its arguments undermined by the board's contradictory statements and the negative votes of trustees Isaac Gomez Jr. and Solomon Seixas, who declared that the appeal was "inviting insult and only intending to create Schisms in the Congregation to a greater extent."[27]

This dispute demonstrated that Jeffersonian republicanism endured within the congregation. Jeffersonians opposed restraints on competition as British-like efforts to create favorites in the marketplace and to limit entrepreneurial opportunity. It also showed the pragmatic nature of republican ideology. Unlike political allegiances, which tended to harden over time, congregants could advocate different strands of republican thought according to their circumstances. While in office, the former trustees championed deferential Hamiltonianism; in opposition, they employed Jeffersonian egalitarianism to oppose the new trustees' rejection of Abrahams. The board, they argued, had jurisdiction in the synagogue, not in the marketplace.[28]

Jeffersonianism emerged in the educational endeavors of Shearith Israel.

The congregation's attempts to maintain a school in the early republic were no more successful than they had been in the colonial era, despite a $900 grant in 1801 from Myer Polony to support a Talmud Torah. The enthusiasm of its first teacher, Hazan Seixas, who believed that education was "the first thing that ought to be pursued in life, in order to constitute us rational," and that children deserved "a compleat and full knowledge of the Hebrew language," did not prevent enrollment from shrinking to a dozen students. After Seixas stepped down, the school often failed to meet because the congregation was unable to hire a competent teacher.[29]

Jeffersonian thought supported common school education in the belief that a democratic society required an educated citizenry. In 1811, Shearith Israel learned that Albany was considering funding a common school system. This was an opportunity for educational revival. The trustees, with the help of Mayor DeWitt Clinton, applied for state funds. Persuaded "that the Legislature will look with an equal eye upon all occupations of people who conduct themselves as good and faithful citizens," the trustees argued that the Jewish community deserved "the same countenance and encouragement which has been exhibited to others." After an initial rejection, the congregation received $1,565.70 "for the instruction of poor children in the most useful branches of common education."[30]

Funding dropped markedly when the legislature voted to devote the bulk of its funds to nondenominational schools. In 1813, learning of the establishment of Free School No. 1 and lawmakers' intent, the trustees petitioned Albany. Acknowledging that education was the "best pledge of republican institutions," the congregation yet found the free school "exceptionable on the score of religious instruction." Its five hundred pupils would not receive spiritual education there or from "irreligious parents." The appropriation would "encourage parents in habits of indifference to their duties of religion," leading children's minds toward "fraud and deception." The petition failed. The Polonies Talmud Torah continued to struggle. At one point, it had but two students. In the Age of Jefferson, Jewish parents, integrated into New York society, did not look to the synagogue for the education of their children.[31]

Jeffersonian civil libertarian ideals became an issue at Shearith Israel in 1823 when the board suspended David Seixas, son of the late hazan, from receiving honors for a year for insulting the new hazan with "passion and temper inconsistent with decorum due" to the "Holy Place of Worship." The board's failure to maintain Seixas's widowed mother at the agreed amount angered him. Seventeen congregants wrote the trustees that its decision was a violation of bylaws, which allowed a member charged with insulting the parnas in the discharge of his duties the right to a hearing before the board. Seixas never received that opportunity. The petitioners, ready to "attest that there was nothing inconsistent with decorum" in Seixas's actions, reasoned that if this action was permitted, they too could be subject to "similar ex parte interpretations." Indeed, "laws . . . enacted for the rights and Liberties of individuals ought not to be thus precipitously disrespected." Nothing should be done to weaken members' allegiance to the congregation's constitution, a charter in conformity "with that universal law of our country which requires the accuser and accused to be confronted." Eschewing deferential expectations, these members invoked egalitarian republicanism to defend their rights.[32]

■ Secession

The final and most significant example of Jeffersonianism came with the revolt of Ashkenazi members, leading to the formation of a second congregation, B'nai Jeshurun, in 1824. In the 1776 Declaration of Independence, Jefferson affirmed that a people under a government that denied them the "unalienable Rights" of "Life, Liberty and the Pursuit of Happiness" possessed the right "to institute new Government." While Jefferson was not writing of Jewish congregations, B'nai Jeshurun was born within this spirit.

The movement began with an incident of synagogue discipline. English Ashkenazi pawnbroker Barrow Cohen refused to make an offering when called to the Torah. (Though Cohen was of low economic standing, his status as a Kohen, a Jew whose ancestry was among the priestly tribe of ancient Israel, allowed him significant synagogue honors.) The Board of Trustees summoned Barrow for a hearing. With Ashkenazi Jews an ever-increasing majority of the congregation's membership, and Cohen's recognized position as a leader of dissident Ashkenazi, the board understood that this was more than the usual case of disruption. It decided that no one but the president could ask questions. Other trustees would have to submit queries in writing; if the president deemed the request improper, Cohen would be asked to leave while the board discussed the issue.[33]

After seceding from Shearith Israel in 1825, the members of the new congregation, B'nai Jeshurun, purchased the First Coloured Presbyterian Church on Elm Street and remodeled it with new chandeliers and brick columns. It seated six hundred, twice the capacity of Shearith Israel. (Courtesy Collections of the New-York Historical Society)

At the hearing, Cohen, while admitting he made no offering, stated that he acted "according to the Constitution of th[e] Congregation." If the trustees proceeded "contrary to the Constitution," he would "apply elsewhere." He made no offering, because "as a Congregator his rights were taken from him." Trustee Haym Salomon became irate, declared the proceedings "illegal," and left the hearing. Attempting to avoid internal conflict, the board declared that Cohen was ignorant of the law and had no desire to insult the trustees. Thus, it only directed him to behave properly while attending "Divine Worship." It also repealed the requirement of offerings for those who were called to the Torah. Spurning this offer of reconciliation, Cohen wrote the board that its "insinuation" to his "future behavior" merited "nothing but contempt."[34]

Cohen's hearing rallied the Ashkenazi faction against what they saw as a domineering board insensitive to their concerns. They next requested permission to conduct their own services in the morning, at a time when the synagogue was not in use. Their request, they stated, was not meant as separation but to operate independently within the synagogue. They pledged to collect offerings, "keep a regular account," and use the customary Sephardic "*minhog*" (tradition). They expressed their confidence in the trustees, who had "no ground for refusal": "The trustees will cheerfully concur in the promotion of our zeal and attention to the worship of our holy religion."[35]

The Ashkenazi faction organized its own society, Hevra Hinuch Nearim (Society for the Education of Youth), in 1824. Its constitution pledged loyalty to Shearith Israel, strict performance of Jewish law, and regular attendance at services "at such times and places as shall be directed." An executive committee of five elected members was to govern the society for three-month terms; then a new committee would take on authority. Committee meetings were open to the public. The hazan would possess no greater standing than any other member of the society, nor would he dress differently, except when wearing tallit. A member of the synagogue could join the society if he received a majority vote of members. This rule was "not intended to exclude any brother Yehudah" from "joining therein, provided he conduct himself with propriety." The society would distribute honors "in such a manner that each person shall have an equal portion"; offerings were lowered from two shillings to six and a quarter cents. The society intended to foster Ashkenazi identity and increase religious observance. Egalitarian governance would replace the authoritarianism of Shearith Israel.[36]

The Board of Trustees responded in two ways. First, they rejected the petition "under the full conviction that they cannot recognize any society or association for religious worship distinct from Shearith Israel." They were backed by fifty-three members, who gave the trustees "full and entire approbation of their conduct," in opposition to measures that have "a tendency to destroy the well known and established rule and customs of [their] ancestors as have been practiced . . . for one hundred years past." Second, with the advice of an attorney, the trustees interpreted their act of incorporation as allowing them to restrict membership. With a vote required for all new members, the congregation rejected all but two of the first sixteen to apply. The synagogue also sought Jewish legal sources to forbid Barrow Cohen from receiving honors even if he were the only Kohen present, including the priestly benediction. Immigration of Ashkenazi Jews created fear, distancing one part of the membership from its republican roots while driving the other into radical republican remedies.[37]

The final step was secession. In October, the Ashkenazim met at Washington Hall and established a new congregation. In a letter to Shearith Israel's trustees, the founders of the new society stated that being "educated in the German and Polish minhog," they found it "difficult" to practice the Sephardic ritual. Second, despite the still small Jewish population in New York and sparse synagogue attendance, the Ashkenazi dissidents contended that an increasing Jewish community made it impossible for Shearith Israel to handle all the Jewish congregants, "particularly on Holidays." Finally, "the distant situation of the shool" from their homes made it difficult to attend services. The secessionists "respectfully trust[ed]" that their decision would be "Satisfactory" to the board. They did not "capriciously . . . withdraw" from the "ancient and respectable congregation," but acted only from "motives of necessity." In closing, they invoked the "religious and . . . equitable claim" that, they said, "we have as Brethren of one great family." As part of a community larger than any one synagogue, the new congregation, B'nai Jeshurun, trusted that their endeavor would "be recognized." Shearith Israel's board considered the letter, postponed action, and never responded.[38]

Prominent members of Shearith Israel, including Noah and Hendricks, both Ashkenazim, signed the secessionists' letter. It was time to let their brethren go; the growing city could encompass more congregations. The new synagogue filed articles of incorporation with the state and drafted a constitution whose preamble praised the "wise and republican laws of this country . . . based upon universal toleration given to every citizen and sojourner the right to worship according to the dictate of his conscience." Within a year, with the help of Hendricks, the congregation purchased the First Coloured Presbyterian Church on Elm Street, in the heart of Five Points, a mixed working-class neighborhood that included many Jewish residents. The sanctuary, remodeled with chandeliers and brick columns, seated six hundred, twice the size of

Shearith Israel. Soon the two congregations treated each other on a friendly basis. Shearith Israel loaned B'nai Jeshurun four scrolls for the dedication of the Elm Street synagogue in 1827, and prayers were offered in each synagogue for the welfare of both sets of trustees.[39]

B'nai Jeshurun was the first of many new synagogues. Bolstered by increasing numbers of immigrants, congregations split and split again. Historian Hyman Grinstein contends that if Shearith Israel had been more forthcoming, secession might have been avoided, even with new congregations. Instead, "they destroyed the very institution both sought to save—the united Jewish community of New York." The dream that Shearith Israel would become "the largest congregation in the New World" would not come true. The founding spirit of Shearith Israel, threatened by attacks on its authority, withered as egalitarian republicanism blossomed in the new Ashkenazi society. B'nai Jeshurun, representing a younger generation with fewer men of wealth and prestige, would become one of the largest synagogues in the city.[40]

■ Republican Jewish Women

Did republicanism alter the lives of New York's Jewish women? Immediately after the Revolution, it will be recalled, the three Judah sisters defied Shearith Israel's Board of Trustees over their seat assignments. When they were denied what they considered their rightful seats, they told the board, "when the Gentlemen Trustees can convince us that we are subject to any laws they choose to make which is to hinder us from attending Divine Worship, they may endeavor to exercise authority." They did not stop their confrontation until a judge in civil court ruled against them. Yet this act of defiance to male authority did not herald a new era of politically active Jewish women, demanding a greater role in congregational governance or in ritual observance. Nor did women, Jew and non-Jew, find significantly greater opportunities in the marketplace. However, the new nation, building on the heightened political awareness and ideology of the Revolution, expected women, including female Jewish citizens, to be educated "republican mothers" whose moral behavior would nurture republican children. The success of the republic depended on their virtue.[41]

Shearith Israel found that its female scholars, if few in number, were highly motivated. Seven girls were among the thirty-five students receiving Hebrew

Grace Nathan, wife of merchant Simon Nathan, was an educated correspondent with her relatives. Devoted to Shearith Israel and her brother Reverend Gershom Seixas, she composed poetry expressing her strong religious feelings. (Courtesy American Jewish Historical Society)

instruction when its school opened in the 1790s. In 1808, six girls attended, three from the Seixas family. The next year, five of them received prizes, as opposed to only three of sixteen boys. In the synagogue, two women applied to be shamash in 1788, though neither won appointment. The removal of the balustrade in the remodeled 1818 synagogue allowed greater participation in the service. The proportion of women's seats increased to 44 percent. A mixed choir sang at the dedication. In 1820, Richa Levy, first vice president of the Female Hebrew Benevolent Society, an organization "established by the Ladies of [the] congregation for the relief of indigent females *particularly*," sent the Board of Trustees a letter from The "Board of Managers" seeking permission to solicit offerings at the synagogue for the society. Their petition granted, the society continued for fifty years. Women composed a larger part of attendance at religious services and were more active in synagogue affairs, but within a segregated, auxiliary role.[42]

Republican New York housed more educated women than had the colonial seaport of Abigaill Franks. Unfortunately, few of their writings survive. Reverend Seixas's daughter Sarah, married to Jewish scholar Isaac Kursheedt, for example, wrote informative letters to her father, but, unlike her father's responses, none remains. However, seven letters written to her by Hazan Seixas's sister, Grace Nathan, a woman of wide literary tastes, are extant. Like Abigaill, Grace read voraciously, consuming all of Lord Byron's work with relish and approval. Her letters contain French and Spanish phrases, and her grammar and syntax are without error. Like brother Gershom, she was an ardent nationalist. In 1814, she wrote her niece, "I am so true an American, so warm a patriot that I hold these mighty [British] Armies and their proud-arrogant-presumtious, and over-powering nation as Beings that *we* have conquered and *shall* conquer again—this I persuade myself will be so. And may the Lord of Battles grant that it may be so."[43]

Grace Nathan focused her life around family affairs and faith. Family was foremost. Discussing the troubles of her aunt Zipporah, she wrote that despite her sorrows, "she has some resources of comfort, her own conscience and the kindnesses of her children. Can there be in nature more lasting Enjoyment?" Grace continued, "I answer, there *cannot* be." The lives of children and relatives, celebration of the Sabbath and holidays, trips to the synagogue, Jewish ritual and customs, weddings and funerals, and the business of Shearith Israel were always on Grace's mind. Jewish festivals were particularly important: "I will now wish you a happy Yom Tov and hope you may go out on these approaching Sacred days [Shavuoth]. Tis a Festival I always took pride & pleasure in & I contemplate going to shool. I shall throw off some of my *deep* mourning [for her husband] and wear white Bonnet and Handkerchief."[44]

Grace Nathan lived nearly seventy-nine years, a long life for the late eighteenth and early nineteenth centuries. She witnessed a great deal of suffering, including painful fatal illnesses of both her beloved husband, Simon, and brother, Gershom. Never bitter, she was a woman of consolation; friends and relatives went to her for succor when in bad health. She reported to Sarah in one letter that Mrs. Gideon Moses was confined to her room; Hetty Seixas was "bringing up blood" for three weeks, which doctors attributed to "tight corsets"; the mind of Sarah's uncle was "almost a blank"; cousin Sarah (a different woman) was in bed sick with "gout in the stomach"; Becky Hart suffered from "the burnings of St. Anthony's fire." The lesson of these infirmities: the "mutability of Life." Not that the suffering and loss she witnessed and endured made her callous. Five years after the death of her husband, auctioneer Simon Nathan, despite attempts to cleanse herself of a constant sorrow, she lamented, "I carry that within no time can change however it can soften."[45]

Nor did tribulation make Grace a religious skeptic, despite her admiration of Byron's romanticism. When niece Sarah was in distress, tormented by her son Asher's life-threatening accident and by the grave business troubles of her husband, Israel Baer, Grace assured Sarah that she will "offer up Morning & Evening Prayer for his [Asher's] well being—and coming from a Contrite heart God will hear it." For Sarah's husband's difficulties, Grace counseled the "Lesson of Submission to the Divine Will." As Grace neared the end of her life, she wrote her son, "I am perfectly resigned to meet the last earthly event—grateful to God for the blessings He has given me. I die in the full faith of my religion."[46] In her private moments, Grace Nathan composed poetry. Perhaps anticipating Virginia Woolf, she wrote, "I still hold possession of my Room, & God only knows if ever I shall hold any other." In that room, she read other poets and wrote "her productions In the Rhyming way." One, composed in 1822, was a dedicatory poem for the new cemetery of Shearith Israel:

> Within these walls made sacred to the dead,
> Where yet no spade has rudely turned a sod,
> No requiem chanted for a spirit fled,
> No prayer been offered to the throne of God.
>
> There in due form shall holy rites be given,
> And the last solemn strain float so high in air,
> That listening Angels shall bear it to Heaven,
> And the soul of the just be deposited there.

Many of her poems find analogies between the lives of plants and those of men and women. In a verse written shortly before her passing, a vine brought thoughts of the seasons of life and death:

> A vine late luxuriant and gay,
> Which I ever beheld with delight
> Is now falling with Autumn's decay
> And leaf by leaf leaving the sight.

It soon will be stript so entire
That only the vine will remain
Again I may live to admire
The quitting it will not cause pain.

For either event I'll prepare
And tho' I am called from the view
The vine will continue to bear
The root will the foliage renew.

To this vine I have likened my day
I have flourished thro' seasons—been blest
And when nature may call me away
I shall hope for the sunshine of rest.[47]

Grace Nathan's letters reveal one of the worlds of Jewish women in early national New York. Women affiliated with Shearith Israel formed a network of friends and relatives, their lives centered on Jewish ritual and the Jewish calendar. Within the limits permitted women, they maintained a sense of independence and dignity and were knowledgeable of national affairs, evincing the passion and optimism of American republicanism. Nathan's life also exposes the limitations of an intellectually gifted woman in the early nineteenth century. Though she possessed an excellent education and intellect, the latter improved by reading contemporary literature, a separate career or literary life was unlikely—not that Grace Nathan would have found this a problem.[48]

Much less is known about Jewish women unaffiliated with Shearith Israel. With the freedom available in republican society, their families lived lives with fewer Jewish ties and mixed freely with the Christian world in the open republican society. Some women emerging from these families would intermarry. While most would not, their identification with Jewish society and with Shearith Israel, while not broken, was weaker than in the close synagogue community of colonial New York.[49]

Because the Jewish community so deeply incorporated the republican values of the new American republic, republicanism deeply influenced the Jewish spiritual life of both women and men, a life still largely centered on congregation Shearith Israel. Republican divisions that sundered the American political community also divided congregants. The republicanism that so pervaded all aspects of American public life and penetrated into the private lives of the nation's citizens took root among the Jewish community of New York, which fashioned a unique combination of traditional practices and republican ideology.

The Reverend Gershom Mendes Seixas in 1784, as he was retaking the position of hazan at Shearith Israel after the Revolution; artist unknown. (Courtesy Museum of the City of New York)

CHAPTER 7

New York's
Republican Rabbi
and His Congregation

*As spiritual leader of Shearith Israel from the late colonial period
to the end of the War of 1812, Gershom Seixas lived in three separate eras of
American history. The only Jewish trustee of Columbia College in the nineteenth
century, he represented Judaism in early national New York. A Jeffersonian republican and a devout, traditional Jew, his life was also a model for Jews in New
York who strove to be Jewish citizens of the new republic.*

Born in New York of an obscure merchant, Gershom Seixas, under the influence of Hazan Joseph Jeshurun Pinto, gravitated to the synagogue from
an early age, becoming hazan in 1768, when he was only twenty-two. Except
for the war years in Philadelphia, he served until his death in 1816. During
his tenure, Seixas led daily, Sabbath, and holiday prayers; circumcised Jewish boys; taught school; conducted weddings, funerals, and bar mitzvahs; and
comforted the sick and bereaved. In addition to being the first Jewish trustee
of Columbia College, he also served on the board of the city's Humane Society. He mixed with John Jay and Alexander Hamilton and was likely present
at Washington's inauguration. A man of average height and stature, eschewing a beard, and known for his generous but not outgoing personality, Seixas
dressed in the manner of the city's divines, in a black gown with a double white
collar. Over the years, "his integrity, his innate dignity and his sound judgment
in all his dealings with the Jewish and Christian communities" made him both
a beloved leader of the congregation and the chief representative of the Jewish
people in the nation's largest city.[1]

Seixas knew the problems of Shearith Israel. During the War of 1812, he anguished over the "state of the finances of the synagogue." Regarding internal disputes, Seixas wrote his daughter, "There is talk of doing something to rectify the affairs of the Shule. How much it will be affected I know not." Another letter complained that "Shule affairs" were in the "same mismanagement" as when she had left them, with "no prospect for the better." Respected as he was, the Board of Trustees considered him an employee and not a policymaker. He could not curb the divisive forces in the congregation. But if he was unable to heal the wounds of the synagogue, he could set an example and offer comfort as a spiritual leader.[2]

■ Seixas and Jeffersonianism

Jefferson's religious convictions were entwined within Jeffersonian republicanism. Historians identify two major historical strands of republican thought. The first, classical republicanism or civic humanism, dating from Aristotle's Athens and Machiavelli's Florence, stressed virtue and the common good. In a republic, each citizen's duty is to place the good of the whole ahead of his or her personal concerns. Republican society would succeed or fail to the extent that the republic contained virtuous citizens willing to make personal sacrifices needed for the welfare of the commonwealth. The second strand, based on the writings of John Locke, emphasized individual liberties. The state allows each citizen full access to the public square and the marketplace to pursue his or her goals unobstructed by the state, church, or aristocratic privilege. The two strands were not mutually exclusive; New York's Jeffersonians held aspects of each. They expressed a sense of patriotic public duty and sacrifice, with distaste for excessive extremes of wealth and for a deferential society. They also championed an egalitarianism that allowed ambitious artisans and merchants to enter the marketplace unfettered by traditional and deferential barriers. Jeffersonians detested opposition "aristocrats" (Federalists) who used economic coercion to maintain a deferential society.[3]

Jefferson's republican religious creed centered on his belief in the power of science. Two of his three heroes, Francis Bacon and Isaac Newton, were scientists. Jefferson possessed absolute faith that scientific law controlled the world according to the dictates of reason. A monotheist, he had no patience for the supernatural. He regarded Jesus as a great moralist, but when he made his edition of the Bible, he excised all miracles. Concepts such as the Trinity had no place in modern religion. Jefferson considered Judaism one of many American religious sects, each with the same "moral basis, on which all our religions rest." Finally, Jefferson passionately championed religious liberty and the separation of church and state; he considered the passage of the Virginia Statute for Religious Freedom, which he drafted, one of his greatest accomplishments. He wrote Shearith Israel that American law protected "our religious, as they do our civil rights, by putting all on an equal footing."[4]

Although no American read as many books as Thomas Jefferson did, Seixas was an avid reader. Both read the English deists Tindal, Bolingbroke, and Priestly, and both were familiar with Voltaire and the French philosophes. Jefferson numbered many scientists as friends, and Seixas was close to New York chemist and congressman Samuel Latham Mitchill. Jefferson was an admirer of Tom Paine, whose *Age of Reason*, a critique of Christianity as contrary to reason, was the largest-selling religious book in the eighteenth century, going through seventeen editions from 1794 to 1796. Staunchly republican printer Naphtali Judah, whose shop insignia included an image of "Paine's head," published Seixas's 1798 sermon critical of the Federalists during the height of Federalist repression, with journalists under arrest for printing tracts critical of the government.[5]

In Philadelphia, fighting for the rights of Jews in the new republic, Seixas echoed Jefferson's belief in the separation of church and state and in religious equality. Back in New York, his sermons—given at important occasions, commonly days of special prayer, thanksgiving, and celebration—reflect the influence of Jeffersonian republicanism.

Seixas shared Jefferson's faith in science based on a rational universe, governed by "nature and nature's god." He viewed God as the prime mover or designer. In 1789, Seixas spoke of the "works of an almighty providence" that enabled humanity to contemplate the future and increase knowledge, specifically the "movements of the heavenly spheres," which proved "the necessity of a great first cause." Ten years later, he described humanity "called into an existence from Nothing," endowed with the power to distinguish between good and evil and to "prefer the good and refute the evil." In 1803, he described the "disinterested benevolence of our Creator," which humanity must strive to imitate. God endowed humanity with "the faculty and power of reasoning," a great gift, as "it is by reason we arrive to the knowledge of infinite Goodness." Seixas's faith in human understanding and research made him confident that "the sacred text of scripture" would be "verified" in his day by science.

Commenting on methods to combat yellow fever, he stated that "supernatural means are never used upon any occasion where natural means can affect any particular purpose."[6]

Like Jeffersonian republicanism, Seixas despised excessive inequality. During the deadly yellow-fever epidemics that plagued New York in the 1790s and early 1800s, he sympathized with the middling and wealthy classes who had been forced to relinquish the "advantages of trade," but he focused on the plight of the "poorer class of people" who could not leave the city. While leaders of the congregation fled, Seixas stayed behind in every epidemic, founding a relief society, Kalfe Sedaka Mattan Basether (Collection for Charity Given Secretly). He displayed Jeffersonian egalitarianism when he disparaged "a myriad of fattened lambs" in comparison to "purity of Heart" and "sincerity of worship." A man must "subdue the passions of his carnal appetite," for "worldly riches" are "as nothing when put in competition to the promised state of happiness." The duties of a righteous person were to God, to "ties of consanguinity," and to society, "each and every individual." Doing God's work included the classical republican duty: responsibility for the common good. "Virtue" was not "of a passive nature." It must be "active, fulfilling the Law of God, exercising ourselves in good works, and by an exemplary Life, inducing others to pursue the path of righteousness." A citizen's duty was to "ameliorate" the condition of his or her brethren.[7]

Seixas was circumspect. He never publicly referred to Jesus, using the Hebrew word *talui*, meaning "crucified one," when discussing him. However, in a personal letter to his daughter, he described an encounter with George Bethune English, a Harvard linguist who had written a book that sought to undermine the New Testament. Although Seixas would not assist English, he had no doubt that his plan to "explode the trinatarial system gradually" through rational argument would be "accomplished." He believed that English "adduced many stronger proofs against the pretended Messiaship of the Talui." Jefferson, too, rejected the Trinity and supernatural renditions of Jesus's life. Seixas saw Christianity as an irrational religion. For Jefferson, it was a true religion, once excesses of historical misunderstanding were corrected. But both placed human reason and scientific investigation at the forefront.[8]

Republican, revolutionary patriotism pervades Seixas's writings. In a Hebrew oration written for the Columbia graduation address of Sampson Simson, Seixas recalled the moment that the "inhabitants of North America" crushed the "Yoke of subjection." At that time, "Jews from throughout the Union, placed their lives in their hands," and, as "the Lord was with them," achieved "freedom and Independence."[9] In other sermons, Seixas clarified the meaning of the Revolution for the city's Jewish community. The struggle to achieve American republicanism expressed God's will. The "conclusion of the last war" and the "establishment of public liberty" were "a wonderful display of divine providence," including the "general approbation and adoption of the new constitution." What were the responsibilities of Jews in a republican society? Jews were fortunate to live in a country where they "possess every advantage that other citizens of these states enjoy," under a "magistracy" that sanctioned "every religious mode of worship" and a government "earnestly endeavoring to promote their spiritual happiness." In return, the Jewish community must "support that government which is founded upon the strictest principles of equal liberty and justice." In the language of classical republicanism, Seixas asked congregants to join fellow citizens for the "public good," suppressing "every species of licentiousness." They must "not be deficient" in promoting "the welfare of the United States" and must "return thanks to benign Goodness" for placing them "in a country where they are free to act, according the dictates of conscience," where "no exception is taken from following the principles of [their] religion." This was the most they could expect "in this captivity."[10]

Seixas entered American politics as a revolutionary. In the political battles of the 1790s, uncomfortable with Federalists' deferential expectations, his allegiance was with the Jeffersonians and their egalitarian stance. In condemning the partisanship of the era, he invoked the classical republican ideal of national unity, seeking an end to party politics, a restoration of national unity, and "peace and tranquility" among the nation's political leaders. During the War of 1812, Seixas's republican revolutionary spirit reemerged, overcoming his hatred of war as the "greatest of punishments that could be inflicted" on humanity. The Jewish community had to support the conflict; it was "sufficient" that their "rulers . . . have declared war." It was their "bouden duty to act as true and faithfull Citizens, to support and preserve the honor—the Dignity —& the Independence of the United States of America! That they may bear equal rank, among the Nations of the Earth." Describing soldiers on the New York frontier as "destitute of food, of raiment and of every necessarie of life," facing "mercenaries" of "an implacable inhuman enemy," he beseeched God:

"deliver us . . . from those that rise up against us" and "frustrate the designs and machinations of the enemy." Shearith Israel held three services in support of the war effort; despite the Jewish community's small size, it collected a ninth of the city's relief funds. For Seixas, at stake was the rescue of American republicanism.[11]

■ A Traditional Rabbi

While Seixas and Jefferson enjoyed reading common authors, Seixas devoted many more hours to books Jefferson could not and did not read. Seixas spent most of his days studying the Hebrew Bible and its commentaries, most notably the medieval scholar Rashi and sixteenth-century rabbi Joseph Caro, who compiled the *Shulchan Aruch*, a comprehensive code of Jewish law. It is unlikely Seixas studied in any depth either the Talmud, the key Jewish text of European yeshivot (centers of religious study), or nineteenth-century Jewish thought. Seixas's religious outlook was rooted in a careful reading of Hebrew Scriptures, particularly the Pentateuch and the Prophets. Significant changes to Jewish theology following the destruction of the Second Temple (70 CE) and in the medieval and early modern eras did not play a large role in his perspective.[12]

Republicanism and Seixas's orthodoxy shared a common acceptance of monotheism. Seixas declared, "there is no part of our belief so highly obligatory upon us as acknowledging the Unity of God." It was the "most essential doctrine of the Jews," who would suffer "pangs and tortures . . . rather than to deny it." Monotheism also fit within Jefferson's Unitarian concept of God. Other religious doctrines were more difficult to reconcile.[13]

Salvation emerged as a central theme of Seixas's sermons. In 1789, he reminded his congregants that "the Almighty" was "ever watchful over his people." God was "weighing their actions" and "rewarding and punishing them according to their merit or demerit." All men and women must be aware that "when divested of their bodily affections" with only the "immortal part" of their existence remaining, they would have to "give an account of [their] actions." Only those with a "firm belief in God" could "truly hope for Salvation." But "faith alone" was "not sufficient to procure salvation." Only following God's commandments led to "happiness both here and hereafter." The "fear of God" must be constantly in mind.[14]

Sin and reformation were intertwined with salvation. Seixas provided congregants with evidence of God's wrath as a consequence of sin. The ten lost tribes were dispersed because the Jews were "sinners in the eyes of the sight of their Creator," unwilling to "follow His commandments." The Romans destroyed the Temple because of the "abominations" of the Jews, who were "so refractory they were never at peace." And the "late melancholy visitation" of the yellow-fever epidemic (1799) was "a manifestation of his displeasures," a moment when "the finger of God" pointed out "the atrocities of our sins." These events of ancient and current history called for "strict reformation." Each Jew must review his or her behavior: "Examine well yourselves and you will speedily discover wherein you have deviated from that path of rectitude. See that you have not defrauded the Widow and the Orphan, that you have acted honestly in your dealing with each other. Have you distributed charity to the Poor: have you been ready to assist your brother, in the time of his distress?" Seixas viewed the most grievous sinners as those who violated ethical commandments; his most constant criticisms fell on those who failed to help the less fortunate. Those who truly changed their character for the good could take comfort that the "visitation of Justice" in the form of yellow fever "was still blended with mercy." Survivors must "rejoice that he has saved us alive, that we may have time to repent us our manifold Sins, and to become *regenerated.*"[15]

Salvation implied a day of judgment, a world to come. Influenced by New York's Protestant environment, Seixas warned congregants, "awaken from your lethargy before it is too late." Life "becomes a burthen" to a man who "denies the Providence of his maker," even if he possesses "worldly riches." Pity him on his deathbed, "calling for mercy in his last moments." While moving through life "in the slough of dissipation," he looked at God as "afar off." Now, facing the "presence of infinite justice," he has only "horror" for his prospects. In "paroxysms of Phrenzy," he beholds the "moment of his dissolution," the "abyss of destruction." This is the "miserable end of sinners" who "persist in wickedness."[16] "Were it not for the hopes and promises of an hereafter," what person would wish to be "a creature of this transitory existence," with its troubles and pains. For the pious, though "the blessings of this life are many," they cannot compare "with those of the life to come." While humanity can conquer the "ills of life" only with "grace," Seixas yet taught that behavior "depended entire upon the freedom of the will." Humanity possessed the "glorious prerogative" of "the power of free agency." The choice of a life of "virtue" prepared humans for their "future state, when our immortal Soul shall be freed from this unstable tenement of flesh." God "leaves us to choose between the extremes of Good & Evil, with their subsequent reward or punishments." With this awesome fate in mind, who would not "forego the transient pleasures of this precarious Life"?[17]

Seixas articulated a third traditional theme: restoration. The "sins of [Jews'] progenitors" transformed Jews into "wandering exiles through the habitable Globe." But the long banishment was nearing an end. The war convulsing the world in 1798, revealing the "depravity and corrupt state of human nature," signaled that "the glorious period of redemption is near at hand," when God would keep "his divine promise" to collect "the scattered remnant of Israel." The scourge of yellow fever, "certain evidence of the authenticity of divine revelation," was, "to a reflective mind," also a signal of "that great and glorious day" when the "people of Israel, . . . purged of [their] Sins," would be released from "their long and gloomy captivity" and be "reinstated in [their] land, there to dwell in Safety, in Peace, in Happiness." Though American Jews had "the good fortune to live in a free land," they could not "perform the rites and ceremonies of [their] temple service." These rituals could "only be observed in the holy land," within a rebuilt "sanctuary." While Seixas always believed that true "reformation of [Jews'] conduct" hastened the day when God would "fulfill his divine promise," when it was clear that revolutionary events gave no evidence of restoration, Seixas provided the cause: the "spirit of disobedience"— the failure of Jews to follow God's laws such as observance of the Sabbath and dietary laws led to "Misery and Desolation! continuance of captivity and the oppressions of Man." Toward the end of his life, he wrote his daughter, "[Only] a reformation among ourselves, . . . repentance and amendment, [will] reinstate us in the sight of our Creator, to obtain his divine Grace, to restore us to our own Land, where we may dwell in Peace—in happiness! According to the words of our sacred Prophets."[18]

■ Reconciling Seixas's Theology

There are compelling contradictions between Jeffersonian republicanism and aspects of Seixas's religious outlook. It is possible to reconcile classical republicanism and the biblical prophets, both demanding that the common good come before individual advancement, disdaining excessive inequality, and insisting on the primacy of virtue. Parallels also exist between republican millennialism and Jewish millennialism. Many republicans, most notably Thomas

Jefferson, believed that the American Revolution heralded a new age in world history, one that overthrew centuries of traditional governance and ideology for a new republican creed. So, too, Judaism looked to a messianic age of national restoration. Seixas held both visions. In the throes of revolutionary enthusiasm, while working for changes in the Pennsylvania constitution to allow Jewish citizens to participate fully in revolutionary liberty, Seixas was studying the calculations of a medieval German rabbi that, based on a reading of the book of Daniel, the world as known would end in 1783. He also preached that the end of the war would bring a "permanent Peace . . . until time shall be no more." On another occasion, he expressed confidence that the false logic behind the concept of the Trinity would be undermined "before the coming of the great day." Both Judaism and republicanism anticipated a new age in history. Jefferson, however, would not have countenanced the coming of a messiah to lead the Jews back to Palestine to resume superstitious, ancient customs. Too, Seixas's sturdy patriotism lay uneasily with his sense that American Jews remained in captivity, awaiting restoration in Palestine. In sum, Seixas had only partial success in his attempt to blend Jeffersonian republican ideals and biblical Judaism.[19]

Jefferson's concept of a benevolent God who shuns the supernatural, seems to contradict Seixas's declarations that God was yet punishing Jews with pestilence. Moreover, the idea of personal salvation and a world to come where the righteous are rewarded and the wicked punished, compelling concepts in Seixas's sermons, are difficult to reconcile with deistic Jeffersonian thought. Jefferson accepted an afterlife and the fear of reward and punishment as a means to maintaining a moral society. That was not Seixas's understanding.[20]

However, it is important to understand that whereas Gershom Seixas's early career took place during the Revolution and its aftermath, in his later years he lived in New York during the Second Great Awakening, a time of rising evangelical religious sentiment. Deism attracted fewer and fewer Americans. Jefferson's belief that America would become a nation of Unitarians proved a false prophecy. As Mark Noll, a prominent interpreter of the history of American Christianity, has shown, the Christian Protestant churches of America, especially the evangelical sects, synthesized Christian theology with the tenets of republicanism, blending a communal quest for virtue with a liberal republican quest for individual freedom. Their fundamentalist thought encompassed reason, including the maxims of Scottish commonsense philosophy that God gave humanity a universal moral sense, the basis for ethics and moral absolutes. Thus, "by taking on a version of republicanism, evangelicals put themselves in position to offer their religion to the new nation as a competitor to the rational, moralistic faith of the founders." And the "struggle was almost no competition." The founders' deistic ideals found little welcome among the young men and women of the new republic, while evangelicalism rapidly expanded.[21]

Seixas knew and frequently associated with the Protestant ministers of New York, a community that included figures such as Methodist bishop Francis Asbury and Presbyterian minister Samuel Miller. Though Seixas had strong differences over the divinity of Jesus, he would have been familiar with their writings and some of the books that they read. This likely accounts for the prominent place in his sermons of doctrines such as salvation, a day of judgment, and concern for the hereafter, dogmas not commonly stressed in contemporary Jewish thought. Moreover, he would have read the works of Christian thinkers that provided a synthesis between orthodox religion and republicanism. While it is impossible to know with any certainty, the evolving pietistic republicanism, replacing in part Jeffersonian thought, may have offered Seixas resolution between his republican and his biblical outlook. His sermons never raise any doubts about the compatibility between traditional Jewish doctrine and republicanism.

Nor does Seixas's life display mental anguish over conflicting ideological worlds. While during his last seven years "disease marked him as a proper victim," subjecting him to a "tormenting and chronic complaint," even "sufferings beyond the ken of human understanding," he remained cheerful and affable to the end, comforted by his "old friend Job." He continued to delight in informal merriment with his wife and fourteen living children, good food, and festive occasions such as the holiday of Purim. He died in 1816, one of New York's most beloved citizens, at peace with himself. Near the end of his life, he wrote his daughter that fifty years earlier, he read Voltaire and Rousseau, European philosophes whose anticlericalism would have been impossible to reconcile with evangelical concepts of republicanism, implying that he no longer found their ideas influential. He also wrote that that he now cautioned friends, "we are not in the Latter days yet"; and he said that "the latter days in Scripture" referred to subsequent ages, and until then, the world would continue as it is. By 1815, it is likely that along with his Jeffersonian republican fervor, perhaps replaced by a new more fundamentalist republicanism, the millennial excitement of revolutionary ideas in a revolutionary environment had also diminished.[22]

■ Jewish Identity in Republican New York

Historian and biographer Jacob Marcus stated that the Reverend Seixas "had one foot in the nineteenth century." That is, part of him still lived in the world of Jewish textual study, and part of him was at home in republican New York, conversing with Christian divines on salvation and the nature of the soul. But what of the rest of New York Jewry? Unlike Seixas, New York's Jews had little or no understanding of the evangelical republican synthesis. (More a pastor than a theologian, Seixas did not use his sermons to resolve potential contradictions.) Seeing the widespread distribution of tracts aimed at the Jewish community by missionary societies, Jews distrusted Protestants' motivations. Jews' religious framework contained no room for a messiah, much less a personal rebirth into the arms of a once-human God in whom they did not believe. Did they find republicanism compatible with a stronger devotion to Orthodox Judaism in the manner that Christians found harmony in the piety of Baptist and Methodist churches? Could Jews remain faithful to their heritage and traditions, withstanding the assimilationist tendencies of a republican society that accepted them as full citizens? Or, unlike their Christian neighbors, would they become less attached to religious practices, finding that Jewish rituals prevented their integration into the new republic?

Entering republican society, including the maelstrom of party politics, Jews of republican New York left the tight-knit synagogue community of the colonial era. The transition came with momentous changes to Jewish practices that formerly kept Jews and Gentiles apart, particularly the dietary laws and laws of Sabbath observance. Some Jews remained observant. Harmon Hendricks and his family kept their rolling mill closed on the Sabbath and strictly observed kashrut. When on the road, "they were ready to live on bread and rice if kosher food was not available." Sampson Simson, law graduate of Columbia, was "a very pious man, . . . an uncompromising orthodox Israelite" who was "so precise in his religion" that he had "his Matzos baked in his own house." Hendricks and Simson were financially independent, like Jacob Franks of the colonial era. Their money and its influence broke down interfaith barriers.

But those without fortunes who wanted fewer barriers between themselves and their fellow citizens often discarded practices that separated them from their Christian neighbors. Republicanism weakened Jewish religiosity. Given the small attendance at the synagogue's school and services, many Jews maintained their rituals, if at all, within their homes. Mordecai M. Noah, for example, observed the High Holy Days, kept a kosher kitchen, and fasted on Tisha B'Av, but as an editor, he worked on the Sabbath when necessary. Dining with many non-Jews, he did not maintain kashrut outside his home. He deemed prayer with phylacteries a custom of "Israelites of old." He and many fellow Jews did not permit Jewish observance to interfere with their integration into republican America.[23]

Historian Hyman Grinstein argues that a number of factors caused the falling off of ritual observance, including the cessation of inquiries into the practices of members of Shearith Israel, much less those of the Jewish community as a whole. These factors include increased mixing of Jews and non-Jews, economic circumstances forcing Jews to work on the Sabbath or fall behind their Christian competition, lack of religious education, and the rise of deist doctrines. Most important, the republican environment fostered the separation of church and state, removing religion from the public square. Jews could enter the public sphere no longer needing the shelter of the synagogue community; they could rely on the state instead.[24]

Integration, though, did not mean loss of identity as Jews. Although the rate of intermarriage doubled in the early national era to about 30 percent, 70 percent still married within their faith, limiting their choice of spouse to less than 1 percent of the population, a strong signal of a common identity. Unlike Abigaill Franks's offspring, conversion was not a requirement for acceptance in American society. To be sure, that a Jew did not maintain kashrut out of one's home did not mean he or she abandoned it. Concern with the practices of the shochet indicates that a significant number of Jews followed dietary laws at home. That a Jew did not attend synagogue regularly did not mean that he or she was not present on High Holy Days. Most seats were sold. That a family did not send its children to a Jewish school did not mean it did not expose them to Jewish customs. Jews adapted, each family in its own way, as most strove both to remain Jewish and to enter the mainstream of republican life. There was no single path. Manuel Josephson, a learned Jewish merchant who lived in New York until the Revolution, declared that "North American congregations . . . in reality . . . have no regular custom." Marcus has termed the early republic an era when "there were almost as many Judaisms as there were individuals."[25]

Seixas represents, better than any other citizen living in New York in the first two hundred years of Jewish settlement, the synthesis of republican ideology and traditional Jewish thought. This was an not an easy synthesis: Jeffersonian thought and orthodox Jewish doctrine, like reason and revelation, are not easily reconciled. Yet his life and his sermons demonstrate that Jews were able to embrace republican America and yet retain their singular identity. Republican New York drew its Jewish community into the heart of its culture, and the community splintered but did not disintegrate. Bonds of ethnicity and nationhood remained strong enough to maintain Jewish identification. The character, standing, and words of Reverend Seixas undoubtedly contributed to the maintenance of Jewish identity. A much beloved man—at his death, two long eulogies were given, and the Jewish community went into profound mourning—his example and presence provided an important living symbol of the Jewish embrace of republican society and thought. When the first wave of European immigrants arrived in the 1830s, they found a recognizable Jewish population, but one becoming increasingly different from the Jewish society of the old world.

Beginning in 1862, the annual Purim Ball was the highlight of the season for prominent members of the Jewish community. No costume was too spectacular or extravagant. *Frank Leslie's Illustrated Newspaper*, 1 April 1865. (Courtesy Library of Congress)

CHAPTER 8

Beyond the Synagogue in Antebellum New York

Historian Naomi Cohen argues that Jewish "emigration foreshadowed a secularization of their faith." The act of choosing to emigrate, separating from the community in Germany, as well as other central European countries, in itself repudiated tradition. Jewish newcomers wanted to fit into American society as quickly and easily as possible. Yet, while many immigrants grew lax in observing ritual law and chose not to join a congregation, they did not cease to identify as Jews. The vast majority married within their faith. For these Jews, institutions beyond the synagogue allowed them to maintain a coherent unity.[1]

New York in the Antebellum Era

When Isaac Mayer Wise, the future leader of the Reform movement in America, disembarked in New York in 1846, he recalled witnessing "such rushing, hurrying, chasing, running," the likes of which he had never seen before. The culture of this "large village" did not impress him. The source of his displeasure stemmed from New York's entrepreneurial energy as the city, in the three decades before the Civil War, became the nation's most vibrant municipality. Spurred by the emergence of the Erie Canal as the entrance to the West, by the city's enterprising merchants, by an industrious workforce, and by a massive influx of Irish and German immigrants, New York grew from a seaport of 200,000 in 1830 to a metropolis numbering 814,000 individuals in 1860 (and a metropolitan area of well over a million).[2]

The growth in entrepreneurial energy that Wise encountered, to be matched by an ever more vigorous democratic politics and a maturing American culture, was part of the second phase of American republicanism, also known as the Age of Jackson and the antebellum era. A population rapidly growing from the inflow of immigrants from Germany and Ireland witnessed major advances in industry and agriculture, the growth of manhood suffrage, and an ever more competitive and hard-fought political scene. This was the period of Alexis de Tocqueville's *Democracy in America*, stressing the pervasiveness of the democratic spirit throughout the United States, an ethos that reinforced the republican disdain of aristocracy and privilege. It was also an age that produced enormous wealth, much of it concentrated among the elite entrepreneurs who lived in American's prominent cites, men such as I. M. Singer, inventor of the Singer sewing machine, an instrument that revolutionized the garment industry. No city was more representative of these new strains of republicanism than New York, America's cultural and financial capital.[3]

At the hub of the nation's growing rail system, Gotham became America's leading manufacturing center. The city housed the nation's garment trade, major iron works, and a multitude of assorted industries such as the Singer Sewing Machine Company. New York's merchants established the country's first department stores.

New York became the axis of the nation's communication network. Telegraphy permitted almost instantaneous news of business and current events. The rise of the rotary press, with a capability of producing two hundred thousand copies per hour, allowed an 80 percent drop in the price of a newspaper. Dailies and weeklies blossomed, and their pages enticed both the elite and working classes with news, politics, sports, court trials, theater, investigative exposés, and gossip about the rich and famous. They ranged from the *New York Herald* (circulation of fifty-two thousand in 1853) to low-circulation weeklies. The latter included two English-language newspapers aimed at the Jewish population, the independent *Asmonean*, edited by English immigrant Robert Lyon, and the Orthodox *Jewish Messenger*, edited by Reverend Samuel Isaacs, rabbi of congregation Shaaray Tefilah, newspapers that give us an invaluable picture of the Jewish community in the 1840s, 1850s, and 1860s.[4]

Housing the New York Stock Exchange and the Gold Exchange, New York was the American center of market speculation. Its banks provided the investment capital for the West and the South. The California gold rush brought the city both capital in newly minted gold and an outlet for its manufactories supplying western speculators. New York developed close ties to the South: its bankers accepted slave property as collateral; its brokers sold southern

New York was a city of immigrants prior to the Civil War. The first place in the new world that an immigrant would see was the reception center at Castle Garden, on the southern tip of Manhattan. (Courtesy Museum of the City of New York)

railroad and state bonds; its wholesalers sold southerners household goods; its traders and ship owners monopolized the sale of cotton.[5]

The city's wealth produced an affluent elite; the number of families worth more than $100,000 multiplied sevenfold in the antebellum era. Both old wealth such as the Astor, Schermerhorn, Beekman, and Livingston families and new wealth in such figures as Peter Cooper, George Templeton Strong, and August Belmont moved uptown into mansions and brownstones, where these genteel families lived in an elegant lifestyle north of Union Square and Grace Episcopal Church on Tenth Street and Broadway. Many built summer homes in Queens, Brooklyn, and Long Island. Female dress attained new heights of ornamentation, preventing fashionable ladies from doing domestic work. A new opera house opened at Astor Place, a new theater on Park Place, and a new Academy of Music on Fourteenth Street. Works by Mozart, Donizetti, and Verdi were performed regularly.[6]

In the thirty years before the Civil War, thousands of immigrants settled in New York. Pushed out by a potato famine in 1845 that spread from Ireland to the southern and western German states, the failure of the German Revolution

By 1860, the city extended northward toward Central Park. Kleindeutschland, the home of many of the city's immigrant German Jews, is the large bulge at the center of the picture. (Courtesy Eno Collection, New York Public Library)

of 1848—an unsuccessful movement to bring democratic government to central Europe—and unemployment in Britain, an average of 157,000 immigrants arrived at Castle Garden in New York each year. In 1854, 319,000 entered Manhattan. Approximately one of every five or six remained in the city, where they joined thousands of native-born Americans who left their farms or workshops to try their luck in the metropolis. By 1855, over half the population of the city was immigrants, with 176,000 from Ireland and 98,000 from Germany. Two of every three adults in Manhattan were born abroad. New York was an immigrant city.[7]

While life for most newcomers was better than in Europe, with more meat and nicer furniture, the immigrants remained one bad recession from the pawn shop. Many German arrivals lived in tenements in Kleindeutschland in Lower Manhattan, stretching from Canal to Rivington Streets, pushing east to Avenue D and north toward Fourteenth Street. A tenement there, twenty-five feet by seventy feet, three to five stories, with twenty-four two-bedroom apartments each, with only a single window for the families and their boarders, usually housed more than 150 tenants.[8]

About 150,000 Jews figured among the immigrants arriving in America in the 1830s, and especially the 1840s and '50s. While many traveled on to Chicago, Cleveland, and St. Louis, thousands remained in the city. Before large-scale immigration began in the 1820s, Jews composed less than 0.5 percent of the city's population. By 1840, their population had reached seven thousand (2.2 percent), and then sixteen thousand in 1850 (3.1 percent), and by 1859, they numbered near forty thousand (5 percent), half of whom were German Jews. By the mid-1840s, New York was home to a quarter of the American Jewish population. These newcomers included eastern European Jews from Russia and Poland who either came through Germany or who became German due to German annexation of their towns.[9]

Most immigrants arrived poor; the wealthy and more highly educated preferred to stay in Europe. Many were single men and women. They came from lands that were intermittently hostile to Jews, restricting access to professions, trades, real estate, and even marriage. In New York, much of the nonimmigrant Jewish population moved to the west side as far north as Thirty-Seventh

Many German immigrants sold used clothing along with other ware in the Chatham Square area, which become well-known as a Jewish business neighborhood. This is an 1859 scene. (Courtesy Museum of the City of New York)

Street but congregated most commonly near Fourteenth Street and Seventh Avenue. Immigrant Jews settled among the Catholic and Lutheran German immigrants. In the 1830s, the Five Points neighborhood attracted many poor Jewish immigrants. By the 1850s, most new Jewish arrivals, especially those of German descent, lived in Kleindeutschland in an area bounded by Grand, Stanton, Ludlow, and Pitt Streets. In 1856, the *New York Times* reported two dwellings housing thirty-two families, "mostly German Jews," on Hester Street. Toward 1860, immigrants moved as far north as Twentieth Street. Immigrant synagogues could be found in both Five Points and Kleindeutschland.[10]

In the early 1830s, with the Jewish population between one and three thousand, most Jews worked as small merchants, clothiers, or brokers. Immigrants seeking to join the ranks of their brethren received the advice "to go and peddle." Given a "hastily fixed up basket," they headed "into the country." Perhaps half of immigrant German Jews took up peddling when they arrived. The other common alternative was the needle trades. By 1855, 95 percent of tailors in the city were born abroad, 55 percent in Germany. The majority of Jewish immigrants did not ascend the socioeconomic ladder. They remained small grocers and shopkeepers, workers in the garment industry, and craftspeople from jewelers to carpenters, eking out a living as their families squeezed into crowded tenements. Most spoke no English and were uncomfortable with American customs. Struggling to make ends meet, they became a "troubled, unhappy generation."[11]

Though most Jews remained in the lower and lower-middle classes, opportunity and mobility were possible. Some peddlers made the transition to merchant standing within five to ten years, while workers in the garment industry joined successful peddlers and native-born Jews in manufacturing and selling clothes, wholesale or retail. The value of the clothing market in New York rose to $17 million by 1861. The used-clothing market grew rapidly, as many New Yorkers were unable to buy made-to-order goods. Jews in New York acquired a reputation for their shops in the Chatham Square neighborhood that sold secondhand clothing, or "slops." In *New York in Slices*, journalist George Foster described this area, known as "Jerusalem":

> Clothing stores line the southern sidewalk without interruption, and the coat-tails and pantaloons flop about the face of the pedestrian. . . . In front of each, from sunrise to sundown, stands the natty, blackbearded and fiercely moustached proprietor. . . .

Stooping as you enter the low, dark doorway, you find yourself in the midst of a primitive formation of rags, carefully classified into vest, coats and pantaloons.

Isaac Mayer Wise termed the area a "disgrace." However, many of these clothiers were far from aggressive petty retailers, their reach extending to the southern and western trade. In the robust economy of the era, at least a quarter of the immigrant Jewish population rose to the middle class by the 1850s, joining native-born Jews as merchants, wholesalers, retailers, skilled craftspeople, and professionals.[12]

A few did even better; an 1861 publication listed nine German Jewish firms with over $100,000 in capital. (Four were in the garment trade, three were importers, one manufactured iron, and one processed tobacco.) During the Panic of 1857, a harrowing recession caused by the overextension of banks and a fall in the price of wheat, the *Asmonean*, hoping to persuade wealthy Jews to help those without work, published the names of fifty leading Jewish firms, averaging 278 employees each. Most were in textiles; a few worked in importing and dry goods. The shirtmaking firms of Einstein & Jacobs and Stettheimer & Rosenbaum each employed eight hundred workers, while the clothing manufacturer Laisch, Stubblefield & Barnett employed fifteen hundred. An 1853 list of the "Principal Merchants" of the city included at least 105 Jewish firms, or 4 percent of the total. The 1850s was a fertile decade for Jewish enterprise. In 1853, for example, 51 Jewish firms imported "Dry Goods, Fancy Goods, Straw Good, Hats, Caps and Furs"; six years later, there were 141. The number of importers of watches and jewelry rose from two to twenty in the same period. Many of these men had connections in the South and West, including Joseph Seligman, whose family firm made a fortune supplying first the California gold rush and then the Union cause, and New York merchant Levi Strauss, who became a legendary success outfitting miners in California, while his purchasing office and manufacturing operations remained in New York. This wealth, immigrant and nonimmigrant, provided the resources to build Jews' Hospital and the Hebrew Orphan Asylum, to patronize the arts, to organize lavish balls, and to construct elaborate synagogues.[13]

It is important to note that the German Jewish immigrants, who composed perhaps 15 percent of the German community, did not identify as a distinct subgroup. Rather, they maintained their German identity and mixed harmoniously with their fellow Germans, whether in trade-union activity or singing societies or other German cultural events. While there was considerable anti-Semitism in Germany, there was little among Christian Germans in America. The Jewish and non-Jewish Germans lived together in Kleindeutschland as immigrants in a new world with far more in common than not.[14]

What kind of Judaism would survive within this new Jewish community, rich and poor, increasingly foreign born, and increasingly German? Already in the early republic, the synagogues were failing to fulfill the needs of Jewish republican citizens, who sought to enter more deeply into the life of the new nation. Immigrants, particularly German immigrants, equated Orthodox religion and practices with the European ghetto and political servility. The Judaism they had known carried a shameful social stigma. Isaac Mayer Wise reminisced that in 1846 New York, most poor Jews were ignorant of Jewish learning, while the better-off "kept aloof from Hebrew society" and "despaired of the future." Yet neither the native born nor the immigrant community abandoned Judaism. Immigrant Jews needed each other in a foreign land, and common ties of ethnicity, language, and culture remained strong, while deeply ingrained tradition, practice, and commonality caused many of the older generations to maintain loyalty. But if the synagogue, despite a strong presence in New York, would not or could not fully satisfy needs for bonding, where would these yearnings find an outlet?[15]

■ Fraternity

For immigrants living in tenement houses, simple ties of neighborhood counted most in the early years. Once immigrants acquired a foothold in the city and overcame the anxieties of subsistence, they sought deeper bonds in benevolent and fraternal organizations, adding to those of the native born and immigrants of an earlier generation. Though Jews composed less than 5 percent of the population, no less than ninety-three Jewish organizations flourished between 1843 and 1860. In comparison, non-Jewish ethnic and religious groups formed ninety-six organizations.[16]

In the 1840s, Henry Kling, who worked in the paper business, and Isaac Dittenhoefer, who owned a dry-goods store, began meeting Sunday mornings at Stensheimers' Café in Kleindeutschland with like-minded German immigrants including a cantor, a shoemaker, and a jeweler. These gatherings culminated in 1843 in the formation of B'nai B'rith (Sons of the Covenant), a secular fraternal organization combining the traditions of Judaism and Freemasonry and replacing the synagogue with a "lodge room." They called the president of a lodge the Grand Nasi, the vice president the Grand Aleph, and the secretary the Grand Sopher. The lodges, incorporating special handshakes and passwords, conducted their meetings in German for the first decade. B'nai B'rith spoke to the concerns of immigrants. Concerned with "the deplorable condition of Jews" in their "adopted country," members attended to the needs of the sick, poor, and needy. They also strove to support "science and art." Jewish peddlers found fellowship in lodges in many American cities. The society sought to bridge the gap between immigrant standing and citizenship. By 1851, New York had seven hundred members, with new lodges opening each year.[17]

As B'nai B'rith grew, it determined to remain a Jewish organization helping immigrants integrate into American society and to work toward universalist goals. Responding to a Baltimore lodge's request to admit non-Jews, the New York chapters replied that the order was "adapted . . . solely for Israelites." Members organized the Maimonides Library "to provide instruction for the masses." By the end of the 1850s, with immigrants attaining greater economic standing, the lodges switched to English and dropped many rituals. These changes represented an ideal, stated in the preamble of the society's constitution, of a "dignified representation of the Israelites in America in a religious and a social point of view, and the elevation of the masses in a moral and intellectual direction." Lodge members also participated in the discussion society that led to the formation of Temple Emanu-El, the city's first Reform congregation. Dr. Leo Merzbacher, rabbi of Emanu-El, wrote the preamble of the society's constitution and was spiritual adviser to B'nai B'rith.[18]

Anniversary dinners revealed lofty patriotic ideals. In 1851, the Lebanon Lodge, the first lodge "working in the English language," held its "ordinary exercise," listened to an address by President Sigismund Waterman, a highly knowledgeable Israelite who graduated from Yale's medical school after immigrating from Germany, and then proceeded to New York's Masonic Hall for an elegant dinner. There members toasted sister lodges, "valuable links in the great chain of brotherhood," the "glorious West and the Impulsive south," and "the United States," their "adopted country," the "Palestine of the modern Hebrews." The final toast, to the "Unity of Israel throughout the world," expressed "the destiny of the Order," the "quiet haven of universal brotherhood and happiness."[19]

As B'nai B'rith grew in size and standing, it became increasingly concerned with the character of its members and its appearance. At the installation of a new Jordan Lodge in 1852, Grand Nasi Henry B. Jones, the head of B'nai B'rith, warned that the organization could be damaged by the admission of "bad men, capable of imposition and fraud." The lodges' "investigating committees" had to be "strict and close" in winnowing out unworthy candidates— three black balls barred any applicant—and in expelling unseemly members. Jones warned that sometimes "an officer is elected to the President's chair who is not able to read correctly." To encourage a greater "desire for literary cultivation," lodges must avoid disseminating printed work "full of typographical and grammatical errors." Members must consider themselves "priests in the service of the order of the promotion of intelligence, morality and purity of character."[20]

B'nai B'rith lodges acted as adult literary societies, guided by the ideas of German liberal intellectuals. The society's pride, the Maimonides Library Association, held eight hundred books available for loan for a dollar a year. Lodges sponsored cultural evenings on such subjects as "Religious Education," "Ideas on a Universal Religion," "A Solution to the Slavery Question," and "The Condition of Political Parties in America." Speeches were replete with radical statements, inspired by leaders of the failed liberal revolution of 1848. Henry Jones called on members to "forget every distinction which position and wealth, intellect and education creates between man and man." President Julius Bien declared, "*Science* is the *Messiah* of the human race, leads to human happiness and leads toward the realization of the 'brotherhood of man.'"[21]

Immigrants founded B'nai B'rith to find common fraternity in a foreign world and then to make America their "Palestine," to become literate, moral citizens of their "adopted land." Advocating a creed of brotherhood and commonality and a devotion to science and humanity, lodges provided important benefits to widows and children—all beyond the synagogue.

Some young men of ambition created an alternative fraternal outlet in the 1850s in the literary society. Prompted by a notice in the *Asmonean*, the founders of the Young Men's Literary Society met and recruited twenty young men. Though the club stated that it did not want many of the "lower classes who sought admission," the majority were workingmen. After delivering the inaugural lecture at Stuyvesant Hall, "Literature: Biblical and Post Biblical," Reverend Morris Raphall, spiritual leader of B'nai Jeshurun and the foremost religious leader in the city in the 1850s, declared that he was glad to assist "efforts to promote mental culture and to spread and popularize knowledge among [the Jewish] people." He advised the young men on the importance of mental cultivation: "You are American Jews. You are citizens of the glorious commonwealth in which the predominance of mind over matter has been most fully established." At the next lecture, Isaac Mayer Wise journeyed through world history, concluding that commerce and art were central to the overthrow of despots and that Russian Jewish merchants spurred the downfall of serfdom.[22]

Members held optimistic visions for their people in the young America of 1853. In the society's second year, spokesman Mosely Lyon declared the society's "manifesto to the world": "We are the young men of Israel, Joined together to raise from its position of mediocrity the literary fame of the great mass of the Jewish race. . . . We number among our elders the peers of any wise men of the Gentile, but perhaps with a few exceptions, their labors are confined to the quiet closet of the student and a chief quality of their character is their retiring modesty." Lyon declared that the society revered the "kings of Intellect" that marked the Jewish people "from the time of Moses . . . to the day of Mendelssohn." While persecutions had held back the Jewish people's intellectual advance, in the "mighty republic of WASHINGTON" Israelites witnessed the "victory of reason, love and knowledge over the cankering remains of prejudice, hatred and superstition." The "men of the Ten Tribes" would soon be "awaking from their lethargy."[23]

At the society's third anniversary, in the presence of both sexes, it considered whether "a woman ought to move in the same sphere as men." In 1857, during the Panic, it debated whether fashion was beneficial to humanity, deciding in the negative. At another meeting, Dr. Waterman compared Russian serfdom and American slavery. Because of the work of the society, President James Seligman declared, young men who once could barely "give utterance to a thought" were now "proficient in extemporaneous speaking and forensic discussion," and those "of limited pecuniary Means" were able to peruse "the chronicles of past and present."[24]

A fissure in leadership in the 1850s led to the formation of the rival Touro Society, which gave its lectures in German. In 1856, young attorney A. J. Dittenhoefer spoke at the Touro Society of the benefits of tolerance and the importance of a literary life. A merchant must be well-read. Dittenhoefer, noting that critics censured the Touro Society for admitting ladies to its library and lectures, declared that there was no reason to continue the "cold and icy prejudices of the dark ages."[25]

Literary societies reflected attempts by German Jewish immigrants, joined by non-German newcomers and native-born Jews seeking greater refinement, to provide a means of fraternization, to integrate into American society, and to discuss critical contemporary issues. These societies were both Jewish and secular. Their ambitions were perhaps premature, as they failed to enroll significant numbers of members. The *Jewish Messenger* deplored the lack of interest of young men in careers in letters. But the Jewish community of the 1850s focused on attaining an economic foothold in the new country. Relatively few, even of the successful, displayed interest in pursuing a literary life. Far more, however, expressed support for philanthropy.[26]

■ Philanthropy

Benevolent charity societies that began prior to 1830 generally centered in synagogues, including the most notable citywide organization, the Hebrew Benevolent Society (HBS), which originated in Shearith Israel in 1822 and moved to B'nai Jeshurun before becoming independent. Its president for years was Mordecai M. Noah, New York's most prominent Jewish citizen. The society's funds available for charity increased from $600 a year in the late 1820s to $17,000 annually in the late 1850s. In 1841, it distributed $1,763 among 195 indigents; in 1858, it gave $3,567 to 2,025 different recipients. Funds came from membership dues and donations.[27]

The HBS, while it admitted Germans, was the bastion of the native born. Both a charitable and fraternal society for prominent Jews in the city, it served as the center of social and benevolent enterprise for the English-speaking community. The festivities of the charitable organization resembled those of fraternal societies. In 1849, for example, at its annual celebration (joined this one time by the German Hebrew Benevolent Society) in the Apollo Saloon, at Broadway near Canal Street, HBS members dined to orchestral accompaniment. City alderman and rabbinical luminaries attended, including Isaac Leeser of Philadelphia. Arms of the states decorated the room. Reverend Samuel Isaacs of Shaaray Tefilah, noting that he was once saved by assistance, spoke of the centrality of charity to Judaism. Dr. Max Lilienthal of Anshe Chesed spoke in German of the enduring suffering of Jews in Hungary and Russia.[28]

All anniversaries of the HBS's founding, as well as those celebrating the founding of other societies, rejoiced in the glory of being a Jew in America. Reverend Isaacs spoke of the wonder of America, where "Jew and Gentile

[were] meeting together for mutual advantage, without reference to creeds or parties," where the "Hebrew" was accepted as a "friend and citizen." Reverend Raphall lauded America as "the only Christian nation not stained by spoliation, cruelty or any wrong of any kind committed against the Jew." He declared, "[I had not seen] religious liberty in its full extent—which is the perfect equality of all men before the law—until I set my foot on the shores of this, the State of New York." Extolling America's destiny following the victories of the Mexican War, Raphall predicted that America would soon hold "a leading rank among the nations of the earth," while Europe was convulsed in "a mighty struggle" in search of "Liberty, Civil and Religious."[29]

Community respect was as much a goal of the HBS as were charity and patriotic demonstration. The society received donations from Governor Hamilton Fish and letters from President Millard Fillmore and Senator Daniel Webster. In 1851, Reverend J. J. Lyons recited the prayer after meals "in a dignified and harmonious manner, eliciting the admiration of all the Gentile visitors, to whom the Hebrew service was novel." The 1852 drive raised over $3,000, including donations from "esteemed Christian friends," many from "Broad and Wall Street firms." The *Asmonean* declared these men of commerce worthy of "the support of Hebrew merchants." As the HBS rejoiced in its deeds, it celebrated its standing in non-Jewish society.[30]

As economic conditions worsened in the 1850s, the focus on charity sharpened. Reverend Raphall advised merchants attending the banquet that "they could not invest . . . in a better cause" than charity for an immigrant fleeing the "stringent laws against the Hebrew," landing penniless in "this land of liberty." The HBS "takes him by the hand," producing "an honest and worthy citizen." In 1852, President Harris Aronson, who succeeded Noah after Noah's death in 1851, declared that "within the last two years there had been many applicants for relief from the society." Since the poor lived in obscurity, "but few could tell of the misery and distress which was to be found in the city of New York." In 1854, he reported that "the groans of hunger are more louder [*sic*] and more numerous than ever." The "ship loads" of people from the "old world" who sought to find "the star of hope . . . in the West" exhausted the society's funds. Reverend Isaacs pitied the "creatures . . . who pined in wretchedness." When God "in his inscrutable wisdom" deemed that some should "pine in sorrow," he endowed "his more favored children" with "innate love." Charity, the "unseen cement," bound the world in concord.[31]

The declining economy pushed the HBS to its limits. In 1855, the *Asmonean* complained of "the great distressed state of the operatives in this city," made worse by the benevolent societies' bylaws limiting the distribution of their resources to a percentage of their collections and endowment. In December, Reverend Raphall, warning of the "alarming increase of pauperism among the Hebrews in this city, and the pernicious influence over their moral and religious conditions," advocated construction of a "House of Industry." During the Panic of 1857, which threw thousands of people out of work, the HBS held its annual meeting at B'nai Jeshurun without a celebratory dinner. In November, the society held a "speculation" (fundraiser) of music, using the "whole of the able corps of artists, vocal and instrumental." The sense of charity, however, seemed absent when participants complained that *Il Trovatore* was "thrust at them" instead of *I Puritani*. Early the next year, Raphall thanked God that 1858 was "in full bloom."[32]

Though the HBS was the foremost Jewish charity, it was but one of many. Second in size stood the German Hebrew Benevolent Society, which held similar festive anniversaries and which also attracted Dr. Lilienthal, Reverend Isaacs, and Reverend Raphall. President Joseph Seligman, of the rising mercantile family, noted that though the "Society is but Young," he rejoiced in the "vigor and strength caused by its youth," its harmony, and its "holy work." Seligman described the "distress and suffering" of Jewish immigrants, of visiting committees who witnessed families "cramped up in a small room, prostrate with disease, no fuel to warm them, scarcely any clothing to cover them, no healing draft to alleviate their suffering." He, too, spoke of the grandeur of America, a land where the nobility was not a social class but the "noble and liberal constitution," accompanied by "free schools" and "free speech." By 1860, the German Hebrew Benevolent Society's disbursements equaled those of the HBS.[33]

In 1851, the Young Men's Hebrew Benevolent Society, composed of "working men . . . who not only lend their names to a charity but give their time and labors to promote its ends," numbered two hundred men, held funds of $1,725, and collected eighty tons of coal for the poor. That year they sponsored a presentation of *A School for Scandal*, at which, the *New York Herald* noted, "a most dazzling concentration of the beauty . . . of the fair daughters of Israel were in the ascendant." Nine hundred dollars was raised. The Hevra Bikur Cholim Vkadischa, a traditional charitable society of Poles, celebrated anniversaries that were "a source of much delight" to Jewish immigrants, as they brought back "reminiscences of the customs of home." The society, which administered to the sick and the dead, reported collections averaging $1,300 to $1,900 per year. At one dinner, a large American flag was displayed, accompanied by the banner of Hungary in support of Hungarian independence. Polish Jews toasted the United States, a land "great generous and free: the home of the wanderer, the asylum of the oppressed . . . we love and bless it every day of our lives."[34]

Though synagogues were relegated to a lesser benevolent role, they took care of their members, providing women with a singular opportunity to participate in community affairs. In October 1850, the women of Shaaray Tefilah announced a capital fund of $700 devoted not only to the sick and dying but to the poor, "with a liberal hand." In 1856, Shearith Israel's sisters produced a fair to benefit the indigent; there a visitor could gaze on tableaus of a Jewish wedding, an infant school, "dolls in every variety of costumes, . . . giant scarfs [tallit], smoking caps, pincushions and all the various specimens of ladies work, . . . [displaying] the skill of the lovely Jewess, for fine embroidery," as well as a "beautiful melodeon and a sewing machine."[35]

Given the patriotic pride that charitable societies expressed at America's progress, including the western conquests and migration, it is not surprising that the German Hebrew Benevolent Society provided immigrants with "the means to emigrate further West" and that the HBS declared that it "furnished means to a large number of individuals and families to depart from" New York City. In 1837, a new organization, the Society of Zeire Hazon (Tender Sheep), sought to purchase farm land and to aid immigrants building their farms. Both this plan and a similar effort in 1838 of a society centered at congregation Anshe Chesed to purchase land in Ulster County failed.[36]

In 1855, the president of the Lebanon Lodge of B'nai B'rith founded the American Hebrew Agricultural and Horticultural Association to buy land for immigrants. The society declared that as long as Jews practice "exclusively the commercial interest, it is clear that [they] pursue a course inimical to the welfare of [the] country." Dr. Waterman argued that Jews occupied "an unnatural position" in the American economy, as almost no Israelite chose to become a "solid man of the soil." The farmer, "far from the temptations of commerce," enjoyed more independence than a merchant did. New immigrants were told to get a basket and peddle. Why not become a farmer instead of competing with country merchants? An *Asmonean* contributor agreed, writing that Jews were subject to "reproach" for their "exclusive pursuit of commerce," with "some good show of reason." At a meeting "crowded to capacity," Reverend Raphall produced an "electric influence" with his portrayal of Jewish contentment in ancient agricultural society. Another attendee, however, opposed the plan because it led to Jewish separatism. Jews should not work in segregated colonies. D. E. M. Delara also protested on grounds of equality. Did Christian merchants in New York and Philadelphia pursue a course inimical to the country? Commerce "spreads civilization and peace, political order and law, supports the arts and sciences." Societies, he averred, should be cautious before making statements that could incite anti-Semitism. The idea of returning Jews to agriculture, a long and vexing issue, repeatedly rose and died.[37]

In May 1847, congregation Shearith Israel held a service to encourage members to contribute to the relief of "the people of Ireland suffering from the severest dispensation of a wise Providence," the potato famine. This was an exceptional plea. Although this was an era of nationwide reform movements, including sabbatarianism, temperance, women's rights, and abolition, and although New York City was headquarters for many of these campaigns, Jews did not lead these movements, nor did the community express much interest. There are a number of reasons for this. Foremost may be that many reform movements were led by Protestants, whom Jews held in contempt and fear for missionary efforts that peaked in the antebellum era. Second, reform was largely a Whig effort, and most Jews were Democrats. Finally, a lingering "siege mentality," the product of centuries of European persecution, made Israelites cautious of exposing themselves by pointing out flaws in society, and this mentality took time to dissipate. Their quest for acceptance in America preoccupied them instead.[38]

In 1830, Dr. Daniel Peixotto, member of the New York Medical Society and son-in-law of Gershom Seixas, addressed the issue of the lack of Jewish participation in reform efforts at an anniversary dinner of the Society for the Education of Poor Children and the Relief of Indigent Persons of the Jewish Persuasion. Noting the "benevolent spirit which so peculiarly illustrates the character of the present century," Peixotto remarked that many Jews were "indifferent, if not hostile" to reform movements. Why did this society limit its efforts to the needs of the Jewish community? Because the first duty of a citizen was "to provide for his own wants." The "proudest badge of any sect" should be that no member was "dependent on public eleemosynary institutions." The limitation of Jews' benevolence came not from "illiberality" but from "a sincere desire of rendering that good which is in [their] power." In Peixotto's view, in taking care of their own, Jews fulfilled their civic responsibilities.[39]

■ Jews' Hospital

Leaders of the Jewish community often expressed concern over the failure of the Jews of New York to act in unity—and with good reason. Immigrants who settled in Kleindeutschland apart from most other Jews, who spoke only German, and who tended to congregate among themselves created a sense of separation and, undoubtedly, resentment and antagonism among those Jews who had already put down roots in the community, spoke English regardless of their origins, and were comfortable in American culture. These differences appeared in the failure of the Hebrew and German Hebrew Benevolent Societies to form an umbrella philanthropic organization. Rather, the German community formed its own society, working in a separate sphere, despite pleas from both the *Asmonean* and the *Jewish Messenger* to unite for the good of the overall community. Even during the Panic of 1857, when thousands of people were out of work, the HBS, a "Sephardic stronghold," feared that if the two organizations merged, most beneficiaries would be Germans. Divisions were also visible in the secession of some members of the Young Men's Literary Society to form their own German-speaking organization and in the formation of B'nai B'rith, devoted to the needs of immigrants.[40]

A similar problem prevented construction of a community hospital. New York suffered serious epidemics: in 1849, cholera raged through the city, killing up to 40 a day and in one week carrying away 714, mostly from the crowded areas housing immigrants. The city contained a number of hospitals, including Bellevue, New York Hospital, a charity hospital for the poor on Blackwell's Island, Lincoln Hospital for blacks, and St. Vincent's, a Catholic institution. Yet no medical facility existed where Jews could obtain kosher food and avoid missionaries. The *Asmonean* asked readers to consider a poor Israelite, forced to enter a city hospital that housed patients of "the lowest grade of society." Though this soul may not have been observant before, "the approach of death makes us wondrous orthodox." If he refused the hospital's nonkosher food, he would die; if he ate, he would suffer pangs of conscience. Nor could he put on tephillin without being subject to the "derision of the fellow sufferers or the jeers of their fellow inmate." *Israel's Herold*, a short-lived German-language weekly, carried an article by Dr. N. Waterman that declared that the city's hospitals were of little use for the city's German Jews, as "the doctors, who speak only . . . the English language, do not understand these sick people and cannot recognize their illness from their appearance." An "invalid," alone and afraid, "throws himself into his death bed in indescribable despair."[41]

First attempts to found a hospital failed. In 1847, a movement fell apart because of "the evil which works itself into, and rankles in all our public undertakings, WANT OF UNITY." In 1850, the *Asmonean* noted that three organizations, the Hebrew and German Benevolent Societies and the Young Men's Benevolent Society, set apart funds and created a board headed by President Noah to collect contributions for a hospital. Given the "divisive spirit of the times," they attempted "to do too much." The German Hebrew Benevolent Society stated that it was "thrill[ed] with joy" at the prospect, but the projected hospital was not "founded on republican and just principles"; in short, German Jews were underrepresented on its board.[42]

With the charities at loggerheads, a notice in the *Asmonean* announced a ball at Niblo's Saloon at Broadway and Prince Street, one of the city's eminent dining spots. The president of the sponsoring society, the Jews' Hospital in New York, was seventy-two-year-old Sampson Simson, now a reclusive philanthropist. Wealthy members of Shearith Israel and Shaaray Tefilah joined him, including real estate dealer John D. Philips, Benjamin Nathan of the New York Stock Exchange, and Henry Hendricks of the copper-manufacturing family.[43]

The ad caused considerable excitement and intrigue. A "delegate to the Original Hospital Committee" asked the *Asmonean* for intelligence. Editor Lyon replied, "we have no information to afford." The society's ball, covered in detail in the *New York Times*, raised, after expenses, more than $1,000, a significant sum. Two years later, in November 1853, the founding committee laid a cornerstone, formed a board of directors, and drafted a constitution giving the board control of the hospital. No German joined the board. The hospital, organized privately, reflected the work of Jews with deep roots in the community, many affiliated with Sephardic Shearith Israel, who were able to find Christian donors if German Jews proved reluctant to contribute because of their exclusion from governance. While Israelite employees were difficult to procure, the constitution did state, "all persons employed in carrying out the objects of this Society shall, as far as practicable, be of the Jewish faith." For the first time in American history, the directors proclaimed, "a refuge for the needy Israelite

Jews' Hospital soon after it opened in 1855. Jews' Hospital was the greatest collective achievement of the city's Jewish community prior to the Civil War. After the war, it was renamed Mt. Sinai and became public, open to the city's entire population. (Courtesy Mt. Sinai Archives)

requiring surgical and medical aid" stood ready to receive patients. Given the hospital's "invaluable benefit to the Israelites in the United States," they appealed to the "benevolence and liberality" of the Jewish nation. Any congregation or society contributing fifty dollars a year had the "privilege" of sending the hospital one patient per year "not disqualified [through a mixed marriage] by the laws of the society." This provision revealed that the sense of exclusiveness found in synagogues was also present in Jewish secular institutions.[44]

With $7,000 in hand, the hospital began to rise on land donated by Simson on the south side of Twenty-Eighth Street between Seventh and Eighth Avenues. At a celebratory dinner, Simson declared that soon the "last dying sigh of the expiring Hebrew" would be "heard by attending and sympathizing Jews." Reverend Isaacs stated that Jews often claimed that city institutions "supplied all the necessities . . . without any additional trouble or expense." They were wrong. While Jews shared common interests with all Americans, their religion was "perfectly distinct and separate from all other beliefs." More than a medical institution, the hospital was a dwelling for the "spiritual happiness" of the Jewish community.[45]

The hospital's consecration took place on May 17, 1855, after an unsettling dispute when the board refused to augment the number of German Jewish trustees. Built of brick and accommodating up to 150 patients, it rose four stories, with a wing on each side and a garden and courtyard in the center. Ceilings were a spacious sixteen feet high. The basement, used for a refectory and washroom, included a tablet "to the memory of Judah Touro," the New Orleans philanthropist who bequeathed $20,000. The hospital's synagogue housed a tablet with donors' names. Despite festering ethnic and generational divisions, the hospital marked a major advance in the self-respect and standing of New York's Jewish community.[46]

The consecration ceremony resembled that of a synagogue, including seven circuits of the Torah. It also celebrated how far the Jewish community had advanced in greater New York society. Attending the ceremonies, covered extensively by the *New York Times*, were Jewish dignitaries, the mayor, and the lieutenant governor. The president of the hospital sat under a flag featuring an image of George Washington. One patriotic toast declared, "Our Country, may she always be right, but right or wrong, our country." Reverend Raphall proclaimed, in ecumenical spirit, "[Jews work in] fellowship to Catholic and Protestant, because we feel that we are the children of one Father, and servants of one God, who has created us." Lieutenant Governor Henry Raymond responded that the Jewish community was "taking on the responsibilities of the state herself!" He pledged aid from the legislature.[47]

The staff of Jews' Hospital included consulting physicians Chandler Gilman, professor of obstetrics at Columbia; William Detmond, an orthopedic surgeon from Germany; and two attending surgeons, including Jewish physician Israel Moses. Except in cases of emergencies, the hospital admitted only Jews. At first, fearful of epidemic, it refused to accept typhoid victims, but it soon relented. The hospital regularly submitted reports detailing patients treated. Its first report in 1856 recorded sixty-nine male and forty-one female patients, twenty of whom could pay; the largest number in the hospital at any one time was twenty-three.[48]

In 1856, a dispute over autopsies erupted at the hospital. Physician Simeon Abraham stated that though it was an unpleasant duty, the safety of the living required it. Referring to passages in the Talmud, he argued that the hospital followed Jewish law. Maimonides, he wrote, stated that it was not forbidden to examine a corpse before burial to ascertain the cause of death. The hospital's board consulted with the chief rabbi of England, Dr. N. M. Adler, who replied that autopsies were forbidden desecrations that could only be performed in cases of suspected murder or to save lives in the context of an unknown disease. The directors acceded to Dr. Adler's response but in practice often granted exceptions. This did not end the controversy. Physician Abram Arnold of Baltimore wrote that Dr. Adler's decision was "a slur on the medical art, and is a discredit to any body of Jews which endorses it." Should it be "published to the world" that Jews were willing to benefit by the "investigations undertaken by others, while [they] den[y] the means employed to attain them?"[49]

Jews took great pride in the work of the hospital. Jewish newspapers reported many dramatic stories. A Bavarian woman betrothed to a man in America journeyed across the Atlantic only to fall ill. After a miraculous recovery at Jews' Hospital, she found and wed her beloved. A man with a fractured thigh had undergone treatment for six months "without any benefit." After an operation at the hospital, he was discharged, "able to use his leg." Seven-year-old John Roth, unable to support himself "on account of a congenital deformity of the feet and legs," gained entry after being denied assistance elsewhere. After surgery, he walked home. Seven-year-old Henrietta Barnett, suffering from "scrofulous sores and diseased bone" and considered a candidate for amputation in London, was admitted in June and discharged in October "much improved." Hanna Ahrens, "in the most abject state of distress" from severe chronic rheumatism, left the hospital "in perfect health." In addition to healing, the hospital also brought "brethren back to their faith, rescuing them from public charities," restoring them to "health and the abiding force and truth of Judaism." One dying man of sixty had been a "philosopher" for years but at life's end confided, "my philosophy fails." Despairing of years of infidelity, he expressed thanks for "Jewish soup" that, he declared, possessed "an extraordinary healing power." As death neared, he affirmed, "happy the child of mortality who, on the brink of the grave is here, his pillow softened by the members of his own community, his last moments attended by the voice of true sympathy."[50]

Though never filled to capacity, Jews' hospital kept as many patients as revenues permitted. In 1857, the hospital admitted 220 patients, 85 percent of whom were immigrants from Poland and Germany. In 1858, it reported that 54 of its 250 patients were peddlers, "a fact ascribable to so many immigrants being cast upon our hospitable shores without profession or trade." It admitted forty-nine female domestics under similar conditions.[51]

Some tensions between the German-immigrant community and the Sephardic and native-born dissipated by the end of the 1850s. In 1857, the board amended the constitution in a manner to permit more German Jews to join. Lack of adequate financial support concerned the directors, given that the "Hebrew proportion [of the city] is increasing" and that "its members are participating in equal ratio with their fellow citizens in the accumulation of wealth." Another signal of eased tension appeared in 1859, as the German and Hebrew Benevolent Societies merged, creating a unified organization. These two events symbolized that the maturing German-immigrant community had won acceptance as peers of the established Jewish community.[52]

Original plans called for an orphan asylum to accompany the hospital. Though this did not materialize, in the early 1860s the *Jewish Messenger* campaigned for this institution, expecting a "speedy response" from Jews whose "worldly affairs are in such a position as can enable them to do good to others without detriment to themselves." Shortly after merging with the German Benevolent Society, the Hebrew Benevolent Society purchased a four-story building on West Twenty-Ninth Street. The cornerstone for the Jewish Orphan Home was laid on July 29, 1862, with great ceremony. U.S. Representative Roscoe Conkling declared that the "greatest and guiltiest rebellion [Civil War] that the world has ever seen" was "filling the land with orphans," and Reverend Isaacs praised this "labor of love," inspired by "principles of humanity" and by the aid of the city and state. In 1864, with the asylum open, the *Jewish Messenger* argued that it should accept no orphans of illegitimate birth or doubtful Jewish parentage. Should an applicant "born in sin" share "equal rights with those whose parents have lived a life of purity?" "Certainly not." Though this may seem "harsh and unfeeling," the institution must "do justice" to poor Jewish children. There is no evidence that the institution adopted this policy, but the argument indicates that some Jews sought to use their communal institutions to enforce religious norms.[53]

Jewish Women in Antebellum New York

While most Jews did not join national reform movements, Ernestine Rose did. Born Ernestine Potowski, the only child of a devout Polish rabbi, she rebelled against his authority and escaped an arranged marriage by fleeing to England. There, under the influence of utopian socialist Robert Owen, she renounced organized religion and embraced the movement for legal and social equality of the sexes. After marrying William Rose, a non-Jewish Owenite, in a civil ceremony, she and her new spouse immigrated to New York, where William worked as a watchmaker and engraver, enabling Ernestine to launch her career as a free thinker, abolitionist, and spokesperson for women's rights. A spellbinding orator, Rose declared that "whenever human rights are claimed for man, moral consistency points to the equal rights of women." Never a figure in the New York Jewish community, she seldom mentioned her background. However, in 1852, at the third convention for women's rights, introduced as an Israelite, she contended that as the daughter of a "down trodden and persecuted people called the Jews," she understood the need for equal rights on a personal level. In 1864, she entered into a debate with a progressive yet anti-Semitic Boston editor, defending the Jewish people as sober and industrious citizens, even if they unfortunately believed in God (but not in a Trinity). Her most recent biographer attributes her debating skills and quick intellect to her Jewish upbringing. She was the most significant Jew in the antebellum national reform movements.[54]

Aside from Rose, few if any Jewish females participated in the women's rights movement, a cause that sought a world in which women claimed equality within nineteenth-century standards. The Jewish community was conscious of the Seneca Falls convention of 1848 and its manifesto that "the history of mankind is a history of repeated injuries and usurpations on the part of man toward woman, having in direct object the establishment of an absolute tyranny over her." The *Asmonean*, for example, printed a parody of the proclamation from the *Philadelphia Evening Bulletin* that maintained that it was time for the women of the nation to "break off the chains which Fashion has thrown among them" and to assume dress that "the laws of nature and a

The *Jewish Messenger* ran these ads in 1865. That so many piano companies were willing to appeal to the Jewish community is a sign of the growing wealth and embourgeoisement of the Jewish population, and the demands for the refinement that a musical education afforded a middle-class woman of the nineteenth century. It also indicates greater aspirations to fitting into New York 's cosmopolitan society, often to the detriment of Jewish religious commitment. (*Jewish Messenger*, 28 July 1865)

regard for their health" require, including "the privilege to dress in frocks and trowsers,—a right most inestimable to them and formidable to tyrants only."[55]

The majority of essays in Jewish newspapers, written by men, rejected Seneca Falls, echoing nineteenth-century middle-class norms that women did not belong in the marketplace or the public square, but belonged in the home, at the center of domestic life. An 1850 article by "B.H.A." titled "On the Necessity of the Religious Instruction of Females" affirmed the importance of education for women, but only to strengthen feminine qualities, notably "mildness, tenderness, softness and sincerity," reflected in "pleasing bashfulness, silent grace and tenderness of feeling." In response to a claim in the New York press that only Christianity would "ultimately redeem her sex from an unjust bondage to ignorance and human will," a female contributor responded that Jewish women accomplished many acts of benevolence. An essay titled "Woman" praised females as God's creation whose strength resided in her dependence. In comparison to men's "individuality," women's ambition was for a "union with man." Women's innate gullibility and trust endangered them if not under a man's protection.[56]

Orthodox commentator "Here and There" was an exception. He regretted that the world was "slow to admit that women were intellectually and morally the equal of man." A woman possessed the ability to "comprehend the most abstruse sciences." Her "delicate touch" made her a "skilled practitioner of the crafts." Yet men thwarted her any time "she contemplates supporting herself." The solution was not for women to dress as men or to enter politics but for mothers to cease training their daughters for "parlor distinction" and for women to cease placing marriage as the "acme of their ambitions." A number were already succeeding in new "duties and occupations."[57]

Were women "beyond the synagogue"? While a significant number of women found religious consolation within the city's sanctuaries, and others secured the opportunity to join congregational societies, the majority of New York's female Jewish population received a secular education and found religious training and participation peripheral to their lives. Too, middle-class Jewish women responded to the appeal of the arts, evidenced by pages of advertisements for pianos in Jewish newspapers and women's attendance at concerts, dramas, and operas. They accepted invitations to literary-society festivities and Purim balls. Though few affiliated with the women's rights movement, many participated in New York society, far from the synagogue gallery.

■ Arts and Entertainment

Jewish intellectual enterprise, once restricted to the synagogue, found new outlets in the arts. In 1836, a Jewish musical prodigy, Daniel Schlesinger, arrived in New York from Germany. Playing "at the home of a German patriarch," he won over his audience with "musical eloquence, poetry, and genius." He could perform the classical repertory or "clothe Yankee Doodle in music." Schlesinger studied American folk music, from the national anthem to "African melodies." Alas, with a public "in whom even Beethoven's name could not have then awaked a glow," he found no receptive audience. He tried teaching, at one time instructing three pupils in his dreary lodgings. An attempt to present "a series of *Chamber-Concerts*," failed, though before his untimely death in 1838, he gave successful recitals. He was the forerunner of many more successful Jewish artists.[58]

A decade after Schlesinger's death, Jews numbered among the promoters and patrons of the arts. Nowhere was this more evident than in the Italian Opera Company under the direction of Max Maretzek. Born in Moravia, Maretzek, a Jewish violinist, came to America as conductor at the Astor Opera House. In 1848, he formed his own Italian Opera Company, heavily patronized by fellow Jews. Many artists were also Jewish. He achieved success: in 1850, the *New York Herald* reported that five-year subscribers to the opera expressed "entire and unqualified approbation of his conduct as manager of the Astor Place Opera House" and recommended re-leasing the building to Maretzek. That December, the *Asmonean* described the "Gala Night" opening the season. Noted soprano Teresa Parodi enchanted the reviewer with an "astonishing vocalization and performance in *Lucretia* and *Norma*." The following fall, however, the tone changed. The paper criticized the house for charging European prices for inferior performances; a tenor could not hit the "high notes"; a soprano sang *Norma* in an "incomplete, slovenly and inefficient" manner. Could the "petted and *spoilt* Maretzek," a critic wondered, preserve the enterprise "from absolute and total failure?" Given "the many sacrifices which have been made to establish an Italian Opera in New York," how could the management fall into the hands of "charelatans and humbugs?" By next February, the director had returned to good graces: "the promptitude with which Max Maretzek has adopted *our advice* and reduced the price of admission to *Fifty cents*" again produced "crowded audiences."[59]

The *Asmonean*, declaring that in "no city in the world" was dancing as popular as in New York, reported the opening of a school run by Israelite Henry Wells and his sister. Wells had lived in Paris and studied at the Royal Academy. The paper also recognized a visual Jewish artist, D. Davidson of Stanton Street, who was preparing an exhibition for the Crystal Palace that "he hopes will reflect credit on the Jews." He designed ten "Scriptural Pieces—five engravings, and five in writings replete with ornament." The larger pictures depicted the Feast of Tabernacles and the Ten Commandments and the "sacred Menora or Chandelier."[60]

Jews avidly attended the theater. The *New York Times* reported that the dress circle of the City Theater was filled "with men and women, handsomely dressed and of genteel manners, including a large sprinkling of Jews." The *Asmonean* reported regularly on theatrical events. One week it noted that Barnum's Museum was presenting plays that were "more intensely effective representations of real life . . . than any other establishments in the city." It announced performances of the German National Theater, the "first permanent German Theater in this city." That Mr. C. P. Farret, "one of the most prominent leaders" of the 1848 Revolution, stood at its helm, the paper said, gave it "further claim on us." In addition, Niblo's Garden was "crowded" at every performance, while the popularity of Fellow's Minstrels—an entertainment parodying blacks, with whites wearing blackface and imitating black dialects—"continued unabated." Though New York owed much to "her Hebrew Citizens" for "enterprise in the advancement of the trade, commerce and amusements of this metropolis," nothing surpassed the new theater of Jewish producer Harry Eyttinge, which cost $250,000. The playhouse sported a stage fifty-five feet deep and a hundred feet wide, seats for more than four thousand playgoers, fresco paintings, and twenty-five chandeliers. A one-price system of fifty cents gave entrance "to all parts of the house." Productions of *Camille*, *Phedre*, and *Adrienne Lecouvreur* filled the parquette and amphitheater, while the upper circles, where the affluent congregated, contained a "numerous and highly intelligent audience." During the "financial revulsion of 1857," opera halls yet held "supremacy over the people," while music publishers continued to "multiply their productions."[61]

The *Jewish Messenger* also kept readers abreast of cultural events. Performances of *Rigoletto* and *La Traviata* in 1859 were "splendid successes." Pointing to productions of the operas *La Juive* and *Nebuchadnezzar*, it stated, "citizens of New York at the present moment, owe their principal sources of amusement to Israelite and Jewish subjects." Jews tended to "monopolize the management [and] the talent" of New York opera and were among "the most critical and sensible spectators" of "current dramatic productions."[62]

What was the source of the strong Jewish interest in the arts? The intellectual energy that went into religious life and study, so predominant in European Jewish culture, perhaps found a secular outlet in a secular society in the arts, a world in which perplexing questions could be posed and difficult solutions offered to profound dilemmas. As important, participation in the arts offered the middling and newly affluent Jewish community an opportunity to mix with the Christian population on equal terms. Social acceptance in the broader community could be attained through patronage of the arts.

In addition, Jews of the middling classes embraced ever more lavish festive occasions. Dinners of literary and benevolent societies included music and dancing. The most notable events were balls in celebration of Chanukah and especially Purim. In 1860, Myer S. Isaacs, the twenty-one-year-old son of the editor of the *Jewish Messenger*, Reverend Samuel Isaacs, founded the Purim Association. Its annual Purim Ball quickly became the social event of the year, despite the ongoing Civil War. The demand for invitations was intense; nobody of means wanted to be left off the list. More and more tickets were printed, as upward of three thousand fashionable Jews attended. Perhaps the 1863 ball was the most sumptuous. The Seventh Regiment band, with sixty-five musicians, played dance numbers, including quadrilles, waltzes, polkas, and a Virginia reel. Lavish costumes included "many elaborate marchionesses and duchesses with hair powdered en regle," Queen Margaret of Valois dressed in "crimson velvet bordered with ermine" mingling with both a "Grecian maiden in white" and Andalusian flower girls. Italian and Hungarian peasants, Little Red Riding Hood, Joan of Arc, and Old Mother Goose wandered in, joining the Queen of the Night, Joseph in his coat of many colors, Marie Stuart, and the "Hot Corn Girl and Tambourine Girl." Adopting Christians' New Year's Day tradition, fashionable Jewish homes were open for visits on Purim. The Purim Ball marked the end of the "ball season," a season that encompassed synagogue and benevolent-society affairs, "sociables of a more private and exclusive character," as well as public lectures and concerts. Listing the new events of the coming fall season, the *Messenger* noted, "our people were intent to turn from the horrible realities of war to the gay and festive, the charitable and intellectual."[63]

By the end of the 1850s, more and more of New York Jewry, including immigrants, had advanced in economic and social standing. As the city moved up-town, so did they, purchasing brownstones north of Union Square. What was the meaning of this movement? Did Jews want to dissociate from their brethren and disappear within New York society? Perhaps this solution appealed to the quarter of the community that intermarried. Affluent financier and Rothschild agent August Belmont, for example, claiming that his "liberal views on religion" kept him distant from the "requirements of the Jewish Talmud" and that Jews in America were "too disagreeable," married in an Episcopal church and, though he never converted, moved solely within the Christian community. But most Jews still wanted to associate with other Israelites as they also sought entry into main-stream New York. On the one hand, in the formation of B'nai B'rith, the founding of Jews' Hospital, and the inception of ninety-three different organizations rang-ing from small burial societies to the Hebrew and German Benevolent Societies, Jews determined to bond with each other, often divided by nationality. On the other hand, as we shall see, Jewish families welcomed the public school, the insti-tution that offered the quickest mode of acceptance for immigrant children into a larger urban community. In their immersion in the arts, as in business, Jews chose to join Christian New Yorkers without distinction as they sat side by side at the Astor Opera House, the Academy of Music, and the Broadway Theater. Jew-ish identity and Jewish integration both remained appealing goals as Jewish life increasingly centered beyond the synagogue.[64]

There is a republican theme to the New York Jews' propensity to participate in so many ways beyond the synagogue. Alexis de Tocqueville in his famed classic, *Democracy in America*, notes that one of the most important forms of American democracy in the Jacksonian era was the propensity for Americans to exercise their democratic spirit by forming voluntary associations in every nook and cranny of the United States, thus participating in the life of the re-public. As we have seen, the Jews of New York City took on this American democratic pathway with great zeal, forming many societies. And within these societies, they expressed the increasingly aggressive patriotism, the sense of manifest destiny that often characterized the republican spirit after the elec-tion of Andrew Jackson in 1828. As Jews had participated in and incorporated the republican spirit of the American Revolution, so too the much larger pop-ulation of the 1830s, '40s, and '50s, bolstered by tens of thousands of immi-grants, took on the new democratic values, enterprise, and sense of destiny that characterized the growing nation.[65]

Representative of the elegant synagogues built in the 1840s and 1850s is the Rodeph Shalom sanctuary of a congregation of German Jews. Built in the Round or Romanesque Style, its stylish chandelier, lofty ceilings, and grand design represented a new visibility for the Jewish community of New York and a sign of their worldly success. (Rachel Wischnitzer, *Synagogue Architecture in the United States: History and Interpretation* [Philadelphia, 1955]; courtesy Jewish Publication Society)

CHAPTER 9

Division, Display, Devotion, and Defense: The Synagogue in Antebellum New York

On the eve of Shavuot 1850, Anshe Chesed consecrated its new syna-
gogue on Norfolk Street between Houston and Stanton Streets, a Gothic sanctu-
ary seating twelve hundred. In the presence of the mayor and members of the
Common Council, the elders paraded the congregation's Torahs around the new
sanctuary and through the aisles. The procession passed by twelve young men
and women, the latter clad in white dresses with blue sashes. New York's promi-
nent spiritual leaders delivered sermons in German and English. A year later,
in a modest ceremony, Bene Israel, a congregation of Dutch Jews, consecrated
a small sanctuary on Pearl Street, with only Reverend Raphall in attendance.
The rapid growth of the Jewish population created a remarkably diverse reli-
gious community.[1]

■ Synagogue Growth and Division

While a great deal of Jewish communal and personal life took place beyond
the synagogues in the antebellum era, these venerable institutions remained
viable and ever more visible, even if their significance and their role in Jewish
life were far more limited than in the colonial and early republican eras.

Jewish newcomers from Germany, Poland, and other European nations
stimulated the rise of new synagogues. From 1730 to 1824, a single congregation served the Jewish community; Ashkenazim and Sephardim coexisted
without great difficulty. The founding of B'nai Jeshurun in 1824, however, signaled the growing importance of nationality and immigrant standing. Four
years later, German, Dutch, and Polish Jews split from B'nai Jeshurun to form
Anshe Chesed. In 1837, Polish Jews, defecting from B'nai Jeshurun and Anshe

Chesed, founded Shaaray Zedek. In 1839 and again in 1842, factions of German Jews left Anshe Chesed to form Shaaray Hashamayim and Rodeph Shalom. The Polish synagogue Shaaray Zedek fell victim to division in 1845, leading to the establishment of Beth Israel. In 1844, a number of the original founders of B'nai Jeshurun, dissatisfied with their congregation, founded Shaaray Tefilah, a congregation composed largely of English- and American-born members. In 1845, members of a German "cultus society," an informal religious/literary discussion society, established Temple Emanu-El, the city's first Reform synagogue. Polish, Russian, French, and Dutch Jews formed their own synagogues. In thirty-five years, the number of congregations grew from one to twenty-seven, or nearly one per year.[2]

Divisions occurred for a number of reasons. An admission fee and the refusal of B'nai Jeshurun to admit a wife who had converted to Judaism initiated the exodus of the founders of Shaaray Zedek in 1837. The B'nai Jeshurun schism of 1844, which ended in civil court, resulted from a contested Board of Trustees election. Prior to the court case, internal disputes divided the synagogue. Its hazan, Samuel Isaacs, demanded greater religious observance, even to the point of denying nonobservers membership. He gave sermons in English to a predominantly German audience. The congregation experienced additional problems with its shochet, with intermarriage, and with disruptive members. Finally, increasing resentment arose against new immigrant members who had the potential to make a faction a majority.[3]

The disputed Board of Trustees election in B'nai Jeshurun was so controversial that the congregation hired four policemen to oversee the proceedings. When the winners prevailed by two votes, supporters of the losing candidates claimed that legitimate members were denied the right to vote. The testimony of Morland Micholl, former president of the Board of Trustees, spelled out the central contention. The synagogue, he testified, had to protect its assets, worth over $25,000. Recent years had brought New Yorkers to the congregation who were "utterly unknown to the people among whom they came." The elders tried numerous remedies to "exclude those who were calculated . . . to disturb . . . the peace and welfare of [the] congregation," including rules differentiating seat holders from electors, increasing the residency requirement for membership from six months to three years, imposing an admission fee up to $250, and requiring applicants to win the assent of two-thirds of the members. Why? To protect "places of public worship" from "ignorant immigrants" who

Consecrated in 1834, the new home of Shearith Israel was lavishly decorated with five gas chandeliers, Brussels carpet, and a masterfully fashioned ark, whose interior was lined with crimson red silk and whose exterior was covered with red brocade drapery. It seated 174 men and 204 women. (Courtesy Congregation Shearith Israel)

could become the "tools of ambition" of members who did not hold the good of the synagogue foremost in mind. Resolution of the conflict came with the exodus of leading figures of B'nai Jeshurun, including Hazan Isaacs, to form Shaaray Tefilah, assisted by a payment of $5,000. Antagonism against immigrants, added to internal dissension, led to both court and secession.[4]

Another telling schism took place at Beth HaMidrash, a congregation begun by twelve Russian Jews who rented a garret on Bayard Street for eight dollars a month. Russians were not welcomed by their Polish counterparts.

Consecrated in 1850 on Norfolk Street, the magnificent home of Anshe Chesed, one of the city's first and largest German congregations, seated one thousand and represented the neo-Gothic architectural style that was popular throughout the country. (Rachel Wischnitzer, *Synagogue Architecture in the United States: History and Interpretation* [Philadelphia, 1955]; courtesy Jewish Publication Society)

Congregation Shaaray Zedek forbade any new Russian members after 1844. As the congregation grew, it moved to a store front on Canal Street and then to the upper story of a building on Pearl Street. It was "the only institution in the country at the time where religious studies were pursued according to traditional East-European pattern[s]." In 1855, the congregation divided over the hiring of a shochet. While Galician rabbis approved the appointment, the synagogue's leader, Rabbi Ash, did not, and the shochet's supporters left to form a minyan on Bayard Street. Rabbi Ash's contingent, Beth HaMidrash, bought a Welsh Chapel on Allen Street with a bequest from philanthropist Sampson Simson. Soon Ash and his parnas grew incompatible. This dispute ended in court, with Parnas Joshua Rothstein prevailing. With $300 from Beth HaMidrash, Ash's followers formed another congregation, Beth HaMidrash HaGadol, renting a floor on Forsyth Street, near Grand Street. In 1861, the Forsyth synagogue split. After a dispute over an open window during High Holy Day services, a number of members left with Rabbi Ash to form a Hasidic "Stuebel" on Delancey Street. They purchased their own synagogue on Ludlow Street in 1872. These synagogues of Russian Jews again demonstrate the divisive nature of the antebellum Jewish community and its tendency to factionalize over internal disputes, ethnicity, personality, and ideology. Cash payments notably eased the friction of synagogues that split after bruising internal struggles.[5]

■ Grandeur

The growth of new synagogues also reflected a new, larger, and rapidly growing Jewish community, no longer centered on a single congregation but, even with the internal divisions, more self-assured and visible. The splendor of synagogues built between 1830 and 1867 testifies to a new assertiveness. Shearith Israel, the city's first synagogue and still home to many of its notable Jewish citizens such as Mordecai M. Noah and Harmon Hendricks, finally left Mill Street in 1834 for a sanctuary on Crosby Street near Broome and Spring Streets. Clergy from Trinity Church, the Dutch Reformed Church, St. Patrick's Cathedral, and the Unitarian Church attended the consecration. Like many other institutions built at that time, Shearith Israel chose a Greek Revival style in honor of the Greek Revolution. The synagogue seated 174 men, while its women's gallery, supported by fluted columns of the "Greek ionic order" held 204 seats. The new structure had a basement chapel and five gas-powered chandeliers. The *New York Times* described the ark, enclosed by "a pedimented structure on Corinthian columns and pilasters," as "one of the most exquisite specimens of workmanship and architecture we have ever seen." Shearith Israel used this site for only twenty-two years. In 1859, the congregation moved to West Nineteenth Street and Fifth Avenue and sold the Crosby Street synagogue for use as a minstrel hall. The new building, 50 percent larger and costing nearly $100,000, was constructed in a seventeenth-century Baroque style and became known for its octagonal dome supported by Corinthian columns. It was the tallest building above Fourteenth Street.[6]

Synagogues that began in Five Points and other working-class neighborhoods also moved uptown to more fashionable neighborhoods, to be replaced by new and smaller congregations. In 1850, B'nai Jeshurun sold its Elm Street home to the New Haven Railroad and moved to a fashionable neo-Gothic building on Greene Street near Houston. Spending the princely sum of $50,000, the congregation prayed under a fifty-six-foot-high dome featuring windows with ornamented paintings. Columns and buttresses supported a paneled sanctuary. At the same time, Anshe Chesed moved to a large Gothic-style synagogue seating twelve hundred (seven hundred men and five hundred women), with enclosed pews, stucco walls, stained-glass windows, and a controversial rendering of the Ten Commandments in glass rather than in tablets.[7]

Temple Emanu-El's growth astonished observers. Its founders rented a room in 1845 on Clinton Street. In 1847, the city's first Reform congregation purchased a church building on Chrystie Street for $12,000. Seven years later, the congregation transformed a Baptist church on Twelfth Street between Third and Fourth Avenues into a neo-Gothic sanctuary. Fifteen years later, the synagogue erected a towering Moorish Revival structure on Fifth Avenue and Forty-Third Street at a cost of $650,000. Attracting the support of many successful German immigrants, it became one of the most influential congregations in the city. The lavish synagogues constructed in the 1850s were located in the fashionable center of Manhattan Island, just below Union Square, a much different neighborhood from the immigrant streets of Kleindeutschland that housed the smaller congregations. Beginning in 1859, synagogues moved beyond Fourteenth Street, into neighborhoods not distinctively Jewish, where members of these affluent institutions lived.[8]

An educated prospective immigrant who resided in New York from 1853 to 1854 before returning to Germany wrote that the average Jewish sanctuary cost over $12,000, while only the Unitarian and Dutch Reform Christian congregations spent over $10,000. He also remarked that the synagogue "building exteriors collectively resemble Christian churches," with golden letters over the entrance. This observer believed that "synagogue building" represented "the Jews' adaptation to American morality or immorality." Regardless of morals, the elegant synagogues symbolized the Jewish community's rise in wealth and social standing, marking it as a worthy peer of proper Christian society.[9]

Growth in population and affluence within the Jewish community allowed larger congregations to bring to New York men who were well versed in Jewish learning, both biblical and Talmudic, and in secular studies, men who could match architectural elegance with knowledge of Jewish thought. Their arrival transformed New York into the intellectual center of American Judaism. The most prominent orthodox leaders were Samuel Meyer Isaacs of Shaaray Tefilah, Morris Raphall of B'nai Jeshurun, and Max Lilienthal of Anshe Chesed. Isaacs, son of a Dutch merchant, moved to London in 1814 at age ten. Following a stint as principal of a Jewish day school, he came to America in 1839 to become hazan/rabbi at B'nai Jeshurun but left to lead Shaaray Tefilah, where he remained thirty-three years, also serving as editor of the *Jewish Messenger*. Raphall, born in Sweden and educated in Scandinavia and Germany, settled in England in 1825 at age twenty-seven; there he edited the *Hebrew Review and Magazine of Rabbinical Literature* and translated the Mishnah into English. A gifted speaker never reluctant to enter political debate or to defend Jewish rights, he served as spiritual leader and headmaster of the Birmingham Hebrew Congregation and was one of England's most prominent Jewish spokesmen. Dissatisfied with the low cultural level and aspirations of British Jewry and the Birmingham congregation's inability to pay him a worthy compensation, in 1849 he accepted an invitation to come to B'nai Jeshurun for the substantial salary of $2,000. His arrival represented a major event for the city's Jewry. As New York's most prominent Jewish clergyman, he spoke at every significant occasion in the Jewish community and at synagogues throughout the country. The first rabbi invited to address Congress, he published lectures titled "The Poetry of the Hebrews" and "Post-Biblical History of the Jews." Unlike earlier hazans, Raphall and Isaacs gave sermons on holidays and other special occasions. This added gravity to the services and attracted the attention of Christian audiences.[10]

Max Lilienthal, who attained both ordination from a traditional yeshiva and a doctorate from the University of Munich, was selected at age twenty-five by the Russian government to modernize the Jewish school system in Russia. The opposition of traditional Jews and his inability to win Russian Jewry full citizenship rights convinced him of the futility of this mission. In 1844, not quite thirty, he moved to New York and became, simultaneously, rabbi of three separate German congregations, most notably Anshe Chesed. Although respected for his learning and experience, Lilienthal encountered difficulties with the duties required by the boards of trustees and resigned in 1850. Shearith Israel, though the oldest synagogue in the city, did not hire a learned leader until 1855, when it appointed Dr. Arnold Fischel, a Dutch scholar living in England, to work with its hazan, J. J. Lyons. A less effective speaker, Fischel was respected but not as influential as Isaacs and Raphall and Lilienthal. Lyons, a noted archivist, continued to represent Shearith Israel on charitable organizations and at synagogue consecrations.[11]

The emerging Reform movement had its strongest advocates living in and near New York, adding to the city's wealth of highly educated Jewish religious leaders. Max Lilienthal, while running his boarding school, moved into the

Reform camp. Rabbi Leo Merzbacher arrived in New York in 1830 from Bavaria, where he received a traditional yeshiva education followed by study at the University of Erlangen. Like Lilienthal, when he arrived in New York, he was a traditional rabbi, taking positions at the German synagogues Rodeph Shalom and Anshe Chesed. His increasingly Reform outlook led him to join Temple Emanu-El as its first rabbi in 1845, and he remained there until his premature death in 1856. Merzbacher's successor, Samuel Adler, the son of an Orthodox rabbi, studied at a yeshiva and at the universities of Bonn and Giessen. Unlike Lilienthal, he served as a Reform rabbi in Germany, introducing mixed seating, abolition of the second day of festival observance, and changes to the liturgy. He emigrated in 1857 both to advance his family and to escape state supervision of religious institutions. His brother was imprisoned during the Revolution of 1848; Samuel sympathized with its ideals.[12]

In 1846, Isaac Mayer Wise arrived in New York from Bohemia. The son of a very poor family, Wise received his Jewish education from his father, a teacher, and from yeshiva and secular university studies in Prague. He, too, served as a rabbi in Bohemia before coming to America. Although he took a pulpit in Albany, he remained an integral part of the New York scene, where he lectured, examined students, spoke to literary societies, and edited the literary section of the *Asmonean*. He quickly assumed the helm of the Reform movement in America.[13]

Rabbinical leadership in nineteenth-century New York was a new phenomenon. Yet despite rabbis' superior knowledge of Jewish religion and Jewish history, they deferred to boards of trustees, who remained by law governing bodies of the congregations, and zealously guarded their prerogatives. Each considered its rabbi an employee, along with the shochet and shamash, even though rabbis often represented the Jewish community to the Christian world. The boards did not want any employee, including its prominent leaders who joined the distinguished clergy of the city, speaking about controversial subjects, jeopardizing Jewish standing in the community. The boards also maintained discipline in the synagogue, fining members who spoke out of turn or insulted or threatened the authority of the parnas, the president of the board.[14]

■ The Synagogue at Work

Synagogues continued to play a role in the lives of Israelites. Julius Bien, a leader of B'nai B'rith, recalled that "it became a social necessity for a man of family to join a congregation," though the meaning of membership was in question. The High Holy Days remained solemn events for the Jewish community. Peddlers returned home. Jews filled synagogues; many "temporary places for worship" were "fitted up." Jewish retailers, unwilling to give up Saturdays for business, closed on Rosh Hashanah and Yom Kippur. For observant Jews, synagogues remained critical, monitoring kashrut and providing the means and necessities for Jewish rituals. Boards of trustees continued to spend hours ensuring that certified kosher meat and matzos were available. They worked hard to maintain cemeteries, as city ordinances required burial grounds to be moved outside city limits, often creating conflict with Jewish law. With the arrival of educated Jewish leaders, a few synagogues became focal points for sophisticated religious discussion. The elegant sanctuaries also provided their members considerable prestige.[15]

Synagogues served as the site for life-cycle ceremonies from the bris (circumcision) of a newborn baby boy to bar mitzvah, marriage, and death. Wedding ceremonies for family members of small congregations often occurred at home, while the more prominent used the major synagogues. These were often large festive affairs, with merrymaking following the nuptials under the canopy. Processions through the city, particularly for notables, often preceded funerals, a Jewish tradition dating to the colonial era. In 1851, when Mordecai M. Noah died, a "dense crowd" thronged the streets near his home on Broadway between Bleecker and Houston. Doctors, authors, merchants, editors, and artisans walked behind the hearse to the cemetery on Twenty-First Street, along with members of benevolent and literary societies, B'nai B'rith, and synagogue representatives. The ceremony was held outdoors to accommodate the throng.[16]

Synagogue decorum continued to bedevil the trustees, as they sought to emulate the dignity of Protestant services. In 1854, Shearith Israel's board received a memorial from members complaining of the rapid reading of prayers that no one could understand, of absurd and meaningless motions of the body, of long services, and of the absence of lectures to rekindle piety. An anonymous contributor to the *Asmonean*, "W," wondered why the "liberal and philosophic" spirit of the synagogue had vanished. He urged members dissatisfied with the stubborn conservatism of the Board of Trustees, which branded dissenters as infidels, to "be of good courage" and to "fear not those who walk among us as living mummies." Change will come, and "truth will triumph."

In response, the trustees posted signs in "conspicuous" places in the sanctuary stating that "in case of impropriety of conduct or too much CONVERSA-TION the parties offending would be removed . . . by the Shamash upon the order of the Parnas." Shearith Israel was not alone. In 1844, Anshe Chesed banned conversation during services and proposed fines for anyone who read prayers aloud or chanted with the choir. B'nai Jeshurun's board removed Barrow Cohen, Shearith Israel's former nemesis, from his office as secretary for calling a member a "damned liar." (He first denied the charge, then apologized and was reinstated.)[17]

In antebellum New York, the growing Jewish population of single men and women mingled freely with the non-Jewish population. Not surprisingly, intermarriage increased, as did requests for conversion. The exact proportion of Jews who intermarried is unattainable but is estimated at one-quarter. Until the 1830s, synagogues adopted a moderate approach, allowing the Jewish member of an intermarriage to retain his or her seat, and even to be an elector. After the 1830s, this attitude changed. In 1835 and 1847, Shearith Israel's trustees ruled that no seat could be held by anyone "married contrary to [its] Religious Laws" and prepared a responsum equating intermarriage with idolatry. Consequently, any man participating in an illegal marriage had to be expelled from the congregation. Other synagogues followed suit. In 1852, the *Asmonean* reported that B'nai Jeshurun barred a man who was allegedly married by a Baptist minister. Marriages performed outside of synagogues challenged synagogue authority. In 1850, Reverend Samuel Isaacs termed Rabbi Henry Goldberg a "criminal" deserving "punishment" for divorcing and marrying Jews contrary to Jewish law.[18]

The synagogues' hostility to intermarriage reflected a communal attitude. Bavarian Christian immigrant Franz Schano wrote a telling letter to his in-laws in 1853 about his sister-in-law, Babett, who became pregnant by a young Jewish man. The father of the child-to-be refused to marry Babett, stating that he had not promised marriage and that "he was Jewish and wouldn't abandon his faith and didn't want to hurt his family." He ultimately agreed to pay Babett $100 to settle his responsibility. The point of this story is as much the strong ties binding Jewish families and community as the youth's unfortunate behavior.[19]

Nor were congregations willing to convert prospective spouses. In 1835, Shearith Israel turned down two requests for conversion. Denouncing a charlatan rabbi in the *Jewish Messenger*, Reverend Isaacs asserted, "we want no proselytes." Experience demonstrated that "changing the outer garb fails in altering the inner feeling." Admitting converts would only "tarnish the bright banner" of their "blessed religion." Ten years later, he charged congregation Rodeph Shalom with allowing the marriage of a proselyte converted outside of Jewish law. (Rodeph Shalom denied the act.) "What do we want of converts?" he asked, as "such neophytes" were "seldom heard of again." Since Jewish law allowed conversion, the *Messenger* advocated an intensive investigation prior to any ceremony to "preserve the purity of Israel" from the stain of "commixture or admixture." The "purity of Israel" emerged as a significant issue in the mid-nineteenth century, perhaps enhanced by the heated contemporary controversies over slavery and race. Did the Bible not demand purity among the Hebrews?[20]

While Isaacs represented the norm, there were dissenters. Writing in the *Asmonean*, "A Friend of Truth" argued that "Jews may accept of proselytes"; they were received from the earliest days of Jewish history: for "our religion is for the world, . . . not for us alone." Indeed, "the more friends Judah acquires, the more its benevolent and simple doctrines penetrate the walls of prejudice." Isaacs's views were "extreme, untenable and unJudaic." Proselytes should know that, if synagogues refused them entrance, the "bone and sinews of the Jews will gladly admit them." The Reform movement accepted converts. In 1859, Rabbi Samuel Adler of Temple Emanu-El converted a Christian woman in an English ceremony—to the consternation of the Orthodox.[21]

■ The Synagogues and Jewish Education in Antebellum New York

The education of Jewish children, traditionally a synagogue responsibility, fell solidly into the hands of the public school system in the mid-nineteenth century, though not without competition from the city's congregations. By the 1840s, the Public School Society dominated education, opening branches throughout New York. Despite its Protestant-tinged curriculum, most Jewish parents sent their children to these schools. Shearith Israel and B'nai Jeshurun, reluctant to cede their role in educating Jewish youth, joined seven Catholic schools in 1840 in an unsuccessful petition for public aid. These efforts instead persuaded the state to require that its money be used exclusively for secular education and to institute a public board of education. Unlike Catholics, Jews gradually came to see the public schools as an opportunity for free education and admission to the economic and social opportunities of the republic.[22]

Despite reorganizations, a Protestant outlook remained in the curriculum. In 1843, Jewish residents complained to public school trustees of the Fourth Ward, a district in the Lower East Side with a large Jewish population, that a number of books in use were either anti-Jewish or promoted Christianity. One book, for example, *Conversations* by reformer Dorothy Dix, declared that "the gospel was first sent to them [the Jews], but they, with the exception of a few disciples, rejected its precepts and ignominiously crucified their Savior," and a popular speller lamented that a Jew would not "give a shekel to a starving shepherd." The Board of Education rejected the complaint on the grounds that "Jews have not . . . and cannot have the same privileges as those who embrace the Christian religion." Providing free education did not "give them the right of changing or interfering with [Christians'] own religious institutions." The New Testament was part of the national culture during the Second Great Awakening in the early to mid-nineteenth century. The Jewish community continued to resist this influence and, under pressure, the board allowed local schools to control Bible readings. By the mid-1850s, the state legislature and Board of Education moved toward "tolerance and local option." If the Bible was read, no commentary was permitted. This made the public schools in the wards where most Jews dwelt more acceptable.[23]

Attempting to counter the popularity of public education, in the 1850s, a number of congregations, following the example of Anshe Chesed, which began the first parochial synagogue school in 1845, established Jewish day schools offering secular courses taught by non-Jews and a Jewish curriculum taught by Jewish instructors. Eight synagogues and as many as 850 Jewish children, perhaps 10 percent of the Israelite school-age population, participated. In 1853, Shaaray Zedek, seeking to educate children "in the tenets of their holy and Venerable Religion" and in the "elements of moral and social truths" and to "enable them to claim an equal right, and uphold a due rank among their American fellow citizens," began a school whose Judaic curriculum included Hebrew reading, writing, and translation; the codes of the *Shulchan Aruch*; and the Torah with commentaries. English education incorporated reading, writing, arithmetic, grammar, geography, science, history, and bookkeeping; girls received instruction in needle work and drawing. Each day opened and closed with a Hebrew prayer.[24]

The most celebrated school, the B'nai Jeshurun Educational Institute, opened its own building with great fanfare in 1854, with a floor each for the primary school, the school for older boys, and advanced classes for young ladies. The congregation's leader, Morris Raphall, predicted that, with proper education, a Jew "in a few years" might occupy the "Presidential Chair of the United States." At the school's dedication, Jewish leaders declared education the "pole-star of the Jews throughout their long history," allowing them to preserve "enlightenment through centuries of barbarism." Soon New York's schools would compare to the academies in Babylon. The school's public examinations were a source of pride. Drs. Max Lilienthal and Isaac Mayer Wise officiated in 1854 as children from six to twelve responded in Hebrew, German, and English.[25]

The institute lasted only two years, a year less than Shaaray Zedek, each school closing because of financial losses. (Anshe Chesed's school closed in 1857.) Too few parents were willing or able to pay the tuition. The demise of parochial schools caused "great confusion" in the Orthodox Jewish community. The decline in Hebrew education meant that fewer boys read the haftorah portion at their bar mitzvah services. The *Messenger* foresaw peril for the Jewish community. Editor Isaacs noted that while Jewish children trained to become good citizens and industrious workers, their education as Jews was deplorable. Parents would be held "responsible at the Bar of unerring Justice" for this sin. The city had "splendid synagogues" but scarcely a nursery or "proper school house." Learning to read but not understand Hebrew, Jewish children lacked "a chart and compass to guide them through the rough storms of life, [and they are] compelled to grope their way in mental darkness." Moreover, the public schools threatened the "perpetuity of Israel." Would children not inevitably hear Christian doctrine? How many young Israelites would feel the "blush of shame" when they heard their religion denigrated and their ancestors vilified by schoolmates? They were too young to defend their faith. "J.C." admonished parents that these "Christian schools" taught religion in every subject, including the sciences.[26]

The failure of the synagogue academies meant that Jews voted with their feet for the public schools. The *Asmonean* likely represented popular sentiment when it editorialized that the city's schools were "unrivalled . . . for the amount and quality of instruction" they afforded to their pupils. There was "no degradation" in placing Jewish children in these schools, no "sting of charity." The public system strengthened Judaism in the city: "entwining more closely the social ties which connect us with our fellow citizens, and fully carrying out that fraternization of which American liberty and equality are the basics." Improvements, of course, were warranted. One correspondent reported a petition to have Hebrew taught with Latin and Greek. Another complained that Protestants chose Bible selections "indiscriminately"; rather, "the Public Schools should be held perfectly free from religious or political taint." Editor Lyon lobbied for a public supplementary education system for Jewish education.[27]

What could be done for Jewish education? As a first step, the *Messenger* urged each congregation to open a Sunday school "for the improvement of the young." This solution proved as popular in New York as in Philadelphia, where Rebecca Gratz first introduced it. In 1861, five synagogues were open on Sunday for instruction—one with 250 students. As opposed to public schools, "Robinson Crusoe [was] abandoned for the catechism, negro melodies for the inspiring Hebrew hymns, and tops and marbles for the instruction books." Without Sunday schools, Jewish children "would have remained totally ignorant of their God and His wondrous doings!"[28]

One morning a week was, of course, insufficient. In the 1860s, the day school movement, responding to the threat of missionaries, struggled to initiate a Jewish public school. In 1865, Free School No. 1 opened with the moral support of the mayor and a donation of furniture by the Board of Education. Jewish spokesmen praised the city for demonstrating the "liberality of our American institutions," which understood that the Jewish faith "requires a distinct course of training," and praised the Jewish community for providing poor Jewish children the "spiritual food" and "religious comfort" that their parents could not afford. However, without public fiscal support beyond the donation of tables and chairs, no network of Jewish free schools could survive. Public schools continued to be vehicles of education of New York's Jewish children.[29]

In 1850, Dr. Lilienthal, unwilling to put up with the arrogance and demands of boards of trustees, shifted his energies back to education, opening the Hebrew Commercial and Classical Boarding School on Tenth Street. Some of the city's prominent Jews sent their children there, including Mordecai M. Noah. Lilienthal taught religion, Hebrew grammar, and translation, and additional instructors gave lessons in history, geography, arithmetic, and bookkeeping and, for an extra fee, music, dancing, and drawing. Influenced by Johann Pestalozzi, a Swiss educator who advocated parental love rather than harsh discipline in the classroom, Lilienthal sought to create a family of teachers and students. He reasoned that in America, where Jewish children lacked a yeshiva background, instruction must proceed from a simple to an enriched catechism expressing the immortality of the soul and the unity of God. As a young Jew, "the child is trained to become a good man," as his faith leads him to become a tolerant and benevolent citizen. Christianity must be taught with respect, enabling these youths to live happily with their neighbors. Lilienthal stressed the importance of mentors; a student "becomes good with a teacher who is true and sincere." The school closed when Lilienthal moved to Cincinnati in 1855.[30]

The Free Academy (to become the City College of New York in 1866) attracted a number of Jewish scholars. The *Asmonean* proudly noted its progress and curriculum in 1851, though the *Messenger* criticized its policy of holding classes on Jewish holidays as harmful to Jewish students who missed classes on these days. But where were Jewish institutions of higher learning? Both the *Messenger* and *Asmonean* called for the establishment of seminaries to train Jewish educators and clergy. The *Messenger* published an ad for a Hebrew high school under Reverend Isaacs, with English, mathematical, and classical departments, but there is no evidence that the school succeeded. Sampson Simson left funds in his will for a Jewish college, but it did not materialize. Despite pleas for higher education, the community did not respond.[31]

The New York City public schools became legendary institutions of Americanization for immigrants of the late nineteenth and early twentieth centuries. These institutions did much the same for German Jewish immigrants of the 1840s and 1850s, as well as for the native born. That most Jews preferred these schools to parochial synagogue schools stemmed in part from their lower cost, but also from a desire that their children integrate into American life.

■ Women and the Synagogue

Nineteenth-century American Christianity underwent a period of "feminization" as women became the mainstay of church congregations, the most reliable attendees at Sabbath services, the most conscientious members of committees, and the most pious element of the membership. Was there any parallel movement in New York's Jewish congregations? While Jewish women hardly achieved the same place in Jewish religious practice that Christian women attained, since many received little religious education and preferred the secular pursuits that the city offered the Jewish community, evidence exists of female

In 1852, Reverend Morris Raphall of B'nai Jeshurun published his Rachama exercises (devotional prayers) to meet the special spiritual needs of women who could not follow or attend regular services. It was an attempt by the Orthodox community to respond to the needs of women in the metropolitan world of New York. (*Asmonean*, 24 April 1852)

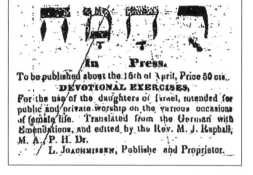

influence. The new synagogues all constructed large women's galleries. Indeed, Shearith Israel's 1834 Crosby Street sanctuary contained thirty more seats for women than for men. Moreover, women maintained female benevolent societies in every large synagogue, contributing to poor relief, and were members of burial societies. There is all too little testimony of the nature of female religiosity. One observer, however, an anonymous visitor from Germany who lived in New York in 1853 and wrote disparagingly of the city's synagogues, declared that the "spirituality" of Jewish women "overcomes the American environment" and that "pious women . . . are often the moving force behind congregations." If his perception has credence, the influence of women, especially their presence at services, was significant.[32]

One female correspondent addressed the issue of women's religiosity in the *Jewish Messenger*, condemning the deportment of the sexes in synagogue and the lack of Jewish religiosity in educated young women. Another young lady, "Une Enfante Terrible," complained that men came to synagogue only on holidays and Sabbaths, when women were certain to be in attendance. She scorned young men in "faultless neck ties" who "sauntered" into the sanctuary when the service was three-fourths over to ogle women instead of reading prayers. Responding to "Enfante," "An Observer" blamed the ladies for encouraging the attention given them; "Enfante," revealing an awareness of the women's rights movement, asked to see even "one solitary man who will give up his right to dictate and rule, to follow the example of one of [her] sex." The "presence of a few score" men would be more effective in filling the "now-vacant seats" in the galleries than lectures were. She found it interesting that when holidays fell on Sundays, and more men were present, "all the ladies attend."

"A Lady" told "Observer" that if he attended Sabbath services, he would see "the gallery full of [her] sex," while the men's section was "a very poor show." These contradictory exchanges show more concern with who is to blame for laxity in attendance than with piety. However, they also hint that women were spiritual mainstays at some congregations.[33]

Orthodox men's response regarding the place of women was strictly paternal. One correspondent wrote that unlike men, "the female mind is inspired by the quiet of domestic life"; as a consequence, "the chief honor of a female is religion." She must, therefore, have a good religious education to bring up her children correctly. "The Voice of Jacob," after detailing the heroic roles of Ruth, Hannah, Miriam, and Judith in Jewish history, and while dismissing the writings of the ancient rabbis as vestiges of a segregated world, reasoned that women should be educated, just not in the "subtleties of theology," which might induce them away "from their proper duties."[34]

The apotheosis of this view came in a book of devotions for women by New York's leading Jewish spiritual leader, Morris Raphall. His introduction noted that women lived "at all times" in the "charmed and charming circle of domestic duty and domestic bliss, of which as wife and as mother, she is the presiding and guardian genius." With little religious education, traditional prayer had limited appeal for women. In the spirit of the *techinoth* (private devotions) of the mediaeval era, it was appropriate to write special prayers for women. These included "Reflections of a Bride" before marriage, with the bride-to-be asking for "understanding, intelligence, strength and ability" in order to "manage [the husband's] household in a manner becoming an affectionate and faithful wife." She prayed that she not indulge in "vain and absurd pretensions" that would take from her husband "the hard earned fruits of *his* industry" and that she "meekly rest content with [the] humble lot" that God chose for her, whether it be joy or sadness. Raphall advised a wife entrapped in an unhappy marriage to understand that the "chastisement" of the unfortunate union was the rightful punishment of God. He instructed her to pray: "Teach me to subdue my stubborn disposition that I may be able to meet [my husband's] censures with meekness, his reproofs with submission, his ill-temper with kindness." A good wife was a good wife forever.[35]

With the decline of the synagogue's ability to educate the young, "Here and There," an occasional columnist for the *Jewish Messenger*, expressed concern with the level of female education, declaring that Jewish girls had "every opportunity of the acquisition of a liberal education" and yet were woefully ignorant of "their faith." They witnessed their parents' nonobservance of Jewish law and followed that path, "unmindful of the danger ahead." Parents who sent their daughters to fashionable schools yet provided no religious instruction failed as mothers and fathers. More was expected from the "Women of Israel." They must become aware of their hallowed traditions and concern themselves with the "jewel" as well as the "casket."[36]

■ Anti-Semitism at Home and Abroad

While congregations guarded their autonomy, synagogues united to protest outrageous foreign acts of anti-Semitism. When in 1840 a Damascene Jew was accused of a ritual murder, thousands gathered in anger. Leading members of congregations sent letters to the president of the United States and received a positive response. The largest outcry arose over the Mortara case in 1858, in which a Jewish child was torn from his home in Italy under Catholic law because his nursemaid secretly baptized him at age six. Synagogues led and hosted protest gatherings. Delegates of twelve synagogues met at the home of Reverend Raphall to plan protests, including a mass meeting of over three thousand Jewish citizens at Mozart Hall. Following speeches by politicians and Jewish leaders, the assembly adopted a resolution stating that the "kidnapping" recalled the "dark ages." President James Buchanan declined to intervene in the affairs of another sovereign country, perhaps concerned about alienating the Catholic Democratic vote. He did, however, personally answer the letter of Benjamin Hart, president of B'nai Jeshurun.[37]

The Mortara affair instigated an effort to found an American Jewish union. There were multiple obstacles. The vast distances between American synagogues in the United States, significant differences and enmities among nationalities, and hostility between Reform and Orthodox congregations posed barriers. The *Jewish Messenger* pleaded for a national board of Jewish congregations to enable Jews to have a greater influence in national affairs. Editor Isaacs preferred a chief rabbi to enforce common standards among synagogues but, knowing that to be impossible, strove for a loose political union. He contended that there were many republics (congregations) but no federal union. After the Mortara affair, representatives of eleven Orthodox New York congregations and twelve congregations from cities ranging from New Orleans to St. Louis met in New York. John Hart of Shaaray Tefilah, Isaac's synagogue, chaired the meeting. In 1859, the Board of Delegates was established with headquarters in New York. It pledged no interference in party politics or internal affairs of congregations, though this did not prevent Reform congregations from boycotting, along with Shearith Israel, which never felt comfortable with Ashkenazi congregations. In 1861, the board led the quest for Jewish army chaplains and, in 1863, expressed the community's shock over General Ulysses S. Grant's expulsion of Jews from his War Department.[38]

Local anti-Semitism prior to 1830 surfaced mostly when Jews entered elective politics, notably during Mordecai M. Noah's run for sheriff in 1824. That occurred when Jews, composing less than 0.5 percent of the city's population, were barely noticeable. With a population nearing 5 percent of city residents, merchants gaining financial standing, areas of the city clearly recognizable as Jewish neighborhoods, and elegant synagogues appearing as noticeable markers of a Jewish presence, anti-Jewish sentiment became far more common. With visibility, the impression of Jews in the press worsened.[39]

Some newspapers and magazines commonly pictured Jews as parvenus rapaciously climbing the economic ladder as they flaunted material success and opulence. Journalists singled out Jewish proprietors of stores on Chatham Street for shame and ridicule as pinchpennies. A *Pen-and-Ink Panorama of New York City* mused that "the old red men scalped their enemies, the Chatham clo' men skin theirs." Even the *New York Times*, a paper favorably inclined to the Jewish community, reported stories confirming a Jewish propensity for dishonest commerce. In 1855, it reported on a customer being maltreated by a Chatham Street merchant by being "abusively ejected into the street," conduct that is "hourly repeated by those people at every clothing store." Their behavior to "respectable young females" was "highly offensive." Another story recounted how "aggrieved parties" took revenge on Jewish clothes vendors for "being taken in and done for." A third notice told of the plight of poor sewing women exploited "by the Chatham St. Jews" (as well as by wealthy Christian store owners). Jews working in the stock market also suffered as common targets. *A Week in Wall Street* described underhanded traders named "Solomon Single-Eye" and "Jacob Broker" and "King Saul," out for "a pound of flesh." By 1860, the term *Jew one down* had entered the American lexicon, nowhere more so than in New York.[40]

Politics continued to be a common source of anti-Semitism, as more Jews attained elective and appointive office. The most important political figure remained Mordecai M. Noah, until his death in 1851. Active in Democratic and conservative Whig politics, an editor of major newspapers, and a judge, Noah was an outspoken politician who maintained a strong Jewish identity. James Gordon Bennett, a Scotch immigrant, former seminarian, and editor of the anti-Semitic *New York Herald*, continuously attacked Noah. In one issue, he doubted whether "Mordecai M. Noah and his better half, with all the fat feathers, and false jewelry she could muster, the first from the sausage stalls of Washington market, the latter from the old clo' shops of Chatham row, could have made a better show."[41]

The 1850s witnessed a revival of evangelicalism and, with it, religiously motivated attacks on the Jewish community. Evangelical Harvey P. Peet, president of the New York Institution for the Deaf and Dumb, wrote a pamphlet, *Scripture Lessons for the Young*, that vividly pictured Jews calling for Jesus's death as they "lead him to the cross" and "reviled him." Ever after, "Jews hated Christians and persecuted them." For their sins, they have been "scattered among all nations." The Episcopal *Churchman* raged against "blaspheming Jews," the "infuriate infidel," the "malicious, bigoted hypocrites." During the Mortara affair, the *New York Tablet*, a Catholic paper, charged that Catholics had always treated Jews well, but, alas, Jews, "with the[ir] acquisitive instinct," have "turned the indulgence of the Pontiffs to the best account and have in many instances made fortunes by it." The *Herald*, commenting on a prayer by a Jewish rabbi before Congress, predicted that soon "we shall have a pawnshop in the basement" of the House of Representatives. On Yom Kippur 1850, a crowd of mostly Irish immigrants broke into a Jewish home in Brooklyn, believing its inhabitants had killed a Christian girl for a Jewish feast.[42]

Educated men also harbored anti-Semitic feelings. Charles King, future president of Columbia College, declared Jews "deficient" in patriotism. *Harper's Magazine*, a weekly catering to the middle class, stated that Jews' "future in this country, as in Europe, is a problem which is well deserving of sober thought." Lawyer and civic figure George Templeton Strong observed that if, during a theater performance, a member of the audience yelled out "Farmer's Loan and Trust Co.," these words would have "an appalling effect on the hook-nosed and black-whiskered congregation." Additionally, he remarked, Jews' form of worship was "utterly unlike that of any Christian culture I have ever witnessed." A Walt Whitman prose sketch described "dirty looking German Jews," and a Herman Melville short story about Manhattan depicted "a Jew with hospitable speeches, cozening some fainting stranger into ambuscade, there to burk him."[43]

Although the city's two Jewish weeklies were not official organs of the synagogue, they became the principal vehicles refuting these charges of anti-Semitism. The *Asmonean*, edited by Robert Lyon, a former merchant and also a member at Shaaray Tefilah and the voice of the emerging Reform movement, and the Orthodox *Jewish Messenger*, edited by the Reverend Samuel Isaacs of Shaaray Tefilah, while focusing on synagogue notices, community news, sermons, and articles about Jewish history and thought, promptly responded to the anti-Semitic charges, particularly those in the mainstream press. When the *Herald* used the Damascus affair as an excuse for publishing an article on the "mysteries of the Talmud" that alleged Jewish blood-libel murder plots, the *Asmonean* accused editor Bennett of "catering to the morbid appetites of ignorant and prejudiced immigrants" by singling Jews out as criminals. The *Asmonean* refuted an article in the *Journal of Commerce* that claimed that Jews were as identifiable in public as the African-American population because of their separate dwellings and behavior. It accused an attorney of anti-Semitism for stating in a trial that "he would not believe a Jew under oath where money is concerned." (The attorney, Chauncey Stouffer, felt compelled to write an apology, stating that he was speaking under "excitement" and that he numbered "among the Israelites of th[e] city" some of his "best and most steadfast friends.") Editor Lyon confronted a New York state senator for accusing German Jews of adulterating the liquor they sold; excoriated a book published in Germany that wrote of a girl being killed in New York on Yom Kippur; and lobbied successfully for Mayor Fernando Wood to investigate police conduct relating to a fire in which the Jewish proprietor of a clothing store was charged with murder for the death of his family. Many tales that disparaged Jews were challenged without timidity.[44]

The *Jewish Messenger* registered particular sensitivity to another form of anti-Semitism, at least in the eyes of the Jewish community: aggressive Protestant missionaries who attempted to convert Jews. Isaac Mayer Wise recalled in his *Reminiscences* that in 1849 the Presbyterian General Assembly issued a manifesto demanding that Jews enter the Presbyterian Church. This aroused both Presbyterian missionaries and those of other Protestant sects, so that "the whole country swarmed with conversion-apostles and the conversion of the Jews was lauded in all pulpits as highly praiseworthy." The *New York Times* published numerous reports of the meetings of the American Society for Meliorating the Condition of the Jews. These missionaries expressed ambivalent attitudes toward the Jewish community, praising their industriousness while yet terming them "infidel Jews." Missionaries sought to provide "an open door of the entrance of the gospel into thousands of Jewish families," particularly as they believed that half the Jews in America never let it be known that they were Jewish. Another report stated that missionaries preached to Jews "in the highways, in their dwellings, in their synagogues, and in Christian churches." The *Asmonean* reported that missionaries tended to visit hospitals and dispensaries seeking out Jewish patients, assuring them that they could not be saved unless they converted. Spiritual leaders and Jewish newspapers constantly condemned these attacks on their community.[45]

The demands and opportunities of the expanding American democracy sharply limited the role of the synagogue. It was no longer the center of Jewish existence. However, to a considerable degree, it carved out a niche compatible with an expanding American and Jewish population living in a sophisticated, cosmopolitan, democratic environment. New synagogues met the needs of the different immigrant nationalities. The growth of costly ornate synagogues and the hiring of prominent spiritual leaders provided an important means for the more affluent Jews to display their integration and success in the American republic. Adapting to the public school, as representative an institution as any of the dominance of a maturing republican ethos, they lowered their expectations to a subsidiary pedagogical role. They continued to maintain a venue for important life-cycle events and for the High Holy Day services, which, if they were less important in providing spiritual content, remained a coalescing communal forum. Indeed, the synagogue's most important role was as a unifying force within the powerful secular and Christian allures of Manhattan society. The synagogue, allied with Jewish newspapers, remained the most important defense against a growing anti-Semitism, the product of resentment of Jews' greater and more visible role in New York society. What the synagogue largely failed to do, however, was to offer a religious path that would appeal to both native-born and immigrant Jews who sought spiritual guidance relevant to a modern society, a society that was in part the product of the European and American Enlightenments. Ideas espoused in the sanctuary often lacked appeal to those who frequented the lodges, literary societies, and theaters.

"Two are better than One, and a Threefold Cord is not quickly broken."

The weekly *Asmonean*, New York's first lasting English-language newspaper intended for the Jewish community, began publishing in 1849 and continued until editor Robert Lyon's sudden death in 1858. Named for the grandfather of Mattathias, head of the Maccabean family of priests, it saw itself as a vehicle for Jewish renewal and became the voice of the emerging Jewish Reform movement. The phrase about the threefold knot refers to the three divisions of Jews—Kohens, Levites, and Israelis—and represents a plea for Jewish unity. (*Asmonean*, 23 November 1849)

CHAPTER 10

The Challenge of Reform

In the summer of 1846, Isaac Mayer Wise, the future leader of American Reform Jewry, only a few weeks in New York after a harrowing sixty-three-day voyage, was in despair. His attempt to teach English had failed, and he had but a few dollars to his name. Fellow Jews advised him to become a peddler. Instead he decided to take one more chance and called at the home of Rabbi Max Lilienthal on Eldridge Street. Their meeting changed the course of American Judaism. Lilienthal welcomed Wise and started him on a momentous career. This meeting of like minds who envisioned radical changes to the practice of Judaism made New York the scene of a momentous contest in American Jewish history.[1]

■ The Synagogue in Crisis

While architecturally graceful and opulent sanctuaries announced the growing standing of the city's Jews, congregations played a diminished spiritual role among the Jewish population. Threadbare attendance at weekly and daily services presaged serious problems. Antebellum New York was not colonial or even republican New York. Its Jewish community was far more diverse and becoming increasingly secular. Moreover, Jews, like the city they lived in, focused on the world of the entrepreneur. How relevant could a synagogue be in such a booming capitalist society?

Visitors' reports reveal problems facing synagogues in antebellum New York. Lydia Child, a favorably inclined liberal Christian reformer from Boston, attended Rosh Hashanah observances at Shearith Israel in 1841. She found the services "a vanishing resemblance to reality; the magic lantern of the past." Men, she reported, wore "fringed silk mantles, bordered with blue stripes" and "dreary" modern European hats. The black silk robes of the hazan reminded her of an Episcopal priest. The hazan led the service, but in fact the chanting consisted of "monotonous ups and downs of the voice, which, when the whole congregation joined in it, sounded like the continuous roars of the sea." The "ceremonies were in a cold mechanical style," less earnest and less pious than those at a Catholic church. The use of only Hebrew made the prayers "a series of unintelligible sounds." In other words, services continued as they had for generations, led by a hazan, with each member praying at his or her own pace. Child, of course, understood no Hebrew, but that was also true of much of the Jewish community. Isaac Mayer Wise declared that the "majority of Israelites" did not understand Hebrew prayers, resulting in a "want of devotion" at services. Decorum was lacking "because the worshippers do not know what they say."[2]

In 1873, Wise reminisced about the state of the synagogues in New York upon his arrival from Bohemia in 1846. Shearith Israel's ritual, he recalled, was "antiquated and tedious." "Crass ignorance" ruled B'nai Jeshurun, as the shamash laughed when Wise asked for a copy of the Mishnah, basic books of Jewish law. He found only ignorance at Polish synagogue Shaaray Zedek, and the German congregations, including Anshe Chesed, were as "ill-behaved as in Germany." The hazan at Anshe Chesed "trilled like a nightingale and leaped out like a hooked fish." Wise could not endure the "intolerable sing-song" of the service. An anonymous German visitor who lived in New York from 1853 to 1854 also criticized Shearith Israel, where, he observed, the presidents sat on "thrones." At the service, the congregation went through the rituals, but "little of the inner self is involved. Spanish self-complacency and American custom combine to smother the seed of life." Great attention was given to ritual detail, while "all else is neglected." Hazan Lyons, "after gurgling out his trill . . . looks around for applause, especially from the women." All congregations were "unkind and un-Jewish" to strangers. A group of "well-dressed, respectable and earnest German Jews" were "brutally kicked out" of a Sukkoth celebration of a non-German congregation. It was not that New York did not contain pious Jews, but "piety is not expressed in congregational life."[3]

By the 1850s, most Jews in New York City did not belong to a synagogue. So that congregations could supplement their income, they allowed Jews to purchase High Holy Day seats without becoming members. The actual number of dues-paying members is unknown. Based on population estimates compared with the number of congregations in the city, it would have taken an average of eight hundred members per synagogue just to reach a 50 percent membership. Many were small; thus, it is likely that no more than a quarter of the population paid membership dues.

Congregations had traditionally overseen and even enforced community adherence to Jewish ritual observance. This prerogative ended. European Jewish leaders referred to nineteenth-century America as a *"terepha"* (unkosher) land. Attempts by synagogues to enforce adherence failed. At B'nai Jeshurun, Samuel Isaacs unsuccessfully sought to exclude the nonobservant from membership. The first trustees of Anshe Chesed decreed that Sabbath violators would be denied seats; this rule went unmentioned after 1840, though officers had to conform to Jewish law (a hazan was suspended for eating with his head uncovered). Shaaray Zedek's bylaw that no member could be "elected to office if he keeps open his Shop on Sabbath" soon became obsolete. Isaac Leeser, Philadelphia editor of the *Occident*, wrote that censure of individuals for an offense against spiritual authority had long been abandoned. He doubted "whether a single Hasid could be found in this country."[4]

Violation of the Sabbath, the cornerstone of Judaism, caused congregational leaders great anxiety and concern. Reverend Samuel Isaacs lamented that "in the days of yore" Sabbath transgressors were "publicly stoned"; today they are given "first honors in the synagogue." The *Jewish Messenger* bemoaned that despite attractive sanctuaries "dedicated to the service of the most High, . . . a melancholy view of empty seats is present on every Sabbath." A correspondent anguished over the "woefully empty benches" of a rainy Saturday. In 1844, Hazan Lyons of Shearith Israel wrote his board that congregants at Sabbath and holiday services often had to wait a quarter of an hour for a minyan of ten men, after which they were compelled to "omit an important portion of the Service." A few years later, Isaac Mayer Wise reported that if he and two strangers had not attended Shearith Israel one Friday eve, "there would have been no minyan" to hear the "benumbed forms of the Middle Ages, . . . the beautiful canons of the age of William the Conqueror."[5]

Jews not only did not attend Sabbath services, but they openly violated its strictures by working on the day of rest. Refuting an article in the *New York Herald* that Jews were adopting Sundays as their Sabbath so they could work on Saturday, the *Messenger* argued that these charges arose from "neglect of religious duties." Were Israelites not aware that "they must be laughed at for supposing their religion unknown because they do business on Sabbath?"

MIKVAH SYNAGOGUE,
GREEN STREET.

MRS. NOOT (wife of the Rev. S. C. Noot,) respectfully begs to inform Hebrew Ladies, that the above
Mikvah is now open, fitted up with every attention to their
comfort, and in strict accordance with the requirements of the
Law,

Mrs. Noot respectfully trusts wives and mothers in Israel
will not take it amiss if she presumes to remind them of an indispensable religious duty incumbent on them, and which can
only be performed in a Mikvah lawfully constructed; any other
mode is unlawful, and therefore, in a religious point of view,
void and altogether useless.

Mrs. Noot will deem it a privilege to be permitted personally
to attend on the Ladies visiting the Mikvah.

New York, June 29, 5713.

According to Jewish law, women were required to immerse themselves in a ritual bath
following their menstrual cycle. However, only 1 percent did so, which points to the
decline in ritual observance. A few synagogues, such as B'nai Jeshurun on Greene Street,
built *mikvehs* and advertised for their use. (*Asmonean*, 9 July 1853)

"Professor B." asked "if Chatham Street is not a crying abuse, a stain, a foul
spot upon the New York Israelites," lowering them in "general esteem." It was
distressing that energetic Jewish merchants who achieved "mercantile success"
would "willfully and publicly violate the Sabbath." Reverend Isaacs asked "every Jewish merchant, importer, tradesman or mechanic, every attorney and
counselor" to follow the example of Jewish communities in Paris, London, and
Frankfort and "make up his mind resolutely to do no work whatever on Sabbath." On "streets abounding with Israelite merchants," Jews should "meet as
brethren to discuss the best means for doing their duty as Israelites."[6]

New York's Jews regularly neglected dietary laws. One correspondent declared, "at the present day, parents, with few exceptions, especially when away
from home, with their family, regard the said law as obsolete and unfit for our
time." Yet these very laws were responsible for the "adamantine wall of separation" that kept Israelites a separate people, "turning back attempts" to "amal-
gamate" with them. As America's first ordained rabbi, Abraham Rice of Baltimore, lamented, "most of the Jews eat forbidden food and profane the Sabbath
openly and nobody pays any attention."[7]

Few women observed the commandments mandating that a married woman immerse herself in a ritual bath (*mikveh*) after her period of menstruation, a ritual that allowed her to resume sexual relations with her spouse. Only a few synagogues maintained *mikvaot*. Hyman Grinstein calculates that only two hundred women out of twenty thousand used the *mikveh* regularly. While no sermons have come to light faulting women for failing to undergo purification, an 1853 advertisement by "Mrs. Noot" to the "wives and mothers of Israel" praised the features of B'nai Jeshurun's *mikveh*, "fitted up with every attention to their comfort, and in strict accordance with the requirements of the Law." She reminded Jewish women of the "indispensable religious duty incumbent on them." Another ad coaxed potential bathers by describing a *mikveh* "refinished in a style of beauty, convenience and elegance." These ads made little headway, as Jewish women in New York declined to observe this ritual.[8]

The lack of spirituality in Jewish youth troubled observers. Covering an 1852 confirmation ceremony at Anshe Chesed, the *Asmonean* observed that students had to be aware of "the violent contradiction between the actualities of life and the doctrines of religious instruction." The *Messenger* declared that it could not "commit to paper a tithe" of what it had "seen and heard." Young men and women, like their parents, openly violated Jewish law. In the holy sanctuary, they arranged dinner parties at the Maison Doree, a restaurant where "forbidden viands" were served in an "inviting style." (The *Messenger* counseled that even in this "enlightened age," the "safe" path for youth was to follow the teachings of the "sages of Israel.") Young Israelites "publicly derided" the "holy Sabbath." "Why," the *Messenger* questioned, "must Friday evening be selected for visits to places of amusement" and "Saturday afternoons to the dancing master, or . . . their piano-forte instructors?" In 1863 and 1864, both the Jewish Clerks Aid Society's anniversary and a Purim Ball took place on Friday night. In all, things were "growing worse and worse" as "a fearful laxity" prevailed. How many "liberally educated young men" were "faithful adherents of Judaism?" Where were the potential Maccabees who would rally to their faith "under severe trials and . . . temptations?"[9]

Aware that the desire to win acceptance in American society encouraged the decline of observance, the *Messenger* argued that failure to follow Jewish law actually harmed a Jew's chances of gaining recognition. In 1862, it wondered how Israelites could "seek the approbation of their fellow citizens," who could not but witness "the many seats vacant in [their] shrines." When Christians saw religious disregard, when they viewed Jews wholly "engrossed in commercial pursuits or devoted to trifling amusements," should they not believe that "Israel has very much degenerated?" It was appalling that an Israelite elected to public office, once in position, forgets "that he is an Israelite in faith, besides being an American socially and politically." Jews maintained fealty to their faith and nationality only when they were "observing the laws and statutes given to [them] for observance, and for transmission to posterity." Standing in the Christian world would come from genuine religious practice.[10]

Immigration "foreshadowed a secularization of faith" in which an "idyllic America" became the "kingdom of God on earth." Modern Judaic philosopher Abraham Joshua Heschel observed that the least pious Jews were those willing to risk fleeing to America. Immigrants were most interested in adapting to their new country and making a better living. Many used the openness of the United States to Americanize, discarding customs that either hindered them in the marketplace or separated them from other Americans. Native-born Jews as well began to drift away from religious practice in the early republic, drawn by the attractions and wealth of American society, a trend that continued in the antebellum era. It was difficult both to make it in America and to follow traditional Jewish rites. As a result, except on High Holy Days, the synagogues, despite their elegance, stood nearly deserted, their authority greatly diminished.[11]

■ The Challenge of Reform

The rise of Reform Judaism constituted the most important religious development in the antebellum era for American Jewry. It triggered a fierce contest of ideas between proponents of orthodoxy and reform. As Jeffersonians and Hamiltonians had contended over the legacy of the American Revolution, so leaders of Orthodoxy and Reform struggled for their vision to become the future of Judaism in the American republic. The movement to reform the Jewish religion in both its outward ceremonies and rituals and in its core religious doctrines divided the community, ultimately leaving the Orthodox a minority among American Jews affiliated with congregations. The battle for the hearts and minds of the American Jews that began in Charleston in the 1820s reached new dimensions in New York in the late 1840s and early 1850s, as accomplished scholars took on the Orthodox establishment.[12]

Reform Judaism took root in Germany in the late eighteenth century with the work of Moses Mendelssohn, an Orthodox philosopher who sought to reconcile German philosophy and Judaism and to make Judaism acceptable to

Temple Emanu-El, the city's only Reform congregation, grew rapidly. Its first sanctuary lasted only seven years. In 1854, the membership purchased a large Baptist church on Twelfth Street, which they transformed into a neo-Gothic sanctuary. It became one of the most influential synagogues in the city, home to many wealthy Jewish German immigrants. (Rachel Wischnitzer, *Synagogue Architecture in the United States: History and Interpretation* [Philadelphia, 1955]; courtesy Jewish Publication Society)

Jews living in an enlightened world. In the generation following Mendelssohn, reformers began with his ideas but went much further. Hostile to mystical trends in Judaism, they forged a new Science of Judaism (*Wissenschaft des Judentums*) to study the history of Judaism and origins of the Bible with the scientific tools of archeology and philology. Reformers intended to maintain Judaism as a living religion by integrating it with the philosophical ideas of Kant and Hegel. Leaders included Abraham Geiger and Samuel Holdheim. The former, an influential scholar and rabbi, understood Judaism as a historical, evolving religion, much different in the nineteenth century than in the ninth. He accepted rituals, provided they were not "devoid of spirit," and advocated a Hebrew service that could be understood in a contemporary framework. Holdheim, more radical than Geiger, rejected the Talmud, adopting the belief that the Bible, including the Torah, was the "human reflection of divine illumination." Reformers established a temple in Hamburg in the early nineteenth century with an organ, a reduced barrier between men and women, weekly sermons, and a liturgy that included traditional themes but excluded

Isaac Mayer Wise arrived in New York in 1846 at the age of twenty-seven and soon became one of the leaders of Reform Judaism in America. Though his pulpit was in Albany, Wise was literary editor of the *Asmonean*, in which he argued for Reform, and regularly traveled to New York to lecture, to examine students, and to speak to literary societies. He was an integral part of the city's Jewish community until his move to Cincinnati in 1854. (Courtesy American Jewish Archives)

prayers seeking the rebuilding of the Temple in Jerusalem and greatly reduced pleas for a return to Zion. New York's Reform leaders, Max Lilienthal, Isaac Mayer Wise, Leo Merzbacher, and Samuel Adler, emerged from the German Reform movement.[13]

The city's first Reform congregation, as we have seen, grew from a small 1830s discussion society of knowledgeable German immigrants into Temple Emanu-El. The founders sought alterations in worship that would allow Jews to "occupy a position of greater respect among [their] fellow-citizens," services that blended devotion to the divine with fidelity to the new age. Initial modifications were limited: men sat in the front, women in the rear; men still wore hats and prayer shawls. The congregation retained the traditional order of service but reduced the number of prayers and introduced new vocal music enhanced by a choir, together with weekly sermons. The next decade, moving to a new synagogue, the congregation adopted radical changes. It ended the separate seating of men and women and the requirement that a bar mitzvah youth read the weekly Torah potion. Services proceeded with the accompaniment of an organ and without the chanting of the hazan. Emanu-El no longer celebrated the second day of festivals. Prayer shawls were abandoned, and, by 1859, hats were no longer required. Lay leaders wanted to totally abolish the practice of covering one's head during prayer, but yielded to more traditional members until 1864, when, with the concurrence of Rabbi Adler, it became mandatory. In 1855, Rabbi Merzbacher completed a prayer book, *Seder Tefilah*, modified by Rabbi Adler, which influenced Reform synagogues throughout the country. The rabbis incorporated German hymns and eliminated mention of restoration to Zion, resumption of sacrifices, the concept of a chosen people, the coming of a personal messiah, and resurrection of the dead.[14]

The tradition of lay control held sway at Emanu-El. While Merzbacher and Adler exerted influence, the temple's trustees, including some of the city's most prosperous German immigrants, the "merchant princes," took the helm. For example, Dr. Merzbacher, while willing to abandon Talmudic traditions and ceremonies, sought to preserve Mosaic institutions, distinguishing between biblical commandments and rabbinic laws. The Cultus (ritual) Committee made no distinction. Merzbacher could conduct no marriage ceremony without the board's permission. When a member, after instructions to dispense with "the wearing of the Tallis in the Temple," responded unsatisfactorily, the board declared that the dissenting member could "according to his request have the Amount paid on his Pews returned." Concerned with decorum, the board cautioned congregational officers not to appear "in a Condition of Dress unsuitable to his office." They conferred with like-minded synagogues, invited leading Reform figures to lecture, and recruited talented, highly educated leaders. Under this spirited management, Emanu-El grew rapidly both in numbers and wealth.[15]

The Reform movement, with Temple Emanu-El as its base, took on the Orthodox establishment in a debate that reverberated in the streets, the pulpits, and the Jewish press. The top figures in the Reform movement, Lilienthal and Wise, assisted by Merzbacher and, after 1858, Adler, gained a significant platform in 1851 when Robert Lyon, editor of the *Asmonean*, New York's only Jewish weekly, decided that Wise was "the man of the future of American Judaism" and appointed him the literary editor of the paper's "theological and philosophical department." Wise opened the *Asmonean* to articles by himself, Lilienthal, Merzbacher, and supportive anonymous correspondents, who detailed Reform's ideology and ambitions to the public.[16]

Reform thinking rested on the primacy of science and reason. Reformers based their creed on the wedding of science and Judaism, arguing that Judaism must stand the test of modern investigation. This included thought and rituals. In 1849, Max Lilienthal defined the role of science for Judaism in a speech to the society Friends of the Light (*Verein der Lichtfreunde*), an organization of intellectually oriented German immigrants.

> We cannot greet this epoch of Jewish science with anything but joy and exultation. . . . Science is aware of its mission, to teach and preach Judaism to the world and to offer it to her purified. . . . Thus scientific enlightenment must clear away the disagreement, must becalm doubt and fear, must reconcile the hearts of Israel in the worship of the One Lord, must banish indifferentism and fanaticism alike and make Israel reconciled in love and peace, the herald of peace for the world.

Lilienthal wrote that "truth has not to shun the torch of investigation; scientific research will but remove superstitions and the darkness of erroneous views, and put religion still more in the halo of its heavenly light." It would be better to have no religion than one "that cannot stand the trial before the forum of science, knowledge and common sense." For the "wheels of human progress" will not halt; "life and science and truth will soon give the answer," and that answer "will but endear our pure and divine religion to every Jewish heart." Echoing Lilienthal, "Ben-Yehuda" declared in the *Asmonean* that modern man needed "natural philosophy, mathematics, history and philosophy of history" to comprehend the Bible. An advocate of Reform must "serve God in a pure and holy manner" and, like the prophets, return Judaism to "its original purity." Free from "prejudice, superstition and fear, he must take the world as it is."[17]

Concurring, Isaac Mayer Wise wrote that "all Post Scriptural Scriptures are exposed to a sound and scientific criticism." Other creeds relied on faith and only faith, while Judaism depended on scientific and philosophical grounds; its doctrines were so strong a creed that "even the most rigid application of philosophical criticism could only endear it to a thinking and reflective mind." Reason, he argued, "like the doctrine of the Jews, is of divine origin, and science is the result of reason." In 1853, Wise regretted that no person was "yet among the mortals" who could translate the Bible into English "upon the solid fundaments of the results of modern criticism." Yet Wise was confident of the future because "the spirit of progress and reform, a proper acknowledgement of the just demands of the age and a desire for the living word of God, advances in spite of all the opposition of literate charlatan and bigoted ciphers." Reason would triumph since "liberty, enlightenment, progress and reform are sisters that go side by side." Progressive Judaism must prevail.[18]

Reform argued that Judaism evolved over the centuries. Where did the

After an unsuccessful attempt to reform Russia's system of education for its Jewish population, Max Lilienthal, a brilliant German-educated rabbi, emigrated to America in 1845 at age thirty; there he was rabbi for three German congregations. He left that position in 1850 to become headmaster of a greatly admired private school for Jewish girls and boys. He developed a strong friendship with Isaac Mayer Wise and turned from Orthodoxy to Reform, becoming, with Wise, one of its leading spokesmen. This image is from his younger days in New York. He moved to Cincinnati in 1855. (Courtesy American Jewish Archives)

Talmud, the jewel in the crown of modern Orthodoxy, fit in Jewish history? Samuel Adler claimed that the Talmud mirrored a distant past, a past containing wisdom but also ceremonies and commandments that were lifeless in the modern era. Jews "of conviction" must work to free their "pure religion" from the "alloy" that the "dark age of the Past . . . mingled with it." Max Lilienthal declared that the Talmud had less and less meaning for the modern Jew because it contained *minhagim* (customs) derived from cultures of nations with whom Jews lived in the Diaspora. The esteemed codification of Jewish law, the *Shulchan Aruch*, derived in part from Persian and Chaldean practices; Slavonic and Russian traditions could also be found in Jewish ritual. How could *minhagim* originating from ancient non-Hebraic societies be binding? Science demonstrated that the Bible was and that rabbinic law (Talmud) was not divine in its creation. Consequently, Lilienthal argued, "our creed will only then shine with the eternal light of its Heavenly truth, when all these foreign elements will be removed, and we again will stand upon the solid rock of the Mosaic law!!" Only when "every humbug and every defect," the "unfounded conglomeration" of earlier eras, was expunged, would Israelites resolve the "contradiction between life and religion" and "feel proud of their Jewish name." Though it might take some time, ultimately all Jews would come around to this truth.[19]

Isaac Mayer Wise went even further than Lilienthal, questioning aspects of Mosaic law. In an essay in *Israel's Herold*, a German-language newspaper that appeared briefly under the editorship of Isidor Busch, a refugee from the failed Revolution of 1848, Wise declared that "Mosaicism has prescribed a ceremonial law which touches on all the conditions of life and consecrates and sanctifies them," moving humanity closer to God. Yet in the present era, "must we still consider this ceremonialism as an essential part of Judaism after it has lost all value and significance? No, we must not." Ceremonies assisting Jews' journey toward "moral perfection, loving the Eternal God, and walking in His way" should be preserved; those with no modern meaning "belong to the past, to hoary antiquity, to the dead, not to the living present."[20]

Reform leaders' historical understanding of Judaism allowed a discerning Israelite to find the original meaning of Judaic faith, cleansed of foreign, outmoded ritual, and encouraged an awareness of the stages of Jewish history from the biblical to the modern era. Ultimately history revealed that "Judaism has the mission to bring its divine principles and ideas to the world at large." A new stage of Jewish history was dawning. Since the mid-eighteenth century, as "evidence of progress" became unmistakable and "reason" triumphed over "authority," the only question was whether "the Jew was to remain solitary and separated from the rest of humanity," as Talmudists desired, or "whether he was to mingle with the rest of the world and become a respected portion of the social order."[21]

Advocates of Reform were not freethinking atheists or agnostics. Rather, in their framework of belief, God, though not the "imagined deity of the vulgar," was the "Creator, Preserver and Governor of the Universe." God was the "first cause," whose "greatness consisted in his Wisdom, Justice and Goodness." He created the universe and "governs it by permanent laws." (These laws are not the laws of the Sabbath or of kashrut but the laws of science, such as the law of gravity.) Man, too, was created "in the quality of his maker." The study of history revealed evidence of divine providence and God's grand plan.[22]

Reform paid considerable attention to the nature of the immortal soul. Stressing the importance of this concept, Lilienthal made it and the unity of God central to the catechism for young children. Wise explained that the soul was immortal, temporarily housed inside the body, to be freed upon death. (If there was any eternal punishment—he sharply condemned the concept of hell and brimstone—it was the soul's inability to rectify errors made when still within the corporeal structure.) As the body decayed, the spirit continued to grow, and death in no way affected its eternal existence. One "of the energies" of the human soul, a central characteristic, was humanity's innate desire to be moral, "to do what is good and right." As a consequence, man differed from other forms of life because "he is the unhappiest of beings if he gratifies all his passions," including the "almost invincible desire to make money." The existence of the "soul" indicated that science did not provide answers to all questions and that divine will was present in the Torah and in the ongoing universe. However, reformers' understanding of religion centered on the investigations of scientists and historians and the corresponding recognition that Judaism was an evolving faith.[23]

What were the consequences of the rise of reformist thought? One was the harsh condemnation of many Jewish rituals. Wise ridiculed the requirement that a man cease shaving for thirty days after the death of a mother or father, the eleven months of mourning, and the mindless repetition of prayers. What was the source of these customs? Were they from the Hasidim, who "are most all ignorant in Jewish literature," or from Kabbalists, who allegedly had "intercourse with the angels?" Kabbalist doctrine derived from Zoroastrian and Brahmin religion, creeds that included idol worship. Judaism too often fell into superstitious sectarianism, proposing the existence of Satan and espousing ascetic practices, such as numerous fast days and hours spent seated on the floor on Tisha B'Av (anniversary of the destruction of the Temples). Those who practiced these rites "never comprehended the spirit of Judaism."[24]

Dietary laws, a bastion of Orthodoxy, came under attack. Lilienthal noted that some Jews transgressed out of "the harsh exigencies of life" and others from personal conviction. "Maccabee," a contributor to the *Asmonean*, argued that the laws stemmed from the "casuistry of the Talmudic rabbis, and later encoded with many other onerous duties in the gendarmerie of the Shulchan Aruch." No Jew should undergo a "species of martyrdom" to maintain an antiquated custom. Not everyone "can pay his cook five thousand francs a year like Rothschild" to maintain a kosher kitchen. It was lamentable "what subterfuges the poor Israelite frequently allows himself to practice, in order to obviate the oppressive and ruinous observance of what is and what is not *Kasher*," and that a kosher table remained the "diploma of a good Jew." The times demanded reform. "Where are the Isaiahs of our day?"[25]

Deserted sanctuaries offered evidence of the impact of outdated customs and superstitious ritual. Many contributors to the *Asmonean* described the state of affairs. "Remy" lamented "synagogues without preachers, Divine worship without devotion or instruction, ministers without learning, but full of arrogance and fanaticism, Sabbaths without rest," and congregations with no peace. "Rational Conduct" condemned practices such as blowing the shofar seventy-two times during High Holy Days, "insufferable repetitions of prayers," and "shaking the willows with an energy and violence, as meaningless as it is ridiculous." The "boisterous and rapid chanting by the congregation" produced a "general effect . . . [of] confusion; one standing, another sitting down, one walking in, anther running out." This "disrespectful attitude" would not be tolerated by an earthly "Sovereign," much less by "the Almighty monarch of countless worlds." "A Jew" mocked prayers offered at "horse race speed," the recitation of six or seven Kaddishes, a service that nine-tenths of the congregation could not comprehend, and a sanctuary "disfigured" by the placement of the reader's platform in the center of the synagogue, requiring the hazan to keep his back to the congregation. "I.S.H." found a service he attended appalling. A child led the liturgy. No one listened to the prayers. At the end of prayers, the few remaining left "like a small lot of Mexican cattle in a stampede." Lilienthal concluded that these practices produced materialism and an indifference to spiritual ideals, while Wise termed the Orthodox sanctuary nothing but an "ancient opera house," the result of remaining "deaf to an enlightened age," of refusing to hear "the voice of reason."[26]

In contrast to disorderly and historically obsolete Orthodoxy, advocates of Reform in the *Asmonean* happily described Temple Emanu-El. "S" portrayed "attractive and soul-elevating" services. Congregants offered no Chaldean prayers unsuitable for an enlightened age. A lecture by Dr. Merzbacher replaced "Sing-song" recitation and the selling of *mitzvot* (the honor of being called to the Torah). "A Member of the Temple" declared that Emanu-El elevated "the ritual in [the] Temple to a state befitting intelligent and reasonable beings . . . [by] clean[ing] the wheat from the chaff." Nor did it censure members who rode to services; if a man could not ride to synagogue, he would "ride to his place of business and devote his Sabbath to Mammon instead of God." Members of Emanu-El worked with a "zeal and unanimity" seldom found in Jewish congregations. They did not found their synagogue because of an internal quarrel. United from the beginning, their principles were "consonant with the dictates of reason . . . and in harmony with the spirit of Revelation," their rituals "free from previous practices."[27]

Another important impact of reform involved rethinking the position of women in Jewish religious practice. Emanu-El's decision to end segregated seating, a move that contradicted longstanding tradition, represented an important step toward female equality. When the congregation moved to a new sanctuary in 1854, a redesigned church, the congregation decided to maintain the existing family pews, allowing husbands and wives to sit together. Emanu-El had already added mixed choirs for regular services in 1847. This too contradicted the tradition that prohibited women's voices in worship. Emanu-El replaced the bar mitzvah service, which made "no impression on the boy," with a new confirmation ceremony. On a "profound Jewish holiday, boys and girls enter to the accompaniment of a choir, are examined by the minister and publicly declare their commitment to Judaism." Confirmation received Jews' "sons and daughters into the same covenant," unlike the bar mitzvah ritual, which was exclusively for males.[28]

Gender egalitarianism reflected, in part, Emanu-El's desire to emulate the dignity and decorum of Protestant churches. Jewish women's fate was entwined with the Jewish community's quest for respectability in the Christian world. To the Protestant world, the women's gallery appeared heathenish, resembling a harem. But this was only one consideration. Its significance went beyond emulation of Protestant society. Reform ideology reinforced the antebellum movement for women's rights, for political, social, and economic equality. Rabbi Merzbacher declared that "the ladies of our day claim more liberty and equal rights even, and will not submit to the restrictions of former time and return into the ghettos of the Synagogues of old." Isaac Mayer Wise termed a traditional morning prayer in which a man thanked God that he was not created a woman "an insolence." Was it not "a rudeness of the meanest kind, that a female is considered as nobody in respect to person?" Judaism had dispensed with many "oriental notions"; it needed to go further.[29]

Defending mixed seating, Wise asserted that when a man sat with his wife and children, "decorum and devotion" and attendance improved. In an exchange with Reverend Henry Henry of Shaaray Zedek, who argued that "canon law did not permit women and men to sit together," Merzbacher contended that Jewish law did not require separation of the sexes and that Talmudic sages would also have condemned much of the clothing worn by the Orthodox. Traditional synagogues, "where gentlemen are seated below the amphitreal seats of the females in the gallery above," with each sex gazing at

each other, were not conducive "to decorum and devotion." Harmony and decorum emerged when "on the side of every gentleman" sat "the guardian angel
of his choice, . . . with the members of his family."[30]

In the early 1850s, New York became the center of American Reform Judaism.
Its leading intellectuals, Lilienthal, Merzbacher, and Wise, lived there or close
by. The movement had a voice in the influential *Asmonean* and a friendly audience among the German-immigrant community. New York housed the nation's
foremost Reform synagogue, a congregation supported by the city's wealthiest
Jews and other dedicated congregants. It boldly advocated an outlook that saw
Judaism as a great religion, firmly in harmony with reason, science, and history.
Reform's adopted mission was to free Judaism from antiquated ceremonies that
drove Jews from their faith, replacing them with a creed and practices compatible with an enlightened era. Orthodoxy, it contended, could not appeal to an
American Jew encountering the opportunities of a democratic, largely tolerant
society in which the government played no role in religion.

■ The Orthodox Response

Learned spiritual leaders Samuel Isaacs, Morris Raphall, and Arnold Fischell gave traditional Judaism the intellectual strength to respond forcefully to
the emergence of Reform Judaism. While their stance differed little from Gershom Seixas's theology, there was an important distinction. Seixas's task was to
integrate republicanism and Judaism, while the cause of the rabbis of the 1850s
was to defend Orthodoxy against the "rationalists." As there was no competing doctrine for Seixas, he cannot be said to have been Orthodox. Orthodoxy
could only exist when there was an opposing standpoint. Consequently these
men were New York's first Orthodox spiritual leaders. They spoke out in their
synagogues, in the *Asmonean*—whose pages remained open to Orthodox
spokesmen—and, after 1857, most prominently in the Orthodox-leaning *Jewish Messenger.*

The shepherds of the city's major Orthodox congregations rejected the major tenet of the reformers, that Orthodox Judaism was irrational, even superstitious. Dr. Raphall, an ardent follower of Moses Mendelssohn's belief in the
Haskalah, or Jewish enlightenment—a doctrine that allowed Jews to participate in modern society but strictly within a traditional framework—declared
it "the happy privilege of the Israelite that his faith is in union with his reason." Dr. Fischel's inaugural sermon argued that Jews possessed in one hand,

Hazan at Shaaray Tefilah, the city's leading English congregation, Samuel Isaacs founded the weekly *Jewish Messenger* in 1858. It became the voice of Orthodoxy, relentlessly attacking the Reform movement and beseeching the community to maintain Jewish ritual and tradition. (Courtesy American Jewish Archives)

their faith, and in the other, "the sword of truth and reason." One *Asmonean* contributor wrote that a Jew could never be a "true convert to another faith" because "there is not a single doctrine inculcated in holy writ that requires of the Jew that he should compromise his reason." Another issue featured Mendelssohn's writings on the "designs of God." Mordecai M. Noah declared, "we have no mysteries, no revelation which are not natural and reasonable." As Judaism held no irrational doctrines such as the Trinity, it had no conflict with reason. Judaism was a logical, consistent religion. However, as Samuel Isaacs's son Myer preached, though "nature alone would suffice to convince us that there is a God . . . preparing the world as a habitation for man," in and of itself "reason" was insufficient. Thus, God provided revelation to instruct humanity "what He would require of us as creatures obedient to His word, dependent upon Him for our existence." Unlike the advocates of reform, Orthodox assertion of reason did not include scientific investigation of Jewish sacred texts or the use of history, archeology, and philology.[31]

To the Reform contention that many laws and customs were alien encrustations deserving of excision, the Orthodox responded that the ceremonies were neither outdated nor superstitious. Many of the laws of the Sabbath and the table predated Abraham and Moses; they were part of the "law of nature." Reverend Raphall used the near sacrifice of Isaac to illustrate that in the modern world God spoke to humanity not directly, as he did to Abraham, but through "the law of life and truth everlasting," including the daily commandments. Dr. Fischel implored congregants to cling to "venerable customs and distinctions" handed down from "the most remote ages by the most pious and most zealous Israelites." The *Jewish Messenger* repeatedly urged observance. There was no excuse, "even in a modern world," for violation of the Sabbath, the "palladium of religion." If Jews were to be in harmony with God's laws and maintain their separate identity in a land where "many sought to mingle the blood of Jew and non-Jew," they needed dietary laws. They remained as relevant in the nineteenth century as in the age of King David. Moreover, the oral law (Mishnah) and the teachings of the Talmud were as binding as laws of the Torah.[32]

The issue of resurrection ignited an unusual direct confrontation between Reform and Orthodoxy. In early 1850 in Charleston, South Carolina, where Wise was interviewing for a position and Raphall was lecturing, the two met privately. Wise spurned Raphall's entreaty to reject Reform as it "had no future in America," replying, "doctor, we will see in twenty years what will be left of orthodoxy in America." At a public debate a few days later, when, by Wise's account, Raphall was faring badly, Raphall abruptly turned to Wise and asked, "Do you believe in the personal Messiah? Do you believe in bodily resurrection?" When Wise answered, "No," in a "loud and decisive voice," Raphall "angrily rushed from the hall." Neither Wise nor other leading Reform figures denied the immortality of the soul, but for them it was a benevolent, abstract concept. To the contrary, the Orthodox argued that bodily resurrection was so vital a principle that "the Jew who persistently denies this doctrine, forfeits all claim to future bliss and is doomed to perdition." In 1850, Reverend Isaacs, responding to a "charge" that in Judaism resurrection only became "general currency" with the rise of Christianity, declared, "the Resurrection of the Dead not an article of Judaism! As well may it be urged, that the Immortality of the Soul is not a dogma."[33]

Reform adamantly rejected the threat of divine punishment; the Orthodox did not. Reverend Isaacs declared that a Jew who worked on the Sabbath will "not even have one day of rest" while alive and, when his end approaches, will "not rest easy" on his "death bed." At New Year's 1860, he asked "nominal Israelite[s]" who appeared in synagogue but once a year seeking repentance to question whether they were "conducting [themselves] . . . as to be entitled to life beyond the grave." He also warned those who disregarded dietary laws that they hazarded "their chances beyond the grave." Israelites who, "in the greatest confidence," trampled on God's law would find that "the most imminent danger" lurked in their "every step."[34]

Reform found the restoration of the Jews to the Holy Land problematic; Orthodoxy did not. During the Civil War, Myer Isaacs argued that while a Jew was as patriotic as any American, "love for Palestine yet burns in his breasts, . . . the blood of the Maccabees flows through his veins." In a Thanksgiving sermon, Reverend Raphall proclaimed that Jews, though in their "temporary sanctuary," were as patriotic as any citizen. The same "revelation" that gave them hope of return to their homeland "commands" them to "promote the land in which [they] dwell."[35]

Mordecai M. Noah remained the most outspoken Jew on restoration. In 1845, he gave a widely reported discourse to an audience that included prominent Christians. The man who once proposed an upstate New York island as a refuge for world Jewry again placed restoration forefront, but this time in Palestine. No longer under the spell of Jeffersonian millenarianism, Noah linked a Jewish homeland in the Middle East with the coming of the messiah. It was in the interest of Christians to see Jews return to Zion. Though Jews in tolerant countries, such as America, would not return, a homeland would be a boon to oppressed Jews throughout the world. A distant age did not interest Noah, nor did he believe that God alone would usher in a Jewish restoration. Given the weakness of the Ottoman Empire, Jews needed to seize the moment for action.[36]

At benevolent-society anniversaries, leaders of both Orthodoxy and Reform mixed, agreeing on the centrality of charity, the danger of "mammon worship," and the need to celebrate the rising glory of America and the freedom it provided Jewish citizens. Raphall, Isaacs, and Fischel attended the funeral of Rabbi Merzbacher of Emanu-El in 1856. Otherwise, Orthodox leaders sharply challenged their rebellious brethren. Raphall declared that he was not "hostile to reform." But the reform he wanted would raise people to the "standard of a heaven born religion" rather than lower them to the "base level of the people's convenience." Most reformers focused on polishing and trimming rather than "improving the mind and purifying the heart." He desired a well-educated community that recognized that Israelites had duties to perform "in

Obedience to God's holy law." Chosen by God, these "religious trusts" distinguished Jews from "the rest of [their] fellow citizens." As Reverend Isaacs stated on the eve of Passover 1860, "The Supreme brought us from Egypt to be our God, and we were to be His People."[37]

Raphall's mild tone was exceptional. For the most part, the Orthodox response was contemptuous and angry. Raphall himself vented such ire when he walked out on Wise in Charleston. For the Orthodox, Reform was a toxic cancer in the community. Its proponents, the *Messenger* charged, "stripped Judaism of its most pleasing features." They would extinguish the life they thought they were saving. Far worse than Karaites, who believed ceremonies were an adjunct to religion, reformers aimed to "destroy all that is sanctified by age, uproot not the weed that they say surround the Judaic Tree, but the very ground in which it has stood implanted thousands of years." The commandments were a "test of a man's religious consistency"; no one possessed the license to ignore or amend them. Should Judaism alter its sacred customs and laws, it would lose its "distinctive character, its historical worth." As a result, "we should have no God to adore." On the eve of Succoth 1858, the *Messenger*, lamenting that "an enemy has arisen in our midst," pleaded with Jews to "hold obeyance" to the faith's holy rituals.[38]

Unthinkable as it was, Orthodox opponents spelled out the consequences should the proponents of Reform succeed in their quest to "ruthlessly destroy" the "noblest fabrics which have stood for centuries the buffeting of the storm." The "spirit of innovation," the abrogation of the laws and rituals of Judaism, would eliminate "the basis of [Jews'] hallowed creed." What few ceremonies reformers retained would be discarded by their children. The synagogue would lie in ruins, while Jewish homes became settings for "the unhappiness of domestic life." The ideology of those creating "din and tumult in the camp of Israel" led directly to "infidelity and deism." Its goal was the "destruction of all and every religion." A reformer's true creed would read, "I do not believe that there is a god; I consider all and every religion, all and every religious ceremony, a perfect humbug." Egotism motivated "all and every reform."[39]

Reform Jews who did not succumb to atheism would fall prey to Christianity, the Orthodox charged. Look at the "new temples." An organ played, but "the worshipper is mute." Within the choir were "Christian voices [who] sing of a Unity, who believe in a Trinity." This "church service," this "farce" at Temple Emanu-El, "failed to improve the Israelite." The move to mixed seating, a flagrant violation of sacred Jewish law, a sacrilege, merely imitated Christian practices. "Lara," a contributor to the *Jewish Messenger*, claimed that reformers embraced mixed seating to imitate Protestant modes, making them appear superior to the "mass of Jews." It said to Christian neighbors, "do not despise me as a Jew, *I* am not one of them. *I* am a reformed Jew, I wish to come as near you as I can. I will, therefore, eat with you. . . . I will marry your daughter" and attend "a church in imitation of your church and a service as near as I can like yours." Thankfully, "the novelty fails to attract." Most Jews remained "true to their synagogue," rejecting mixed seating, mixed choirs, and organs. Perhaps the prodigal sons would rejoin the "vast majority of Israel."[40]

Reform enjoyed only a brief heyday in nineteenth-century New York City. The *Asmonean* ceased publication in 1858, after editor Lyon's sudden death. Lilienthal and Wise moved to Cincinnati in the mid-1850s, and Rabbi Merzbacher died in 1856. Temple Emanu-El remained, with Samuel Adler, its gifted leader, constructing an outlook centering on the concept that God's words were conveyed by the prophets to the people in the form of morality. The synagogue was to mediate between the prophets and Israel. He foresaw Judaism's perception of God becoming a common treasure of humankind. Supported by prominent Jewish New Yorkers, Emanu-El, which built the largest synagogue in the world in 1868, remained a significant presence in New York.[41]

Despite Adler's brilliance, Reform lacked a voice in the press and attracted the allegiance of a minority of affiliated New York Jews in the 1850s and 1860s. The argument moved elsewhere. Within a generation, New York's Orthodox Jews were joined by hundreds of thousands of like-minded immigrants from Poland and Russia.

While Gotham remained the heart of American Orthodoxy, antebellum New York was a seedbed of the American Reform movement and the location of a contest that forever changed American Judaism. Reform Judaism, based on the European Enlightenment, found a home in America's new republic, founded on an American Enlightenment that incorporated many European ideals. Reform soon became the Jewish denomination that was far and away most attractive to America's Jews because it was in harmony with the republican spirit at the center of their quest for full acceptance and full participation in American life. It was fitting, then, that the initial debate over its values and principles took place in New York, home to a quarter of the nation's Jewish population and the center of Jewish intellectual life in the United States.

A Columbia-educated attorney and poet, Leopold Newman joined New York's Thirty-First Regiment and fought at the battles of Bull Run and Antietam. Rising to lieutenant colonel, he was hit by grapeshot in the leg and taken to Washington, D.C., where he died while surgeons amputated his leg. President Lincoln visited him at bedside and promoted him to brigadier general. (Courtesy New York State Military Museum)

CHAPTER 11

Politics, Race, and the Civil War

In September 1863, in the midst of a bloody war, with hundreds of thousands already dead and wounded and hundreds of thousands to follow in the next year at a half, the New York Times *published its annual report of the Rosh Hashanah celebration. After explaining the meaning of the holiday and its rituals, the* Times *remarked, "The present anniversary is, according to the Jewish calendar, the five thousand six hundred and twenty fourth since the creation of the world, and owing to the rapid changes going on in Jewish society, and the many removals and deaths occasioned among them in this country, by the existing war, will be observed with peculiar formality and impressiveness." This was an insightful observation. The Civil War fundamentally altered New York's Jewish community, both its internal understanding of American society and its relationship with the Christian world.*[1]

▨ New York Politics before the Civil War

Antebellum New York politics, volatile and passionate in the 1850s, reached its tensest moments in the years prior to the Civil War. The city was a stronghold of the Democratic Party. Its earlier and still most popular champion, Andrew Jackson, drew a crowd of over one hundred thousand when he visited New York in 1833; Democrats were prosouthern, standing for laissez-faire economics, states' rights, free immigration, noninterference with slavery, and hostility to reform movements. Democrats recruited their strongest supporters from the working classes, particularly the immigrant working classes, German and Irish immigrants, and merchants whose major economic ties were in the South. The party freely used municipal patronage to cement its base.[2]

Until the mid 1850s, the Democrats' major opponents were the Whigs, supporters of a strong central government, federally sponsored internal improvements, a national banking system, and tariff support for manufacturing. Whigs feared immigration and, as supporters of "order, morals and religion," welcomed reform. Bankers and merchants not entwined with the South generally backed Whigs. The Whigs also garnered the votes of middling master craftsmen and, during depressions, of a working class seeking government aid. Democrats won most elections in the city, except for a few mayoralty races lost due to infighting and recession.[3]

In the mid-1850s, Republicans replaced Whigs as the second major political party. With a platform opposing the extension of slavery in the territories, they drew the adherence of the city's small antislavery contingent, including William Cullen Bryant and the Reverend Henry Ward Beecher, along with a number of merchants, including those hoping for a transcontinental railroad. Republicanism never became a popular movement in New York, alienating the white working class with its probusiness, antislavery, and anti-immigrant outlook. In the 1856 presidential election, Republicans garnered only a fourth of the vote in New York, and in a three-way mayoral race in 1859 that elected prosouthern candidate Fernando Wood, the Republican challenger collected only 27 percent of the vote.[4]

Strong economic bonds between New York and the South strengthened Democrats and weakened Republicans. The garment industry, the city's largest business and the trade in which most Jews worked, by 1860 produced 40 percent of the nation's attire; it supplied clothing to southern whites and slaves. The city's economy centered on cotton, the nation's most valuable product. New York merchants controlled its trade and held "a virtual stranglehold on regularly scheduled ships shuttling between northern, southern and European ports." A city merchant's words to an abolitionist illustrate the importance of this trade: "Slavery is a great evil, a great wrong," he admitted. "But a great portion of the property of the Southerners is invested under its sanction; and the business of the North . . . has become adjusted to it. There are millions upon millions of dollars due from Southerners to the merchants and mechanics alone, the payment of which would be jeopardized by any rupture between the North and the South." "We cannot afford, sir," he concluded, "to let you and your associates endeavor to overthrow slavery. It is not a matter of principles with us. It is a matter of business necessity." *Debow's Review*, a respected periodical, commented that without slavery, ships would rot in New York's harbor, grass would grow on Wall Street, and New York would be remembered as were Babylon and Rome. The *Evening Post* declared that "the City of New York belongs as much to the South as to the North." Antiabolitionists broke up meetings of abolitionists; looted the home of merchant Lewis Tappan, a prominent foe of slavery; and threw rocks at black churches and stores owned by abolitionists.[5]

Republicans had strength in upstate New York, electing governors and legislative majorities in the statehouse. Tension between New York City and Albany exacerbated the fraud, coercion, and bullying common to the electoral politics of 1850s. In 1857, New York City had two police forces, one backed by Democratic mayor Fernando Wood and one backed by the Republican state legislature. This, predictably, led to violence and near chaos in the streets.[6]

What were the prewar political allegiances of the city's Jewish community? The Whig Party attracted affluent Israelites. All seven Jews included in journalist Moses Beach's list of the wealthiest New Yorkers in 1845 were Whigs. Otherwise, ever since the age of Jefferson, New York's Jews voted predominantly for Democrats within a solidly Democratic city. The most prominent municipal Jewish officeholders were Democrats. The patriotic spirit and unconditional support of the nation's manifest destiny, prominently displayed at Jewish fraternal celebrations, fit well with Democratic politics. But even if there were a considerable number of Jewish Whigs in New York, there were fewer Republicans. Why were Jews hostile to the Republicans? The key issue was slavery's threat to the union.[7]

■ Slavery and New York's Jewish Leaders

Slavery dominated politics in the antebellum era, reaching a fever pitch in the 1850s. That decade witnessed the Compromise of 1850, which resolved the issue of slavery in territory wrested from Mexico in part by implementing a stronger Fugitive Slave Act; the Kansas Nebraska Act of 1854, which replaced the Missouri Compromise of 1820 (no slavery north of the $36° 30''$ parallel) with popular sovereignty, a referendum determining a state's position on slavery; the *Dred Scott* decision (1857), which by ruling that blacks were not citizens permitted slavery in all territories; and John Brown's failed abolitionist guerrilla raid in 1859 on the Harper's Ferry federal armory that resulted in seven deaths and Brown's execution. The war of words between northern supporters of the South and abolitionists became alarmingly heated.

The most prominent Jewish leaders in New York, reflecting the city's strong southern attachments, were antiabolitionist and, to varying degrees, proslavery. Emmanuel Hart, like many Democratic politicos, worked his way up from captain of a volunteer fire brigade to ward leader to head of the Central Committee of Tammany Hall, the Democratic Party's political organization. Hart won election first to the Common Council and then to Congress, becoming in 1850 the first New York City Jew to sit in Washington. An active member of Shearith Israel, Hart was a leader of the conservative "hunker" wing of the Democrats, a faction that was strongly opposed to any agitation on the slave question and that threw its influence, whenever possible, in support of the interests of the slaveholding states.[8]

Mordecai M. Noah was, to the Christian world, the "most important Jew in America." The Jeffersonian playwright, former American consul at Tunis, sheriff and surveyor of New York, and editor of the *National Advocate* and the *New York Evening Star* became one of the North's foremost southern sympathizers, declaring, "I was always a friend of the south." His southern sympathies reached their height during his period as editor of the *Evening Star* from 1833 to 1840. That daily, "one of the most influential papers in the country," encouraged New Yorkers, particularly merchants, to develop close ties with southerners. Though once critical of slavery, Noah reversed course after the Missouri Compromise, declaring slavery to be a common good. Blacks were "anatomically and mentally inferior a race to the whites, and incapable, therefore, of ever reaching the same point of civilization, or have their energies roused to as high a degree of enterprise and productive industry." They could only be content in servile positions. A field slave found happiness in his cottage, wife, children, and patch of "corn and potatoes," while the house servant, blessed with a "kind master," relished his fine clothing.[9]

Noah feared blacks. Nat Turner's Revolt in 1831, a rebellion led by a literate, messianic Virginia slave that killed fifty-five whites, horrified him. For three months, the *Evening Star*'s editorial page daily detailed the atrocities of an 1839 slave revolt in Santo Domingo. Emancipation would jeopardize the safety of the country. Noah supported the notorious "gag rule" forbidding the House of Representatives from debating slavery. He supported a move to make publication of antislavery literature a punishable offense. While serving as a judge, he ordered the grand jury to indict any member of the American Anti-Slavery Convention, meeting in New York in 1842, who advocated "a project embracing a dissolution of our happy form of government." Noah saw abolitionists as dangerous men. They strained relations between merchants and southern traders. At war with America, they jeopardized the Union.[10]

Robert Lyon, editor of the *Asmonean*, also edited the *New York Mercantile Journal*, a paper that carried "great influence over the minds of many commercial men." His newspapers reached both a local and a national audience. Lyon was a Jewish religious progressive, opening the pages of the *Asmonean* to advocates of Reform Judaism and appointing Isaac Mayer Wise its literary editor. Lyon opposed the Know-Nothing Party, an anti-immigrant political movement—a cause that briefly attracted Mordecai M. Noah—seeing its nativism as a threat to the Jewish community.[11]

Lyon was also a staunch Democrat. Though he did not endorse candidates in 1852, noting that Jewish allegiance divided between Whigs and Democrats, in 1856, with the opposition now the Republicans, Lyon endorsed Democrats James Buchanan for president and Fernando Wood for governor, both known as friends of the South. The *Asmonean*, defending its stand, declared that it placed these names at the top of the masthead with "impartiality." For Lyons, impartiality meant that he made the endorsement after consulting "the wishes and desires of the majority of [the paper's] supporters." The "Hebrews of America" could never support the candidacy of Know-Nothing Millard Fillmore or Republican John C. Fremont, "whose chief aid will be from the bigoted and persecuting New England states." The paper made this endorsement because the election was "of such vital importance to the future of the Union." As Jews had always been "Democrats, and as Buchananites are 'democrats of the right stamp,'" Israelites belonged in their ranks. Buchanan's policies were "progressionist" and Israelites were "progressionists," despising "papacy and priestcraft." Given Lyon's detailed knowledge of the Jewish commercial world, his political leanings likely reflected those of the Jewish business community. (The mercantile community as a whole, formerly known for Whig loyalty, favored Democrat Buchanan in 1856, fearing that a Republican victory would harm its southern trade.)[12]

Lyon despised abolitionists as much as Noah did. In 1850, he published a speech by Senator Lewis Cass of Michigan that warned of the "fearful consequences" of emancipating three and a half million slaves "living in the midst of another and superior caste." The following year, he warned Americans of the "foul Fiend which stalks among us": "Abolitionist traitors." These included British radicals, "Frederick Douglass, the nigger," and a "heterogeneous stew of fanatics and imposters," all of whom clamored to grant the "sons of Africa" the suffrage that "our fathers fought and died for." A "more wild and a more preposterous idea never yet entered the brain of man." Behold Jamaica, its plantations a "wilderness" following emancipation. Or Haiti, sixty years after its slave revolt, "hastening to total irremediable ruin." The issue before the nation was "the relative value of civilization and barbarism." Lyon urged Americans to "resolve this day to put down abolitionism in whatever shape or form it may present itself . . . and to crush out for once and forever the attempt to plunder our Southern citizens of their property."[13]

After a hostile, nearly violent reception forced English abolitionist George Thompson to flee America, Lyon wrote that this was a "lesson to that class of bigots, who sent him here to promote disunion, and to rail at the institutions of our country." If Thompson used his energies to observe his homeland, he would have noticed that the factory workers there endured "far more misery than any suffered by [America's] so called slaves."[14]

The *Asmonean* supported enforcement of the controversial Fugitive Slave Act, which required police to turn over an alleged fugitive solely on the affidavit of a master, denying the fugitive the right to speak in court. The bill was now "the law of the land." In 1851, physician Sigismund Waterman contended that the Union was at the heart of the controversy over this measure. If the "bond of the states" came apart, commerce would fall into a state of paralysis. Centuries of "gloom, despair and servitude" would replace the "happiness and bliss of the present and the past." For Jews the Bible decided the question: "Thou shalt return the slave to his owner." Slavery was part of God's wisdom, as He revealed "the natural law of the superior and the inferior." Jews, once slaves in Egypt, could "appreciate the sorrow of the man of servitude—but there are many conditions of things, we cannot alter nor change." While they might purchase a slave's release, they could not endanger "national and even international peace by gaining his freedom through violence." Jews owed their renewed sense of "manhood" and comfortable position to America; they must "stand by the constitution, now and forever."[15]

Joining Hart, Noah, and Lyon as leading Jewish, prosouthern, and pro-

Morris Raphall, spiritual leader at B'nai Jeshurun, was the city's most eminent Jewish leader. In January 1861, he gave a sermon declaring that the Bible condoned slavery and declaring that it was incorrect to accuse the South of wrongdoing. The speech was very widely circulated in the North and the South. He supported the Union during the war, but never saw the conflict as a great moral cause. (Courtesy American Jewish Archives)

slavery leaders was Reverend Morris Raphall of B'nai Jeshurun, New York's most prominent spiritual leader. In January 1861, with southern states seceding and the Union in peril, Raphall delivered a sermon on the Bible and slavery in his synagogue. While no "friend to slavery in the abstract" and still less "to the practical working of slavery," his personal feelings were, he declared, irrelevant. Invoking the biblical story of Noah and his son Ham, he concluded that, aside from family ties, slavery was the oldest form of social relationship. For viewing his father's nakedness, Ham and his descendants, the black race, were cursed to become slaves. At Sinai, God condoned slavery in his commandment that an owner give Sabbath rest to "thy male slave and thy female slave." The Bible, Raphall explained, differentiated between Hebrew slaves, who were in bondage for limited terms and were to be treated as any other Hebrew, and non-Hebrew slaves and their progeny, who were to remain slaves during the lives of their master, his children, and his children's children. Hebrew slaves bore no relation to southern slavery; heathen slaves did. Hebraic law permitted masters to chastise these slaves, short of murder or disfigurement, and required that a slave who fled from Dan to Beersheba must be returned, as must the slave absconding from South Carolina to New York. The law forbidding Hebrews from returning an escaped slave to his or her master applied only to slaves escaping from foreign lands.[16]

Responding to the Reverend Henry Ward Beecher's contention that the Bible opposed slavery, Raphall proclaimed, "How dare you, in the face and sanction and protection afforded to slave property in the Ten Commandments—how dare you denounce slaveholding as a sin?" What right "do you have to insult and exasperate thousands of God-fearing, law-abiding citizens," placing a citizen of the South on the level of a murderer? While Raphall cautioned southerners that slaves must be protected from lustful advances, hunger, and overwork, he emphatically concluded that the Bible sanctioned slave property.[17]

Raphall's speech created a sensation. Two weeks later, he repeated it at the New-York Historical Society before members of the Democratic Party and the pro-South American Society for Promotion of National Unity. Also attending were supporters of reconciliation favorable to southern demands, including prominent banker August Belmont, and distinguished Jews from Richmond, Montgomery, and New Orleans. Artist/inventor Samuel B. Morse served as chair. At the meeting's conclusion, merchant Hiram Ketcham collected funds to publish and disseminate Raphall's words. Southern sympathizers distributed the sermon throughout the country. Dr. Bernard Ilowy of Baltimore, a rabbi respected for his knowledge of biblical law, supported Raphall. Three New York newspapers published the text in full, and the *Times* printed lengthy excerpts. The *Richmond Daily Dispatch* termed Raphall's talk "the most powerful arguments delivered," and Rabbi Simon Tuska of Mobile declared his reasoning "the most forceful arguments in justification of the slavery of the African race."[18]

In 1856, a straw poll of "twenty-five of the prominent clergy" in New York revealed that twenty-three of them backed Fremont, the Republican candidate for president. (The other two backed Fillmore, the Know-Nothing candidate; none backed Democrat Buchanan.) If Reverend Raphall's (or Lyon's and Noah's) remarks are exemplary, these political sympathies did not extend to Jewish spiritual or secular leaders.[19]

■ Jews and Antislavery

Raphall's sermon did not go unanswered. Jewish Reform leader David Einhorn of Baltimore published a lengthy refutation. Isaac Mayer Wise, while opposed to Republicans and abolition, criticized Raphall's literal interpretation of the Bible. Reverend Leeser of Philadelphia found fault in his argument that the black race descended from Ham. The most important response, however, came from Michael Heilprin, a Jewish, Polish-Hungarian, revolutionary refugee. A deeply learned man, well read in biblical criticism, he had already revealed his political preferences by speaking at an antislavery Democratic rally in Philadelphia.[20]

Responding in the abolitionist-leaning *New York Tribune*, Heilprin regretted that Raphall's "sacrilegious" arguments had not disappeared among the "scum." He condemned the moral sense of slavery's defenders as "depraved" and the minds of their "mammon-worshiping followers" as debauched. Fearing that Raphall's speech might convince the ignorant that the Hebrew Bible condoned slavery, he savagely attacked Raphall's reasoning—citing the German Jewish scholars that influenced the Reform movement. Heilprin, in effect, also attacked the literalist, ahistorical approach of Orthodox leaders to Jewish texts. Heilprin argued that Raphall misunderstood the biblical word for "servant." The word Raphall translated as "slave" also denoted court officers and royal ambassadors. He ridiculed the absurdity of invoking the story of Noah and his son: "Noah, awakening from his drunkenness, curses, in punishment of an insult, a son of the offender, and a race is to be 'doomed for all times'! Doomed by whom, 'preacher in Israel'? By the God whom you teach our people to worship, the God of Mercy, whom our lawgiver proclaims to extend his rewards to the thousandth generation." Heilprin contended that Ham's descendants included the Babylonians, Philistines, and Egyptians. He contemptuously dismissed Raphall's contention that Abraham, Isaac, and Jacob had slaves; they were "peaceable unwarlike nomadic patriarchs" wandering through hostile lands. Those who allied with the patriarchs were "voluntary followers." Raphall's interpretation led to divine approval of bigamy, polygamy, and "traffic in Semitic flesh." Finally, Raphall ignored Moses's most important words to the Israelites: "Forget not that ye have been slaves in Egypt." Catering to southern admirers, he cruelly misinterpreted the Bible.[21]

Reverend Samuel Isaacs, the esteemed editor of the *Jewish Messenger*, knew Professor Calvin Stowe, husband of Harriet Beecher Stowe, and supported Republican Fremont in 1856. He did not, however, allow politics into the *Messenger* until war was declared. The paper breathed not a word of the momentous events of 1860 and early 1861. When the election of 1860 concluded,

Isaacs inserted a short notice that "THE ELECTION OF ABRAHAM LINCOLN as President of the United States . . . having been decided on Tuesday, quiet once again reigns and the " 'long agony' is over." Nothing more. He refused to print essays on Raphall's controversial sermon other than urging Jews to refrain from using the Bible either to defend or to attack slavery. Isaacs's resolve to keep politics out of the *Messenger* faltered on occasion because of his practice of reporting the sermons of major religious figures, including an address by Hazan Lyons of Shearith Israel critical of the American tendency to rely on the voice of the people rather than the voice of God, implying that Lincoln's election should not be allowed to overrule the Bible's acceptance of slavery; and a sermon by Reverend Raphall similar to the notorious talk he delivered a few weeks later. An ardent foe of Reform Judaism, Isaacs did not publish the antislavery remarks of Dr. Samuel Adler of Temple Emanu-El. Raphall's views were representative of Orthodox rabbis. A historian of Jewish abolitionism concluded that "there were no Orthodox Jews in the antislavery movement." However, as Isaacs's largely silent stance reveals, there were exceptions.[22]

While a distinct minority, New York Jewish Republicans numbered in the thousands and included important members of the party. Temple Emanu-El, the only Reform congregation among the city's twenty-seven synagogues, attracted the allegiance of prosperous merchants Joseph and James Seligman and attorney Abram J. Dittenhoefer, the son of a prominent merchant who abandoned the Democratic Party at nineteen because of its stance on slavery. Dittenhoefer served as an elector for Lincoln in 1860, as did German immigrant and supporter of the 1848 Revolution, attorney Sigismund Kaufman. Assistant Attorney General Philip Joachimsen, whose vigorous prosecutions made him a "terror" to illegal slave traders, many of whom operated out of New York, was a member of Shearith Israel. Reform Judaism's willingness to reinterpret the Mosaic code likely attracted Israelites of liberal political temperament, though, as Joachimsen's membership reveals, Republicans also joined other congregations. Some affiliated with secular organizations. *The National Cyclopaedia of American Biography* lists Kaufman as founder and first president of the Turnverein, a German fraternal society.[23]

New York's most outspoken Jewish abolitionist, Ernestine Rose, advocated immediate emancipation. During the war, she urged the adoption of radical measures that Lincoln was yet unwilling to take. When the Emancipation

Proclamation was issued in 1863, she called the document "a mockery" because it only freed "slaves we cannot reach." Disregarding the delicate politics that maintained the loyalty of Maryland, Kentucky, and Missouri, she demanded, "First free the slaves that are under the flag of the Union. If that flag is the symbol of freedom, let it wave over free men only. The slaves must be freed in the Border States." Rose, a friend of abolitionists William Lloyd Garrison and Frederick Douglass, invoked her birth as the daughter of a "down trodden and persecuted people" to strengthen her appeal on the part of the oppressed, even though she did not identify as a member of the Jewish community.[24]

▧ Where Did New York Jews Stand?

Did the forty thousand Jews in New York, a pro-South Democratic city with a minority of Republicans, harbor similar stands on slavery and abolition as their conservative leaders? The American and Foreign Anti-Slavery Society report of 1853 noted that the "Jews of the United States have never taken any steps whatever with regard to the Slavery question. As citizens, they deem it their policy 'to have everyone choose whichever side he may deem best to promote his own interests and the welfare of his country.'" The society found this both puzzling and lamentable, as Jews were frequently "the objects of so much mean prejudice and unrighteous oppression." The society's observations were correct. Most Jews avoided the subject. The *Jewish Messenger*'s refusal to insert a single political article as the country fell apart in 1860 and 1861, despite the editor's Republican leanings, exemplified this timid approach. For years, the Jewish community did its best to make political participation legitimate for Jews, but only as individuals. Many yet worried that Jewish voting blocs would ignite Christian fears of Jews, leading to European-style anti-Semitism, even persecution. Were Israelites to advocate causes particular to their society, they would create obstacles to their aspirations to fit fully into Christian society. Jews observed the problems that the Irish created with their forceful entry into politics, including the rise of the Know-Nothings, a strong nativist party. When Reverend Raphall delivered his controversial proslavery speech, his board of trustees did not reprimand him over his position on slavery but only objected to "the impropriety of intermeddling with politics": "we firmly believe such a course to be entirely inconsistent with the Jewish clerical character, calculated to be of serious injury to the Jews in general and to our congregation in particular." Jews, including their leaders, should not enter politics as a class other than to oppose exceptional incidents of Jewish persecution, such as the Mortara case.[25]

However, the refusal of the board of B'nai Jeshurun, whose members constituted leading members of the city's Jewish community, to specifically condemn Raphall's spirited defense of slavery speaks volumes. The political silence of editor Isaacs was to give no platform to a position unpopular in New York. Other leaders of New York Jewry, however, who represented the majority opinion in Gotham, were willing to violate the Jewish tradition of political noninvolvement (as Jews) and in a loud public voice defend the Democratic Party, the South, and slavery. The American and Foreign Anti-Slavery Society's statement was incorrect if applied to New York's Jewish leadership cadre. The problem was not that they were silent but that they took a strong position at odds with that organization. The question of whether or not the rank and file of the city's Jewish population followed the lead of Raphall, Hart, Lyon, and Noah can be estimated by examining election returns. In 1860, Lincoln commanded but 35 percent of the city's vote. German-immigrant wards where most Jews lived voted two to one against Lincoln. Jews, whose record of voting Democratic began under the leadership of Thomas Jefferson, an opponent of slavery, for the most part continued that tradition into the 1850s, when that party stood full square for the continuation and spread of American slavery.[26]

The reminiscences of Abram J. Dittenhoefer give powerful testimony to the strength and loyalty of the Jewish community to the Democratic Party. Dittenhoefer recalled that when he was a young law student, his father advised him to become a Democrat. Any hope for public office as a Republican "would be impossible in the City of New York." Dittenhoefer recollected, "One can hardly appreciate to-day what it meant to me, a young man beginning his career in New York, to ally myself with the Republican Party. By doing so, not only did I cast aside all apparent hope of public preferment, but I also subjected myself to obloquy from and ostracism by acquaintances, my clients, and even members of my own family." The proslavery stance of prominent Jewish leaders reflected mainstream Jewish political leanings.[27]

By following the lead of Hart, Noah, Lyon, and especially Raphall, New York's Jews, other than adherents to the incipient Reform movement, rejected any parallel between southern slavery and their ancient Egyptian captivity. Annual Passover messages in the Jewish press never equated the two. In March

1861, on the eve of war, the *Messenger's* Passover remarks celebrated "the perpetual commemoration by His chosen people of their deliverance from Egyptian bondage," with no mention of American slavery. Ancestral Jews and black slaves lived in two utterly different worlds—this despite the observation from a German visitor that "female slaves" regularly attended synagogue services. By "slaves," he meant household servants who, he believed, were once in bondage and who, upon receiving their freedom, "chose to remain with their now endeared masters and assumed their religion." They prayed with "true devotion" but also with "the Black's characteristic exaggerations." The *Messenger* omitted any comment about emancipation when it went into effect in January 1863.[28]

By 1860, many of New York's Jews had achieved solid middle-class standing in the empire city, as owners of small shops, garment manufacturers, importers, and professionals. The merchants, wholesalers, retailers, and even garment workers of the city considered the southern trade their lifeblood. Southern planters and merchants owed New York firms $200 million in 1860; war would wipe out that debt. Early in 1861, the businessmen of New York desperately sought compromise, sending delegations to Washington in hopes of preventing secession. One of the New York delegations included former congressman Emmanuel Hart. On 29 January 1860, a special train arrived at the capital bearing the city's leading merchants with a petition of forty thousand businessmen stating that the "perpetuity of the union" was far more important than a controversy over territories. Many of the signatories would have been Jewish entrepreneurs facing loss of trade and the panic of bankruptcy if the Union dissolved. Horace Greeley's *Tribune* disparagingly commented that "rich Jews and other money lenders," together with "great dry goods and other commercial houses," feared Lincoln and supported his opponents. Indeed, after Lincoln's election, New York endured a severe, if short-term, depression. The *New York Herald* reported that in December 1860 ten thousand men were out of work. Bankruptcies doubled. Dry-goods and clothing businesses, the prominent Jewish mercantile occupations, especially suffered.[29]

In addition, Jews in midcentury New York sought acceptance into American society. Raphall's many patriotic sermons and toasts were not inconsistent with his opinion on slavery. Unpopular positions did not win friends, one of the reasons, as noted, that Jews disdained ethnic politics. Undoubtedly the pervasive racism in the North penetrated the Jewish community. Finally, the collapse of the Union imperiled political as well as financial security. The United States Constitution provided protections for Jews that were found in few other places in the world. What would happen to that safeguard if the Constitution collapsed with the Union? For most of the Jewish community, these were persuasive arguments.

■ The War Begins

In April 1861, Confederate forces turned their cannon on ships sent by President Lincoln to resupply Fort Sumter, the Union's last southern outpost. The heavy Confederate cannonade transformed sentiment in New York overnight. The news, New Yorker Walt Whitman declared, "ran through the land, as if by electric nerves." Even in the financial heart of the city, Wall Street, business ceased as men rushed into barrooms, hotels, and public squares to hear the dreaded news. Patriotic fervor gripped the city. American flags flew over every department store and town house, even from the spire of Trinity Church, while Broadway was "almost hidden in a cloud of flaggery." Thousands of young men enthusiastically enlisted in the Union cause. This zeal is nowhere better reflected than in the lead editorial in the *Jewish Messenger*, "Stand by the Flag." Isaacs, unchained from his apolitical vows, wrote an exuberant call to arms, declaring that the *Messenger* wanted to join with the "hearty and spontaneous shout ascending from the entire American people, to stand by the stars and stripes!" Can our former brethren be permitted to tear apart a union that was "reared by the noble patriots of the revolution?" The time for forbearance had passed. Isaacs praised young Jewish volunteers willing to risk their lives in "the cause of law and order." He wished them a speedy return, but if they were to fall, "what death can be so glorious than that of the patriot?"[30]

Like the stores, churches, and townhomes, nearly every synagogue in New York flew the Stars and Stripes above its sanctuary. Inside, sermons reflected the patriotic spirit. Most notably, Reverend Raphall's defense of the South gave way to a passionate commitment to the Union as he proclaimed that Jews would uphold the flag "at the peril of life and limb." Not born in America and not "to the manor born," Jews knew the "difference between *elsewhere* and *here*." Having lived in prosperity, he said, "we flinch not from our hour of peril." Raphall blamed the "foul stimulants of selfish, ambitious leaders" who misled ordinary southern citizens. Northerners were under deadly attack by their brothers. In response, "hundreds of thousands of conservative men of the North, the East and the West take up arms." While slaveholding was not a wrong, he said, "we do find in the Bible abundant warrant for denouncing rebellion as a sin before God." Raphall warned southerners that their struggle was fruitless. Outnumbered and overpowered, they would be remembered as Benedict Arnolds for flying the "black flag of treason." Praising the "brave defenders of the union," he beseeched "the Lord of Hosts to bless their righteous efforts."[31]

New York in the spring of 1861 was a harrowing place. The economy sank quickly as southern deposits disappeared. While the war economy would soon revive many businesses, life remained turbulent. One non-Jewish immigrant, Alexander Dupré, wrote, "New York looks like an army camp. There are armed men everywhere, everyone carries a revolver, and we're living in an absolute torrent of commotion." Tens of thousands of soldiers marched through the city on their way to war, many never to return. Another German immigrant, Julius Wesslau, lamented, "Most of [the men] are in what you know as the militia, and you can well imagine what it's like when out of 800–1,000 riflemen only half are left, the effect that has on their families and the city."[32]

■ Service, Rights, and Recognition

The Civil War presented occasions for New York Jewry to lead American Jews in patriotic service, which in turn brought both rights and recognition. Foremost was combat duty. Young Jewish New Yorkers responded to the martial spirit of spring 1861, serving with distinction. Simon Wolf lists 1,996 known Jewish soldiers from New York State, the vast majority of whom came from New York City. This was more than twice as many as the next state, as the city housed a quarter of the nation's Jewish population. Stories of courage, dedication, and sacrifice abounded. Charles Breslauer fell at Bull Run in 1861, early in the war, as Union forces overconfidently attempted to take Richmond. Isidor Cohen died at Gettysburg in 1863 as the Union held off Robert E. Lee's invasion of the North, and Lieutenant Joseph Abrahams was killed during the battle at Cold Harbor in 1864 when General Grant ordered a frontal assault on Lee's forces, resulting in calamitously heavy casualties. Native-born Leopold Newman, a Columbia-educated attorney who wrote poetry and short stories, joined New York's Thirty-First Regiment, one of the Union's most courageous outfits, and fought in battles from Bull Run to Antietam. Rising to lieutenant colonel, Newman was at home when the War Department asked him to return to duty, even though he had completed his term of service. While leading a charge at Fredericksburg, grapeshot hit his leg. He was taken to Washington, D.C., where he died shortly after surgeons amputated his limb. Before his death, President Lincoln visited him at bedside and promoted him to brigadier general. Edwin Wertheimer, advancing at Manassas and at Chancellorsville, safeguarded New York State's flag in the face of a "murderous" cross fire. Badly wounded, he passed on the banner to a fellow officer. In one New York Jewish family, five members served in the army; in another, a father fought with his three sons; and in a third, three brothers enlisted.[33]

In each issue, the *Messenger* published the names of Jewish officers joining the army. It printed sketches of the war by a Jewish soldier stationed in Washington who described thousands of soldiers and massive equipment, wagons in motion everywhere. He depicted an optimistic portrait of General McClellan's preparation of a well-disciplined army and of the calmness of Lincoln amid the storm. The young soldier trusted that the war would purify the nation, completing the work of the Revolution. He also chronicled Jews' prominent role in the army, how they kept the Sabbath, and how one soldier both fasted and fought on Yom Kippur. Though some soldiers feared becoming the subjects of venomous taunts, he reported no anti-Semitic slurs. In the summer of 1862, a letter from a volunteer noted a large number of Jewish New Yorkers in the field in Mississippi. These soldiers sensed that they were participating in a momentous historic event. They also complained of loneliness and the boredom of soldiering, as the days passed slowly far from home. New York's Jews fought and died alongside their Christian brethren. They were equal cohorts in the effort to preserve the Union.[34]

Congress in August 1861 approved legislation that required all military chaplains to be "of some Christian Denomination," rejecting an amendment to exclude that proviso. Jewish protest began when Rabbi Arnold Fischel of Shearith Israel, responding to a request by a Jewish officer in a Philadelphia regiment, petitioned to be made a chaplain. Secretary of War Simon Cameron declined the request, asserting that but for the proviso, the application would have been given "favorable consideration."[35]

The Board of Delegates, the organization begun by Reverend Isaacs in 1859 to unite American congregations, appointed Fischel its unofficial chaplain in Washington, D.C., with the duty of visiting hospitals, "supervising the spiritual welfare of our . . . co-religionists," and lobbying for a change in the law. Despite hundreds of people waiting to see the president, Fischell gained access and received a warm welcome. He presented Lincoln a memorial declaring that the "oppressive" chaplaincy law, an act of "prejudicial discrimination," violated the Constitution. A few days later, the president agreed to seek a change. Despite protests from a few Christian denominations, to which many other Christian citizens responded with letters supporting the board, a new bill passed in March 1862 that reinterpreted the phrase "Christian denomination" to mean "religious denomination."[36]

Following passage, the Board of Delegates failed to raise the funds needed to support Fischel's mission, forcing him to retire from the field after comforting wounded Jewish soldiers and accompanying the army into Virginia. In 1862, Rabbi Joseph Frankel of Philadelphia, a Bavarian immigrant, became the first Jewish chaplain in the American military, as American Israelites gained greater recognition as a significant segment of the American people.[37]

The Civil War mobilized New York's Jewish women. They met in synagogues to make army provisions, worked in hospitals, and participated in sanitary fairs, large expositions that sold wares, donating the proceeds to the Union cause. Many synagogues organized women's auxiliaries. With Jewish assistance, an 1864 fair raised a million dollars. These fairs combined Jewish and Christian women, another instance of the war integrating the Jewish community into greater New York society, including women, who in the nineteenth century often remained apart from the marketplace and public square.[38]

A milestone patriotic act of the Jewish community was the transformation of part of Jews' Hospital into a military hospital. As noted, the hospital. founded in 1855 after years of planning and disappointment, was the community's most important collective act. It stood as a monument to the Jewish community's commitment to its members' welfare and to the Jewish population's increasingly prominent position in the city. By 1862, the hospital had admitted 117 soldiers and covered their expenses. For the first time, it also appointed leaders of the Jewish Reform movement to its board, an act likely initiated by the receipt of significant bequests from Temple Emanu-El. A visitor noted that most soldiers came from New England, and that their loneliness was eased by the "considerate attentions of visitors of the fair sex," as Jewish women regularly comforted patients. The hospital allowed Israelites a prominent forum to "manifest their sympathy for a noble cause." During the draft riots of 1863, the hospital, located in the midst of the turmoil on Twenty-Eighth Street, admitted victims of the violence. In 1864, the hospital's board voted to accept fifty more Union soldiers. One of its staff physicians, Dr. Israel Moses, resigned in 1861 to serve in the army, where he remained as a lieutenant colonel to the end of the conflict. After the war, the hospital remained open to the public, changing its name to Mount Sinai.[39]

Finance was another major contribution to the war effort. New York Jews played a significant role in funding the war, none more important than the efforts of Joseph Seligman, a German immigrant who moved to the city in 1846. With his brothers, he rose from country peddler to the helm of New York's most prominent Jewish enterprise. A strong Union supporter, he was elected vice president of a mass Union rally the day of the firing on Fort Sumter. His brother William spoke at a similar meeting in September 1864. When war was declared, the Seligmans won a contract to outfit New York's Seventh Regiment. They also helped gather financial backing for a government whose finances were at risk following the withdrawal of southern deposits. During the war, Joseph established a foothold in Washington, D.C., obtaining additional contracts to supply uniforms to the army. When promised Treasury funds seemed in doubt, he despaired that he might have "no alternative but the suspension of [their] house, which will drag down 10 other houses, and throw 400 operatives out of employ." Fortunately, he received nearly $1.5 million by July 1862. That summer, he traveled to Germany to sell bonds for the war effort; there, joined by brothers Isaac and Henry, he sold up to $200 million of securities. The war facilitated the Seligman family's transition from a manufacturing to a banking firm, which began operating in 1862. Joseph was also one of the few Jews (along with his brother) who were asked to join the prestigious Union Club, formed in 1863 to allow conservative businessmen to support the Republicans and to play a greater role in New York's politics. Both the invitation to the Union Club and his highly visible efforts for the Union were noteworthy steps toward Jewish integration into New York society at its highest levels.[40]

Cotton traders Emanuel and Mayer Lehman, two of the South's leading cotton merchants and the founders of Lehman Brothers, commenced business in New York in 1858, opening a branch of their operations in the city that was the center of cotton exchange. The war stranded brother Emanuel in the city, where he sold cotton that Mayer dispatched and that slipped though the Union blockade. During the conflict, Emanuel traveled to London, where he acted as an agent for the purchase of Confederate bonds.[41]

■ The Rise of Anti-Semitism

The Civil War triggered "the worst period of anti-Semitism in the United Sates to date." The most significant incident, a national event that electrified New York's Jewish community, was the notorious General Orders No. 11, "the most sweeping anti-Jewish regulation in all of American history." On 17 December 1862, General Ulysses S. Grant, terming the Jews "a class violating every regulation of trade established by the Treasury Department," commanded their immediate expulsion from his military department, an area encompassing northern Mississippi and parts of Kentucky and Tennessee. Once a Jewish emissary informed Lincoln of the act, he moved immediately to have it rescinded; the orders were revoked on 4 January 1863. But it was too late; the orders had already created fear and rage among Jews throughout the nation, especially in New York. Upon hearing of the edict, the *Messenger* angrily asked, "why single out as the especial objects of his wrath, the *Israelites* residing within his lines? Why inflict upon a general body a penalty due to individual offenders?" There was no reason to sully "the Jewish name" because of the misdeeds of a few. Unless the order was revoked, there was no telling "to what enormities it may lead." The next issue gave telling evidence of the edict's impact. Observing the "exceedingly bitter" mood within the community, the *Messenger* implored fellow Israelites not to turn their anger into sympathy for politicians whose objects were "very, very far from the Jewish heart" or to give credence to the "wild, insincere suggestion that 'Government in Washington is bigoted, intolerant and unfriendly to Jews.'" Grant's order created disaffection in a community never comfortable with the Republican Party, especially when support was faltering in the face of a seemingly endless war.[42]

The *New York Times* reported that when a "committee of Jews" in the city "took it upon themselves" to applaud Lincoln for "annulling the odious order," the "bulk" of the city's Israelites rebuked the committee, declaring that "they have no thanks for an act of simple and imperative justice—but grounds for deep and just complaint against the Government." Grant should have been summarily dismissed. The *Times* declared that even on "selfish" grounds, the order ought not to have been issued, given the high political positions Jews held in Europe and the power of the Rothschilds "to raise or destroy the credit of any nation." But issues more fundamental were at stake. Men "cannot be punished as a class, without gross violence to our free institutions." The rights of American

Jews were "as sacred under the Constitution as those of any other sect, class or race." The *Times* article, along with the *Messenger*'s warnings, reveals the rage and discord that Grant's order created within the Jewish community.[43]

The charges in Grant's order were repeated in other dispatches from scenes of war. The South unleashed the first shots at Fort Sumter, the *New York World* proclaimed, because there was likely an "unrevealed southern Rothschild" backing its decision. One sailor reported that his boat was "as covered with German Jews as a dead carcase with carrion crows." A report from Tennessee claimed that "certain parties in Huntsville were unpatriotic enough to sell their cotton to the Jews who swarmed here from the North." A post from Mississippi noted an order by Colonel Dubois that "all cotton speculators, Jews and other vagrants" who lacked permission to be in the area must leave within twenty-four hours. General Benjamin Butler, in command of troops in New York City in 1864, engaged in a dialogue with the *Messenger* over his use of the word "Jew" when he referred to individuals. Butler replied that he identified Jews as a nationality "though possessing no country." He described what they were known for:

> The closeness with which they cling together, the aid which they afford each other, on all proper, and sometimes improper occasions, the fact that all of them pursue substantially the same employment, so far as I have known them—that of traders, merchants and bankers—the very general obedience to the prohibition against marriage with Gentiles, their faith, which looks forward to the time when they are to be gathered together in the former land of their nation—all serve to show a closer the [tie] of kindred and nation among the Hebrews and a greater homogeneity than belongs to any other nation.

Butler did not consider himself biased, but his characterizations of clannishness and vocation and his subtle questioning of patriotism were common anti-Semitic claims.[44]

The charge that Jews were crooked expanded to include a lack of patriotism, as Israelites were depicted as cowards, a people who remained far from the battlefield while profiting from shoddy war production, even to the extent of fabricating unsafe goods. A doggerel published in *Vanity Fair*, one example of many slanders in the newspapers and magazines, pictured a visitor wandering through the stalls in Chatham, where "Sholomonsh" and his fellow vendors sell tawdry merchandise with "smiles obsequious":

Viewed, as I have, the swindle-stitched disgrace
Of uniforms daubed with sordid lace,
With cheap tag-rags disguised, and paltry loops,
Served out by mean contractors to our troops;[45]

The gold exchange, whose trade volume far exceeded that of the stock exchange, fluctuated wildly depending on the war's progress. As men of wealth often put their money in gold when they believed the Union cause was going badly, it came under harsh critical attack. Perhaps because the most prominent gold trader was the Jewish firm of Hallgarten and Herzfeldt, and because of traditional associations of Jews and gold trading and moneylending, newspapers held Jews responsible for market gyrations. Horace Greeley's *Tribune* titled an angry editorial "Hebrews and Gold." *Frank Leslie's Illustrated Newspaper* reported that Jews "cut a miserable figure as they rushed to and fro, foaming at the mouth, cursing with impotent rage Old Abe and Secretary [of the Treasury Salmon] Chase, who had brought this ruin on the house of their fathers." Three New York newspapers blamed Jewish traders for the volatility of the market: "those hook-nosed wretches speculate on disasters." A visitor wandering to a corner near the Gold Exchange would only observe "descendants of Shylock."[46]

Harper's and the *Herald* charged that all Jews were copperheads (southern supporters). August Belmont, the "the Jew banker of New York," who came to Gotham as a representative of the Rothschilds, was held in special contempt. The *New York Herald* "spoke as though all the Jewish bankers in the world, with Belmont in the lead, were joined together for support of the confederacy." (Belmont, who married a Christian in an Episcopalian church, supported the Union but also urged peace talks with the South and supported Democratic candidates against the Republicans.) Again and again, this wealthy banker with a strong German accent, a man who never associated himself with the Jewish community, was singled out for ridicule. So too was his employer, as a speaker at Cooper Union declared that "there is not a people or government in Christendom in which the paws, or fangs, or claws of the Rothschilds are not plunged to the very heart of the treasury." Other allegations included accusations that a disloyal non-Jew was "a tool of the Hebrew race," that Jews favored the draft, and that Jews set Columbia, South Carolina, on fire. The anguish of a long bloody war, combined with a rapidly growing and ever more visible

Jewish community, a community that included more and more men of wealth and prominence, exacerbated and heightened anti-Semitism and its challenge to New York's Jews, who had largely enjoyed acceptance and approbation from their Christian neighbors.[47]

■ The Draft Riots and the Election of 1864

As the war dragged on, with increasing casualties and no sign of victory, support in New York for the Union cause diminished. The city was the headquarters of the Peace Democrats, who favored making accommodation with the South and ending the war quickly. Democrat Horatio Seymour gained the governor's seat in the fall of 1862, an election in which Seymour ran on an anti-Lincoln platform. Democrats carried every ward in the city and elected all six of their congressional candidates. In 1863, New Yorkers chose for mayor German American C. Godfrey Gunther, who ran as a reformer but was a member of a Democratic faction that supported the "supremacy of the white race." He received strong support from Kleindeutschland, home to many German Jews. There is no evidence of how Jews voted, but they were likely even less sympathetic to Republicans after General Grant's edict.[48]

On a national Fast Day in May 1863, the *Messenger* noted that attendance at the synagogues had declined considerably from previous such occasions and that "it was very evident that less respect was manifested for the recommendation of the Executive," likely a reference to the Emancipation Proclamation. Reverend Raphall's sermon that day reflects disaffection. He preached that the conflict, the result of "demagogues, fanatics and a party Press" of both North and South, had mired the United States "in the third year of a destructive but needless sectional war which has armed brother against brother and consigned hundreds of thousands to an untimely grave." While Raphall found "consolation" that the "cause of the union is the worthiest in the field," he did not mention slavery or the Emancipation Proclamation or discuss any larger meaning to the conflict. His unconditional patriotic enthusiasm of April 1861 disappeared. His words conveyed the disillusionment prevalent in the city, including within the Jewish community. The lavish Purim balls and numerous other "sociables" and the festive Saturday afternoon strolls down "Judenstrasse" (Broadway from Canal to Union Square) gave evidence of the community's attempt to escape the realities of war.[49]

In July 1863, any citizen unlucky enough to be walking the streets of the metropolis heard the crack of rifles and witnessed buildings ablaze, as the worst urban riot in America to that day erupted. Enraged over a lottery draft of men aged twenty to thirty-five, Irish and German workingmen took to the streets. Resentment flamed against blacks, blamed as the cause of the war and already the object of Irish hostility, and against the wealthy, who could buy out of the draft with a payment of $300. For three days, gangs stalked the streets; they blocked avenues and alleys with barricades. Crowds attacked German garment stores, including stores owned by Jews on Grand Street, as well as Horace Greely's *Tribune*, a pro-Union newspaper, and houses in wealthy neighborhoods. Mobs lynched blacks in the streets and set fire to the Colored Orphan Asylum. The official count listed 118 dead, though many more may have perished. The riot ended when Secretary of War Edwin Stanton ordered soldiers from Gettysburg to the city. Jewish General William S. Meyer received a personal note of thanks from President Lincoln for his service during the uprising. Joseph Seligman, a likely target of the rioters, condemned Governor Seymour's attempt to stop the draft, along with the "Copperheadism of the once 'Democratic' party." These Democrats gave "Jeff Davis their moral support and another straw of hope."[50]

The *Jewish Messenger* declined to report details of the riot. Instead, it asked, "how many Jews were among the thousands [who] rose determined to commit every act repugnant to humanity?" The answer: "not one." Not that poor Israelites could afford $300. They could not. The draft weighed as heavily on them as on men of other faiths. But Jews "love the land in which they dwell, and obey the governing powers." In religion, they pray to one God, but in politics, "they obey the law of the country." When the conscript lottery resumed in August, the *Messenger*, noting the names of Israelites chosen, expressed confidence that those with no disability or substitute payment would "shoulder a musket," consoled in the reflection that "their country called and they must obey." The draft, it reported, made soldiers of peacefully inclined coreligionists, including spiritual leaders of a wealthy uptown and an east side immigrant synagogue.[51]

Prior to the election of 1864, newspapers reported that a delegation of New York City Jews visited Lincoln, assuring him that, with only a few exceptions, Israelites would give him their votes. In response, Myer Isaacs, coeditor of the *Messenger*, wrote Lincoln explaining that there was no "Jewish vote." Rather, there were "a large number of faithful Union supporters" among prominent

Jews, but there were also "supporters of the opposition." Israelites were not, as a body, "distinctly Union or Democratic." Isaacs did report that at a recent mass meeting of the German Union Society, the chair of the Executive Committee, two principal speakers, and others on the platform were Jews. But Lincoln carried only 33 percent of the city's vote, despite the fall of Atlanta, which foretold a speedy end of the war. The *Messenger*—noting that on the Union side, Abram Dittenhoefer was a candidate as an elector for Lincoln, while on the Democratic side, Jacob Seebacher was Democratic nominee for assembly—reiterated Isaacs's contention that there was no such thing as "Jewish politics"; Israelites individually followed their conscience. Copperhead accusations to the contrary, the paper remained staunchly behind the Union. It expressed confidence that "an overwhelming majority of Israelites in the States," in their personal choices, shared these sentiments. But what about New York City?[52]

How did New York's Jews vote? By 1864, nearly all major Jewish industrialists and merchants had turned to the Union side. After a difficult initial year, these men of commerce prospered. The Hendricks's copper manufactory, founded by Harmon Hendricks, one of the city's wealthiest Jews, operated at full capacity during the conflict, and garment manufacturers supplied the army's seemingly endless needs. The city poured hundreds of millions of dollars into the war effort, much of it raised in and through the city. Republicans and industrialists formed a common economic bond. Joseph Seligman stated that if the Republicans won in 1864, he "would be in favor of investing in manufacturing as in that case the tariff would hardly be lowered in five years." However, the working classes, especially independent craftspeople and unskilled laborers, did not prosper as did the bourgeoisie. While wages increased markedly, inflation eroded living standards. The price of coal tripled, sugar doubled, and flour rose by a third. The working-class vote created a sizable Democratic majority.[53]

Did the large Jewish German working and middle class join other German workers in voting Democratic, or did they support Lincoln? Kleindeutschland strongly supported white supremacist Godfrey Gunther for mayor and would have been sympathetic to the German Democratic Club's contention that the "Republican war, inflation, taxes, and draft had had harsh economic consequences" for the middling classes. Future Democratic candidate Horatio Seymour wrote in 1861 that the Germans were the "true conservatives of the Democratic Party." While German immigrants were friendlier to the Union

The German born and educated rabbi at Temple Emanu-El, Rabbi Samuel Adler, was the leader of the Reform movement in New York after Rabbi Wise and Rabbi Lilienthal departed and Rabbi Leo Merzbacher died. A strong Lincoln supporter, he saw slavery as the root of the war and its eradication as the great accomplishment of the conflict. (Courtesy American Jewish Archives)

cause than were the Irish, the German wards in Kleindeutschland gave Lincoln's opponent, General McClellan, 69 percent of its votes in 1864. German Jews tended to mingle freely and identify with non-Jewish Germans; indeed, as "they were bound together in an organic unity that lasted for generations," it is unlikely that their vote differed significantly from fellow immigrants. Isaacs was correct: Israelites voted on both sides. But was there a strong proportion one way or the other? Because Jews did not live in enclaves separate from non-Jews, it is impossible to precisely determine their votes. But since they did not disassociate themselves from their German neighbors, it is probable that they voted in a similar pattern. If so, there was a similarly strong Jewish vote against Lincoln.[54]

▪ The Death of Lincoln

The assassination of Abraham Lincoln on April 14, 1865, shocked an entire nation. News of the President's death reached New York on the Sabbath; synagogues quickly filled to capacity, the exterior of each draped in black. At Shaaray Tefilah, Reverend Isaacs spoke of an "appalling calamity" at a moment when the nation was jubilant with news of "peace and reunion." In the *Messenger*, he wrote that this "kind good hearted man, the steadfast, conscientious President," would rank second only to George Washington in the nation's history. At Shearith Israel, with the lectern, pillars, and gallery covered in black, a special Sephardic prayer for the dead was recited, the first time that prayer was recited for a non-Jew. At Temple Emanu-El, the entire congregation stood and recited the Kaddish, the traditional prayer for the dead. Rabbi Adler was so overcome with grief that he could not speak, though a few weeks later he compared Lincoln to Moses, both emancipators of slaves. Learning from nature allowed Lincoln to "fully extirpate slavery," restoring "the land of the free to true freedom," rendering the Union safe, and convincing the world of the stability of republican government.[55]

When Lincoln's body arrived by train in New York, it was taken to city hall to lie in state. Fifteen hundred members of B'nai B'rith, bearing a chain with three links and the banners of the various lodges, marched in the Fourth Division of the funeral pageant. After the funeral train resumed its journey, a massive ceremony convened at Union Square. From Shearith Israel, members of six synagogues and Jewish aid societies paraded to the gathering. Reverend Raphall and five other Jewish leaders sat on the speakers' platform. Speaking for the Jewish community, Reverend Isaacs prayed that God would both remove Lincoln's soul "to the spot reserved for martyred saints" and "soothe our pains and calm our griefs."[56]

German immigrant Marie Wesslau described the scene in New York after Lincoln's assassination: "It was terribly sad to walk through the streets with all the flags on the public buildings at half-mast and almost all the buildings draped in black and white with all sorts of inspirational inscriptions. . . . I don't believe the death of any monarch has ever been as deeply mourned as Pres. Linkol." A city that had rejected his leadership by a two to one margin but six months earlier was now in the deepest sorrow at his death. The profound reaction to the martyrdom of Abraham Lincoln provided the spark that ensured that the Civil War would be a transformational moment for the city's Jewish community. The elements for that transformation were already in place. The willingness of near two thousand New York soldiers to serve with non-Jewish comrades, joining the ranks of officers and infantrymen offering to sacrifice their lives for their country, fused a bond between Jews and the rest of the American population, notwithstanding the outbursts of anti-Semitism. The conversion of Jews' Hospital, the community's most treasured accomplishment and previously reserved exclusively for Jews, to Mount Sinai, open to the needs of the entire city, signaled common citizenship. Yet, in the summer of 1864, nine months before Lincoln's death, with the war grinding on, with casualties mounting by the tens of thousands, with Lincoln's reelection in doubt, and with increasing war weariness and disaffection in the city, the patriotic energy so visible in the Jewish community in the early days of the conflict might have evaporated into the hazy Manhattan air. In 1863 and 1864, the *Messenger* often ignored the war completely.[57]

Moreover, even if most New York Jews supported the war, they offered starkly different interpretations of its meaning. As we have seen, Reverend Raphall, whose son lost his hand in battle in 1863, considered the conflict a "needless sectional war" brought on by "demagogues." He also criticized Lincoln's withdrawal of civil liberties, his willingness to suspend habeas corpus. The conflict was a war of self-defense for "national honor and safety." Rabbi Samuel Adler of Temple Emanu-El took a different view. His Thanksgiving Day sermon compared the nation to a sick patient. Does a physician treat symptoms with temporary remedies or "discover the root of our national malady, and having found it, tear it from the body?" That root was found: "its name is Slavery. Remove that thoroughly, and the fever will lose its power, its nourishment, and this unholy rebellion be crushed beyond all possibility of resuscitation." Jews had a duty to advocate "the eternal immutable principles of liberty and the inalienable right of man."[58]

Early in 1864, it was unclear whether Raphall's or Adler's views of the war's meaning would prevail within the city's Jewish community. Beginning in the fall, events moved quickly. The surrender of Atlanta, Lincoln's reelection, his inauguration, and, forty days later, his assassination galvanized the nation, including the city's Jewish community. Intense patriotism and profound, nearly unendurable sorrow gave Adler's words of radical change a prophetic ring, of a more fitting result of the conflict than the mere restoration of the Union that Raphall advocated. The sacrifices of the battlefield seemed not just necessary but heroic. The achievements of the Union soldiers, resulting in emancipation, loomed as historic, as did the conversion of Jews' Hospital to Mount Sinai. Jews rejoiced in these accomplishments and tearfully mourned Lincoln's death. While the Civil War's outcome was unclear to the end, it ultimately ensured that the sense of national unity and pride, the growing fusion of the Jews into American life, and an expanding Jewish American sense of national destiny were to become permanent.

Lincoln's power to forge a common identity can be heard at the conclusion of an article written forty years later by Myer Isaacs, son of editor Samuel Isaacs, at that date an officer of the American Jewish Historical Society:

This paper will be read on the 12th of February, the birthday of Lincoln. Profane hands, even now, touch the ark which holds sacred the memory of the beloved and martyred President. We of the Jewish Historical Society reverently place our tribute of gratitude by the side of the myriad chaplets in honor of the American who was too great to be sectarian, whose motto was "Malice towards none—charity for all," "doing the right as God gave him to see the right," whose idea of atonement was the Jewish inspiration, "let the oppressed go free."[59]

In the 1850s, New York's Jewish leaders Hart, Noah, Lyon, and Raphall openly supported the southern cause, disdained the black race, and despised the Republican Party. Now the shepherds of the Jewish community uniformly mourned Lincoln and championed the "great emancipator." It may have taken a long, dreadful war and the death of a beloved president, but in 1865 Jews began to join Dr. Adler in articulating a common bond between their Egyptian bondage and the plight of African-American slaves. The Civil War was a transformative moment in the Jewish community's embrace of American democracy and Jews' confidence that they had an increasingly secure place in the growing republic. The shift from Democrat August Belmont to Republican financier Joseph Seligman as the city and the nation's most prominent Jew is but one sign of the beginning of this transition. As the 1904 quotation from Meyer Isaacs indicates, two generations later, Jews were well on their way toward a commitment to and a leadership role in the advocacy of civil liberties and civil rights.[60]

Conclusion

Early in this book, I noted that it would have been inconceivable for one of the twenty-three poor Jewish immigrants from Recife living in the lonely community of New Amsterdam in 1654 to envision that this company outpost would ultimately grow to a city of eight million and a Jewish population of over two million. It would have been equally difficult for them to foresee that the city would number over eight hundred thousand in 1860, including a Jewish population of over forty thousand. Their home in Amsterdam, the most hospitable city in Europe for Jews at the time, numbered only a few thousand Jewish inhabitants. The growth and changes in New York over the two centuries between their landing and the Civil War were remarkable in nurturing both a major Jewish population and a significant center of Jewish culture in the United States.

These changes came step by step over the 211 years after those first Jews arrived at the dreary, distant settlement of the Dutch West India Company. The first decade under Dutch rule, from 1654 to 1664, saw individual Jewish traders striving to gain political and economic rights with personal perseverance and help from their Amsterdam compatriots. They created a legacy that endured through the next two centuries and beyond. The long English colonial era transformed the city into the most hospitable municipality for Jews in the entire world. The small Jewish population of thirty to forty families constructed the first synagogue in North America, Shearith Israel, living as a synagogue community in the tradition of London and Amsterdam. Shearith Israel remained the city's only Jewish house of worship for nearly a century. Jewish leaders became merchants of standing in a city devoted to commerce, and the Jewish community enjoyed widespread acceptance, participating in New York's financial and, to a limited degree, civic and political life. During the years of the early republic, the city's Jewish community embraced the wave of republican enthusiasm, moving from a synagogue community toward fuller integration in the life of the city, including the marketplace, social organizations, and the fierce partisan politics of the 1790s. The antebellum decades witnessed a massive influx of German and other European Jews, causing the Jewish population to increase from five hundred to forty thousand in just thirty-five years. The new population triggered an explosion of new synagogues, some elegant to display the prominence and wealth of leading Jewish citizens, some small to serve the needs of poor immigrants. The Jewish community acquired far more visibility in the city, building a hospital and an orphanage, becoming a force in the Democratic Party, publishing two weekly newspapers, and serving as a forum for debates between advocates of Reform and Orthodoxy. New York entered the international arena as one of the centers of world Jewry.

Following the Civil War, the United States experienced far-reaching economic growth. Major industries in steel, copper, oil, and agricultural equipment, along with the growth of mass-produced consumer goods and the establishment of an advanced banking system, produced vast fortunes and the emergence of financiers and industrialists more renowned than the president of the United States, such as John D. Rockefeller, Andrew Carnegie, and J. P. Morgan. In this world of advanced capitalist development, the ideas and ideals of the American Revolution began to recede into a distant past. Social Darwinism, monopoly capital, and labor-management conflict dominated American society.

For the Jews of New York City, the decades following the Civil War also were a time of momentous changes. Men who had immigrated before the war rose to occupy eminent financial and social positions. The Seligman, Lehman, Schiff, Loeb, and Warburg families built elegant mansions on Fifth Avenue and accumulated vast fortunes. Moreover, in the Gilded Age the city added not tens of thousands of new Jewish immigrants, as in the antebellum era, but hundreds of thousands of new arrivals, largely from eastern Europe. This new population, together with the pre–Civil War generation, transformed New York City Jews into the largest Jewish community in the world. With their growing prominence, New York's Jews aspired to a leadership role in national and even international Jewish affairs.

This large, powerful population owed much to their predecessors. The sense of citizenship, the experience of equality and integration into the American republic, remained an enduring legacy. It empowered Jews to extend their efforts to secure decent living and working conditions. Similarly, the struggles of the emergent Jewish working class and the entrepreneurial ambitions of the growing Jewish bourgeoisie in the antebellum era embedded enduring traditions of economic and social responsibility for fellow Jews. Though the days of British rule, the struggles of 1776 and the early republic, and the turbulent years leading to the conflict between the states undoubtedly seemed remote to Jews living in the modern twentieth-century metropolis, without the Jewish achievement of those years, without the growth of a significant, entrepreneurially and politically integrated population to greet the waves of new immigrants, American Jewish history and New York's Jewish history could have taken a far different path.

Indeed, in looking back two to three centuries, it is easy to underestimate the truly revolutionary change in which the small community of Jews in New York City participated. For millennia, they had been out of the mainstream political loop. The middle ages and early modern era in Europe saw Jews subject to expulsions, pogroms, and ghettoization. Even in areas where violence was not common, Jews suffered onerous legal discrimination, determining who they could or could not marry, where they could live, and what occupations they might or might not pursue. The life of a Jew was aimed at survival within a hostile world, and Jews directed their energies inward, with men focusing on study of sacred texts and women devoting themselves to nurturing families.

While the situation in Holland was far better than in most areas, Jews still lived in an isolated community under their synagogue and community leaders. Thus, it is difficult for the modern citizen of a nation that has long honored human rights and democracy, particularly in the past sixty years, to comprehend what a stark difference the Jewish families of New York encountered. The British by the eighteenth century were so concerned with empire and mercantilism that, despite whatever anti-Semitic beliefs they yet harbored, they lifted all restrictions on Jews in order to ensure tranquility and to maximize profits in trade from their precious colony. Jews could not vote in England; they could in New York. Nor was this an oversight. The Naturalization Act of 1740 specifically exempted colonial Jews from the Test Act that permitted only Anglicans the franchise or office in Britain.

The small Jewish community of New York flourished under this new freedom. Gradually it emerged from its closed synagogue society, whose protections and insularity were no longer needed. However, the bonds of community remained vital to most Jewish residents, still far outnumbered by Christians. By the time of the American Revolution, the Jewish community of New York had so much become a part of the economic, cultural, and even political life of the seaport that its leading members became active revolutionaries. They signed petitions and declarations based on the ideas of such English philosophers as John Locke, a man whose relevance to Jewish communities when he was alive in the seventeenth century would have been unthinkable. Moreover, they put their lives on the line, leaving their synagogues and their homes for an uncertain future based on ideals that had not had a place in Jewish history since the Romans put down the Judean rebellion in the first century.

A revolution occurred in Jewish history, not just in American history, when New York's Jewish community incorporated words of the American Enlightenment, inserting phrases from both the Declaration of Independence and the U.S. Constitution into their synagogue's post-Revolutionary charter. That the leading Jew in New York, Solomon Simson, became the vice president of the Democratic Society, the Jeffersonian organization that continued to support the French Revolution even as it became more and more radical, marked an extraordinary transformation in Jewish society, as did the efforts of the leading spiritual leader, Gershom Mendes Seixas, to integrate republican thought with rabbinic Judaism. The influx of German immigrants in the antebellum era enhanced this heritage, particularly through the growth of communal organizations such as B'nai B'rith and the emergence of German revolutionaries at the heart of the movement to Reform Judaism. New York's revolutionary heritage added strength as Jews learned to respect and use freedom of speech and freedom of the press.

The Civil War, a watershed event in American history, so, too, marked a climactic moment in the history of New York's Jewish community. It fulfilled the republican vision of political and economic integration into American society. Jews served and died on the battlefield, attended to wounded soldiers, sewed uniforms for and opened their hospital to soldiers, and mourned the death of their president with as much depth as the Christian population. Never had American citizenship felt more compatible with Jewish identity.

While the Civil War secured the Jewish community a priceless republican heritage that the generation of the 1860s and earlier generations of New York Jewry passed on to the hundreds of thousands of Jews who landed at Ellis Island, it must be remembered that this treasured legacy came with a price. The unprecedented social, economic, political, and cultural possibilities that the American republic offered New York Jewry also challenged the abilities of the community to become an active part of the new society while yet retaining a cohesive identity. Some members found this impossible and broke away. Some managed to hold on to traditional beliefs and ritual within the bounds of American liberty, while still others sought to form a middle ground between the Judaism of the old world and one that would be in harmony with American democracy. These issues of integration remained as critical dilemmas for future generations of Jewish New Yorkers, individually and collectively, as they confronted (and continue to confront) the complex, promising, and often troubling challenges of American liberty.

Jeff Gutterman, "View of Congregation Shearith Israel Cemetery, New York," photograph, 2011. (Courtesy of the artist)

An Introduction to the Visual and Material Culture of New York City Jews, 1654–1865

DIANA L. LINDEN

Jews have long been referred to as the "People of the Book," signifying the importance of ongoing study and interpretation of the Torah. For scholars of both Jewish history and American history, the written word is also central, with such documents as letters, cemetery records, and membership records of burial societies, synagogues, and labor unions constituting their primary sources.

This visual essay offers a different approach. It explores the beliefs, values, attitudes, and assumptions of early New York Jewish history through an examination of visual and material culture, illuminating what we can learn about this period from man-made artifacts of the time.[1] The positioning of figures in a portrait, adaptations of objects from the surrounding culture for new uses, or even what is *not* included by a painter in a composition all provide insights and clues into the social dynamics, the crafting of identity, the portrayal of class status, and the nature of gender relationships in colonial America.

In the coming pages, we will trace the creation of a new dual identity of "American Jew" during the colonial and republican eras, using visual means to consider the various cultures and histories that produced this syncretic identity in New York, from the legacy of oppression and torture in Spain and Portugal to the cultural traditions of Amsterdam to the emerging religious freedoms of the New World.

In Chatham Square, today part of New York City's Chinatown, the Spanish-Portuguese Cemetery built by Congregation Shearith Israel in 1682 stands as New York's oldest cemetery, although it was the second to be built. Raised above street level, protected from vandals and tourists by its padlocked metal fence, this historic cemetery is exposed to weather and pollution eroding its stones, rendering many epitaphs illegible, and roughly pitting their surfaces. Though it is open only by appointment, a viewer can start a visual dialogue with the gravestones by observing how they are oriented (whether vertical or horizontal), their size, and their design or shape, when standing outside its gates.

Toward the left of center stands a two-foot-tall obelisk placed upon a four-foot-tall stone base that makes it the tallest monument in the cemetery. The presence of an obelisk is unusual for a Jewish cemetery because it is not a traditional funerary Jewish form. Colonial American Jews appropriated the obelisk from Protestant cemeteries; the form originated in ancient Egypt, where it was associated with eternal life and light. Here, the obelisk's singular shape and height broadcasts the deceased's importance to the greater community. Even from a vantage point outside of the gates, it can be assumed that the obelisk honors a man, rather than a woman, since women were kept out of the upper spheres of society where power was brokered and obtained. Indeed, the gravestone's inscriptions herald Reverend Gershom Mendes Seixas, the most prestigious religious official of Congregation Shearith Israel in the first hundred years. Seixas's duties equaled those of ordained rabbis, although he did not possess that title. In addition to serving as the congregation's hazan, Seixas supervised kashrut and officiated at all life-cycle events.

The rest of the tombstones conform to one of two orientations: either vertical slab stones favored by the Ashkenazim or horizontal, flat ledger stones on the ground in the manner of the Sephardim. The tombstones are inscribed with texts that include biblical quotes, loving epitaphs, names, and birth and death dates, written in Ladino, Hebrew, and Dutch, among other languages, acknowledging the differing heritages of New York Jews.

Objects have their own lifetime. While tombstones are generally made to endure, everyday objects as well as the artistic creations of immigrants, slaves, women, and the working class are often lost or overlooked, their possessions or creations used up or discarded rather than collected and preserved. Flyers advertising Purim balls and copies of the newspaper the *Asmonean* (1848–1859) printed on pulpy newsprint were mass-produced for a contemporary audience rather than published with an eye toward posterity. Yet close examination of these historical objects and images that have survived enables us to engage directly with Jews' participation in colonial history and in the making of the nation and its culture.

The geographical starting point for the history of New York City Jewish life might be considered Recife, Brazil, where Dutch Jews lived until 1654, when Portugal seized power and they were exiled. The visual and material culture known to the Jews at Recife traveled with them to "Niew Amsterdam," if only in their minds and impressions. It had its origins even further back in time in fifteenth- to seventeenth-century Spain, Portugal, and Holland. The Jewish refugees who departed in haste from Recife to Dutch New Amsterdam, once settled, wove together, as if plaiting strands of a braid, their Jewish needs and traditions with elements of this Dutch, Spanish, and Portuguese heritage, thus producing in the colonial and republican eras a new syncretic identity, that of "American Jew."

The bird's-eye view topographical map of the Americas on page 264 was a ceremonial document conceived as a bold pronouncement of political power over overseas land claims, rather than as a navigational guide for exploration to the Americas. Diego Gutierrez, a Spanish cartographer, collaborated with Hieronymus Cock, a celebrated engraver from Antwerp, to delineate Spain's claim on the American continent.[2] Originally the work's large format required the map to be printed on six separate sheets of paper that later were joined together. The map's scale equaled the oversized ambitions of the Spanish monarchs. From the fifteenth century onward, the Catholic Church supported those European rulers who laid claim to distant territories without regard to the land rights and cultures of indigenous peoples, with the provision that Catholicism become the religion of the Americas.[3] This attitude parallels how the Church and the monarchy treated the Sephardim, or Spanish and Portuguese Jews.

Phillip II, King of Spain (1556–1598), and his half sister, Margarita de Parma, Regent of the Netherlands (1559–1562), commissioned major works of art and architecture such as this, affirming their imperial power and dominion over the world, its peoples, and nature. In similar fashion, as we will see in the next engraving, Spanish and Portuguese artists produced with confidence art celebrating their control over the lives and the deaths of Jews.

The anonymous artist who engraved the scene of sadistic torture and public execution of Jews on page 265 created a work of social celebration rather than social criticism. We do not know if the represented scene took place in the sixteenth, seventeenth, or eighteenth century. Those who might see the finished

The 1562 Map of America, Hieronymus Cock (Flemish engraver) and Diego Gutierrez (Spanish cartographer), engraving, created 1562, Antwerp. (Courtesy Lessing J. Rosenwald Collection, Geography and Map Division, Library of Congress, Washington, DC)

Burning of Spanish Jews and Others in Portugal, eighteenth-century engraving. (Courtesy General Research Division, New York Public Library, Tilden Foundations, New York)

print would easily imagine themselves among the large crowd of witnesses, including clerics holding crucifixes aloft, gathered to celebrate as Sephardic Portuguese Jews were being burnt alive at the stake as heretics. It is not known if the artist directly witnessed this event or if he re-created it later based on oral and written accounts. We can learn much about the culture in which this work was produced by examining how this piece of art was positioned for its viewers. The engraving's fine attention to detail and artistry, and its large size, made it difficult to reproduce and circulate, indicating that it was not created as a warning to Jews. Rather, the Spanish-Portuguese Catholics depicted here who witness the torture would likely be the same people who viewed the image as one upholding their own actions, social status, and ideological beliefs. This artwork helps us to viscerally grasp the cultural milieu from which the earliest Jews of New York had escaped and illuminates the kinds of cultural memories that fed into their struggles for religious freedom and their crafting of their new colonial Jewish identities in first New Amsterdam and then New York.

In contrast to the previous image, the Spanish master Francisco José de Goya y Lucientes (1746–1828) wanted his audience to empathize with, rather than demonize, the condemned man, a Jew, who stands in the foreground of the drawing shown on the facing page. Goya held the distinguished position of personal painter to the king of Spain until the Peninsular War propelled him to create horrific images of war's brutality as well as caustic satirical and social commentary, for which he lost favor with the monarchy.[4] Goya painted this piece during the reign of Ferdinand VII (1808–1833), who had reinstituted the Inquisition and targeted Goya for his politically charged artwork. Here, the subject of a martyred Jew provided a vehicle for Goya to express his own persecution, as well as that of the Jews of Spain. Shrewdly, Goya turned to centuries of European representations of Christ as the physical prototype for the condemned Jewish man, calculating that Catholics in Spain might empathize with the fate of Jesus. The Jew looks downward in apparent acceptance of his fate. Subtle sepia tones, loosely applied with expressive brushstrokes, convey a sense of quiet and solitude. While the two figures to the man's left and right (one seemingly in clerical robes) are painted with dark brownish tones, the Jew wears white to symbolize his virtue and innocence, a color-coded statement on good versus evil.

Since the Middle Ages, Christian artists had maintained a specific iconography to depict "others," most importantly religious outsiders. Facial carica-

Francisco José de Goya y Lucientes, *Por linage de ebros* (*For Being of Jewish Ancestry Condemned by the Inquisition*), 1814–1824, a brush drawing in brown ink wash. (British Museum, Cabinet of Prints and Drawings; © The Trustees of the British Museum, London, England)

ture and physical disfigurement were typically used to represent the Jews' perceived spiritual "abomination."[5] On the depicted Jew's head is a *coroza*, the distinctive conical hat that Jews and criminals were mandated to wear.[6] Goya pointedly titled his work to question the validity of the man's crime, that of being of Jewish heritage. He portrays the church and state as despicable and not the innocent Jew.

Rembrandt van Rijn (1606–1669), *Portrait of Menasseh ben Israel* (?), 1663, etching on paper, Rijksprententkkabinet. (Courtesy Rijksmuseum, Amsterdam, Holland)

Whereas Goya, who claimed Rembrandt as an artistic inspiration, lived in Catholic Spain, the seventeenth-century artist Rembrandt van Rijn thrived in the Dutch Republic, a Calvinist Protestant mercantile culture where artists worked for the free market rather than solely by commission. During the "Golden Age" of Dutch art, Rembrandt etched a portrait of a Dutch Jewish man, believed by many people to be the Sephardic Rabbi Menasseh ben Israel of Amsterdam. Rembrandt's engraving stands apart from previous representations of Jews by European artists.[7] His detailed etching, with its tight hatch markings, presents a Jewish man who represents himself, a man of physical and mental agency, rather than a social outcast, a type, or a condemned figure. Bearing a calm demeanor, Menasseh looks directly out from the oval frame but does not react or perform a role. The sense of solidity in Menasseh's comportment differs from Goya's image of an anonymous Jew, a condemned man who merits pity but lacks individuality.

The seventeenth-century Spanish Jews who settled in Amsterdam found a rare climate of acceptance and tolerance that they had not previously experienced. Many *conversos* (Jews who had been converted), such as Menasseh ben Israel, reclaimed their Jewish identity. Rembrandt's less prejudicial images emerged from the contemporary Dutch Republic's interest in the powers of direct observation, an increased interest in peoples of foreign cultures, and a more tolerant attitude toward Jews. The desire for truthfulness over caricature also speaks to Rembrandt's precisionist and artistic skills. Such artistic skills of observation and naturalism masked deeper desires of Protestant Amsterdam to redeem Jews and convert them to Christianity. Contemporary Dutch Calvinists perceived Jews through the lens of Protestant philosemitism, a "historical phenomenon entirely distinct from modern secular conceptions of religious tolerance,"[8] art historian Michael Zell has proposed. Yet Rembrandt's vision anticipated the possibility of Jewish dignity, which would come to characterize early New York Jews.

Sephardic Jews fascinated seventeenth-century Dutch Calvinists. Painter Emanuel de Witte evinced this open curiosity by painting three separate

Emanuel de Witte, *Interior of the Portuguese Synagogue*, Amsterdam, c. 1675, oil on canvas. (Courtesy Rijksmuseum, Amsterdam, Holland)

images of Amsterdam's Sephardic synagogue, the Esnoga.⁹ De Witte composed his painting as if a curtain had just lifted on a stage set, with viewers of the service in the foreground, their backs to us. These figures serve as our double, placing us among the Gentile visitors who have come to enjoy the lively, exotic Jews as they worship. Such sites as the Esnoga became a tourists' destination for travelers to Amsterdam, many of whom sought out all three of the city's synagogues to visit. Sephardic Jews, proud of their aesthetic sensibilities, welcomed Christian visitors into their world as a way to promote the community. It was centuries before Jews who settled in New York were able to construct a building of equal grandeur.¹⁰

While de Witte painted the Esnoga for non-Jewish patrons, this portrait of revered Rabbi Isaac Aboab da Fonseca, the first rabbi in the Americas, was created and paid for by the Jewish community. The art of portrait painting became popular in the Dutch Republic, with merchants, civic groups, and guilds commissioning large-scale, multifigured group portraits, and betrothed couples sitting for marriage portraits. Sephardic Jews in Amsterdam sought

Aeronaut Nagtegaal, *Portrait of Isaac Aboab da Fonseca*, 1685, engraving and mezzotint on paper. (Courtesy John Carter Brown Library, Brown University, Providence, RI)

to celebrate and retain images of their revered rabbis, around whom a cult of personality arose. In 1641, Fonseca, shown here with the preferred squared-off beard of Sephardic men, versus the bushy, more "Abrahamic" beards of the Ashkenazim, accepted the request of Jews in Recife, Brazil, to become their rabbi. Born a *converso* in Portugal, Fonseca was a mystic who sought wisdom from the Kabbalah rather than the Torah. The artist etched this portrait of Fonseca upon his return to Holland. Through consideration of Fonseca's portrait, his travels, and his biography, we can track the history and influence of Sephardic culture from Portugal to Amsterdam to Brazil and, finally, to New Amsterdam.

When Portugal seized control of Recife, Brazil, from the Dutch, the Sephardim who lived there fled into exile. In 1654, a small group of men, women, and children, twenty-three in all, journeyed by boat to yet another new home. These early Jewish refugees began the process of building the foundations of the city that was to become home to the largest number of Jews globally: New York. They were also creating rudiments of two new identities, American Jew and New York Jew.

The Dutch governed New Amsterdam and commissioned the map on the following page, showing the city in 1660, a few years after the Recife Jews had arrived. In 1916, John Wolcott Adams and I. N. Phelps Stokes re-created —or what they called "redrafted"—the original 1660 topographical map. They chronicle Lower Manhattan, where the Jewish refugees established their Spanish and Portuguese Cemetery and, soon after, their first synagogue. Designed according to an organic plan in evidence today, the area includes streets and property lines arranged along lines of major topographical features. Streets also align with such man-made elements as wharves, used for trade across the Atlantic. Rather than focus solely on land, the original cartographers, and later Adams and Stokes, rendered the city surrounded by waterways liberally dotted with ships flying masts. By emphasizing the masses of land in relation to the surrounding bodies of water, the map pictorially explains how the growth of New Amsterdam as a port city enabled Jews to arrive, to establish themselves in mercantile trades, and to continue working with businesses in Holland.

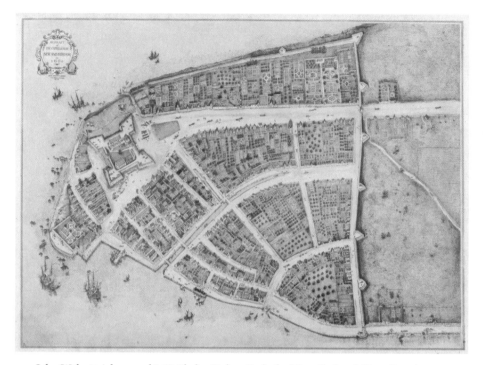

John Wolcott Adams and I. N. Phelps Stokes, *Redraft of Castello* (1916) *Plan, New Amsterdam in 1660.* (Maps Collection, the New-York Historical Society, New York)

The New Yorker David Grim was a youngster during the early 1740s, the period captured in his 1813 map. Grim claimed his rendering, completed when he was seventy-six, to be "a perfect and correct recollection" of the city in its and his own youth. Grim drafted the detailed map for his own "amusement, with the intent that it be on a future day presented to the New-York Historical Society."[11] The map measures a bit less than two feet square, and its once vivid colors have long faded. Grim highlighted monuments to imperial, cultural, provincial, and municipal authority, such as Trinity Church and City Hall. Grim's numbered places "trace the city's ethnic diversity: he listed not only the Anglican Trinity Church but also two Dutch churches, Presbyterian, French, Baptist, and Lutheran churches, a Quaker meetinghouse, and even a Jewish synagogue," ranging in style and scale.[12] His work offers a graphic representation of the range of religions and cultures in New York, including American Jews.

Grim also re-created a city "marked by slavery." Two landmarks represent the site where African slaves were burnt and lynched, a frightening vision to the then four-year-old Grimm, who later asserted, "I have a perfect idea of seeing the Negroes chained to a stake, and there burned to death."[13] His description echoes the anonymous eighteenth-century engraving *Burning of Spanish Jews and Others in Portugal* (p. 265) and testifies to the prevalence of slavery in New York. The interwoven histories of American Jews and peoples of African descent later became a constant subject in New York's visual and social histories.

David Grim, *A Plan of the City and Environs of New York as They Were in the Years 1742, 1743 or 1744*, 1813, pen, ink, and watercolor. (Collection of the New-York Historical Society, New York)

Left: Portrait of Moses Levy, attributed to Gerardus Duyckinck, c. 1735, oil on canvas. (Courtesy Crystal Bridges Museum of American Art, Bentonville, AR; photography by Dwight Primiano)
Right: Portrait of Franks Children with Lamb, attributed to Gerardus Duyckinck, c. 1735, oil on canvas. (Courtesy Crystal Bridges Museum of American Art, Bentonville, AR; photography by Dwight Primiano)

A Dutch merchant-class tradition proliferated in New Amsterdam, with sitting for a portrait an accepted means to mark one's achievement of wealth and status. England also maintained a rich tradition of portraiture, although reserved for the upper echelons of society. Portraits became the most popular form of pictorial expression in colonial America. Moses Levy and his son-in-law Jacob Franks were the most prominent Jewish Anglo-German merchants who settled in New York in the early eighteenth century.[14] Levy and, in the next painting, his family chose to avoid any identifiable Jewish elements in their portraits. Levy wanted the paintings to establish his class position. Indeed, nothing within the paintings distinguishes Levy or his family from their socially prominent Christian neighbors. Painters worked from pattern books containing prints of stock poses, settings, and props derived from portraits of

European aristocrats and royalty. The Franks-Levy Family Portrait Collection comprises six individual canvases, the most extensive surviving program of colonial American portraiture.[15]

In the first painting, Levy gestures out through a window to ships sailing nearby to indicate his merchant status and connections to trade and economic growth. His children in the second portrait are represented to convey their adherence to social mores and appropriate gender roles. The son is shown standing, his arm akimbo so that his elbow overlaps with a window view, or the world beyond a domestic interior. Demurely, his sister sits at his side, sheltered within the home, holding a rose in her uplifted hand and a lamb close to her side. Both the cultivated flower and tamed young animal are symbols frequently included in Protestant and Catholic European paintings to broadcast young girls' virtues, chastity, and impeccable upbringing.

In the portrait of Moses Levy's young daughter, the delicately held blossoms in her hand indicate her youthful purity. It was widely believed that young girls' hands were best kept busy with appropriate activities such as making quilts and stitching samplers. The sampler on the following page was made by the hand of young Rebecca Hendricks. Using silk thread on linen, Hendricks stitched Jewish designs and text into a Christian European form, uniting Judaica with Americana on her linen swatch. Young girls and adult women began to embroider fine needlework beginning in the Middle Ages and, by the sixteenth century, learned their stitches, alphabet, and lessons from set pattern books. Each measured stitch was also a lesson in patience and accuracy. Jewish women adopted embroidery in approximately 1650.[16] Samplers, the most common embroidered works of art and craft, are a literal sampling of different stitches through which women could display their virtuosity with a needle. They were also instructive of social mores, texts, and Bible verses.[17] Texts for colonial-era samplers were usually culled from biblical phrases and aphorisms. Hendricks selected a passage that reflects her dual identity as a colonial girl of breeding and a young Jew. She stitched into cloth verses 1–14 of the 78th Psalm, with the phrase "He commanded our fathers that they should make them known to their children; That they might [not] forget the words of God but keep his commandments" (Ps. 78: 5, 7).[18] The rise of feminist art history in the 1970s, led by Linda Nochlin, a Jewish New Yorker, stimulated scholars to take seriously embroidery and handicrafts by women as works of art.

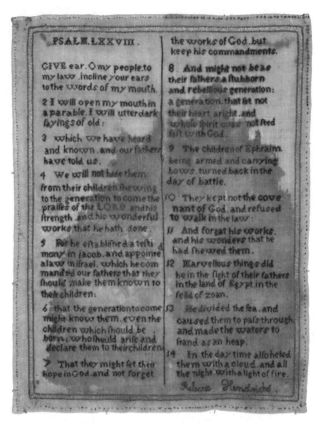

Rebecca Hendricks, *Sampler of the 78th Psalm*, linen with cotton thread, late eighteenth century. (Courtesy American Jewish Historical Society, New York, NY, and Newton Centre, MA)

Artist Susan C. Dessel's work recuperates the names and identities of Jewish women who were denied access to the historical record of New York and of their culture. Her sculptural installation *Still-Lives* acknowledges the six women who were among the twenty-three who sailed from Recife, Brazil, to New Amsterdam in 1654 and who formed the nucleus of Jewish community. Dessel established in her research that colonial society relegated Jewish women and children to a lesser realm than men, an inequality that extended to mortuary rituals and tombstones in Chatham Square. Most epitaphs reduced the whole of a woman's life and her identity to her relationship to men, either as the "daughter of . . ." or "wife of . . ." While a woman's first name was not recorded for posterity, her husband's or her father's full name was inscribed on her stone.[19] In addition to combing cemetery records and studying the burial histories of the Chatham Street Cemetery, Dessel pored over letters that these and other colonial Jewish women wrote and received. In these personal writings, the women express concern for their health and that of their families, an awareness of aging and beauty, and worry about decaying and fragile teeth.

The women's worries and words inspired Dessel to carve a toothbrush from a cow's femur with horsehair bristles and to inscribe each one with a particular woman's name. Each toothbrush bearing names and birth/death dates symbolizes "the women's struggles to take care of the home and the family and to hold on to a sense of self while caring for others' wants and needs."[20] Dessel's work exemplifies how we can continue to explore and examine historical objects, events, and people and their relevance to our current ideas of what constitutes New York City Jewish culture. In lieu of new headstones, Dessel's individualized toothbrushes commemorate these women and their daughters by acknowledging their private concerns and desires while using a contemporary artistic form to bring the women into the present day.

Still-Lives: An Exhibit of Works by Susan C. Dessel, 2009, mixed-media installation, cow bone, horsehair, and hide hair glue. (Courtesy of the artist)

PRAYERS
FOR
SHABBATH, ROSH-HASHANAH, AND KIPPUR;
OR
The SABBATH, the BEGINING of the YEAR;
AND
The DAY of ATONEMENTS;
WITH
The AMIDAH and MUSAPH of the MOADIM;
OR
SOLEMN SEASONS.

According to the Order of the Spanish and Portuguese Jews:

Tranflated by ISAAC PINTO.

And for him printed by JOHN HOLT, in New-York;
A. M. 5526.
1766

Prayers for Shabbat, Rosh-Hashanah, and Kippur, 1765–1766, translated from the Hebrew by Isaac Pinto. (A. S. W. Rosenback Rare Book Collection; courtesy American Jewish Historical Society, New York, NY, and Newton Centre, MA)

When the first Jews arrived in New Amsterdam, the Dutch West India Company ordered Peter Stuyvesant, the last Dutch director of the colony of New Netherland, to permit Jews freedom of religious practice.[21] Just over one hundred years later, Jews were openly practicing their religion in New York without restraint. This prayer book was published in 1765–1766 (5526). Isaac Pinto recognized that the majority of Jews did not know Hebrew and so translated the traditional text into English. The liturgy and order of the prayers follow Sephardic custom. This prayer book (or *siddur*) is believed to have first been published anonymously, probably to avoid raising the ire of traditionalists, who often looked askance at liturgical translations. Such translations of traditional texts were often designed with women in mind; given women's limited role in communal Jewish ritual and worship, they were not fluent in Hebrew, if they knew the language at all.

Just as immigrants and refugees refashioned themselves upon arrival in New York, so too did the Gomez family's ornate mustard pot find a new identity and function. It was transformed from a fancy condiment holder in England to a prized Jewish ritual object—an *etrog* holder. The result is a uniquely American syncretic object that demonstrates the adaptability of the Gomez family.[22] A high-style pot, most definitely a luxury item, made of silver, its body rests upon three cabriole feet and is topped off with a hinged lid. The front displays the family's monogram. Silver was a rare commodity in New York, and Jewish ritual objects available in Europe were not accessible in the New World. For these reasons, the Gomez family transformed their mustard pot into an *etrog* holder for the festival of Sukkoth. The holder stayed within the family for six generations and symbolizes the early American Jewish experience, a blending of Jewish and European—here, British—traditions, styles, and functions, refashioned on American soil.

Unknown maker, *etrog* holder of the Louis (?) Gomez family of New York, late eighteenth century, silver and cobalt blue glass; engraved on front, "E/BG/R/MG," and on back, "C/BG." (Courtesy American Jewish Historical Society, New York, NY, and Newton Centre, MA)

Myer Myers (1723–1795), circumcision clip, c. 1765–1776, silver. (Courtesy Jewish Museum, New York / Art Resource, New York)

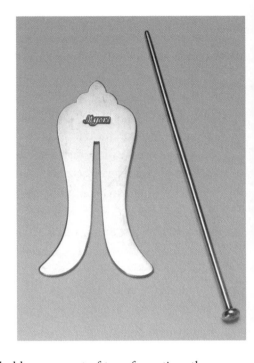

If we consider the Gomez's *etrog* holder as an act of transformation, then this silver circumcision clip made by Myer Myers reflects cultural continuity. "The most ancient sign of Jewish identity within the Jewish community is the circumcision of its males," writes historian Ellen Smith, "as commanded to Abraham by the Lord in Genesis."[23] Very few ritual objects have survived from the colonial and republican eras, which makes Myers's circumcision shield quite rare. This shield belonged to the Seixas family circumcision set, one of two extant sets. On the front of the flat shield, Myers stamped his mark. Silver, a prized and prestigious craft material, was also used as currency at the time, and so silversmiths simultaneously played both the roles of banker and artisan. Myers patterned the shield's curved form on the shape of an inverted lyre, which was the style from at least seventeenth-century Europe. This shield demonstrates that Jewish rituals and European artistic styles survived the transatlantic voyage to the colonies. While Myers is heralded as one of America's premier Jewish artisans, this moniker actually limits his influence and expertise. A contemporary of Paul Revere, Myers was, in fact, one of America's foremost silversmiths. In order to stay financially solvent, Myers did not limit his art to Jewish ritual objects.

Myer Myers was born in 1723 just a block away from congregation Shearith Israel, for which he later made this pair of Torah finials. Given the centrality and sacredness of the Torah in Jewish life, Jews have for centuries used ornaments to honor and beautify the Torah scroll. Myers created three pairs of Torah finials for congregations in Newport, New York (Shearith Israel), and Philadelphia. An inscription on one shaft here reads, "Newport," which suggests that the sets were mixed up at some point—probably during the Revolutionary period, when sacred objects were transferred from New York and Newport to Philadelphia for safekeeping—since the pair now in Newport also bears this inscription on only one shaft. The artistry of the finials conforms to designs typical of Jewish—specifically Sephardic—ritual objects and originated in sacred texts, making these objects rich with symbolism. The gilded bells' chime when the Torah is removed from and returned to the ark is meant to mimic gold bells that once adorned the robe of the high priest. Pomegranates, not indigenous to New York, are intended to recall a biblical verse referring to the brass pillars' capitals with pomegranates that stood on the Temple porch in Jerusalem.[24] Myers brought these antique symbols and meanings to colonial American Jews.

Myer Myers (1723–1795), two Torah finials, 1765–1776, silver. (Photograph by Joanne Savio, in Marc D. Angel, *Remnant of Israel: A Portrait of America's First Jewish Congregation, Shearith Israel* [New York, 2004]; courtesy Congregation Shearith Israel, New York)

Anonymous, *The Mill Street Synagogue*, undated, print on paper. (Courtesy American Jewish Historical Society, New York, NY, and Newton Centre, MA)

During the Dutch period, Jews were required to build their homes close to each other on one side of New Amsterdam, where a de facto Jewish neighborhood emerged. With the British conquest of the city, Jews were free to move but decided to remain centralized around Mill Street. Congregation Shearith Israel began there.[25] This undated print depicts the congregation's first synagogue, which was built by a Gentile mason, Stanley Holmes. At thirty-five square feet, this unassuming structure, consecrated in 1730, stood on a lot approximately 40 by 102 feet on a narrow street often called "Jews' Alley." Shearith Israel was New York's only Jewish congregation until 1825. Despite its modest size, the synagogue contained within all the necessary accoutrements of a Jewish house of worship, including a balcony with seating for women. In addition, the rear garden allowed for the construction of a booth for the festival of Sukkoth. This small cottagelike structure vastly differs from the more elaborate synagogues built in Amsterdam, and nothing about the exterior distinguishes it as a house of worship. New York's Jewish community in the 1730s lacked the population, wealth, and social prestige to build a synagogue approaching the grandeur of the Esnoga in Amsterdam. Instead, in terms of architectural style and scale, the members of Shearith Israel had to start anew. Modernization and relocation required a continuous shifting of artistic styles, so that this Dutch-style house became Jewish by its use. The serene setting of the print, complete with white picket fence and abundant greenery, evidences a familiarity with English landscape art.[26]

Historian Jonathan Sarna writes, "In colonial America, the presence of a Torah scroll served as a defining symbol of Jewish communal life and culture, of Jewish law and love."[27] This scroll, damaged by British soldiers during the American Revolution, comes down to us as a witness to and survivor of the war. That the soldiers were British implies that the synagogue members were British loyalists. In appreciation, the British did not use the synagogue for military purposes, and the British did severely punish the two soldiers who had damaged the scrolls. That the Torah was not buried once it returned to the congregation, as is the custom when a scroll is desecrated, suggests that it was considered to be of value as a historical object. Someone made a choice to give preference to historical interests over religious obligation.

Torah scroll desecrated by two British soldiers during the Revolution. (Photograph by Joanne Savio, in Marc D. Angel, *Remnant of Israel: A Portrait of America's First Jewish Congregation, Shearith Israel* [New York, 2004]; courtesy Congregation Shearith Israel, New York)

Marriage contract of Rachel Franks and
Haym Solomon, 1777. (Courtesy American
Jewish Historical Society, New York, NY,
and Newton Centre, MA)

This *ketubah*, or Jewish marriage contract, marked the union of Rachel
Franks and Haym Salomon on Sunday, July 6, 1777, in New York, then occupied by the British. The groom, a Polish immigrant and a successful businessman and patriot, later provided critical financial backing to the American Revolution. Franks, daughter of a Jewish tailor, was fifteen years old at the
time of the wedding, twenty-one years younger than her husband, but such
a difference in age was not particularly uncommon at the time. The wedding
ceremony was held at congregation Shearith Israel and officiated by Abraham
I. Abrahams.[28] Jewish marriage contracts may be illustrated; however, this example is rather simple. The only decoration is an arch, which imitates fron-
tispieces common in eighteenth-century books. Classical Greek and Roman
designs greatly influenced all areas of American architecture and design from
the nation's beginnings, and this influence filtered into religious artwork. The
neoclassical arch situates this *ketubah* within this era.[29]

Mourning jewelry crafted in the neoclassical style was a popular object in the late eighteenth century and the nineteenth century, "a token and a totem," writes Erin E. Eisenbarth, which brought the face and memories of a deceased loved one to mind while also functioning as a sign of the owner's own mortality.[30] Only wealthy elites could afford to commission jewelry, proof of their status and attention to style. New York was, and remains, a center of the jewelry industry. This exquisitely rendered, detailed mourning pendent typifies bereavement jewelry common to wealthy Christian families, but it is atypical because this piece was commissioned by Jews.

Unidentified artist, memorial pendant for Solomon and Joseph Hays, 1801, hair, gold, pearls, and pigment. (Yale University Art Gallery, promised bequest of Davida Tenenbaum Deutsch and Alvin Deutsch, L.L.B., 1958, in honor of Kathleen Luhrs)

Jacob Hays had this double memorial locket crafted for his wife to mark the deaths of their two sons, Solomon and Joseph, in 1798 and 1801, respectively.[31] The unknown artisan's signature skill, displayed here, was his intricate handling of human hair (from the two sons), beads, pearls, and wire. A lock of Solomon's blond hair forms the weeping willow at left, mirrored by Joseph's brown hair on the right. The craftsman dissolved the boys' hair to paint the left and right portions of the scene, which lends "a golden earthen tone to the background."[32] Chopped and cut blond hair fills the landscape below the memorials, and on the reverse, the two brothers' locks were plaited together, uniting the pair for eternity. Jacob Hays and his wife, along with other wealthy Jews, influenced by their Christian neighbors but without renouncing their Jewishness or abandoning Jewish mourning practices, commissioned bereavement jewelry as a statement of their private grief.

The arrival of slaves in New Amsterdam in 1626 predated the arrival of the Jews from Recife and provided forced labor for the colony. During parts of the seventeenth and eighteenth centuries, New York was home to the largest urban slave population in North America.[33] While the story of slavery is often cast as a southern experience, New York was a slave state until 1827.

New York Jews did not differ from their Christian neighbors who also owned slaves. Jacob Levy Jr. was a prominent figure among New York Jews, connected by marriage to the Seixas family and a member of congregation Shearith Israel. He was also a slave owner. In 1814, George Roper, a slave, appealed to Levy, his owner, for his freedom, which Levy promised to him in three years' time. It appears that Levy was influenced by the New York Society for the Promoting of Manumission of Slaves. Perhaps he was inspired by the pending 1827 deadline to the Gradual Emancipation Act of 1790 to hasten the freeing of his other slaves: Mary Mundy, Samuel Spures, Edwin Jackson, Elizabeth Jackson, and James Jackson.[34] His manumission records, housed within the Manumission Society's holdings, suggests his involvement with abolition. Jewish men who acquired slaves, manumitted them, or chose not to own slaves on moral grounds demonstrated that their communal tenure in America had involved them in one of the fundamental issues of our nation's founding—that of slavery.

Know all Men by these presents, That *Jacob Levy Junr*

do, by these presents, for good and valuable considerations, fully and absolutely *Manumit, make Free, and set at Liberty* a *female* slave, named *Mary Murray* hereby willing and declaring that the said *Mary* shall and may, at all times hereafter, exercise, hold, and enjoy, all and singular the liberties, rights, privileges, and immunities of *a* free *Woman* fully to all intents and purposes, as if *she* had been born free.—And *I* do hereby, for *myself my* Executors, Administrators, and Assigns, absolutely relinquish and release all *my* right, title, and property whatsoever, in and to the said *female Slave Mary* as *my* slave.

In Testimony Whereof, *I* have hereunto set *my* hand and seal, the *fifth* day of *March* one thousand eight hundred and *Seventeen*

Jacob Levy Jr [L.S]

SEALED AND DELIVERED IN
THE PRESENCE OF

I. Morton

City of New York, ss.

On the *sixth* day of *March* 1817 *Jacob Levy Junior* appeared before me, and acknowledged that *he* executed the above instrument, as *his* voluntary act and deed, for the uses and purposes therein mentioned. I allow it to be recorded.

Jacob Radcliff

By *Jacob Radcliff* Mayor, *and* Richard Riker Recorder, *of the city of New-York,*

It is hereby Certified, That pursuant to the statute in such case made and provided, we have this day examined *a* certain Negro Slave named *John Jackson* the property of *Jacob Levy Jr*, aged *four & four months* Slave which slave *is* about to be manumitted, and *The Parents of said Slave* appearing to us ~~to be under~~ *to be able & willing to maintain* ~~forty five years of age, and of sufficient ability to provide for~~ we have granted this Certificate, this *sixth* day of *March* ~~in the year of our~~ Lord, one thousand eight hundred and *Seventeen*

Jacob Radcliff

R. Riker

Certificate of manumission, New York Society for Manumission, New York, 1817. (Collection of the New-York Historical Society, New York)

As more Jews came to America and rose in social prestige, they were less able to control how, where, and why they were represented. The greater New York Jews' ascent into social and political circles, the more public and often-times crude was the public attack. Technological innovations enabled mass printing and distribution of newspapers and broadsides. On the facing page is a parody of a public notice about an attack on Mordecai Manuel Noah, "of no. 57 Franklin Street." Noah, an important early nineteenth-century journalist and playwright, served as editor of the *National Advocate* and later as publisher of the *New York Enquirer* and the *New York Evening Star*. He was U.S. consul to the Kingdom of Tunis, although he was later recalled because of his religion. Noah's activism as a political journalist and a Jew made him the first American Jew to achieve real prominence. In this parody, a large, hook-nosed Noah is being attacked by the puny Elijah J. Roberts, a non-Jewish former business associate with whom Noah had had a falling out. The two men stand on the steps of the Park Theater, and a small playbill on the wall reads,

The Jew
1 act of the HYPOCRITE End with the farce of
THE LIAR

This parody suggests that with public success came hostility and blatant anti-Jewish sentiment. The image of the unusually tall, looming Jew reappeared in cartoons throughout the nineteenth century. Such stereotypical images exaggerating the bodies and faces of Jews originated in the Middle Ages and bypass the naturalism of Rembrandt and Goya. These exaggerated representations of Jews illustrate persistent accusations that Jews held disproportionate amounts of power and social influence.

Common picturesque cityscapes of early New York paint over many of the harsh realities of urban life: streets filled with sewage and animal carcasses, the filth and disease rampant in overcrowded shacks and substandard housing, and the noises and odors that permeated street life. Diseases such as cholera and tuberculosis spread rapidly under such conditions and were often blamed on the latest immigrant group to arrive in the city. These deadly illnesses hit people of all social classes and standing, although the poor were much more vulnerable than others. To address the spread of the disease, and also to plead for protection, congregation Shearith Israel wrote a prayer specifically to

CITY OF NEW-YORK ---ss.

MORDECAI M. NOAH,

Of No. 57, Franklin-street, being

DULY SWORN,

DEPOSETH and **SAITH**, that on the 20th day of June 1828, at the 2d Ward of the *City* of *New-York*, he was violently *assaulted*, by

ELIJAH J. ROBERTS,

Who attacked him on the steps, and

COW-SKINNED HIM!!

without any just justification on the part of the said assailant, wherefore this deponent prays, that the said

ELIJAH J. ROBERTS,

may be bound by recognizance to be of good behaviour and keep the peace, and to answer for the above assault, &c. at the next Court of General Sessions of the Peace, to be holden in and for the said city.

Sworn before me this
20th day of June.
J. HOPSON.

M. M. NOAH.

Satire: Mordecai Manuel Noah, June 20, 1828, woodcut with letter-press broadside. (Courtesy Broadside Collection, Library of Congress, Washington, DC)

Prayer for cholera. (Courtesy of the American Jewish Historical Society, New York, NY, and Newton Centre, MA)

protect congregants from the illness, showing the adaptability of tradition to new surroundings and new challenges.

Even without reading the contents of the Haggadah on the facing page or handling it, consider the many facts that this "quintessential Jewish prayer book for the home" helps to establish. The Haggadah exists because there was a sizable observant Jewish population in 1837 New York.[35] The printer wrote out his name, Solomon Jackson, and profession on the cover page, indicating that Jews had expanded into traditionally Gentile businesses and occupations such as printing; it is likely that by necessity their clientele was not limited to

Jews and that they produced works other than strictly ritual volumes. Notice that Jackson described the Haggadah as the "First American Edition." By labeling it as the first, Jackson announces with confidence that subsequent editions will be needed in the coming years. There was a market for Jewish ritual texts in New York. Finally, the cover provides insight into the makeup of New York's Jewish population at the time. The forty-three-leaf book was published both in the original Hebrew and in English, which suggests that New York's Jews were by and large English speakers. The Haggadah conforms to both the "customs of the German and Spanish Jews," as is written on the cover. These words acknowledge the different linguistic and cultural strains of American Jews. Although the origins of American Jewry began with Sephardic culture, even before the 1820s, Ashkenazi, or German, Jews outnumbered the Sephardim.

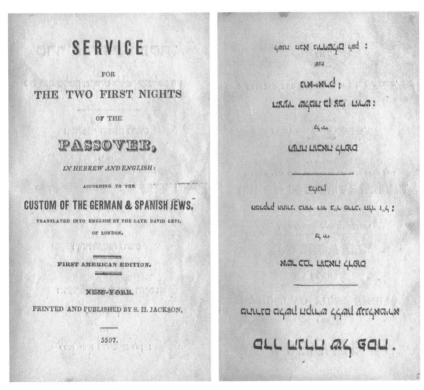

Solomon Jackson, *The First American Haggadah*, 1837. (Hebraic Section, gift Leiner Temerlin, augmented by a grant from Madison Council, Library of Congress, Washington, DC)

"The Jewish Passover of 1858," *Frank Leslie's Illustrated Newspaper*, April
10, 1858. (Courtesy Prints and Photographs Division, Library of Congress,
Washington, DC)

Illustrated newspapers such as *Frank Leslie's* enabled their readers to be armchair voyeurs and anthropologists examining different cultures and peoples, such as New York Jews, from their parlors without having to interact with actual Jews. Founded in 1855, *Frank Leslie's* targeted a rather broad and inclusive "middle" readership, mostly Christians of various denominations who, like the visitors to the Esnoga in Amsterdam painted by Emanuel de Witte, were intrigued by Jews and their culture, which seemed exotic in contrast to their own.[36] These images of matzo production on New York's Chatham Street illustrated a two-page spread titled "The Jewish Passover of 1858." The figures depicted conform to standard racial stereotypes, and the article describes Jews as having "low stature, shining black eyes, crisp inky hair, hooked noses, stooping shoulders and eager movements." The author also asserts that despite Jews' "loose morals" and dishonesty, all are meticulous in their observance of the Passover rituals. Nevertheless, the article concludes with a backhanded compliment that as a whole, the city's Jews are "quiet, law-abiding good citizens, . . . among the very best of the adopted citizens of America." It is notable that a mainstream national newspaper would choose to run a relatively long (the paper was sixteen pages in all), heavily illustrated feature about a minority population. One might also wonder how the journalist went about getting his information, as there are numerous errors, such as the suggestion that beef and fish are forbidden foods on Passover. *Frank Leslie's* typical readership was not poor immigrant Jews. The length of the 1858 illustrated article simultaneously demonstrates a growing awareness and interest in Jewish neighbors by Gentile New Yorkers while also propagating attitudes perceiving exoticism and the need to interpret the mores of new Americans.

Slavery divided New Yorkers. In Abraham Lincoln's senatorial campaign of 1858, he drew on the biblical metaphor of "a house divided" to describe the national split on slavery and abolition. While congregation B'nai Jeshurun's Rabbi Morris J. Raphall opposed slavery as an individual, in his famous 1861 sermon, he insists that according to a literal interpretation of Scripture, slavery was sanctioned by the Torah.[37] Despite his personal views, the fame of his speech and stance led him to be called "The Pro-Slavery Rabbi." In response, Rabbi David Einhorn of Baltimore responded directly to Raphall's sermon with his own antislavery sermon and publication.

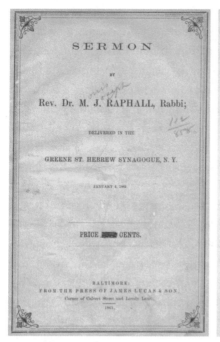
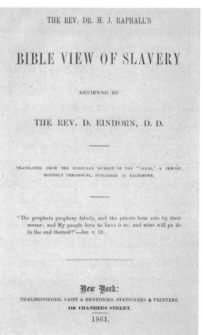

Left: Morris J. Raphall (1798–1868), "Bible View of Slavery: A Discourse, Delivered at the Jewish Synagogue, B'nai Jeshurun, New York, on the Day of the National Fast, January 4, 1861" (New York: Rudd and Carleton, 1861). (Courtesy of the Library of Congress, Washington, DC)

Right: The Reverend David Einhorn, D.D., "The Bible View of Slavery" (New York: Thalmessinger, Cahn & Benedicks, printers, 1861), translated from the February 1861 issue of the *Sinai*, a Jewish monthly periodical published in Baltimore. (Courtesy of the Library of Congress, Washington, DC)

This public altercation between rabbis reveals tensions within the Jewish community, proving that there was more than one way to live as an American Jew. It also shows the degree to which Jews were sufficiently comfortable in America to take on this most decisive of national issues.

The advent of photography in 1839 democratized portraiture and self-representation. Daguerreotypes captured the likenesses of a wider variety of Americans in terms of class, occupation, ethnicity, and religion than was possible with painted portraiture, which remained largely confined to social elites. Studio portraits soon became tied to life-cycle events, such as for newly married Jewish couples. These two men, both soldiers during the Civil

War, possibly brothers, were Jewish New Yorkers who wanted to mark their social status and patriotism. The two men differentiate themselves from each other through each one's choice of dress, hand gestures, and body position. The man at left stands almost in silhouette, his hands limp by his side, with a large-brimmed, nondescript hat on his head. He has turned away from the camera, allowing us to observe him free from his eyes meeting ours. Since people arranged for daguerreotypes in order to preserve their likeness, this sideways stance, which obscures the man's identity, is a rather unusual pose. In contrast, the second man, possibly his brother, stands tall and frontal, his hand in his many-buttoned coat, drawing attention to his uniform. He looks directly at us with pride. What might explain the vastly different poses? It has been suggested that the man at left was a pious Jew who chose not to wear his uniform and would not look into the photographer's camera because of discomfort since the making of a portrait is the making of an image. The man at right, facing proudly forward in his Union uniform, promotes his identity as an American soldier. This photograph depicts this Jewish man as a soldier, with all the brawn and masculinity that accompanies military service. How apt, too, for possible brothers to symbolize the Civil War itself, which pitted brother against brother.[38]

Possibly brothers, an Orthodox Jew and a U.S. Navy engineer pose in New York City during the Civil War, daguerreotype, New York. (Courtesy Robert Marcus)

Solomon Carvalho (1815–1895), *Abraham Lincoln and Diogenes*, 1865, oil on canvas, 44 × 34 in. (Courtesy Rose Art Museum, Brandeis University, Waltham, MA; gift of John J. and Celia Mack, Maurice and Rose Turner, Justin G. and Gertrude Turner)

Born in Charleston, South Carolina, in 1815, artist, explorer, and photographer Solomon Nunes Carvalho was of Spanish-Portuguese Jewish descent. During 1853–1854, he traveled as a photographer with the expedition of explorer John C. Fremont through western territories searching for a possible railroad route to the Pacific Ocean. A few years later, by the early 1860s, Carvalho had settled in New York. True to his birthplace, he supported the South during the ensuing Civil War. His skills as a painter gained him entry to New

York's prestigious and exclusive National Academy of Design, where he exhibited his oils.[39] Despite being a supporter of the Confederacy, he was also simultaneously a great admirer of President Abraham Lincoln, to the point of hero worship. Soon after the assasination of the president in 1865, Carvalho painted this highly unusual posthumous pictorial representation, one of four known allegorical portraits. Carvalho divided his composition so that Lincoln is seated indoors, holding in his hand a scroll that bears words from his second inaugural address. A large swag curtain lifts up at the right, where the Capitol building, symbolizing the Union, is depicted. Behind Lincoln is a statue of President George Washington, draped in a toga as if a Roman leader; no known statue corresponds to this detail. The curtains' red tassle leads the viewer's eye outdoors, where Carvhalo has painted the figure of Diogenes, who, having found his honest man, stands in amazement, his lantern broken on the ground. Carvhalo held high ambitions for his work and envisioned it hanging prominently in Washington, D.C. Instead, it was lost and fell into obscurity until 1952. It is because it is the only known painting by a Jew of Lincoln of that time, rather than its dubious artistic merit, which has brought the work back into public view.

Spanning almost three hundred years, the objects and images offered for consideration in this visual essay serve as passports to the journey of becoming New York Jews. This journey has not been just temporal. Rather, these objects call our attention to a cultural journey in which Jews and Jewish objects have interacted with other cultures, with new materials with which to make art and ritual objects, and with an unfamiliar urban environment in which to establish their new home. While Jews participated publicly in political debates, such as those concerning slavery and the Civil War, through embroidery or portraits we can gain entry into the domestic and private world of Jews in America. In James Baldwin's searing memoir *The Fire Next Time*, the writer states what might seem obvious: that "African American" was a new identity brought about by slavery, and there is no equal to the African American identity in the world and in the African diaspora. His observations are pertinent to American Jews. The formation of New York Jewish identity was not established with the arrival of Recife refugees in New Amsterdam. Rather, the process of identity formation continues to evolve. Tombstones, topographical maps, and Torah finials all serve to shape and announce what it meant historically to be a Jew in New York, as well as what it means today.

NOTES

ABBREVIATIONS

AJA   American Jewish Archives
AJAJ   *American Jewish Archives Journal*
AJH   *American Jewish History*
AJHS   American Jewish Historical Society
AJHSQ   *American Jewish Historical Society Quarterly*
Asm   *Asmonean*
JM   *Jewish Messenger*
MBOT   Minutes of the Board of Trustees (Shearith Israel)
PAJHS   *Publications of the American Jewish Historical Society*

NOTES TO THE FOREWORD

1. Milton Lehman, "Veterans Pour into New York to Find That Its Hospitality Far Exceeds Their Dreams," *New York Times*, 8 July 1945, 51.

2. Ira Rosenwaike, *Population History of New York City* (Syracuse: Syracuse University Press, 1972), 98, 101.

3. Robert A. M. Stern, Thomas Mellins, and David Fishman, *New York 1960: Architecture and Urbanism between the Second World War and the Bicentennial* (New York: Monacelli, 1995), 10, 13–19, 27–28.

4. Moses Rischin, *The Promised City: New York's Jews, 1870–1914* (1962; repr., Cambridge: Harvard University Press, 1977), 294.

5. "Levi Strauss," Wikipedia, http://en.wikipedia.org/wiki/Levi_Strauss (accessed July 13, 2011).

6. Rischin, "Preface to the Paperback Edition," in *The Promised City*, vii.

7. Ibid. "City of Ambition" refers to the 1910 photograph by Alfred Stieglitz taken approaching Lower Manhattan from New York Harbor.

8. In this and the following pages, the text draws on the three volumes of City of Promises: A History of the Jews of New York (New York: NYU Press, 2012).

NOTES TO CHAPTER 1

1. Edwin G. Burrows and Michael Wallace, *Gotham: A History of New York City to 1898* (New York, 1999), ch. 1; Reginald Bolton, *Indians of Long Ago in the City of New York* (New York, 1934).

2. On the expulsion of the Jews from Spain, see Salo W. Baron, *A Social and Religious History of the Jews*, 2nd rev. ed., 18 vols. (New York, 1952–1985), 10:167–219; Daniel M. Swetschinski, *Reluctant Cosmopolitans: The Portuguese Jews of Seventeenth-Century Amsterdam* (London, 2000), 54–56.

3. Baron, *Social and Religious History*, vol. 10, ch. 44.

4. Ibid., vol. 10, ch. 45; Miriam Bodian, *Hebrews of the Portuguese Nation: Conversos and Community in Early Modern Amsterdam* (Bloomington, IN, 1997), 6–17; Jonathan Israel, *European Jewry in the Age of Mercantilism, 1550–1750*, 2nd ed. (Oxford, UK, 1989), ch. 1.

5. Swetschinski, *Reluctant Cosmopolitans*, 57–64; Bodian, *Hebrews of the Portuguese Nation*, 25–28; Eli Faber, *A Time for Planting: The First Migration, 1654–1820* (Baltimore, 1992), 7. The merger of Spain and Portugal in 1580 allowed Portuguese *conversos* to settle in the Spanish American colonies, where they became an important factor in colonial trade. The movement of *conversos* to the Americas was increased by the Inquisition, which persecuted more than five thousand former Jews in the 1620s and 1630s as Marranos, or secret Jews. By the late sixteenth century, as many as six thousand Portuguese Jewish converts were in Spanish America. Until the nineteenth century, there were far more Jews in the Caribbean than on the North American mainland. Jewish expansion in the Americas is well covered in Paolo Bernardini and Norman Fiering, eds., *The Jews and the Expansion of Europe to the West, 1450–1800* (New York, 2001).

6. The most definitive account of the birth of the republic is Jonathan Israel, *The Dutch Republic: Its Rise, Greatness, and Fall, 1477–1806* (Oxford, UK, 1995).

7. Ibid., chs. 11–15; Israel, *European Jewry in the Age of Mercantilism*, 2–3, ch. 2. Simon Schama, *An Embarrassment of Riches: An Interpretation of Dutch Culture in the Golden Age* (New York, 1987); Burrows and Wallace, *Gotham*, 14–17.

8. Jonathan Israel, "The Jews of Dutch America," in Bernardini and Fiering, *The Jews and the Expansion of Europe to the West*, 339; and James Homer Williams, "An Atlantic Perspective on the Jewish Struggle for Rights and Opportunities in Brazil, New Netherland and New York," in ibid., 374–376; Swetschinski, *Reluctant Cosmopolitans*, 91–92, 115–130, 167–224; Bodian, *Hebrews of the Portuguese Nations*, chs. 2–5.

9. Swetschinski, *Reluctant Cosmopolitans*, 102–130; Israel, "The Jews in Dutch America," 335–339. Leo Hershkowitz, "By Chance or Choice: Jews in New Amsterdam 1654," *AJAJ* 57 (2005): 5, 8, notes that Jews constituted 4 percent of major investors in 1656 and increased to 6.5 percent by 1656.

10. Swetschinski, *Reluctant Cosmopolitans*, 109–119; Israel, *The Dutch Republic*, 325–327; Israel, "The Jews of Dutch America," 340.

11. Swetschinski, *Reluctant Cosmopolitans*, 114–119; Israel, "The Jews of Dutch America," 341–342; Williams, "An Atlantic Perspective," 375–378; Hershkowitz, "By Chance or Choice," 3.

12. Arnold Wiznitzer, *Jews in Colonial Brazil* (New York, 1960), esp. ch. 6.

13. Burrows and Wallace, *Gotham*, ch. 2. For the economic background and motives of the West India Company, see Oliver A. Rink, *Holland on the Hudson: An Economic and Social History of Dutch New York* (Ithaca, NY, 1986), chs. 1–3. Russell Shorto, *The Island at the Center of the World* (New York, 2004), is the most recent narrative history; see chs. 1–2.

14. Burrows and Wallace, *Gotham*, 29–40; Shorto, *The Island at the Center of the World*, ch. 6.

15. Burrows and Wallace, *Gotham*, ch. 4; Henry Kessler and Eugene Rachlis, *Peter Stuyvesant and His New York* (New York, 1959), ch. 3.

16. David Franco Mendes, quoted in Samuel Oppenheim, "The Early History of the Jews in New York, 1654–1664: Some New Matter on the Subject," *PAJHS* 18 (1909): 80; Oppenheim's version is on 37–51; Arnold Wiznitzer's revision is "The Exodus from Brazil and Arrival in New Amsterdam of the Jewish Pilgrim Fathers, 1654," *PAJHS* 44 (1954–1955): 93–94. Jacob R. Marcus, *The Colonial American Jew, 1492–1776*, 3 vols. (Detroit, 1970), 1:210. Hershkowitz believes the ship may or may not have been in Cuba. Hershkowitz, "By Chance or Choice," 1–3.

17. Samuel Oppenheim, "More about Jacob Barsimon, the First Jewish Settler in New York," *PAJHS* 29 (1925): 39–49. The importance of Barsimon's mission to the elders of Amsterdam may be found in their decision to send a two-man mission. The second emissary, however, left the ship in London. Hershkowitz, "By Chance or Choice," 4 (quote).

18. Bernard Fernow, *Records of New Amsterdam*, quoted in Oppenheim, "The Early History of the Jews," 9, 67; Leo Hershkowitz, "New Amsterdam's Twenty-Three Jews—Myth or Reality?," in Shalom Goldman, ed., *Hebrew and the Bible in America: The First Two Centuries* (Hanover, NH, 1993), 172; Hershkowitz, "By Chance or Choice," 1–2.

19. Bernard Fernow, *Records of New Amsterdam*, quoted in Oppenheim, "The Early History of the Jews," 68–69, 71–72; Marcus, *The Colonial American Jew*, 1:217; David de Sola Pool and Tamar de Sola Pool, *An Old Faith in a New World: Portrait of Shearith Israel, 1654–1954* (New York, 1955), 9–12. In a letter from Reverend Megapolensis to the classis in New Amsterdam, the dominie argued that though "it would have been proper that these had been supported by their own nation," instead the colony had had to support them to the sum of "several hundred guilders." Oppenheim, "The Early History of the Jews," 72. It is unclear how much property emigrants were permitted to take from Brazil and to what extent the twenty-three were victims of sharp practices by de la Motthe. Given that the dominie and townspeople had to help and that the twenty-three were forced to appeal to their coreligionists in Amsterdam, it is likely that they did not have the means to pay off their debt, despite protestation to the contrary. The newly arrived merchants did not feel it to be their responsibility. Hershkowitz, "By Chance or Choice," 2.

20. Hershkowitz, "New Amsterdam's Twenty-Three Jews," 172.

21. Marcus, *The Colonial American Jew*, 1:217; Peter Stuyvesant to Amsterdam Chamber of the West India Company, 22 September 1654, and approval of the burgomasters on 1 March 1655, in Oppenheim "The Early History of the Jews," 4–5; Hershkowitz, "By Chance or Choice," 2–3; Frederic Cople Jaher, *A Scapegoat in the Wilderness: The Origins and Rise of Anti-Semitism in America* (Cambridge, MA, 1994), 89–91. When head of the Dutch colony in Curaçao, Stuyvesant attempted to prevent the entry of Jewish immigrants. On continuing prejudice toward Jews, see Marcus, *The Colonial American Jew*, 1:228–230.

22. "Request of the Parnassim of Amsterdam to the Mayors of Amsterdam in Behalf of the Jews of New Netherland," in I. S. Emmanuel, "New Light on Early American Jewry," *AJAJ* 7 (1955): 17, 53–54.

23. "Petition of Jewish Merchants of Amsterdam to Directors of the West India Company," in Oppenheim, "The Early History of the Jews," 9–11; Marcus, *The Colonial American Jew*, 1:218–219.

24. Reply of the directors of the West India Company to Peter Stuyvesant, 26 April 1655, in Morris Schappes, ed., *A Documentary History of the Jews of the United States, 1654–1875* (New York, 1971), 4–5; Oppenheim, "The Early History of the Jews," 8; Hershkowitz, "New Amsterdam's Twenty-Three Jews," 172–179; Williams, "An Atlantic Perspective," 378.

25. Marcus, *The Colonial American Jew*, 1:236, 239–40; Oppenheim, "More about Jacob Barsimon," 47; Hershkowitz, "New Amsterdam's Twenty-Three Jews," 176.

26. Classis of Amsterdam to Consistory in New Netherland, 26 May 1656; Rev. John Megapolensis to Classis of Amsterdam, 18 March 1665; and Peter Stuyvesant to board of directors of the West India Company, 26 May 1655 and 6 June 1656, all in Oppenheim, "The Early History of the Jews," 20, 21, 72–73; William Pencak, *Jews and Gentiles in Early America, 1654–1800* (Ann Arbor, MI, 2005), 29–32; Paul Finkelman, " 'A Land That Needs People for Its Increase': How the Jews Won the Right to Remain in New Netherland," in Pamela S. Nadell, Jonathan D. Sarna, and Lance J. Sussman, eds., *New Essays in American Jewish History* (Cincinnati, 2010), 19–44.

27. Letter from directors of the West India Company, 13 March 1656, in Oppenheim, "The Early History of the Jews," 21; Peter Stuyvesant to directors of the West India Company, 14 June 1656, in Schappes, *A Documentary History*, 11-12.

28. Emmanuel, "New Light on Early American Jewry," 56; Oppenheim, "The Early History of the Jews," 7, 19, 24, 32, 61; Marcus, *The Colonial American Jew*, 1:233; Jonathan D. Sarna, "Colonial Judaism," in David Barquist, *Myer Myers: Jewish Silversmith in Colonial New York* (New Haven, CT, 2001), 12; "Naphtali Phillips," *PAJHS* 21 (1913): 183–184; David de Sola Pool, *Portraits Etched in Stone: Early Jewish Settlers, 1682–1831* (New York, 1952), 7–8.

29. Marcus, *The Colonial American Jew*, 3:1226, 1418n. 3.

30. Resolution to exempt Jews from military service, 28 August 1665; and petition of Jacob Barsimon and Asser Levy regarding guard duty, 5 November 1655, in Oppenheim, "The Early History of the Jews," 24–25. Marcus sees the assessments not as discrimination but as signs that the wealthy Jews had brought considerable capital to New Netherland (*The Colonial American Jew*, 1:238).

31. Petition of Abraham de Lucena, Salvador D'Andrada, and Jacob Cohen, regarding right to trade, 29 November 1655; petition of Salvador D'Andrada to purchase home, 17 December 1655; response to petition, 15 January 1656, all in Oppenheim, "The Early History of the Jews," 24, 25, 27, 29, 31–32, and "Naphtali Phillips," 177, 179, 182.

32. Petition to director general and council of New Netherland regarding the right to trade and purchase real estate, by Abraham de Lucena, Jacob Cohen Henriques, Salvador D'Andrada, Joseph D'Acosta, and David Ferera, with response by P. Stuyvesant, Nicasius DeSille, and LaMontagne, 14 March 1656; and West India Company to director of New Netherland, 14 June 1656, all in Oppenheim, "The Early History of the Jews," 31–34; Marcus, *The Colonial American Jew*, 1:226.

33. Petition of Asser Levy to be admitted to burgher standing, 11 April 1656; and petition regarding denial of Asser Levy's petition by Salvador D'Andrada, Jacob Cohen Henriques, Abraham DeLucena, and Joseph D'Acosta, 20 April 1657, both in Oppenheim, "The Early History of the Jews," 35–36; Max J. Kohler, "Civil Status of the Jews in Colonial New York," *PAJHS* 6 (1898): 88–89; Hershkowitz, "Amsterdam's Twenty-Three Jews," 178–179.

34. Marcus, *The Colonial American Jew*, 1:234–240; Stephen Fortune, *Merchants and Jews: The Struggle for British West Indian Commerce, 1650–1750* (Gainesville, FL, 1984), 141.

35. Fortune, *Merchants and Jews*, 230, 234–237; Hershkowitz, "New Amsterdam's Twenty-Three Jews," 176–178; Max J. Kohler, "Jewish Activity in American Colonial Commerce," *PAJHS* 10 (1902): 59; Max J. Kohler, "Phases of Jewish Life in New York before 1800," *PAJHS* 2 (1894): 80; Oppenheim, "The Early History of the Jews," 16, 52–57, 81–86; Faber, *A Time for Planting*, 33.

36. Marcus, *The Colonial American Jew*, 1:239.

37. Leo Hershkowitz, "Asser Levy and the Inventories of Early New York Jews, " *AJH* 80 (1990): 21–39; Hershkowitz, "New Amsterdam's Twenty-Three Jews," 171–175, 179–181; Malcolm H. Stern, "Asser Levy—A New Look at Our Jewish Founding Father," *AJAJ* 26 (1974): 66–70; Simon W. Rosendale, "An Early Ownership of Real Estate in Albany New York, by a Jewish Trader," *PAJHS* 3 (1895): 61–71; Leon Huhner, "Asser Levy: A Noted Jewish Burgher of New Amsterdam" *PAJHS* 8 (1900): 9–22.

38. Noah L. Gelfand, "A Transatlantic Approach to Understanding the Formation of Jewish Community in New Netherland and New York," *New York History* 89 (2008): 375–396. Gelfand notes that Levy, an Ashkenazi not involved in Sephardic Atlantic trade patterns, more easily adapted to the patterns of New Amsterdam. Samuel Oppenheim argued that the promise of the new colony of Western Guiana drew the Jewish inhabitants from the city. This is unlikely. Oppenheim, "The Early History of the Jews," 21; Emmanuel, "New Light on Early American Jewry," 17, 56. The Torah was sent to the Jewish community of Amersfort, near Utrecht. Marcus, *The Colonial American Jew*, 1:244–245.

■ **NOTES TO CHAPTER 2**

1. Jacob R. Marcus, *The Colonial American Jew, 1492–1776*, 3 vols. (Detroit, 1970), 1:258–275, 282–290; Jonathan D. Sarna, "Port Jews in the Atlantic: Further Thoughts," *Jewish History* 20 (2006): 213–216.

2. Edwin Burrows and Mike Wallace, *Gotham: A History of New York City to 1898* (New York, 1999), 78–79; Max J. Kohler, "The Civil Status of the Jew in Colonial New York," *PAJHS* 6 (1898): 89, 93, 94.

3. Kohler, "The Civil Status of the Jew," 96; Simon W. Rosendale, "An Act Allowing Naturalization of Jews in the Colonies," *PAJHS* 1 (1893): 93–98; Menasseh Vaxer, "Naturalization Roll of Jews of New York (1740–1759)," *PAJHS* 37 (1947): 369–389; Leo Hershkowitz, "Some Aspects of the New York Merchant Jewish Community, 1654–1820," *AJHSQ* 66 (1976–1977): 13–18; Eli Faber, *A Time for Planting: The First Migration, 1654–1820* (Baltimore, 1992), 101; Holly Snyder, "Rights and Redemption: The Negotiation of Jewish Status in British Atlantic Port Towns, 1740–1831," *Jewish History* 20 (2006): 152–155.

4. Three of the most important works on New York's colonial history are Michael Kammen, *Colonial New York: A History* (New York, 1975); Patricia U. Bonomi, *New York: A Factious People* (New York, 1971); and Alan Tully: *Forming American Politics: Ideals, Interests, and Institutions in Colonial New York and Pennsylvania* (Baltimore, 1994).

5. The population of the colony of New York, only 9,000 at the British conquest in 1664, grew to about 20,000 in 1700, 75,000 in 1750, and to 160,000 by 1770. Kammen, *Colonial New York*, 91, 145, 179, 279; James T. Gilchrist, ed., *The Growth of the Seaport Cities, 1790–1825* (Charlottesville, VA, 1967), 28. Burrows and Wallace, *Gotham*, 87; Faber, *A Time for Planting*, 34; Hershkowitz, "Some Aspects of the New York Merchant Jewish Community," 10–11, 19–20; Max J. Kohler, "Phases of Jewish Life in New York before 1800," *PAJHS* 3 (1895): 85.

6. Todd M. Endelman, *The Jews of Britain, 1656 to 2000* (Berkeley, CA, 2002), chs. 1–3, esp. 23–24, 31–38, 41; Todd M. Endelman, *The Jews of Georgian England, 1714–1830: Tradition and Change in a Liberal Society* (Philadelphia, 1979); Todd M. Endelman, *Radical Assimilation in English Jewish History, 1656–1945* (Bloomington, IN, 1990), chs. 1–2.

7. Faber, *A Time for Planting*, 28.

8. Leo Hershkowitz, "Original Inventories of Early New York Jews (1682–1763)," *AJH* 88 (2002): 297–315, 316–322; William Pencak, *Jews and Gentiles in Early America, 1654–1800* (Ann Arbor, MI, 2005), 34; Samuel Oppenheim, "Benjamin Franks, Merchant, and Captain Kidd, Pirate," *PAJHS* 31 (1928): 229–235. Other early Sephardic merchants include the synagogue's second hazan, Abraham de Lucena, who requested special exemptions from the governor as a "Minister of the Jewish Nation" and died with British debtors owing him £800; Isaac Rodriguez Marques, who had sixteen separate imports from the islands to New York in 1704–1705 alone; and Isaac Pinheiro, who also lived in Madrid, Amsterdam, London, and Martinique and Nevis. In the case of Lucena, it is clear that mercantile duties were as important, measured by time and effort, as being the spiritual leader of the congregation. David de Sola Pool, *Portraits Etched in Stone: Early Jewish Settlers, 1682–1831* (New York, 1952), 456–459.

9. Pool, *Portraits Etched in Stone*, 218–223; Max J. Kohler, "Jewish Activity in American Colonial Commerce," *PAJHS* 10 (1902): 60; Kohler, "Phases of Jewish Life before 1800," 79–80.

10. Pool, *Portraits Etched in Stone*, 197–201; for other early commercial enterprises, see Kohler, "Jewish Activity in American Colonial Commerce," 58–66.

11. Pool, *Portraits Etched in Stone*, 461; Michael Ben-Jacob, "Nathan Simson: A Biographical Sketch of a Colonial Jewish Merchant," *AJAJ* 51 (1990): 16–17.

12. Leon Huhner, "Daniel Gomez, a Pioneer Merchant of Early New York," *PAJHS* 41 (1951–1952): 107, 109, 112. On the myriad partnerships of Jewish merchants, see Marcus, *The Colonial American Jew*, 2:592–597.

13. Huhner, "Daniel Gomez," 113–123.

14. Hershkowitz, "Aspects of the New York Merchant Jewish Community," 28; Faber, *A Time for Planting*, 25. On marital interrelations, see Marcus, *The Colonial American Jew*, 2:600–603.

15. Letter of Jacob Franks to Naphtali Franks, November 22, 1743, in Leo Hershkowitz

and Isidore Meyer, eds., *The Lee Max Friedman Collection of American Jewish Correspondence: Letters of the Franks Family* (Waltham, MA, 1968), 123–128. Also on business, see letter of David Franks to Naphtali Franks, 14 March 1743, in ibid., 112–113.

16. Jacob R. Marcus, ed., *American Jewry: Documents, Eighteenth Century* (Cincinnati, 1959), 320–321, 374–380; Marcus, *The Colonial American Jew*, 2:584, 712–718; Jacob R. Marcus, *Early American Jewry* (Philadelphia, 1951), 65. Franks become embroiled in collecting payment after charges of fraud were leveled at Oglethorpe. It was not only the Franks and Gomez families who benefited from imperial warfare. An ad from a lesser merchant in the *New-York Mercury* during the French and Indian War indicates the depth to which many Jewish merchants penetrated British commercial military supply: "To be sold, by Hayman Levy, in Bayard Street, Camp Equipages of all Sorts, Best Soldiers English Shoes, White and Brown thread Soldiers Hose, Best Soldiers Shirts, Regimental Shoes, Knee and Stock Buckles, Hair Cockades, Scarlet Broad Cloths, [and other items that made up the] pomp and circumstances of glorious war." Kohler, "Phases of Jewish Life before 1800," 85. For other mercantile activities, see Marcus, *American Jewry*, ch. 4; and Marcus, *Early American Jewry*, chs. 3–4. Franks also outfitted a number of privateers.

17. For Franks's residence, see Hershkowitz and Meyer, *Letters of the Franks Family*, 118n. 6. All the letters refer to political, financial, and international issues as well as family matters. Pencak, *Jews and Gentiles*, 41; Edith Gelles, ed., *The Letters of Abigaill Levy Franks, 1733–1748* (New Haven, CT, 2004), xxv.

18. Ben-Jacob, "Nathan Simson," 23–26; Noah L. Gelfand, "A Transatlantic Approach to Understanding the Formation of Jewish Community in New Netherland and New York," *New York History* 89 (2008): 395–396.

19. Ben-Jacob, "Nathan Simson," 21–26; Wilm Kloster, "The Jews in Suriname and Curaçao," in Paolo Bernardini and Norman Fiering, eds., *The Jews and the Expansion of Europe to the West, 1450–1800* (New York, 2001), 353–368. Marcus, *The Colonial American Jew*, 2:614–652, 769–779, gives a detailed analysis of the business world of the eighteenth-century Jewish merchant.

20. Marcus, *The Colonial American Jew*, 2:653–696.

21. Hershkowitz, "Some Aspects of the Merchant Community," 10–11, 19–20, 25–27; Marcus, *Colonial American Jew*, 2:636; *New-York Gazette*, 26 October 1761.

22. Hershkowitz, "Some Aspects of the Merchant Community," 22–24; Marcus, *The Colonial American Jew*, 2:542–545, 779–783. For an example in which merchants used a noted attorney, James Alexander, to defend a prize, see Lee M. Friedman, "A Great Colonial Case and a Great Colonial Lawyer," *PAJHS* 42 (1952–1953): 71–81.

23. David Barquist, *Myer Myers: Jewish Silversmith in Colonial New York* (New Haven, CT, 2001), 25–34, 42–44; Leo Hershkowitz, "Powdered Tin and Rose Petals: Myer Myers, Goldsmith and Peter Middleton, Physician," *AJH* 71 (1982): 462–467; Marcus, *The Colonial American Jew*, 2:539. Myers's first wife died after twelve years of marriage and four children. Two years later, he married her cousin Joyce Mears, who gave birth to eight more children and lived until 1824.

24. Barquist, *Myer Myers*, 35–40, 47–62.

25. Ibid., 45–47.

26. Ibid., 61, 152–162; Guido Schoenberger, "The Ritual Silver Made by Myer Myers," *PAJHS* 43 (1953): 1–12.

27. Marcus, *The Colonial American Jew*, 2:535–540; *Rivington's New-York Gazetteer*, 24 June 1773; *New-York Gazette and the Weekly Mercury*, 24 December 1770; *New-York Mercury*, 9 October 1758, 15 November 1762; *New-York Gazette*, 14 November 1748, all in Oppenheim Collection, AJHS.

28. Pool and Pool, *An Old Faith*, 473; *Rivington's New-York Gazetteer*, 19 January 1775; Marcus, *The Colonial American Jew*, 2:545–547; Leon Huhner, "Jews in the Legal and Medical Professions Prior to 1800," *PAJHS* 22 (1914): 116; *New-York Gazette*, 7 September 1761; "Manuscripts: Items Relating to Congregation Shearith Israel, New York," *PAJHS* 27 (1920): 19.

29. Marcus, *American Jewry*, 14–17, 100; Marcus, *The Colonial American Jew*, 2:820–821, 826–828; "Advertisement, 1729," in Morris Schappes, ed., *A Documentary History of the Jews of the United States, 1654–1875* (New York, 1971), 20–22. Hershkowitz states that Jews ranked just above the Gentile population in tax assessments. Hershkowitz, "Aspects of the Merchant Community," 10.

30. "Unwritten History: Reminiscences of N. Taylor Phillips," *AJAJ* 6 (1954): 82.

31. Burrows and Wallace, *Gotham*, 126–129, 375; Graham Russell Hodges, *Root and Branch: African Americans in New York and East Jersey, 1613–1863* (Chapel Hill, NC, 1999), 272–275.

32. Eli Faber, *Jews, Slaves, and the Slave Trade: Setting the Record Straight* (New York, 1999), 132; Leo Hershkowitz, ed., *Wills of Early New York Jews, 1704–1799* (New York, 1967), 15, 21–23, 135, 129; Hershkowitz, "Powdered Tin and Rose Petals," 463.

33. Hershkowitz, *Wills of Early New York Jews*, 60, 136; Pool, *Portraits Etched in Stone*, 477.

34. New York represented a minor part of the Atlantic slave trade, which was centered in the Caribbean. Faber, *Jews, Slaves, and the Slave Trade*, 132–135; Leo Hershkowitz, "Anatomy of a Slave Voyage, New York, 1721," *de Halve Maen* 76 (2003): 45–51; Ben-Jacob, "Nathan Simson," 26–30; Hodges, *Root and Branch*, 98; James G. Lydon, "New York and the Slave Trade, 1700–1714," *William and Mary Quarterly* 35 (1978): 375–394; Hershkowitz, *Wills of Early New York Jews*, 79n. 1, 158n. 1; Pool, *Portraits Etched in Stone*, 468–469; David Brian Davis, "The Slave Trade and the Jews," *New York Review of Books*, 22 December 1994.

35. Burrows and Wallace, *Gotham*, 98; Jill Lepore, *New York Burning: Liberty, Slavery, and Conspiracy in Eighteenth-Century Manhattan* (New York, 2005), 166, 226, 189, 226, 250, 252, 254, 258; Hodges, *Root and Branch*, 91–98; "Miscellaneous Items Relating to Jews in New York," *PAJHS* 27 (1920): 380–382. Cohen died shortly after the trial, at which time he willed Hereford to his wife. He was a prosperous merchant and shopkeeper, a parnas of the synagogue, and a major figure in the Jewish community. Hershkowitz, *Wills of Early New York Jews*, 65. Testimony at the 1741 trial is from Daniel Horsmanden, *The New York Conspiracy; or, A Negro Plot, with the Journal of the Proceedings against the Conspirators, at New York, in the Years 1741–42*, 4th ed. (New York, 1810).

■ NOTES TO CHAPTER 3

1. David de Sola Pool, *Portraits Etched in Stone: Early Jewish Settlers, 1682–1831* (New York, 1952), 195–197.

2. Leo Hershkowitz, "The Mill Street Synagogue Reconsidered," *AJHSQ* 53 (1963–1964): 404–414; "Unwritten History: Reminiscences of N. Taylor Phillips," *AJAJ* 6 (1954): 78; Albion Morris Dyer, "Site of the First Synagogue of the Congregation Shearith Israel, of New York," *PAJHS* 8 (1900): 25; Jacob R. Marcus, "The Oldest Known Synagogue Record Book in North America," in *Studies in American Jewish History* (Cincinnati, 1969), 44–53.

3. David de Sola Pool and Tamar de Sola Pool, *An Old Faith in the New World: Portrait of Shearith Israel, 1654–1954* (New York, 1955), 40–45; Jacob R. Marcus, *The Colonial American Jew, 1492–1776*, 3 vols. (Detroit, 1970), 2:890–1892; Doris Groshen Daniels, "Colonial Jewry: Religion, Domestic and Social Relations," *AJHSQ* 66 (1976–1977): 381–382. There was of course, at this point, no rabbi ("rabby"). Nor would there be one for a hundred years. The sand that covered the floor, similar to the synagogue in Barbados, may have symbolized the sand the Israelites crossed on their journey from Egypt to Palestine, or it may have been a remnant from the medieval era, when sand covered unheated public buildings for hygiene. Marcus, *The Colonial American Jew*, 2:890–892. Miscellaneous letters on fund raising can be found in "Manuscripts: Items Relating to Congregation Shearith Israel, New York," *PAJHS* 27 (1920): 1–5. This includes a request from the hazan in Curaçao that "the asquenazum or Germans" who were "more in number" than the Sephardim in New York not be permitted "any More Votes nor Authority than they have had hitherto." The congregation ignored this request.

4. Jonathan D. Sarna, *American Judaism: A History* (New Haven, CT, 2004), 12–14; Jonathan D. Sarna, "Colonial Judaism," in David Barquist, *Myer Myers: Jewish Silversmith in Colonial New York* (New Haven, CT, 2001), 12–16; Sheldon Godfrey and Judith Godfrey, "The King vs. Gomez et al.: Opening the Prosecutor's File over 200 Years Later," *American Jewish History* 77 (1991): 401–406; Leo Hershkowitz, ed., *Wills of Early New York Jews, 1704–1799* (New York, 1967), xxix, 52, 67, 70, 80, 88, 125, 130, 140; Pool and Pool, *An Old Faith*, 92.

5. "The Earliest Extant Minutes of the Spanish and Portuguese Congregation Shearith Israel in New York, 1728–1786," *PAJHS* 21 (1913): 4; Pool and Pool, *An Old Faith*, 259, 286–287; Jacob R. Marcus, *The Handsome Young Priest in a Black Gown: The Personal World of Gershom Seixas* (Cincinnati, 1970), 4. Deference implies voluntary deferral to the more learned, more educated, and more wealthy in the community.

6. Eli Faber, *A Time for Planting: The First Migration, 1654–1820* (Baltimore, 1992), 55–56; Pool and Pool, *An Old Faith*, 264–267, 502; Marcus, *The Colonial American Jew*, 2:906–911.

7. Faber, *A Time for Planting*, 58–66; "The Earliest Extant Minutes," 3 (15 September 1728), 53 (9 September 1746), 62–63 (22 October 1748).

8. "The Earliest Extant Minutes," 75 (7 December 1755); see also 39 (3 March 1736). A letter seeking a "Single: modest: Sober" person as teacher was sent to Jamaica, noting

that the salary was forty pounds in addition to the tuition from parents who could pay. "Manuscripts: Items Relating to Congregation Shearith Israel," 17–18 (15 December 1760); Faber, *A Time for Planting*, 71; Leo Hershkowitz and Isidore S. Meyer, *The Lee Max Friedman Collection of American Jewish Correspondence: Letters of the Franks Family, 1733–1748* (Waltham, MA, 1968), 4n. 9 (7 May 1733), 13nn. 8–9 (7 October 1733); Edith Gelles, ed., *The Letters of Abigaill Levy Franks, 1733–1748* (New Haven, CT, 2004), xxi–xxii; Pool and Pool, *An Old Faith*, 211–214. Jacob Kabakoff, "The Use of Hebrew by American Jews during the Colonial Period," in Shalom Goldman, ed., *Hebrew and the Bible in America: The First Two Centuries* (Hanover, NH, 1993), 19; Marcus, *The Colonial American Jew*, vol. 3, ch. 68.

9. "The Earliest Extant Minutes," 3 (27 May 1729), 29 (11 September 1730), 74 (18 September 1755), 76 (7 July 1756), 84 (30 January 1760); "From the 2nd Volume of Minute Books of the Congn: Shearith Israel in New York," *PAJHS* 21 (1913): 92 (17 November 1765); Faber, *A Time for Planting*, 71–72; Pool and Pool, *An Old Faith*, 341–347.

10. "Unwritten History," 96–97; Daniels, "Colonial Jewry," 399–400; Frank Zimmerman, "A Letter and Memorandum on Ritual Circumcision, 1772," *PAJHS* 42 (1952–1953): 71–80.

11. Hershkowitz and Meyer, *Letters of the Franks Family*, 87 (21 June 1741); Peter Kalm, *Travels in North America: The English Version of 1790*, 2 vols. (New York, 1964), 1:631; William Pencak, *Jews and Gentiles in Early America, 1654–1800* (Ann Arbor, MI, 2005), 52.

12. "The Earliest Extant Minutes," 79–80 (28 March 1758), 70–72 (13 September 1752); see also 68–70 (October 1747, 10 April 1752); "Second Volume of Minute Book," 32–33 (23, 24 December 1771). Throughout the minutes, there is discussion of the appointment and pay of the shochet and bodek. Hazan of Curaçao to Shearith Israel, 1753, in "Manuscripts: Items Relating to Congregation Shearith Israel," 6–7. See also letter from Kingston, Jamaica, 1758, expressing concern over kashrut because Shearith Israel was temporarily without a hazan. Ibid., 10–11.

13. "The Earliest Extant Minutes," 77–78 (14 September 1757), 78–79 (28 March 1758); Daniels, "Colonial Jewry," 400.

14. Kalm, *Travels in North America*, 1:130; Hershkowitz and Meyer, *Letters of the Franks Family*, 7–8 (9 July 1733).

15. "The Earliest Extant Minutes," 39 (7 August 1737), 55–56 (16 April 1747); Marcus, *The Colonial American Jew*, 2:912–916. In accord with the hierarchical structure of society, dues at Shearith Israel were assessed according to wealth and standing, as were seats. (Unlike its sister London synagogue, Bevis Marks, it did not have a sales tax, and its annual income in 1732 was £180. compared to the London synagogue's income of £6,742.)

16. "The Earliest Extant Minutes," 68–69 (10 April 1752).

17. Ibid., 2 (15 September 1728), 16 (27 September 1731).

18. Ibid., 53–54 (1 December 1746); Pencak, *Jews and Gentiles*, 48, 53.

19. "The Earliest Extant Minutes," 59 (9 October 1747), 61–62 (22 October 1748); Hershkowitz, *Wills of Early New York Jews*, 118.

20. "The Earliest Extant Minutes," 74 (10 October 1755); Godfrey and Godfrey, "The King vs. Gomez et al.," 40.

21. Godfrey and Godfrey, "The King vs. Gomez et al.," 41–42; Holly Snyder, "Queens of the Household: The Jewish Women of British America, 1700–1800," in Pamela S. Nadell and Jonathan D. Sarna, eds., *Women and American Judaism: Historical Perspectives* (Hanover, NH, 2001), 17.

22. "The Earliest Extant Minutes," 84 (30 January 1760).

23. Ibid., 83–84 (24 June 1760); "From the 2nd Volume of Minute Books," 83, 84, 87 (17 July 1760, 6 and 10 August 1760, 11 September 1763); Pencak, *Jews and Gentiles*, 54–55; Snyder, "Queens of the Household," 116–117.

24. Hershkowitz, *Wills of Early New York Jews*, 1, 15, 33, 65; Pool and Pool, *An Old Faith*, 161; Marcus, *The Colonial American Jew*, 2:949–950. That the original Chatham Street cemetery was named "Beth Haim" could possibly indicate that some sense of resurrection lived in 1728, when the new cemetery was bought. For details on the cemetery, see Pool, *Portraits Etched in Stone*, chs. 1–8.

25. Gomez quote is from Holly Snyder, " 'Under the Shado of Your Wings': Religiosity in the Mental World of an Eighteenth-Century Jewish Merchant," *Early American Studies* 8 (2010): 584; Marcus, *The Colonial American Jew*, 2:947; Hershkowitz, *Wills of Early New York Jews*, 75; Jacob R. Marcus, ed., *American Jewry: Documents, Eighteenth Century* (Cincinnati, 1959), 14–17.

26. "Manuscripts: Items Relating to Congregation Shearith Israel," 11–15; Herman P. Salomon, "Joseph Jeshurun Pinto (1729–1782): A Dutch Hazan in Colonial New York," *Studia Rosenthalia* (1979): 18–20. Shortly after Pinto arrived, he was evidently asked to resign over a transgression not mentioned in the minutes. He wrote the elders, "I searched my inmost soul and examined my actions from my earliest childhood," studied biblical and Talmudic texts, fasted, and sought repentance. Pleading that he had crossed "the dangerous seas," he now feared becoming a "Wanderer and fugitive upon the earth." He offered to carry out his duties until Rosh Hashanah (two months): "without any pay to see whether I do my duty." The congregation accepted the offer, and Pinto became Shearith Israel's first learned religious leader. The congregation's decision shows an increased appreciation for religious sophistication.

27. Salomon, "Joseph Jeshurun Pinto," 20–28; Pool and Pool, *An Old Faith*, 88.

28. Joseph Jeshurun Pinto, *The Form of Prayer Which Was Performed at the Jews Synagogue in the City of New-York on Thursday October 23, 1760* (New York, 1760) 1, 4.

29. *Prayers for Shabbath, Rosh-Hashanah and Kippur . . .* , trans. Isaac Pinto (New York, 1766), iii–iv, 1–29. The "Barchu" is the opening invocation; the "Ahavat Olam," is a prayer of God's grace and love; the "Shema," central to Jewish prayer, is an affirmation of the oneness of the deity; the "Kedusha" is a statement of the holiness of God and the Sabbath; the "Kaddish" is a prayer of adoration that is part of the service and also said in remembrance of those who have died. A portion of the Torah, the first five books of the Old Testament, is read during each service, accompanied by traditional sung prayers. "Musaph" refers to an additional service performed on the Sabbath and holidays. The Hebrew literacy of New York's Jews is a subject of dispute. There is agreement that many knew enough to follow prayers, but whether there was any true ability to comprehend except by a few is open to question. Marcus details a few colonial New Yorkers with collections

of Hebrew books and discusses Isaac Pinto's work. Pinto was eulogized at his death by a New York newspaper as "an historian and philosopher." Marcus, *The Colonial American Jew*, 2:568–569, 968–970, 973; 3:1075–1077. See also Pool, *Portraits Etched in Stone*, 260–262; Nathan M. Kaganoff, "Hebrew and Liturgical Exercises in the Colonial Period," in Goldman, *Hebrew and the Bible in America*, 184–190; and Jacob Kabakoff, "The Use of Hebrew," in ibid., 191–197.

30. Kalm, *Travels in North America*, 1:130; Lee M. Friedman, "Dr. Hamilton Visits Shearith Israel," *AJHSQ* 40 (1950): 183–184.

31. Hershkowitz and Meyer, *Letters of the Franks Family*, 66 (17 October 1739), 76 (6 July 1740).

32. Ibid., 57–58 (5 June 1737).

33. Ibid., 78 (31 August 1740), 9 (9 July 1733), 87 (21 June 1741); Leo Hershkowitz, "Another Abigaill Franks Letter and a Genealogical Note," *AJHSQ* 59 (1969–1970): 224.

34. Hershkowitz and Meyer, *Letters of the Franks Family*, xv–xvi, 139, 141–142 (30 October 1748), 60, 62 (20 November 1738), 5 (7 May 1733), 15 (16 October 1733); Gelles, *The Letters of Abigaill Levy Franks*, xxxi.

35. Hershkowitz and Meyer, *Letters of the Franks Family*, 118n. 5, 17–20 (16 December 1733), 23–27 (9 June 1734), 4 (7 May 1733); Marcus, *The Colonial American Jew*, 3:1150–1151. One political event Abigaill hardly comments on is the Negro Plot of 1741, though a slave of her husband's was implicated. She notes the "somewath Mellancholly" news, but her letters show no fear. Hershkowitz and Meyer, *Letters of the Franks Family*, 87–88 (21 June 1741). The court party refers to English politics and the party favoring monarchical power, in this case, the governor's authority; the country party favored an enhanced role of Parliament, in the case of the colony, the Assembly.

36. Hershkowitz and Meyer, *Letters of the Franks Family*, 60 (5 June 1737), 66–67 (17 October 1739), 76 (3 August 1740), 100 (20 December 1741).

37. Ibid., 76 (3 August 1740), 142 (30 October 1748).

38. Ibid., 7 (9 July 1733), 40 (15 June 1735), 108 (5 December 1742).

39. Ibid., 110 (5 December 1742).

40. Ibid., 110 (5 December 1742), 116 (7 June 1743).

41. Ibid., 109–110 (5 December 1742), 116–121 (7 June 1743); letter of Jacob Franks, in ibid., 124–125 (22 November 1743). Phila and Oliver lived outside town in the Delancey country seat in Greenwich Village and then in Bloomingdale prior to the Revolution. Ibid., 116–117n. 4; Pencak discusses Oliver's proclivity to violence, including a tavern brawl in which he nearly murdered a physician. Pencak, *Jews and Gentiles*, 46.

42. Hershkowitz and Meyer, *Letters of the Franks Family*, 131 (25 November 1745); N. Taylor Phillips, "The Levy and Seixas Families of Newport and New York," *PAJHS* 2 (1894): 197. Abigaill's daughter Richa left for London in 1772 after her father's death in 1769, seeking, perhaps, a Christian spouse. Pencak, *Jews and Gentiles*, 47. Samuel Oppenheim describes Richa's departure in "The Chapters of Isaac the Scribe, a Bibliographical Rarity, New York, 1772," *PAJHS* 22 (1914): 39–41. Her fate is unknown.

43. Gelles, *The Letters of Abigaill Levy Franks*, xl; N. Taylor Philips comments that David Franks, "being so constantly in the society of Christians, was never particularly

faithful in the discharge his religious duties, and such cares rested lightly on him." The same, Philips states, applied to sister Phila. Philips, "The Levy and Seixas Families," 197.

44. Hershkowitz and Meyer, *Letters of the Franks Family*, 100 (20 December 1741); Mary Beth Norton, *Liberty's Daughters: The Revolutionary Experience of American Women, 1750–1800* (Ithaca, NY, 1980), part 1; Marcus, *The Colonial American Jew*, 2:561–563; Pool and Pool, *An Old Faith*, 493; Daniels, "Colonial Jewry," 403; Snyder, "Queens of the Household," 24.

45. Leo Hershkowitz, "Original Inventories of Early New York Jews (1682–1763)," *AJH* 88 (2002): 293–296; Hershkowitz, *Wills of Early New York Jews*, 11–14, 79; Marcus, *The Colonial American Jew*, 2:538; Snyder, "Queens of the Household," 18.

46. "Unwritten History," 87, 88, 92; Snyder, "Queens of the Household," 24–25.

47. Daniels, "Colonial Jewry," 403; Hershkowitz, *Wills of Early New York Jews*, 12, 51, 81. Pool and Pool, *An Old Faith*, 44. The sixty-five seats were adequate for weekly services but not for High Holy Day services. Sarna, *American Judaism*, 47; Karla Goldman, *Beyond the Synagogue Gallery: Finding a Place for Women in American Judaism* (Cambridge, MA, 2000), 37–45, 59. The women of the congregation also contributed "White decorations" for the Torah scrolls and a "Curtain" for the ark for High Holy Days, which the congregation celebrated with a special blessing.

48. Snyder, "Queens of the Household," 22–23.

49. Ibid., 23–24.

50. Pencak, *Jews and Gentiles*, 48; Robert Cohen, "Jewish Demography in the Eighteenth Century: A Study of London, the West Indies and Early America" (Ph.D. diss., Brandeis University, 1976), chs. 5–6; on intermarriage, see ibid., 112; Daniels, "Colonial Jewry," 389–392; Snyder, "Queens of the Household," 26–27.

51. Cohen, "Jewish Demography," 392; Marcus, *The Colonial American Jew*, 3:1232; Marcus, *American Jewry*, 187–188; "Manuscripts: Items Relating to Congregation Shearith Israel," 27.

52. Marcus, *The Colonial American Jew*, 3:1188–1190; Leo Hershkowitz, "Some Aspects of the New York Merchant Jewish Community, 1654–1820," *AJHSQ* 66 (1976–1977): 13; Marc D. Angel, *Remnant of Israel: A Portrait of America's First Jewish Congregation* (New York, 2004), 33; Pinto, *The Form of Prayer*, 1, 4. Pencak, in *Jews and Gentiles*, 45, sees the election to the lower offices as a sign of discrimination. However, constables were exempt from militia service and jury duty, and the willingness of a number to run and serve may indicate that they did not see the office as dishonorable.

53. Hershkowitz, "Original Inventories," 297, 299; Hershkowitz, "Some Aspects of the New York Merchant Jewish Community," 20; Leon Huhner, "Daniel Gomez, a Pioneer Merchant of Early New York," *PAJHS* 41 (1951–1952): 120. In the *New-York Journal* of 8 May 1749, the Coentjes Club declined to congratulate a Jewish neighbor who had lately moved to "Fudge Corner" because he had the habit of paying too much rent and raising the rent for the neighborhood. He was addressed as "An Israelite of the Tribe of Juda."

54. Marcus, *The Colonial American Jew*, 3:1127–1131; "Disgraceful Acts of a Mob at a Jewish Funeral in New York, 1743," *PAJHS* 31 (1928): 240–241 (from the *New York Weekly Journal*, 16 May 1745); Pencak, *Jews and Gentiles*, 49–50.

55. Max J. Kohler, "Civil Status of the Jew in Colonial New York," *PAJHS* 6 (1898): 99; Pencak, *Jews and Gentiles*, 41–44, 55. Jews continued to participate in municipal elections. By the Revolution, they were again voting in Assembly elections. Whether there was a hiatus in their privileges at that level or how long it lasted is yet undetermined.

56. Pencak, *Jews and Gentiles*, 41; Samuel Oppenheim, "The Jews and Masonry in the United Sates before 1810," *PAJHS* 19 (1910): 1–16; Kalm, *Travels in North America*, 1:129; Pool, *Portraits Etched in Stone*, 209; *New-York Gazette*, 5 November 1750; Marcus, *The Colonial American Jew*, 3:1214.

■ NOTES TO CHAPTER 4

1. "Items Relating to Gershom M. Seixas," *PAJHS* 27 (1920): 128; Thomas Kessner, "Gershom Mendes Seixas: His Religious 'Calling,' Outlook and Competence," *AJHSQ* 58 (1968–1969): 453; Jacob R. Marcus, *United States Jewry, 1776–1985*, 4 vols. (Detroit, 1989), 1:289; Gershom Seixas, *A Religious Discourse Delivered . . . November 26, 1789* (New York, 1789), 6.

2. For population figures, see Edwin Burrows and Mike Wallace, *Gotham: A History of New York City to 1898* (New York, 1999), 194. The literature on the Revolution in New York City and Colony is vast. A recent work is Joseph Tiedemann, *Reluctant Revolutionaries: New York City and the Road to Independence, 1763–1776* (Ithaca, NY, 1997). Books by Edward Countryman and Gary Nash are among the most influential: Edward Countryman, *A People in Revolution: The American Revolution and Political Society in New York, 1760–1790* (Baltimore, 1981); Gary Nash, *The Urban Crucible: Social Change, Political Consciousness, and the Origin of the American Revolution* (Cambridge, MA, 1979). *Gotham* gives an excellent summary. For an introduction to the historiography of the Revolution in New York City, see Clifton Hood, "Prudent Rebels: New York City and the American Revolution," *Reviews in American History* 25 (1997): 537–544.

3. Burrows and Wallace, *Gotham*, chs. 13–14.

4. Ibid., ch. 14; "Some New York Jewish Patriots," *PAJHS* 26 (1918): 237–238; Eli Faber, *A Time for Planting: The First Migration, 1654–1820* (Baltimore, 1992), 102; Jacob R. Marcus, *The Colonial American Jew, 1492–1776*, 3 vols. (Detroit, 1970), 2:1264; *New-York Gazette*, 1 October 1770, 23 July 1770, Oppenheim Collection, AJHS.

5. *New-York Gazette*, 30 July 1770; *New-York Journal*, 9 August 1770, both in Oppenheim Collection, AJHS.

6. *New-York Mercury*, 21 May 1764, 14 January 1765; *New-York Gazette*, 15 April 1770, 28 June 1770, 9 July 1770, 7 January 1771; *New-York Journal*, 14–28 March 1771, all in Oppenheim Collection, AJHS.

7. *New-York Gazette*, 18 November 1771, 6 September 1773; *New-York Journal*, 29 June 1773, all in Oppenheim Collection, AJHS; David de Sola Pool, *Portraits Etched in Stone: Early Jewish Settlers, 1682–1831* (New York, 1952), 349–350.

8. "From the 2nd Volume of Minute Books of Congn: Shearith Israel in New York," *PAJHS* 21 (1913): 12 (28 June 1767), 17–18 (21 March 1768), 24 (8 September 1771), 28 (15 December 1771), 34 (4 October 1772), 55 (29 March 1775), 56–57 (2 April 1775).

9. Hidden minutes of Shearith Israel, as quoted in William Pencak, *Jews and Gentiles in Early America, 1654–1800* (Ann Arbor, MI, 2005), 56–59. That Josephson and Hays publicly used words that could reinforce traditional anti-Semitic libels that accused Jews of ritual murder and, more commonly, of conniving to cheat unwitting consumers reveals the intensity of disputes in pre-Revolutionary years.

10. Ibid., 60–62. Josephson was reinstated when his fine was paid by Isaac Moses.

11. Ibid., 58.

12. On the Battle of New York, see David Hackett Fischer, *Washington's Crossing* (New York, 2005); and David McCullough, *1776* (New York, 2005). On the politics of New York, see Tiedemann, *Reluctant Revolutionaries*; and Burrows and Wallace, *Gotham*; as well as Bernard Mason, *The Road to Independence: The Revolutionary Movement in New York* (Lexington, KY, 1966); and Richard M. Ketchum, *Divided Loyalties: How the American Revolution Came to New York* (New York, 2002).

13. N. Taylor Philips, "Family History of David Mendez Machado," *PAJHS* 2 (1894): 55–56.

14. Samuel Oppenheim, "Letter of Jonas Phillips, July 28, 1776, Mentioning the American Revolution," *PAJHS* 25 (1917): 128–130. The letter never made it to Europe but was intercepted by the British fleet.

15. Letter of Oliver Delancey to Moses Franks, 4 January 1775, Franks Collection, AJHS; on David Franks, see Edwin Wolf 2nd and Maxwell Whiteman, *The History of the Jews of Philadelphia from Colonial Times to the Age of Jackson* (Philadelphia, 1956), 47, 86–91, 181–182.

16. N. Taylor Phillips, "The Levy and Seixas Families of Newport and New York," *PAJHS* 4 (1896): 206. Pool, *Portraits Etched in Stone*, 350–351. Jacob Marcus argues that while Seixas was "a whole-hearted Whig," there is "no evidence whatsoever to substantiate the legend of patriotic leadership." He was one of the many who joined the American cause. Jacob R. Marcus, *The Handsome Young Priest in the Black Gown: The Personal World of Gershom Seixas* (Cincinnati, 1970), 15.

17. "Unwritten History: Reminiscences of N. Taylor Phillips," *AJAJ* 6 (1954): 84–85.

18. Marcus, *The Colonial American Jew*, 3:1257–1261, 1280–1282.

19. Jay, quoted in Pencak, *Jews and Gentiles*, 68–69; Frederic Cople Jaher, *A Scapegoat in the Wilderness: The Origins and Rise of Anti-Semitism in America* (Cambridge, MA, 1994), 121.

20. Burrows and Wallace, *Gotham*, 242–256; Stephen Birmingham, *The Grandees: America's Sephardic Elite* (New York, 1971), 175.

21. "Address of Loyalty to the Conquerors," in Morris Schappes, ed., *A Documentary History of the Jews of the United States, 1654–1875* (New York, 1971), 50–52; Samuel Rezneck, *Unrecognized Patriots: The Jews in the American Revolution* (Westport, CT, 1975), 142.

22. David de Sola Pool and Tamar de Sola Pool, *An Old Faith in a New World: Portrait of Shearith Israel, 1654–1954* (New York, 1955), 46, 169–170; Rezneck, *Unrecognized Patriots*, 143.

23. *New-York Gazette*, 4 August 1777, 22 September 1777, 12 January 1778, 15 June 1778;

Royal Gazette, 13 January 1779, 2 June 1779, 5 December 1781, 7 August 1782, all in Oppenheim Collection, AJHS.

24. *New-York Gazette*, 6 January 1777, 12 January 1778, 4 May 1778, 16 and 23 November 1778, 12 April 1779, 17 May 1779, 25 October 1779; *Royal Gazette*, 9 May 1781, all in Oppenheim Collection, AJHS.

25. Abram Vossen Goodman, "A German Mercenary Observes American Jews during the Revolution," *AJHSQ* 59 (1969–1970): 227.

26. Cecil Roth, "A Jewish Voice of Peace in the War of American Independence: The Life and Writings of Abraham Wagg, 1719–1803," *PAJHS* 31 (1928): 33–74; Pencak, *Jews and Gentiles*, 63–64.

27. Jacob Marcus, ed., "Jews and the American Revolution: A Bicentennial Documentary," *AJAJ* 27 (1975): 141–144, 194–198; Birmingham, *The Grandees*, 175–176.

28. Marcus, ed., "Jews and the American Revolution," 189–190.

29. Petition of New York Officers to the Committee of Safety for the Province of New York, 21 September 1775, in Franks Papers, AJHS; "Miscellaneous Items Relating to Jews in New York," *PAJHS* 27 (1920): 392.

30. Marcus, ed., "Jews and the American Revolution," 23, 56–62. On Eleazar Levy, see Herbert Friedenwald, "Memorials Presented to the Continental Congress," *PAJHS* 2 (1894): 124–125. For a complete list, see Pool and Pool, *An Old Faith*, 329–330.

31. Rezneck, *Unrecognized Patriots*, 35–36, 183–184, 208–209; petition of Isaac Franks for a revolutionary pension, 6 April 1818, in Franks Papers, AJHS.

32. Leon Huhner, "Jews Interested in Privateering in America during the Eighteenth Century," *PAJHS* 23 (1915): 163–164.

33. Rezneck, *Unrecognized Patriots*, 70; "Items Relating to the Moses and Levy Families, New York," *PAJHS* 27 (1920): 331–335; Max J. Kohler, "Phases of Jewish Life before 1800," *PAJHS* 3 (1895): 83; Pool, *Portraits Etched in Stone*, 384–387.

34. "Prayer for Peace during the American Revolution with a Note of Rev. Gershom Seixas to Mr. Isaac Moses," in "Items Relating to Gershom M. Seixas," *PAJHS* 27 (1920): 126–127.

35. Wolf and Whiteman, *The History of the Jews of Philadelphia*, ch. 7.

36. Ibid., 146–152; Pencak, *Jews and Gentiles*, 21–230; Memorial of Rabbi Gershom Seixas and others to Council of Censors, December 1783, in Marcus, ed., "Jews and the American Revolution," 214–216. Pennsylvania had a long strain of anti-Semitism which may have caused many of New York's Jews to leave Philadelphia after the war. The Test Act was in part the work of the Lutheran senior minister Henry Muhlenberg, who accused the Jews of both atheism and declaring that the Christian messiah was an "imposter."

37. Herbert Friedenwald, "A Letter of Jonas Phillips to the Federal Convention," *PAJHS* 2 (1894): 107–109.

38. Burrows and Wallace, *Gotham*, ch. 17.

39. *New-York Packet*, 20 November 1783, 1 January 1784, 10 and 27 May 1784, 6 December 1784, 5 January 1785, 16 December 1788; *Loudon's New-York Packet*, 8 July 1784, 23 August 1784, 27 September 1784, 20 June 1785, 22 May 1786, 17 August 1786, 26 December

1787; *New-York Journal*, 3 May 1787, *New-York City Directory* (New York, 1786) (item for 24 November 1786), all in Oppenheim Collection, AJHS.

40. Burrows and Wallace, *Gotham*, 279, 280; *New-York Packet*, 5 August 1785, 22 May 1786, 24 November 1786, 16 December 1788, and *New-York Journal*, 3 May 1787, all in Oppenheim Collection, AJHS; Marcus, *United States Jewry*, 1:142.

41. Burrows and Wallace, *Gotham*, ch. 19; *New-York Packet*, 5 August 1788.

42. Pencak, *Jews and Gentiles*, 66–69. (When it came to Sunday laws, however, the legislature did not make an exemption for the Jews.) "From the 2nd Volume of Minute Books," 45 (9 December 1783); Pool and Pool, *An Old Faith*, 250, 320. Benjamin Jacobs married Elizabeth anyway, but she deserted him two years later, claiming cruel treatment by her husband; "Manuscripts: Items Relating to Congregation Shearith Israel, New York," *PAJHS* 27 (1920): 33–34.

43. "Manuscripts: Items Relating to Congregation Shearith Israel," 35–37.

44. Letter of Gershom Seixas to Shearith Israel, 21 December 1783, in Marcus, ed., "Jews and the American Revolution," 217–219; Pool, *Portraits Etched in Stone*, 353–354.

45. Tension between the New York and Philadelphia congregations flared for a moment, but then Philadelphia accepted as its hazan New York's Jacob Raphael Cohen. "Items Relating to Gershom M. Seixas," 130–131; Marcus, *The Handsome Young Priest*, 12.

46. A discussion of New York's religious incorporation law may be found in Hyman B. Grinstein, *The Rise of the Jewish Community of New York, 1654–1860* (Philadelphia, 1945), 45–46; Isaac Jerushalmi, "Cultures, Practices, and Ideals of a New York Sephardic Congregation as Reflected in the Minutes of Shearith Israel, 1784–1789," unpublished paper, AJA, 1–4; Pool and Pool, *An Old Faith*, 260–262; letter of Gershom Seixas to Board of Trustees of Shearith Israel, 22 September 1785, Seixas Papers, AJHS.

47. "From the 2nd Volume of Minute Books," 163–164 (31 May 1786), 164–165, (27 June 1786), 165–167, 167–168, 168–169 (3, 16, 25 July 1786), 169–171 (28 August 1786); Pool, *Portraits Etched in Stone*, 94–101; Pool and Pool, *An Old Faith*, 352–253; Grinstein, *The Rise of the Jewish Community*, 70, 74. The elders' proposed conditions were that funds collected must also go toward the synagogue's expenses. The trustees did allow, after initial refusal, the society to repair and maintain the congregation's hearse. MBOT, 1786, Box 23, Oppenheim Collection, AJHS. (Minutes from the Board of Trustees for the 1780s are at the AJHS; minutes from the 1790s through the 1860s are on microfilm at the AJA.)

48. Seixas actually accepted £140 and responsibility for firewood. Pool, *Portraits Etched in Stone*, 355–356; MBOT, 8 August 1784, 19 August 1787, Box 23, Oppenheim Collection, AJHS; Petition of Rev. G. Seixas to Electors of Congregation Shearith Israel, in "Items Relating to Gershom M. Seixas," 134–135. Seixas was requesting a greater salary.

49. Jerushalmi, "Cultures, Practices, and Ideals," 6–8; MBOT, 35, 46–47 (26 August 1785), 1786, Box 23, Oppenheim Collection, AJHS; letter of Gershom Seixas to Board of Trustees regarding seats, Seixas Papers, AJHS; Pool and Pool, *An Old Faith*, 272–273; Pencak, *Jews and Gentiles*, 72. The board also dealt with Manuel Myers, who put a lock on his seat to stop Lion Hart from using it. MBOT, 26 August 1785, 7 Av 1786, Box 23, Oppenheim Collection, AJHS.

50. For recent interpretations, see Jonathan D. Sarna, *American Judaism: A History* (New Haven, CT, 2004), ch. 2; Jonathan D. Sarna, "The Impact of the American Revolution on American Jews," in Jonathan D. Sarna, ed., *The American Jewish Experience* (New York, 1986), 20–30; Faber, *A Time for Planting*, 106; Marcus, *United States Jewry*, 1:76–84.

▪ NOTES TO CHAPTER 5

1. The poor also lived in small communities just north of the city, such as Bowery village, soon swallowed by the expanding metropolis. Edwin Burrows and Mike Wallace, *Gotham: A History of New York City to 1898* (New York, 1999), 372, 387–391; David T. Gilchrist, ed., *The Growth of the Seaport Cities, 1790–1825* (Charlottesville, VA, 1967), 40; Hyman B. Grinstein, *The Rise of the Jewish Community of New York, 1654–1860* (Philadelphia, 1945), 469.

2. The most recent survey of the early national era is Gordon Wood, *Empire of Liberty: A History of the Early Republic, 1789–1815* (New York, 2009). For New York City, see Burrows and Wallace, *Gotham*, chs. 20–27. The references in *Gotham* cover nearly all the published literature to 1999.

3. Burrows and Wallace, *Gotham*, ch. 22; Howard B. Rock, *Artisans of the New Republic: The Tradesmen of New York City in the Age of Jefferson* (New York, 1979), ch. 6.

4. Jacob R. Marcus, *United States Jewry, 1776–1985*, 4 vols. (Detroit, 1989), 1:211–212; Jerome C. Rosenthal, "A Study of Jewish Businessmen in New York City as Reflected in the City Directories, 1776–1830," unpublished paper, AJA, 1977; see also Ira Rosenwaike, "The Jewish Population of the United States as Estimated from the Census of 1820," *AJHSQ* 53 (1963–1964): 131–135; Ira Rosenwaike "An Estimate and Analysis of the Jewish Population of the United States in 1790," *AJHS* 50 (1961): 23–47; Ira Rosenwaike, *On the Edge of Greatness: A Portrait of the American Jew in the Early National Period* (Cincinnati, 1985), 95–96. Rosenwaike finds a similar propensity to mercantile trades in 1830 but breaks them into sixteen categories including pawnbrokers and clothiers. There are nineteen merchants and six clothiers and pawnbrokers. No other category, such as broker or dry-goods proprietor or grocer, has more than three (out of a total of fifty-nine) in the mercantile trades.

5. Mark Bortman, "Paul Revere and Son and Their Jewish Correspondents," *PAJHS* 43 (1953): 198–234; Marcus, *United States Jewry*, 1:190–191; Robert Martello, *Midnight Rides, Industrial Dawn: Paul Revere and the Growth of American Industrialism* (Baltimore, 2010), 261–262; Rita Susswein Gottesman, *The Arts and Crafts in New York, 1800–1804* (New York, 1965), 237; Stephen Birmingham, *The Grandees: America's Sephardic Elite* (New York, 1971), 191–199.

6. Marcus, *United States Jewry*, 1:181–182, 199, 358–359, 560, 642; David de Sola Pool, *Portraits Etched in Stone: Early Jewish Settlers, 1682–1831* (New York, 1952), 282–285, 384–392, 414–418; Edmund Clarence Stedman, ed., *The New York Stock Exchange*, vol. 1 (New York, 1905), 24; Gustavus Hart, "A Biographical Account of Ephraim Hart and His Son, Dr. Joel Hart, of New York," *PAJHS* 4 (1896): 215–219; Samuel Sokobin, "The Simson-Hirsch Letter to the Chinese Jews, 1795," *PAJHS* 49 (1959–1960): 39; Grinstein, *The Rise of the Jewish Community*, 416–419.

7. On Jacques Ruden, see Pool, *Portraits Etched in Stone*, 302–305; and Ralph Bennett, "The Jews Who Built City Hall," unpublished paper, courtesy of Leo Hershkowitz. Also see Marcus, *United States Jewry*, vol. 1, chs. 4–5.

8. Rosenthal, "A Study of Jewish Businessmen"; Pool, *Portraits Etched in Stone*, 333; David de Sola Pool and Tamar de Sola Pool, *An Old Faith in a New World: Portrait of Shearith Israel, 1654–1954* (New York, 1955), 483; Marcus, *United States Jewry*, 1:186. In 1824, Rebecca Gomez, immigrant cousin of the Gomez family from Barbados, apprenticed her son as a jeweler.

9. Gottesman, *The Arts and Crafts*, 108, 117, 125, 380.

10. Marcus, *United States Jewry*, 1:191–196; Gottesman, *The Arts and Crafts*, 307–308. Judah's ads appeared in the *American Citizen* and the *New-York Gazette*.

11. Theodore Cohen, "Walter Jonas Judah and New York's 1798 Yellow Fever Epidemic," *AJAJ* 48 (1996): 23–34.

12. Shane White, *Somewhat More Independent: The End of Slavery in New York City, 1770–1810* (Athens, GA, 1991); Malcolm M. Stern, "Some Additions and Corrections to Rosenwaike's 'An Estimate and Analysis of the Jewish Population of the United States in 1790,'" *AJHSQ* 53 (1963–1964): 385; "Manumitting Slaves, 1806–1809," and "A Slave Promised Freedom," in Morris J. Schappes, ed., *A Documentary History of the Jews of the United States, 1654–1875* (New York, 1971), 118–121, 134; Rosenwaike, "The Jewish Population," 131–139; Pool and Pool, *An Old Faith*, 483.

13. MBOT, 24 November 1805, 9 December 1806, 7 February 1807, 1 November 1807, 24 December 1807, 13 March 1813, 12 July 1819. (All minutes after 1790 are on microfilm at the AJA.) On the Panic of 1819, see Daniel Walker Howe, *What Hath God Wrought: The Transformation of America, 1815–1848* (New York, 2007), 142–144.

14. Pool, *Portraits Etched in Stone*, 336, 396; "Items Relating to the Gomez Family, New York," *PAJHS* 27 (1920): 303; Marcus *United States Jewry*, 1:203–208.

15. *Sachem* referred to a leader of the Tammany Society, at first a fraternal and then a Jeffersonian society. It was based on Indian lore and thus used the term *sachem* for its top officeholders. "Miscellaneous Items Relating to Jews in New York," *PAJHS* 27 (1920): 396–400.

16. Ibid., 394–398; Marcus, *United States Jewry*, 1:426–429, Grinstein, *The Rise of the Jews of New York*, 103; Hart, "A Biographical Account of Ephraim Hart," 215–219.

17. On the history of Freemasonry, see Steven C. Bullock, *Revolutionary Brotherhood: Freemasonry and the Transformation of the American Social Order, 1730–1840* (Chapel Hill, NC, 1996). Samuel Oppenheim, "The Jews and Masonry in the United States before 1810," *PAJHS* 19 (1910): 1–16; Edmund R. Sadowski, "A Jewish Masonic Prayer," *PAJHS* 48 (1958–1959): 134–135; "Burying the Dead," in Schappes, *A Documentary History*, 112.

18. Burrows and Wallace, *Gotham*, ch. 21; the literature on the Hamiltonian-Jeffersonian debate is enormous. A good starting point would be Stanley Elkins and Eric McKitrick, *The Age of Federalism: The Early American Republic, 1788–1800* (New York, 1995); and Sean Wilentz, *The Rise of American Democracy: The Crisis of the New Order, 1787–1815* (New York, 2007).

19. Morris U. Schappes, "Anti-Semitism and Reaction, 1795–1800," *PAJHS* 38 (1948–

1949): 145; William Pencak, *Jews and Gentiles in Early America, 1654-1800* (Ann Arbor, MI, 2005), 74. Simson, Judah, Gomez, and Seixas, as well as Isaac Levy, were original founders of the Tammany Society, a club that became the center of the Democratic-Republican Party. Noah Jackson and Mordecai Myers were later leaders of Tammany. Lawrence H. Fuchs, *The Political Behavior of American Jews* (Glencoe, IL, 1956) 26-28.

20. Gershom Seixas, *A Discourse Delivered . . . the Ninth of May, 1798* (New York, 1798), 6, 14-15; Gershom Seixas, 1799 sermon, 28-29, Lyons Collection, AJHS; Gershom Seixas, 1803 sermon, 19-20, Lyons Collection, AJHS; Schappes, "Anti-Semitism and Reaction," 122-126.

21. Schappes, *Documentary History*, 84-89; Marcus, *United States Jewry*, 1:579; Jacob R. Marcus, ed., *American Jewry: Documents, Eighteenth Century* (Cincinnati, 1959), 309; Pencak, *Jews and Gentiles*, 77.

22. Jacob R. Marcus, *Memoirs of American Jews, 1775-1865*, 2 vols. (Philadelphia, 1955), 1:52-61; Marcus, *United States Jewry*, 1:95-97; "Miscellaneous Items," 397-398.

23. Jonathan D. Sarna, *Jacksonian Jew: The Two Worlds of Mordecai Noah* (New York, 1981), 1-13.

24. Ibid., ch. 3, esp. 35-44.

25. Mordecai M. Noah, *Oration before the Tammany Society . . .* (New York, 1817), 5, 7, 22, 24; Mordecai M. Noah, *Address Delivered before the General Society of Mechanics and Tradesmen . . .* (New York, 1822), 11, 13.

26. Sarna, *Jacksonian Jew*, 48-49; "Noah's Preface to 'The Grecian Captive,'" in Joseph L. Blau and Salo W. Baron, eds., *The Jews of the United States 1790-1840: A Documentary History*, 3 vols. (New York, 1963), 2:415; Mordecai M. Noah, *She Who Would Be a Soldier* (New York, 1819), 8, 23, 31, 40, 43, 58, 73. Noah also comments on American-Indian relations. In his play, the Indian is asked by the Americans to live in peace with his neighbors: "let concord reign among us." He accepts if the general can "guard their wigwams from destruction" and "soften their prejudices and remove their jealousies." Then "the red man is your friend." Michael Schuldiner, "The Historical Drama of Mordecai Noah's *She Who Would Be a Soldier*," in Michael Schuldiner and Daniel J. Kleinfeld, eds., *The Selected Writings of Mordecai Noah* (Westport, CT, 1999), 11-24. For a close reading of this play that sees it as an exploration of Jewish/American identity, see Craig Kleinman, "Pigging the Nation: Staging the Jew in M. M. Noah's *She Would Be a Soldier*," *ATQ* 3 (1996): 201-219; for more background on Jews and theater in this era, see Heather S. Nathans, *Early American Theater from the Revolution to Thomas Jefferson: Into the Hands of the People* (Cambridge, UK, 2003).

27. Sarna, *Jacksonian Jew*, 51-53; Mordecai M. Noah, *Essays of Howard, on Domestic Economy* (New York, 1820), reprinted in Schuldiner and Kleinfeld, *Selected Writings*, 79-81, 84-86, 92-94.

28. Noah, *Essays of Howard*, 87-89, 101-104.

29. Mordecai M. Noah, *Discourse Delivered at the Consecration of the Synagogue K. K. Shearith Israel . . .* (New York, 1818), 7, 18, 19, 24-25.

30. Ibid., 31-32; Sarna, *Jacksonian Jew*, 140-143.

31. Noah, *Discourse Delivered*, 20-23; Lewis Abraham, "Correspondence between

Washington and Jewish Citizens," *PAJHS* 3 (1895): 90–91. Madison also replied that he observed "with pleasure" that Noah's "sect" shared the "common blessings afforded by our Government and laws." Ibid., 92. Jefferson himself had mixed attitudes toward the Jews. He championed the rights of Jews but also attacked the Old Testament theology that preached ideas of God that were "degrading and injurious" and termed their ethics "often irreconcilable with the sound dictates of reason & morality." Frederic Cople Jaher, *A Scapegoat in the Wilderness: The Origins and Rise of Anti-Semitism in America* (Cambridge, MA, 1994), 130. This dualism is found also among Hamilton, Lydia Child, and other prominent figures. Jonathan D. Sarna, "The 'Mythical Jew' and the 'Jew Next Door' in Nineteenth-Century America," in David A. Gebner, ed., *Anti-Semitism in American History* (Urbana, IL, 1986), 59–61.

32. Jacob R. Marcus, "The *Modern Religion* of Moses Hart," in *Studies in American Jewish History: Studies and Addresses by Jacob R. Marcus* (Cincinnati, 1969), 121–154; Marcus *United States Jewry*, 1:620–622.

33. Sarna, *Jacksonian Jew*, 62, 63, 138; Noah, *Discourse Delivered*, 19, 27. For a background on other attempts at settlement, see Bernard D. Weinryb, "Noah's Ararat Jewish State in Its Historical Setting," in Abraham J. Karp, ed., *The Jewish Experience in America*, 5 vols. (New York, 1969), 2:136–157.

34. Sarna, *Jacksonian Jew*, 64–65.

35. Ibid., 66; "Noah's Proclamation to the Jews," in Blau and Baron, *The Jews of the United States*, 3:894–897; Eran Shalev, " 'Revive, Renew and Reestablish': Mordecai Noah's Ararat and the Limits of Biblical Imagination in the Early Republic," *AJAJ* 62 (2010): 5–7.

36. "Noah's Proclamation to the Jews," 3:897–900.

37. "Editorial from *Commercial Advertiser*, New York, October 16, 1822," in Schappes, *Documentary History*, 157–160; "Mordecai M. Noah: A Letter to Him, Dated 1822, from Eduard Gans and Leopold Zunz, Relating to the Emigration of German Jews to America," *PAJHS* 20 (1911): 147–148; Sarna, *Jacksonian Jew*, 64.

38. Sarna, *Jacksonian Jew*, 72–74; "Unfavorable American Reaction," in Blau and Baron, *The Jews of the United States*, 3:902. For a Zionist perspective, see Robert Gordis, "Mordecai M. Noah: A Centenary Evaluation," *PAJHS* 41 (1951–1952): 1–27.

39. Rejoinders in the *Daily Advertiser* condemned Rivington's words as "one of the most impudent performances" of any era and censured his "invidious and personal remarks . . . not only on an individual, but also upon a numerous class of citizens who are certainly, at least, more sincere in their attachments to the interests of America than yourself." Schappes, "Anti-Semitism and Reaction," 119; Pencak, *Jews and Gentiles*, 73–79; Alfred F. Young, *The Democratic-Republicans of New York: The Origins, 1763–1797* (Chapel Hill, NC, 1967) 185; David Hackett Fischer, *The Revolution of American Conservatism: The Federalist Party in the Era of Jeffersonian Democracy* (New York, 1965) 164.

40. Sarna, *Jacksonian Jew*, 45–46; Jaher, *A Scapegoat in the Wilderness*, 137.

41. Marcus, *United States Jewry*, 1:495, 525, 539, 556. In a study of Jewish characters in plays presented in America—and most were seen New York—Edward Coleman, while noting that one play included the character Shadrach Boaz, "the most repugnant stage Jew of the century," states that most Jews were presented in a favorable light. None of the

Jewish American playwrights introduced Jewish characters. Edward D. Coleman, "Plays of Jewish Interest on the American Stage, 1752–1821," *PAJHS* 33 (1934): 171–197; Jaher, *A Scapegoat in the Wilderness*, 128.

42. "From Frey's 'Narrative,'" in Blau and Baron, *The Jews of the United States*, 3:715–722; Marcus, *United States Jewry*, 1:543–548.

43. "Address to the Board by Mr. [Bernard] Jadownicky," in Blau and Baron, *The Jews of the United States*, 3:726–732.

44. "Jewish Opposition to Missionary Activity, 1820," in ibid., 3:758–773. On missionary societies, see Jonathan D. Sarna, "American Christian Opposition to the Jews, 1816–1900," *Journal of Ecumenical Studies* 23 (Spring 1986): 225–238; and Jonathan D. Sarna, "The American Jewish Response to Nineteenth Century Christian Missionaries," *Journal of American History* 68 (1981): 35–51.

■ NOTES TO CHAPTER 6

1. Jacob R. Marcus, *American Jewry: Documents, Eighteenth Century* (Cincinnati, 1959), 154–156.

2. Ibid., 149–150.

3. Ibid., 151–154, 157–158, 163–166.

4. Ibid., 161–163, 165–166. Marcus notes that the distinction in the constitution between yehidim and other Jews likely referred to Jewish members of Shearith Israel and nonmembers who were "members in potentia." See also Jonathan D. Sarna, *American Judaism: A History* (New Haven, CT, 2004), 43; Eli Faber, *A Time for Planting: The First Migration, 1654–1820* (Baltimore, 1992), 118–119, 123.

5. Lewis Abraham, "Correspondence between Washington and Jewish Citizens," *PAJHS* 3 (1895): 93–95.

6. Jacob R. Marcus, *United States Jewry, 1776–1985*, 4 vols. (Detroit, 1989), 1:240. Hannah Adams quotes Hazan Seixas that there were seventy to eighty subscribers out of fifty families plus some unmarried. "From Hannah Adams's 'History of the Jews,'" in Joseph L. Blau and Salo W. Baron, ed., *The Jews of the United States, 1790–1840: A Documentary History*, 3 vols. (New York, 1963), 1:91; MBOT, 28 May 1815, 27 July 1817, AJA.

7. Marcus, *United States Jewry*, 1:256, 598; MBOT, 27 March 1814, AJA; "The Younger Haym Solomon on Religious Laxity, 1825," in Blau and Baron, *The Jews of the United States*, 2:546–548.

8. MBOT, 18 May 1806, 1 November 1807, 27 October 1812, 15 February 1813, 13 March 1813, 11 July 1813, 7 May 1815, AJA.

9. MBOT, March 1812, 21 July 1812, 12 August 1812, 5 July 1814, 14 August 1814, 13 April 1815, 17 November 1819, AJA. Clerk Gomez was granted "a certificate" due in twelve months; the congregation could do no better. In 1813, a trustee voted against an increase in the shamash's wages (still fifty dollars) because "the finances of the Congregation [was] such that they [did] not admit" salary increases.

10. David de Sola Pool and Tamar de Sola Pool, *An Old Faith in A New World: Portrait of Shearith Israel, 1654–1954* (New York, 1955), 352–357, 358, 361–362; Hyman B. Grinstein, *The Rise of the Jewish Community of New York, 1654–1860* (Philadelphia, 1945), 144–146.

"Miscellaneous Items Relating to the Jews of North America," *PAJHS* 27 (1920): 226–227; "From the Notebooks of Rev. J. J. Lyons, Transcribed from Various Sources, Relating to Congregation Shearith Israel," *PAJHS* 27 (1920): 252–255.

11. Hendrik Hartog, *Public Property and Private Power: The Corporation of the City of New York in American Law, 1730–1870* (Ithaca, NY, 1983); Edwin Burrows and Mike Wallace, *Gotham: A History of New York City to 1898* (New York, 1999), 419–422.

12. *Bye Laws of the Congregation of Shearith Israel as Ratified on the 24 June 1805*, Lyons Collection, AJHS. Most of this constitution is reprinted in "Constitution of Shearith Israel, 1805," in Blau and Baron, *The Jews of the United States*, 2:518–521.

13. MBOT, 21 July 1805, 11 January 1807, 8 May 1814, 16 January 1824, AJA. The board had its own rules of procedure, including a requirement of personal notification of every trustee at least six hours before a meeting, a $2.50 fine for speaking out of turn, and a $10 fine for leaving the meeting without permission. With regard to finances, only in the 1820s did the synagogue regain fiscal health. For example, the expenses for salaries in 1814, a dark war year, were $1,350. In 1824, a year of growth and prosperity, they were $8,427. The board never disciplined Hazan Seixas, but he had limited influence with them.

14. Sarna, *American Judaism*, 47; MBOT, 8 March 1818, 5 April 1818, AJA.

15. MBOT, 23 February 1809, 6 September 1820, 26 October 1825, AJA; see also MBOT, 10 July 1825, AJA, for a petition by congregants against changes to the service. The minutes of 26 October 1825 are reprinted in "On Wearing the Tallith, 1825," in Blau and Baron, *The Jews of the United States*, 2:533–534.

16. Lee M. Friedman, "An Early Reference to the Jews," *PAJHS* 24 (1917): 131.

17. MBOT, 25 August 1816, 27 July 1817, 23 November 1817, 28 December 1817, 8 March 1818, AJA.

18. MBOT, 18 October 1817, AJA; Pool and Pool, *An Old Faith*, 48–51. A proposal in 1815 to establish a branch of the synagogue in Greenwich Village was defeated.

19. MBOT, 12 October 1806, 6 October 1807, 16 April 1809, 22 October 1809, AJA.

20. MBOT, 15 July 1813, 25 April 1818, 2 October 1820, 4 February 1821, 1 August 1823, AJA.

21. MBOT, 15 October 1811, 19 and 20 November 1811, 30 August 1812, 11 July 1813, 3 October 1824, AJA.

22. "Manuscripts: Items Relating to Congregation Shearith Israel, New York," *PAJHS* 27 (1920): 90–91; MBOT, 14 July 1814, 12, 13, and 23 April 1815, AJA.

23. Samuel Oppenheim, "A Question of Kosher Meat Supply in 1813 with a Sketch of Earlier Conditions," *PAJHS* 25 (1917): 31–50; MBOT, 7 February and 20 November 1805, AJA.

24. MBOT, 12 December 1812, AJA; Oppenheim, "A Question of Kosher Meat," 48–52.

25. Oppenheim, "A Question of Kosher Meat," 38–42; MBOT, 10 January 1813, AJA.

26. MBOT, 14 February 1813, AJA; Oppenheim, "A Question of Kosher Meat," 52–55.

27. Oppenheim, "A Question of Kosher Meat," 54–60; MBOT, 4 and 14 February 1813, AJA.

28. On republicanism and monopolies, see Howard B. Rock, *Artisans of the New Republic: The Tradesmen of New York in the Early Republic* (New York, 1979), ch. 7.

29. Jacob I. Hartstein, "The Polonies Talmud Torah of New York," in Abraham J. Karp, ed., *The Jewish Experience in America*, 5 vols. (New York, 1969), 2:45–63. "Manuscripts: Items Relating to Congregation Shearith Israel," 52–56, 82–83; MBOT, 6 June 1809, 3 March 1812, AJA. Seixas signed a contract in 1793 to instruct students in secular and Judaic subjects, on Sundays from ten to one and weekday afternoons, for a salary of £135. Seixas stepped down after a few years. On New York education, see Carl Kaestle, *Evolution of an Urban School System: New York City, 1750–1850* (Cambridge, MA, 1973).

30. "Talmud Torah, 1808," and "State Aid to Parochial Schools," in Morris Schappes, ed., *A Documentary History of the Jews of the United States, 1654–1875* (New York, 1971), 113–114, 126–127; Hartstein, "The Polonies Talmud Torah," 52–59; MBOT, 15 and 20 July 1814, 28 December 1817, 4 February 1821, 5 March 1821, 9 September 1821, 2 December 1821, 2 March 1822, 30 June 1822, AJA. (In 1822, the synagogue rented a room for a school to Mr. Rivero as a private concern.) Pool and Pool, *An Old Faith*, 214–221; Grinstein, *The Rise of the Jewish Community*, 228–238.

31. "Manuscripts: Items Relating to Congregation Shearith Israel," 93–98. The school received small payments of from fifteen to fifty dollars into the 1820s.

32. MBOT, 8 August 1823, AJA. The petition was referred to a committee. No report was issued.

33. MBOT, 1, 3, and 27 April 1825, AJA.

34. MBOT, 27 April 1825, 8 May 1825, 7 September 1825, AJA; "The Barow Cohen Case," in Blau and Baron, *The Jews of the United States*, 2:537–539; Grinstein, *The Rise of the Jewish Community*, 39–42. Barrow Cohen's letter was dated May 11 but was not included in the minutes until September.

35. "Division in the New York Community, 1825," in Blau and Baron, *The Jews of the United States*, 2:540–541.

36. Ibid., 2:542–545; Grinstein, *The Rise of the Jewish Community*, 43–44.

37. Grinstein, *The Rise of the Jewish Community*, 45–47; MBOT, 27 June 1825, 10 and 31 July 1825, 6 September 1825 (at home of hazan), AJA.

38. MBOT, 19 and 26 October 1825, AJA; Grinstein, *The Rise of the Jewish Community*, 48–49. The city's Jewish population did not significantly increase until after 1825. The letter of separation is reprinted in Israel Goldstein, *A Century of Judaism in New York: B'nai Jeshurun, 1825–1925* (New York, 1930), 52–53.

39. Goldstein, *A Century of Judaism*, 54–62.

40. Grinstein, *The Rise of the Jewish Community*, 44–45, 49; David de Sola Pool, *Portraits Etched in Stone: Early Jewish Settlers, 1682–1831* (New York, 1952), 305. The hope that Shearith Israel would become the world's largest congregation was made by its president, Jacques Ruden.

41. See Linda Kerber, *Women of the Republic: Intellect and Ideology in Revolutionary America* (Chapel Hill, NC, 1980).

42. Grinstein, *The Rise of the Jewish Community*, 246; Sarna, *American Judaism*, 47–51; Pool and Pool, *An Old Faith*, 361–363.

43. Grace Nathan to Sarah Kursheedt, 14 November 1814, 27 March 1817 (?), Nathan

Family Papers, AJHS; David de Sola Pool, "Some Letters of Grace Nathan, 1814–1821," *PAJHS* 37 (1947): 203–211.

44. Grace Nathan to Sarah Kursheedt, 7 December 1817, 27 March 1817, 4 June 1821, Nathan Family Papers, AJHS. Aunt Zipporah was daughter of Hayman Levy and widow of Benjamin Mendes Seixas. Pool, "Letters of Grace Nathan," 210–211.

45. Grace Nathan to Sarah Kursheedt, 4 June 1821, Nathan Family Papers, AJHS. These women are part of the Seixas extended family.

46. Grace Nathan to Sarah Kursheedt, 5 June 1820, Nathan Family Papers, AJHS; Pool, "Letters of Grace Nathan," 210–211.

47. Papers of Grace Nathan, AJHS. See also "Grace Nathan, the First of Her Clan, 1810–1827," in Jacob Marcus, ed., *The American Jewish Woman: A Documentary History*, 2 vols. (New York, 1981), 1:72–74.

48. Marcus, *United States Jewry*, 1:349, 456, 583; Pool, *Portraits Etched in Stone*, 438–441.

49. On intermarriage, see Malcolm H. Stern, "Jewish Marriage and Intermarriage in the Federal Period (1776–1840)," *AJAJ* 19 (1967): 142–144. The rate was approximately 30 percent.

▪ NOTES TO CHAPTER 7

1. As Seixas left only a handful of letters to his daughter late in life, along with scattered documents involving his service and half a dozen sermons, there is no full-scale biography. Two short studies exist. The first, an article by Thomas Kessner, depicts Seixas as deeply influenced by his roots in the Marrano community of Spain and Portugal. Kessner depicts a religious figure scrupulously observing Jewish law, a man of limited intellect who avoided controversy and preached obedience to government, freedom of the will, the importance of religious observance, and the ultimate restoration of the Jews to Palestine. Kessner maintains that Seixas's closeness to the Christian community was likely the source of Christian doctrines in his sermons, such as original sin. Thomas Kessner, "Gershom Mendes Seixas: His Religious 'Calling,' Outlook and Competence," *AJHSQ* 58 (1968–1969): 444–471. In the second study, Jacob Rader Marcus describes, in a seventy-page biography, the reverend's family life, garrulous personality, widespread reading, and interest in science. Marcus finds Seixas's sermons lacking both organization and a coherent theology, a fault he attributes to his lack of seminary training. He could write Hebrew, but only with considerable errors. Marcus portrays a superb pastor, well versed in the Bible and codes, though rhetorically limited. Like Kessner, Marcus attributes great influence to the milieu in which Seixas lived, seeing him as a neo-Orthodox Jew influenced by deism, "torn between God and the Philosophers." He concludes that Seixas believed in resurrection and the restoration of Jews, though he never probed the subtleties of these concepts. Jacob R. Marcus, *The Handsome Young Priest in the Black Gown: The Personal World of Gershom Seixas* (Cincinnati, 1970), quote on 22. See also the biographical entry in David de Sola Pool, *Portraits Etched in Stone: Early Jewish Settlers, 1682–1831* (New York, 1952), 345–368. For Seixas's personal home life, see David de Sola Pool, "Gershom Mendes Seixas' Letters, 1813–1815, to His Daughter Sarah (Seixas) Kursheedt and

Son-in-Law Israel Baer Kursheedt," *PAJHS* 35 (1939): 189–193. See also Robert Franzin, "The Sermons of Gershom Mendes Seixas," unpublished paper, AJA.

2. Gershom Seixas to Sarah Kursheedt, 27 March 1814, 11 July 1814, 24 November 1814, Seixas Papers, AJHS.

3. For a picture of the debate over republicanism at its height in the mid-1980s, see Lance Banning, "Liberal and Classical Ideas in the New American Republic," *William and Mary Quarterly*, 3rd. series., 43 (1986): 3–19; and Joyce Appleby, "Republicanism in Old and New Concepts," *William and Mary Quarterly*, 3rd. series, 43 (1986): 20–34. For the debate's application to New York City, see Joyce Appleby, *Capitalism and a New Social Order: The Republican Vision of the 1790s* (New York, 1984); Howard B. Rock, *Artisans of the New Republic: The Tradesmen of New York City in the Age of Jefferson* (New York, 1979), chs. 1–5; Sean Wilentz, *Chants Democratic: New York City and the Rise of the American Working Class, 1788–1850* (New York, 1984), chs. 1–2.

4. Silvio Bedini, *Thomas Jefferson: Statesman of Science* (New York, 1990); Paul Conkin, "Priestly and Jefferson, Unitarianism as a Religion for a New Revolutionary Age," in Ronald Hoffman and Peter Albert, eds., *Religion in a Revolutionary Age* (Charlottesville, VA, 1994), 290–307; Paul Conkin, "The Religious Pilgrimage of Thomas Jefferson," in Peter I. Onuf, ed., *Jeffersonian Legacies* (Charlottesville, VA, 1993), 19–49; Charles B. Sanford, *The Religious Life of Thomas Jefferson* (Charlottesville, VA, 1987); Charles B. Sanford, *Thomas Jefferson and His Library* (Hamden, CT, 1977), 115–153; Thomas Jefferson to Mordecai Noah, 28 May 1818, in Lewis Abraham, "Correspondence between Washington and Jewish Citizens," *PAJHS* 3 (1895): 92–94; Thomas Jefferson to Dr. Jacob De La Motta, 1 September 1820, in Morris U. Schappes, ed., *A Documentary History of the Jews in the United States* (New York, 1950), 57; Mark A. Noll, *America's God: From Jonathan Edwards to Abraham Lincoln* (New York, 2001), 161, 206.

5. Marcus, *The Handsome Young Priest*, 34–35; William Pencak, *Jews and Gentiles in Early America, 1654–1800* (Ann Arbor, MI, 2006), 77; Gordon Wood, *Empire of Liberty: A History of the Early Republic, 1789–1815* (New York, 2009), 199–200. Seixas was also familiar with English literature and was an admirer of both Shakespeare and Alexander Pope.

6. Gershom Seixas, *A Religious Discourse Delivered . . . November 26, 1789* (New York, 1789), 9; Gershom Seixas, 1799 sermon, 4, 22, Lyons Collection, AJHS; Gershom Seixas, 1803 sermon, 3, 14, 16, 22, Lyons Collection, AJHS; Isidore E. Meyer, "The Hebrew Oration of Sampson Simson, 1800," *PAJHS* 45 (1956–1957): 48.

7. Seixas, 1803 sermon, 6–7, 9, Lyons Collection, AJHS; Gershom Seixas, *A Discourse Delivered . . . The Ninth of May, 1798* (New York, 1798), 21.

8. Gershom Seixas to Sarah Kursheedt, 23 January 1813, Seixas Papers, AJHS; Marcus, *The Handsome Young Priest*, 24–25; Seixas, 1803 sermon, 14, Lyons Collection, AJHS.

9. Meyer, "The Hebrew Oration," 41–48; Kessner, "Gershom Mendes Seixas," 463–464.

10. Seixas, *A Religious Discourse*, 13–14; Seixas, *A Discourse Delivered*, 23–24; Seixas, 1803 sermon, 7.

11. MBOT, 15 August 1812, 15 July 1813, 19 January 1814, AJA; Gershom Seixas to Sarah Kursheedt, 14 November 1814, in Kenneth Libo and Abigail Kursheedt Hoffman, *The Seixas-Kursheedts and the Rise of Early American Jewry* (New York, 2001), 41; Roger H.

Brown, *Republic in Peril: 1812* (New York, 1964); Gershom Seixas, 1814 sermon, 1–3, Library Manuscript Collection, AJHS.

12. Marcus, *The Handsome Young Priest*, 38–41.

13. Gershom Seixas, sermon, undated, Box 61b, Lyons Collection, AJHS.

14. Marcus, *The Handsome Young Priest*, 42; Seixas, *A Religious Discourse*, 9–10; Seixas, 1799 sermon, 2–3, 12, 22; Seixas, 1803 sermon, 6, Lyons Collection, AJHS.

15. Seixas, *A Religious Discourse*, 11–12, Seixas, *A Discourse Delivered*, 11–12; Seixas, 1799 sermon, 4–7, 23–24, Lyons Collection, AJHS; Marcus, *The Handsome Young Priest*, 53.

16. Seixas, 1799 sermon, 18–19, Lyons Collection, AJHS.

17. Seixas, *A Discourse Delivered*, 12; Seixas, 1799 sermon, 13, 14; Seixas, 1803 sermon, 3–4, Lyons Collection, AJHS. Seixas preached in a similar vein in 1799 when he stated, "what could be more consonant to the feelings of humanity, than the hopes of hereafter?" The continued prevalence of faith in resurrection and the world to come is found on the tombstone of Walter Jonas Judah, the young medical student who died treating victims of yellow fever in 1798. It reads, in part, "Declare him and his soul happy. May they prepare for him his canopy in Paradise. And there may he have refreshment of soul until the dead live again and the spirit renter into them." Theodore Cohen, "Walter Jonas Judah and New York's 1798 Yellow Fever Epidemic," *AJAJ* 48 (1996): 31.

18. Seixas, *A Religious Discourse*, 10; Seixas, *A Discourse Delivered*, 10, 29; Seixas, 1799 sermon, 25–26; Seixas, 1803 sermon, 12, 13, Lyons Collection, AJHS; "Items Relating to Gershom M. Seixas," *PAJHS* 27 (1920): 131. When Napoleon convened the Sanhedrin in 1807, Seixas thought a new age might be at hand. He asked the "God of Israel" to keep the French Jewish elders from "every possible evil" and to keep the "Emperor" under the influence of "divine grace." Would the Sanhedrin bring about Jews' "reestablishment if not as a nation in [their] former territory," then as a "particular society" with the rights of all other societies? Was he giving up the hope of a return to Palestine? How was this different from the American situation? Kessner, "Gershom Mendes Seixas," 469. Gershom Seixas to Sarah Kursheedt, 23 January 1814, 11 July 1814, Seixas Papers, AJHS.

19. Gershom Seixas to Sarah Kursheedt, 23 January 1814, Seixas Papers, AJHS; "Items Relating to Gershom M. Seixas," *PAJHS* 27 (1920): 126–127, 131; Ruth Bloch, *Visionary Republic: Millennial Themes in American Thought, 1756–1800* (New York, 1985), 103–104.

20. Conkin, "Priestley and Jefferson," 292.

21. Noll, *America's God*, 161, 206, 217, chs. 5, 6, 10, 11. See also Robert M. Calhoon, "The Evangelical Persuasion," in Hoffman and Albert, *Religion in a Revolutionary Age*, 156–183.

22. Gershom Seixas to Sarah Kursheedt, 5 May 1814, Seixas Papers, AJHS; Pool, *Portraits Etched in Stone*, 373–375.

23. Jacob R. Marcus, *United States Jewry, 1776–1985*, 4 vols. (Detroit, 1989), 1:91; Myer Isaacs, "Sampson Simson," *PAJHS* 19 (1910): 112, 116; Jonathan D. Sarna, *Jacksonian Jew: The Two Worlds of Mordecai Noah* (New York, 1981), 140.

24. Hyman B. Grinstein, "The American Synagogue and the Laxity of Observance, 1750–1850" (M.A. thesis, Columbia University, 1936), 30–46.

25. Josephson quoted in Jacob R. Marcus, ed., "Jews and the American Revolution: A Bicentennial Documentary," *AJAJ* 27 (1975): 253–254; Marcus, *United States Jewry*,

1:597–613 (quote on 613); Malcolm H. Stern, "Jewish Marriage and Intermarriage in the Federal Period (1776–1840)," *AJAJ* 19 (1967): 142–144.

■ **NOTES TO CHAPTER 8**

1. Naomi W. Cohen, *Encounter with Emancipation: The German Jews in the United States, 1830–1914* (Philadelphia, 1984) 42; Hasia Diner, *A Time for Gathering: The Second Migration* (Baltimore, 1992), 138–141; Malcolm Stern, "Jewish Marriage and Intermarriage in the Federal Period (1776–1840)," *AJAJ* 19 (1967): 142–143.

2. Isaac Mayer Wise, *Reminiscences* (New York, 1901), 18. The source of information on antebellum New York in the following five paragraphs is Edwin G. Burrows and Mike Wallace, *Gotham: A History of New York City to 1898* (New York, 1999), chs. 31–47. The figures on population growth and immigration may be found on pages 736–777. A classic book on the ascendance of New York City is Robert Albion, *The Rise of New York Port, 1815–1860* (Boston, 1939).

3. The most recent and finest survey of the era is Daniel Walker Howe, *What Hath God Wrought: The Transformation of America, 1815–1848* (New York, 2009); see also Edwin Pessen, *Riches, Classes, and Power before the Civil War* (Boston, 1973).

4. Burrows and Wallace, *Gotham*, ch. 27.

5. Ibid., ch. 38.

6. Ibid., ch. 41; Frederic Cole Jaher, *The Urban Establishment: Upper Strata in Boston, New York, Charleston, and Los Angeles* (Urbana, IL, 1982), 202–208.

7. Burrows and Wallace, *Gotham*, 725–727; Diner, *A Time for Gathering*, 8–13, 24–36.

8. Stanley Nadel, *Little Germany: Ethnicity, Religion, and Class in New York City, 1845–80* (Urbana, IL, 1990), ch. 2; *New York Times*, 14 March 1856.

9. Burrows and Wallace, *Gotham*, 748; Hyman B. Grinstein, *The Rise of the Jewish Community of New York, 1654–1860* (Philadelphia, 1945), 469. Population figures for 1860 are tentative. Some estimates are as low as eighteen thousand. Jonathan D. Sarna, *American Judaism: A History* (New Haven, CT, 2004), 63.

10. Burrows and Wallace, *Gotham*, 745; Robert Ernst, *Immigrant Life in New York City, 1825–1863* (New York, 1979), 46; Nadel, *Little Germany*, 99–103; Diner, *A Time for Gathering*, 91, ch. 3; Beverly Hyman, "New York Jewish Businessmen, 1831–1835," unpublished manuscript, AJA; *New York Times*, 14 March 1856. For more detail on immigrant neighborhoods, see Annie Polland and Daniel Soyer, *Emerging Metropolis: New York Jews in the Age of Immigration* (New York, 2012), chs. 1–2.

11. Jacob R. Marcus, *United States Jewry, 1776–1985*, 4 vols. (Detroit, 1989), 2:225–226; Ernst, *Immigrant Life in New York City*, 85; Egal Feldman, "Jews in the Early Growth of the New York City Men's Clothing Trade," *AJAJ* 13 (1960): 5–6; Burrows and Wallace, *Gotham*, 742–743; Rudolph Glanz, "German Jews in New York City in the 19th Century," in *Studies in Judaica Americana* (New York, 1970), 125–126.

12. Glanz, "German Jews in New York City," 127–128; Feldman, "Jews in the Early Growth," 3–7; Cohen, *Encounter with Emancipation*, 31; Wise, *Reminiscences*, 24.

13. *Asm*, 30 October 1857; Glanz, "German Jews in New York City," 128–131; Feldman, "Jews in the Early Growth," 7–14; Vincent Carosso, "A Financial Elite: New York's

German-Jewish Investment Bankers," *AJHSQ* 66 (1977): 66–74; Stephen Birmingham, *"Our Crowd": The Great Jewish Families of New York* (New York, 1967), chs. 2–9; *The New York City Directory, 1856–57* (New York, 1857), available at www.ancestry.com. There were no Jews listed in the 1845 *New York Sun's* list of property owners with more than $100,000 in real estate. Edmund Clarence Stedman, ed., *The New York Stock Exchange*, vol. 1 (New York, 1905), 106–108. Overall, by 1855, one-fourth of the city's top ten thousand taxpayers were immigrants. Burrows and Wallace, *Gotham*, 739.

14. Stanley Nadel, "Jewish Race and German Soul in Nineteenth-Century America," *AJH* 77 (1987): 6–26.

15. Cohen, *Encounter with Emancipation*, 39–63; Sefton D. Temkin, *Isaac Mayer Wise: Shaping American Judaism* (New York, 1992), 38.

16. Diner, *A Time for Gathering*, 102.

17. Edward E. Grusd, *B'nai B'rith: The Story of a Covenant* (New York, 1966), ch. 1; Deborah Dash Moore, *B'nai B'rith and the Challenge of Ethnic Leadership* (Albany, NY, 1981), 1–13; Diner, *A Time for Gathering*, 109–113; Grinstein, *The Rise of the Jewish Community*, 109–114.

18. Moore, *B'nai B'rith*, 13–23; Grusd, *B'nai B'rith*, 33–48; Julius Bien, "History of the Independent Order of B'nai B'rith," *Menorah* (1886–1889): 123–125.

19. *Asm*, 11 June 1851, 4 July 1851.

20. *Asm*, 9 December 1852.

21. Grinstein, *The Rise of the Jewish Community*, 197–205; Bien, "History of the Independent Order," 165, 325.

22. *Asm*, 6 and 24 May 1852, 19 July 1852, 12 November 1852, 24 December 1852, 11 February 1853.

23. *New York Times*, 28 October 1855.

24. *Asm*, 19 January 1854, 3 February 1854, 3 February 1855, 2 March 1855, 20 April 1855, 1 June 1855, 17 July 1857.

25. *Asm*, 23 February 1855, 16 May 1856. The society's inauguration is detailed in the *New York Times*, 21 February 1855. Reverend Raphall there expressed concern that among Israelites "as a class there is not exhibited that zeal and love of literature there should be."

26. *JM*, 11 March 1859, 20 May 1859, 10 September 1859, 21 June 1861, 3 September 1864.

27. Grinstein, *The Rise of the Jewish Community*, 145–147.

28. *Asm*, 26 November 1849.

29. *Asm*, 15 November 1850, 5 December 1851.

30. *Asm*, 15 November 1850, 5 December 1851, 23 April 1852, 26 November 1852, 3 December 1852, 11 November 1853, 22 September 1854, 29 November 1854.

31. *Asm*, 26 November 1852, 9 December 1852, 11 November 1853, 29 November 1854.

32. *Asm*, 19 January 1855, 2 March 1855, 14 and 28 December 1855, 19 January 1857, 2 March 1857, 13 November 1857, 14 and 28 December 1857, 8 January 1858. For elaborate circulars of concerts at Dodworth's Academy and Niblo's Saloon in February 1855, including arias, piano, harp, and violin pieces, see Lyons Collection, AJHS.

33. *Asm*, 1 November 1850, 19 November 1852, 10 November 1854. For more detail on

the charitable functions of the organizations, especially the distribution of matzo at Passover, as well as specific conditions, see Polland and Soyer, *Emerging Metropolis*, ch. 2.

34. *Asm*, 18 and 25, January 1850, 15 November 1850, 10 October 1851, 28 January 1852, 31 December 1852.

35. *Asm*, 12 December 1856, 9 January 1857, 18 October 1850; *JM*, 18 April 1862, 14 November 1862, 12 December 1863.

36. Grinstein, *The Rise of the Jewish Community*, 115–130; HBS circular, 1842, Lyons Collection, AJHS.

37. *Asm*, 4, 11, 18, and 25 May 1855; "A Call to Establish a Hebrew Agricultural Society, 1855," in *Constitution of the American Hebrew Agricultural Association* (New York, 1855), Lyons Collection, AJHS; Cohen, *Encounter with Emancipation*, 35–39.

38. Call for special meeting at Shearith Israel, 1847, Lyons Collection, AJHS; Cohen, *Encounter with Emancipation*, 67; Temkin, *Isaac Mayer Wise*, 39.

39. "A Physician on Philanthropy, 1830," in Joseph L. Blau and Salo W. Baron, *The Jews of the United States, 1790–1840: A Documentary History*, 3 vols. (New York, 1963), 2:597–601. The society that Peixotto spoke to was small, with only eighteen members in 1855. Composed of Ashkenazi members of Shearith Israel, it disbursed over $1,100 in 1854 to "Jewish families, comprising helpless women and tender children, pleading at our doors for relief." Circular, January 1855, Lyons Collection, AJHS; Grinstein, *The Rise of the Jewish Community*, 148–149.

40. Cohen, *Encounter with Emancipation*, 124.

41. *Asm*, 20 December 1850; Guido Kirsch, "*Israel's Herold*: The First Jewish Weekly in New York," *Historia Judaica* 2 (1940): 82.

42. Joseph Hirsh and Beck Doherty, *The Mount Sinai Hospital of New York, 1852–1952* (New York, 1952), 4–13; Grinstein, *The Rise of the Jewish Community*, 155–157; *Asm*, 18 October 1850, 30 November 1850, 21 February 1851, 16 and 23 April 1851, 13 June 1851.

43. *Asm*, 16 January 1852.

44. *Asm*, 30 January 1852, 5 March 1852; "Constitution and By-Laws of the Jews' Hospital of New York," Mount Sinai Hospital Archives.

45. *Asm*, 25 November 1853; Hirsh and Doherty, *The Mount Sinai Hospital*, 18–23; *New York Times*, 29 November 1853, 28 January 1854.

46. *Asm*, 18 and 25 May 1855.

47. *New York Times*, 9 and 18 May 1855; *Order of Service at the Inauguration of the Jews' Hospital* (New York, 1855), Mt. Sinai Hospital Archives; Grinstein, *The Rise of the Jewish Community*, 158.

48. Hirsh and Doherty, *The Mount Sinai Hospital*, 37–38; *Asm*, 18 and 26 January 1856.

49. *Asm*, 1, 8, and 15 February 1856, 11 April 1856, 27 June 1856, 11 July 1856.

50. *Asm*, 18 and 25 January, 12 March 1856; *Annual Report of the Directors of the "Jews' Hospital in New York"* (New York, 1857); *Asm*, 6 December 1857, 16 January 1858.

51. *JM*, 19 November 1858, 25 February 1859, 22 March 1861.

52. *Asm*, 9 May 1856; Hirsh and Doherty, *The Mount Sinai Hospital*, 38–39.

53. *JM*, 3 April 1860, 3 October 1862, 29 July 1863, 12 February 1864.

54. Carol A. Kolmerton, *The American Life of Ernestine A. Rose* (Syracuse, NY, 1997),

4–9, 68, 96, 240–242; "Speeches by Ernestine L. Rose at the Third National Woman's Rights Convention, Syracuse, N.Y., September 8–19, 1852," in Morris Schappes, ed., *A Documentary History of the Jews in the United States, 1654–1875* (New York, 1950), 324–332.

55. Karla Goldman, *Beyond the Synagogue Gallery: Finding a Place for Women in American Judaism* (Cambridge, MA, 2000), ch. 3; *Asm*, 11 July 1851.

56. *Asm*, 2 November 1849, 7 December 1849, 8 and 22 February 1850, 7 March 1851, 19 March 1852.

57. *JM*, 3 March 1865.

58. "Obituary of Daniel Schlesinger, 1839," in Blau and Baron, *The Jews of the United States*, 2:484–493.

59. *Asm*, 22 February 1850, 3 March 1850, 6 December 1850, 29 August 1851, 12 September 1851, 7 November 1851, 12 December 1851, 6 February 1851, 14 September 1855, 16 October 1857. For Maretzek's views, see his autobiography regarding his time in New York, *Crotchets and Quavers* (New York, 1855). He is quite cynical in his view of the cultural level of New Yorkers. As to religion, he states, "I believe in God, and endeavor to do my duty without calling myself Roman Catholic, Episcopalian, member of the Greek Church, Lutheran or Presbyterian." He states that before he turned eighteen, he had determined to shape his creed "to suit everybody." He was to belong to "all tastes and creeds, political and spiritual, in a general way, but to none in particular." Judaism, his born religion, is not mentioned. The *Asmonean* was proud of his Jewish origins, but Maretzek was not, and he never mentions it. He was clearly not an active or identifying member of the Jewish community.

60. *Asm*, 10 October 1851, 4 February 1853.

61. *New York Times*, 27 December 1858; *Asm*, 16 April 1851, 8 September 1854, 12 December 1854, 14 September 1855, 22 February 1856.

62. *JM*, 30 January 1857, 11 November 1859, 11 May 1860. See also *JM*, 2 February 1860, 7 and 28 November 1862.

63. *JM*, 3 March 1860, 20 March 1863, 24 and 31 October 1863; see also for description of other Purim and Chanukah balls, *JM*, 14 December 1860, 1 March 1861, 31 January 1862, 21 March 1862, 7 November 1862, 26 December 1862, 5 February 1864, 1 April 1864, 3, 17, and 24 March 1865; Philip Goodman "The Purim Association of the City of New York, 1862–1902," *PAJHS* 40 (1950–1951): 134–144.

64. David Black, *The King of Fifth Avenue: The Fortunes of August Belmont* (New York, 1981), 35, 66–67, 76–77. The Jewish community repudiated Belmont, considering him an "outcast," even though he made occasional donations to Jewish charities and to the Reform synagogue in Albany in support of Isaac Mayer Wise.

65. Alexis de Tocqueville, *Democracy in America*, ed. Isaac Kramnick (New York, 2007), 452–455.

■ **NOTES TO CHAPTER 9**

1. *Asm*, 24 May 1850, 21 April 1851.

2. Hyman B. Grinstein, *The Rise of the Jewish Community of New York, 1654–1860* (Philadelphia, 1945), 49–53, 472–478.

3. Israel Goldstein, *A Century of Judaism in New York: B'nai Jeshurun, 1825–1925* (New York, 1930), 81–90; Robert T. Swierenga, "Samuel Myers Isaacs: The Dutch Rabbi of New York," *AJAJ* 54 (1992): 607–621; minutes of B'nai Jeshurun, 25 November 1827, 12 May 1828, 28 December 1828, 6 June 1830, 7 and 21 August 1836, Jewish Theological Seminary.

4. Leo Hershkowitz, "Those 'Ignorant Immigrants' and the B'nai Jeshurun Schism," *AJH* 70 (1980): 168–179; Goldstein, *A Century of Judaism*, 93–94; minutes of B'nai Jeshurun, 16 June 1833, and note on inside cover, Jewish Theological Seminary; Leon A. Jick, *The Americanization of the Synagogue, 1820–1870* (Hanover, NH, 1976), 26. Shearith Israel also instituted strict admission rules including a year of residency and a two-thirds vote of members. Shearith Israel circular, 7 August 1837, Lyons Collection, AJHS.

5. J. D. Eisenstein, "The History of the First Russian-American Jewish Congregation," *PAJHS* 9 (1901): 63–72; Alfred A. Greenbaum, "The Early 'Russian' Congregation in America in Its Ethnic and Religious Setting," *AJHSQ* 62 (1972–1973): 162–169; Grinstein, *The Rise of the Jewish Community*, 172; "Appeal for the Support of the *Beth Hamidrash* by Rabbi Abraham Joseph Ash, New York, March, 1857," in Morris Schappes, ed., *Jews in the United States: A Documentary History* (New York, 1950), 373–375.

6. Rachel Wischnitzer, *Synagogue Architecture in the United States: History and Interpretation* (Philadelphia, 1955), 33–37; David de Sola Pool and Tamar de Sola Pool, *An Old Faith in a New World: Portrait of Shearith Israel, 1654–1954* (New York, 1955), 53–60. The 1834 sanctuary had eleven more seats for men, thirty more for women.

7. Wischnitzer, *Synagogue Architecture*, 52–55; *Asm*, 3 May 1850, 3 October 1851.

8. Myer Stern, *The Rise and Progress of Reform Judaism: Temple Emanu-El of New York* (New York, 1895), 13–38; *Asm*, 7 April 1854, 27 May 1857, 9 April 1858; Wischnitzer, *Synagogue Architecture*, 48–50, 72–76.

9. Gershom Greenberg, "A German-Jewish Immigrant's Perception of America, 1853–54," *AJHSQ* 67 (1977): 321–322.

10. In New York, the term for Jewish spiritual leaders varied. *Rabbi* was used, though often rabbis such as Isaacs and Raphall were not ordained in Europe by either a yeshiva or the state. In New York, there was a gradual transformation from *hazan* to *reverend*, both of which applied to Gershom Seixas and Samuel Isaacs. *Hazan* became obsolete, and Jewish spiritual leaders before the Civil War were referred to as "Reverend," "Doctor," and "Rabbi." "Doctor" would apply to German spiritual leaders, as the German state required all Jewish clergy to have secular doctorates. Max Lilienthal and Samuel Adler were ordained in Germany. Goldstein, *A Century of Judaism*, 110–114, 119–124; Israel Finestein, *Anglo-Jewry in Changing Times: Studies in Diversity, 1840–1914* (London, 1999), 168–195; Grinstein, *The Rise of the Jewish Community*, 91–92; Swierenga, "Samuel Myers Isaacs," 607–615.

11. David Philipson, *Max Lilienthal, American Rabbi: Life and Writings* (New York, 1915), 46–59; Bruce L. Ruben, "Max Lilienthal and Isaac M. Wise: Architects of American Reform Judaism," *AJAJ* 55 (2003): 1–29; Pool and Pool, *An Old Faith*, 190–191. On Lilienthal's separation from his duties as a rabbi, see Grinstein, *The Rise of the Jewish Community*, 513–517.

12. Bernard N. Cohen, "Leo Merzbacher," *AJAJ* 6 (1954): 21–24; Philipson, *Max Lilien-*

1 January 1857, 9 September 1858, 21 October 1859, 4 and 11 November 1859, 18 December 1859, 10 February 1860, 1 June 1860, 21 September 1860, 22 February 1861, 21 August 1863, 24 June 1865; Grinstein, *The Rise of the Jewish Community*, 432–439; Allan Tarshish, "The Board of Delegates of American Israelites, 1859–1878," *PAJHS* 49 (1959–1960): 16–36. In 1849, newly arrived Isaac Mayer Wise, together with Isaac Leeser, attempted to assemble a national conference to discuss the state of the American congregations. The meeting was never held; indifference and apathy prevailed. Bertram W. Korn, "American Jewish Life in 1849," in Bertram W. Korn, ed., *Eventful Years and Experiences: Studies in Nineteenth-Century American Jewish History* (Cincinnati, 1954), 35–38.

39. Jaher, *A Scapegoat in the Wilderness*, 170, 186. See also Robert Rockaway and Arnon Gutfeld, "Demonic Images of the Jew in the Nineteenth Century United States," *AJH* 89 (2001): 355–373.

40. Jaher, *A Scapegoat in the Wilderness*, 222, 237–238; *New York Times*, 25 July 1852, 4 April 1855, 27 May 1858.

41. Quoted in ibid., 186.

42. Ibid., 214–218.

43. Ibid., 220–231.

44. *Asm*, 12, 19, and 26 April 1850, 23 May 1851, 20 and 27 February 1852, 6 March 1852, 10 June 1853, 6 August 1853, 30 March 1855, 10 and 17 August 1855, 12 June 1857, 20 November 1857; *JM*, 27 July 1858, 30 March 1860, 23 April 1860, 18 June 1860, 13 November 1863, 5 December 1863.

45. Jaher, *A Scapegoat in the Wilderness*, 140–150; *New York Times*, 25 April 1853, 16 May 1854, 29 June 1855; Isaac Mayer Wise, *Reminiscences* (New York, 1901), 121–122; *Asm*, 9 November 1849, 26 October 1850, 26 August 1853, 8 December 1854, 10 July 1857; *JM*, 30 March 1860.

■ NOTES TO CHAPTER 10

1. Isaac Mayer Wise, *Reminiscences* (New York, 1901), 1–20; Bruce L. Ruben, "Max Lilienthal and Isaac Mayer Wise: Architects of American Reform Judaism," *AJAJ* 55 (2003): 1–3.

2. Lee M. Friedman, "Mrs. Child's Visit to a New York Synagogue in 1841," *PAJHS* 38 (1948–1949): 177–178; *Asm*, 24 April 1852, 27 August 1852.

3. Wise, *Reminiscences*, 21–23; Gershom Greenberg, "A German-Jewish Immigrant's Perception of America, 1853–54," *AJHSQ* 67 (1977): 315–317, 327. The visitor had complimentary comments about the Dutch and English congregations, which "perceive the structures which enforce belief" (324–325).

4. Hyman B. Grinstein, "The American Synagogue and the Laxity of Observance, 1750–1850" (M.A. thesis, Columbia University, 1936), 19–26, 31–38.

5. Grinstein, "The American Synagogue," 19; *JM*, 13 August 1858, 1 June 1860; *Asm*, 9 December 1852; Hazan Lyons to Board of Trustees, 19 Sivan 1844, Lyons Collection, AJHS.

6. *JM*, 18 and 25 November 1859, 14 September 1860; *Asm*, 1 June 1854.

7. Grinstein, "The American Synagogue," 26; *JM*, 10 June 1859, 10 September 1859, 6 April 1860, 18 May 1860.

8. Karla Goldman, *Beyond the Synagogue Gallery: Finding a Place for Women in American Judaism* (Cambridge, MA, 2000), 68–75; Hyman B. Grinstein, *The Rise of the Jewish Community of New York, 1654–1860* (Philadelphia, 1945), 297–298n. 29, 573.

9. *Asm,* 9 September 1850, 6 June 1852, 9 December 1852; *JM,* 9 October 1859, 20 January 1860, 30 January 1863, 7 February 1863, 13 May 1864; Jeremiah J. Berman, "The Trend in Jewish Religious Observance in Mid-Nineteenth-Century America," *PAJHS* 37 (1947): 33–35.

10. *JM,* 1 June 1860, 14 December, 28 February 1862, 18 March 1862, 23 May 1862, 13 May 1864.

11. Naomi W. Cohen, *Encounter with Emancipation: The German Jews in the United States, 1830–1914* (Philadelphia, 1984), 42; Jacob R. Marcus, *United States Jewry, 1776–1985,* 4 vols. (Detroit, 1989), 2:222–226; Grinstein, *The Rise of the Jewish Community,* 339–347; Berman, "The Trend in Jewish Religious Observance," 33–42.

12. America's first Reform synagogue, founded in Charleston, South Carolina, in 1825, was modeled more on American Unitarianism than on the German Reform movement. Jonathan D. Sarna, *American Judaism: A History* (New Haven, CT, 2004), 57–58, 84–87.

13. The most important history of Reform Judaism is Michael A. Meyer, *Response to Modernity: A History of the Reform Movement in Judaism* (New York, 1988), chs. 1–4. See also Michael A. Meyer, *The Origins of the Modern Jew: Jewish Identity and European Culture in Germany, 1749–1824* (Detroit, 1967).

14. Grinstein, *The Rise of the Jewish Community,* 353–371; Myer Stern, *The Rise and Progress of Reform Judaism: Temple Emanu-El of New York* (New York, 1895), 13–24, 30–31, 38–40; Benny Kraut, *From Reform Judaism to Ethical Culture: The Religious Evolution of Felix Adler* (Cincinnati, 1979) 5.

15. Minutes of Temple Emanu-El, 4 June 1854, 3 September 1854, 1 October 1854, 7 January 1855, 1 July 1855, 12 August 1855, Temple Emanu-El Archives; Grinstein, *The Rise of the Jewish Community,* 501–507.

16. Wise, *Reminiscences,* 200–202; Sefton D. Temkin, *Isaac Mayer Wise: Shaping American Judaism* (New York, 1992), 86; Hyman B. Grinstein, "The 'Asmonean': The First Jewish Weekly in New York," *Journal of Jewish Bibliography* 1 (1939): 67–70.

17. Guido Kirsch, "*Israel's Herold:* The First Jewish Weekly in New York," *Historia Judaica* 2 (1940): 77–78; *Asm,* 19 April 1850, 10 May 1850, 13 January 1854, 4 August 1854, 8 September 1854; Ruben, "Max Lilienthal and Isaac Mayer Wise," 9–10, 14–16.

18. *Asm,* 19 April 1850, 8 October 1852, 22 July 1853, 3 February 1854.

19. *Asm,* 19 May 1854, 23 and 30 June 1854, 30 May 1856; Gershom Greenberg, "The Dimensions of Samuel Adler's Religious View of the World," *Hebrew Union College Annual* (1975): 395–402; Ruben, "Max Lilienthal and Isaac Mayer Wise," 14. Another contributor to the *Asmonean,* "Liberality," condemned the "complacency" of the Orthodox, wedded to the "dilapidated" tenets of rabbinic Judaism. *Asm,* 19 May 1854.

20. Kirsch, "*Israel's Herold,*" 78–79.

21. *Asm,* 5 and 26 November 1852.

22. "Letter of Acceptance of the Rev. Dr. Wise to the Respected Society of Friends," *Occident* 7, no. 5 (August 1849): 274–275; *Asm,* 1 October 1852.

23. *Asm*, 16 June 1852, 10 and 17 September, 15 October 1852, 15 September 1854; "Future Reward and Punishment," *Occident* 7, no. 2 (May 1849): 86–89.

24. *Asm*, 13 August 1852, 20 May 1853.

25. *Asm*, 30 May 1856, 21 August 1857; Ruben, "Max Lilienthal and Isaac Mayer Wise," 12.

26. *Asm*, 11 July 1851, 26 August 1853, 8 September 1854, 23 February 1855, 2 March 1855; Ruben, "Max Lilienthal and Isaac Mayer Wise," 16.

27. *Asm*, 5 and 12 April 1854, 24 October 1856, 18 September 1857.

28. Goldman, *Beyond the Synagogue Gallery*, 86–87; *Asm*, 24 March 1854. See also "Women and the Ceremony of Confirmation, 1854," in Jacob R. Marcus, ed., *The American Jewish Woman: A Documentary History*, 2 vols. (New York, 1981), 1:186–189. Anshe Chesed introduced a mixed choir in 1849. Its hazan, Jonas Hecht, moved between the choir and the reader's platform because he believed that the women's voices should only be heard when he sang with them. When Hecht was dismissed, Anshe Chesed continued the mixed choir but otherwise retained Orthodox traditions.

29. Goldman, *Beyond the Synagogue Gallery*, 93–99. When Shearith Israel opened its Crosby Street synagogue in 1832, there were more seats in the ladies' gallery than in the men's section below. No other synagogue, however, had more seats for women than for men. *Asm*, 24 March 1854, 4 January 1856.

30. *Asm*, 24 March 1854, 4 January 1856; Grinstein, *The Rise of the Jewish Community*, 356; Jonathan D. Sarna, "The Debate over Mixed Seating in America," in Jack Wertheimer, ed., *The American Synagogue: A Sanctuary Transformed* (New York, 1987), 363–371; Goldman, *Beyond the Synagogue Gallery*, 94–99; Ruben, "Max Lilienthal and Isaac Mayer Wise," 15.

31. *Asm*, 22 February 1850, 21 March 1851, 3 October 1851, 26 September 1856; *JM*, 15 September 1863; Mordecai M. Noah, *Address Delivered at the Hebrew Synagogue on Crosby Street, New-York*, in Michael Schuldiner and Daniel J. Kleinfeld, eds., *The Selected Writings of Mordecai Noah* (Westport, CT, 1999), 156. On Raphall's Mendelssohnian beliefs, see Israel Finestein, *Anglo-Jewry in Changing Times: Studies in Diversity, 1840–1914* (London, 1999), 168–178.

32. *Asm*, 2 November 1849, 10 May 1850, 3 October 1851, 26 September 1856, 12 February 1857; *JM*, 13 March 1857, 12 February 1858, 6 May 1859, 10 June 1859, 1 June 1860.

33. Temkin, *Isaac Mayer Wise*, 62–65; Wise, *Reminiscences*, 145–149; *Asm*, 18 January 1850, 3 October 1851; *JM*, 13 March 1857, 26 August 1859.

34. *JM*, 6 April 1860, 18 May 1860, 14 September 1860, 28 February 1862.

35. *Asm*, 30 November 1849, 7 December 1849, 12 December 1850; *JM*, 23 March 1860, 15 September 1863.

36. Mordecai M. Noah *Discourse on the Restoration of the Jews* (New York, 1845), in Schuldiner and Kleinfeld, *Selected Writings*, 125–148; Noah, *Address Delivered*, in ibid., 149–159; Jonathan D. Sarna, *Jacksonian Jew: The Two Worlds of Mordecai Noah* (New York, 1981), 152–157. A second address at Crosby Street foresaw the progressive leaders of Christianity withdrawing from a belief in the divinity of Jesus, thus allowing even greater possibilities of cooperation between Jews and Christians. Ibid., 154. It is noteworthy that

Noah could be involved in the intricacies of New York state politics while he advocated a restoration in his time.

37. For Raphall on charity, see *Asm*, 12 December 1850, 9 December 1852, 4 December 1857; *JM*, 14 January 1859, 9 September 1859. Raphall on reform: *Asm*, 7 January 1853; *JM*, 18 May 1860; Myer Stern, *The Rise and Progress of Reform Judaism: Temple Emanu-El of New York* (New York, 1895), 51.

38. *JM*, 24 September 1858, 11 November 1859, 9 October 1863.

39. *JM*, 5 and 19 June 1857, 6 November 1857, 10 and 24 September 1858, 11 November 1859, 20 July 1860, 20 October 1863; *Asm*, 12 May 1854.

40. *JM*, 5 and 19 June 1858, 10 and 24 September 1858, 6 November 1858, 11 November 1859, 11, 18, 25, and 20 July 1860, 20 October 1863; *Asm*, 22 December 1855, 4 and 11 January 1856. The anonymous 1853 visitor from Germany was critical of Emanu-El, describing its services as a "theater party." The "crowding" was also "offensive," as was the "ferocity" of synagogue officials who would let nobody leave before services ended, even to attend the bathroom. Greenberg, "A German-Jewish Immigrant's Perception of America," 323.

41. For an analysis of Adler's theology, see Greenberg, "The Dimensions of Samuel Adler's Religious View of the World," 398–412.

■ NOTES TO CHAPTER 11

1. *New York Times*, 14 September 1863.

2. An excellent survey of New York antebellum politics and society is Edward K. Spann, *The New Metropolis: New York City, 1840–1857* (New York, 1981).

3. Edwin G. Burrows and Mike Wallace, *Gotham: A History of New York City to 1898* (New York, 1999), 621–625.

4. Ibid., 858–863.

5. Ibid., 664, 860; Philip Foner, *Business and Slavery: The New York Merchants and the Irrepressible Conflict* (Chapel Hill, NC, 1941), 4, 14; Sven Beckert, *The Monied Metropolis: New York City and the Consolidation of the American Bourgeoisie, 1850–1896* (New York, 2001), 12; Ernest A. McKay, *The Civil War and New York City* (Syracuse, NY, 1990) 18. Clifton Hood's forthcoming book, "In Pursuit of Privilege: New York City's Upper Class and the Making of the City since 1753," will have important work on the structure of the merchant class.

6. Burrows and Wallace, *Gotham*, 551–560, 838–841.

7. *Asm*, 16 July 1852; Jonathan D. Sarna, *Jacksonian Jew: The Two Worlds of Mordecai Noah* (New York, 1981), 101, 192. The seven wealthy Whigs cited were Emmanuel Michael, A. L. Gomez, David Hart, the Hendricks family, Rebecca & Bell Judah, and Captain Uriah Levy. "Miscellaneous Items Relating to the Jews in New York," *PAJHS* 27 (1920): 406. Lawrence H. Fuchs, *The Political Behavior of American Jews* (Glencoe, IL, 1956), 26–30; Ira Forman, "The Politics of Minority Consciousness," in L. Sandy Maisel, ed., *Jews in American Politics* (New York, 2001), 141–147.

8. Gustavus Myers, *The History of Tammany Hall* (New York, 1901), 166–167; Fuchs, *The Political Behavior of American Jews*, 29; "Biographical Profiles: Emmanuel Hart," in Maisel, *Jews in American Politics*, 351.

9. Sarna, *Jacksonian Jew*, 109–113, 119; *Evening Star*, 18 February 1834, 15 September 1835, quoted in Leonard I. Gappelberg, "M. M. Noah and the Evening Star: Whig Journalism, 1833–1840" (Ph.D. diss., Yeshiva University, 1970), 156–157, 168; *Asm*, 30 October 1857.

10. Sarna, *Jacksonian Jew*, 111–112; *Evening Star*, 9 November 1839, quoted in Gappelberg, "M. M. Noah and the Evening Star," 184–185.

11. For Know-Nothing articles, see *Asm*, 13 and 27 April 1855, 15 June 1855, 27 July 1855.

12. *Asm*, 25 July 1856, 8 and 15 August 1856, 5 September 1856. Some Jews were attracted to the Know-Nothing Party for its attacks on the papacy and the Catholic Church and for its fear of immigrants, in this case, Irish Catholic immigrants. Bertram Korn, "The Know-Nothing Movement and the Jews," in *Eventful Years and Experiences: Studies in Nineteenth-Century American Jewish History* (Cincinnati, 1954), 64–65; Foner, *Business and Slavery*, 138; *Asm*, 30 October 1857, 19 March 1858.

13. *Asm*, 4 July 1851.

14. *Asm*, 13 December 1850, 4 April 1851.

15. *Asm*, 26 October 1850, 10 January 1851, 5 June 1851. In the *Asmonean's* January 10, 1851, issue, Lyon quoted from both the Hebrew Bible and the New Testament to explain how biblical literature can be misused and that the Bible supported the law.

16. Israel Goldstein, *A Century of Judaism in New York: B'nai Jeshurun, 1825–1925* (New York, 1930), 110–114, 119–124; Hyman B. Grinstein, *The Rise of the Jewish Community of New York, 1654–1860* (Philadelphia, 1945), 91–92.

17. "'Bible View of Slavery,' a Discourse by Rabbi Morris Jacob Raphall before Congregation B'nai Jeshurun, New York, on the National Fast Day, January 4, 1861," in Morris U. Schappes, ed., *A Documentary History of the Jews of the United States, 1654–1865* (New York, 1950), 405–418; Max J. Kohler, "The Jews and the American Anti-Slavery Movement," *PAJHS* 5 (1897): 154–155.

18. "Bible View of Slavery," 405–406; Jayme Sokolow, "Revolution and Reform: The Antebellum Jewish Abolitionists," in Jonathan D. Sarna and Adam Mendelsohn, eds., *Jews and the Civil War: A Reader* (New York, 2010), 187–189; Bertram W. Korn, *American Jewry and the Civil War* (New York, 1951), 16–19; Kohler, "The Jews and the American Anti-Slavery Movement," 154–155.

19. *New York Times*, 2 October 1856.

20. Sokolow, "Revolution and Reform," 180, 188–189; Gustav Pollack, *Michael Heilprin and His Sons* (New York, 1912), 3–12; "Michael Heilprin Replies to Dr. Raphall, the *New-York Daily Tribune*, January 15, 1861," in Schappes, *Documentary History*, 419.

21. "Michael Heilprin Replies to Dr. Raphall," 418–428; see also Benjamin Braude, "The Sons of Noah and the Construction of Ethnic and Geographical Identities in the Medieval and Early Modern Periods," *William and Mary Quarterly* 54 (1997): 103–142.

22. Sokolow, "Revolution and Reform," 183; Robert R. Swerienga, "Samuel Meyer Isaacs: The Dutch Rabbi of New York City," *AJAJ* 44 (1992): 616; *JM*, 9 November 1860, 4, 18, and 25 January 1861. Korn believes that the *Messenger's* refusal to take a political position before the war was done out of fear. Korn, *American Jewry*, 249.

23. Myer Stern, *The Rise and Progress of Reform Judaism: Temple Emanu-El of New*

York (New York, 1895), 40, 55–57; Sokolow, "Revolution and Reform," 183–185; Kohler, "The Jews and the American Anti-Slavery Movement," 147–149, 152; Korn, *American Jewry*, 161; Fuchs, *The Political Behavior of American Jews*, 36; Isaac Markens, *The Hebrews in America* (New York, 1888), 209; *The National Cyclopaedia of American Biography*, vol. 2 (New York, 1892), 413.

24. Quoted in Stanley R. Brav, "The Jewish Woman, 1861–1865," *AJAJ* 17 (1965): 62. Max Kohler notes that a German Jew, perhaps a New Yorker, Mr. Lazar, was active at the meeting of the American and Foreign Anti-Slavery Society in New York in 1853. Kohler, "The Jews and the American Anti-Slavery Movement," 144.

25. Naomi W. Cohen, *Encounter with Emancipation: The German Jews in the United States, 1830–1914* (Philadelphia, 1984), 129–135; Sokolow, "Revolution and Reform," 125.

26. "Government and Politics," in Kenneth Jackson and Fred Kameny, eds., *The Almanac of New York City* (New York, 2008), 367–368; *JM*, 25 March 1861, 2 January 1863; Stanley Nadel, *Little Germany: Ethnicity, Religion, and Class in New York City, 1845–80* (Urbana, IL, 1990), 136.

27. Abram J. Dittenhoefer, *How We Elected Lincoln* (New York, 1916), 2–6.

28. *JM*, 22 March 1861; Gershom Greenberg, "A German-Jewish Immigrant's Perception of America, 1853–54," *AJHSQ* 67 (1977): 320.

29. Foner, *Business and Slavery*, 251; Edmund Clarence Stedman, ed., *The New York Stock Exchange*, vol. 1 (New York, 1905), 128. A more recent book that covers the same ground generally confirms Foner's findings while noting that manufacturers at times had different interests from merchants, notably in seeking tariff protection. Sven Beckert finds that Republicans, while a small minority of New York's middle class, were most likely to be merchants involved in the western trade and manufacturers. Manufacturers were four times more likely to be Republicans than merchants. However, the bulk of Jewish manufacturers were in the garment trade, a trade deeply attached to the southern trade. Beckert, *The Monied Metropolis*, ch. 3; Basil Leo Lee, *Discontent in New York City, 1861–1865* (Washington, DC, 1943), 8–13; Burrows and Wallace, *Gotham*, 864.

30. Adam Goodheart, *1861: The Civil War Awakening* (New York, 2011), 177, 188. The quotation about Broadway is from the *New York Herald*, 19–21 April 1861. *JM*, 26 April 1861. Replying to this editorial, the Jews of Shreveport, Louisiana, canceled their subscription and published the resolves of their congregation stating their intent: "as law abiding citizens, . . . to stand by and honor the flag, . . . of the Southern Confederacy with all that is dear to us." They scorned both the *Messenger*, a "black republican paper," and editor Isaacs, who they compared to Brutus, plunging a dagger into Caesar's heart while kissing him. *JM*, 7 June 1861.

31. *JM*, 26 April 1861, 24 May 1861; other sermons may be found in the May 24 issue.

32. Walter D. Kamphoefner and Wolfgang Helbich, eds., *Germans in the Civil War: The Letters They Wrote Home* (Chapel Hill, NC, 2006), 44 (Alexander Dupré, 26 April 1861), 61 (Julius Wesslau, 23 July 1861).

33. Simon Wolf, *The American Jew as Patriot, Soldier and Citizen* (Philadelphia, 1895), 111, 236–301; "Standing by the Union," in Schappes, *Documentary History*, 689–690n. 2; Jacob R. Marcus, *United States Jewry, 1776–1985*, 4 vols. (Detroit, 1989), 3:39–41. See also

"Identifying the Jewish Servicemen in the Civil War: A Re-appraisal of Simon Wolf's *The American Jew as Patriot, Soldier and Citizen*," *AJHSQ* 59 (1969): 357–369. The percentage of Americans living in Union states that served in the Union army was about 11 percent. The percentage of New York Jewry would have been about 4 percent, based on a population of forty thousand. This likely reflects continuing disaffection by the majority of New Yorkers for the Republicans and their cause, a disaffection that continued throughout the war, following a brief moment of patriotic enthusiasm in the spring of 1861.

34. *JM*, 3 and 17 May 1861, 7 and 21 June 1861, 9 August 1861, 17, 24, and 31 January 1862, 7, 14, and 21 February 1862, 11 July 1862, 27 August 1862.

35. Korn, *American Jewry*, 56–67; Myer S. Isaacs, "A Jewish Army Chaplain," *PAJHS* 10 (1904): 128–130.

36. Korn, *American Jewry*, 68–72; Isaacs, "A Jewish Army Chaplain," 31–33; Marcus, *United States Jewry*, 3:43–45; *JM*, 31 January 1862, 5 May 1862. The Reform movement did not recognize the Board of Delegates' claim to represent all of American Jewry, as it was composed only of Orthodox synagogues. After the board sent its protest to Washington, six Reform leaders including Rabbis Wise, Lilienthal, and Adler publicly protested that while they supported the legislation, it was their "duty" to dispute the Board of Delegates' assumption that they represented American Jewry. Korn, *American Jewry*, 77–74; *JM*, 11 July 1862.

37. Korn, *American Jewry*, 74–80. Fischel returned to Holland, where he lived the rest of his life.

38. Ibid., 100–104.

39. *JM*, 20 June 1862, 18 July 1862; Joseph Hirsh and Beka Doherty, *The Mount Sinai Hospital of New York, 1852–1952* (New York, 1952), 4–13, 42–44; Grinstein, *The Rise of the Jewish Community*, 155–157.

40. Korn, *American Jewry*, 161; George S. Hellman, "Joseph Seligman, American Jew," *PAJHS* 41 (1951–1951): 27, 34–35; Elliott Ashkenazi, "Jewish Commercial Interests between North and South: The Case of the Lehmans and the Seligmans," *AJAJ* 17 (1965): 25–29; Thomas K. McGraw, "Immigrant Entrepreneurs in U.S. Financial History, 1775–1914," *Capitalism and Society* 5 (2010): 14–15; Ross L. Muir and Carl J. White, *Over the Long Term: The Story of J. & W. Seligman & Co.* (New York, 1964), 24–30, 44–48; Ron Chernow, *The House of Morgan: An American Banking Dynasty and the Rise of Finance* (New York, 1990), 13; Beckert, *The Monied Metropolis*, 112; Peter Chapman, *The Last of the Imperious Rich: Lehman Brothers, 1844–2008* (New York, 2010), 10; Marcus, *United States Jewry*, 3:53–54. There is debate about the success of Joseph Seligman as a bond seller in Germany. The records that led an early biographer to make the claim of $200 million sold are no longer extant. See also Hood, "In Pursuit of Privilege."

41. Stephen Birmingham, *"Our Crowd": The Great Jewish Families of New York* (New York, 1967), 77–78.

42. Leonard Dinnerstein, *Antisemitism in America* (New York, 1994), 30; Korn, *American Jewry*, ch. 6; "Revoking General Grant's Order No. 11," in Schappes, *Documentary History*, 472–476, 702–704; Marcus, *United States Jewry*, 3:48–50; *JM*, 9, 16, and 23 January 1863.

43. *New York Times,* 8 January 1863; see also *New York Times,* 19 December 1862, 5 and 7 January 1863, 8 February 1863.

44. *New York World,* 16 April 1861; *New York Times,* 2 and 7 April 1862, 19 December 1862, 23 November 1863, 28 February 1864; *JM,* 19 December 1863.

45. Quoted in Gary J. Bunker and John J. Appel, "Shoddy Antisemitism and the Civil War," in Sarna and Mendelsohn, *Jews and the Civil War,* 314.

46. Korn, *American Jewry,* 161; *New York Tribune,* 13 March 1863; *Frank Leslie's Illustrated Newspaper,* 21 March 1863, quoted in Gary L. Bunker and John J. Appel, " 'Shoddy' Antisemitism and the Civil War," in Sarna and Mendelsohn, *Jews and the Civil War,* 320. Edmund Stedman does not list any Jews in his lengthy discussion of the gold trade and its fluctuations. Gold was critical to government finances during the war. Stedman, *The New York Stock Exchange,* 150–152.

47. Korn, *American Jewry,* 158–164, 173; *JM,* 21 November 1862, 19 December 1862, 20 June 1863. Many of Korn's references are to the *Jewish Messenger.* McKay, *The Civil War and New York City,* 276; Stedman, *The New York Stock Exchange,* 162. Other instances of anti-Semitism were recorded in the *New York Times,* 11 January 1861, 28 September 1862, 8 February 1863, 2 April 1863, 27 July 1863, 2 November 1864. See also Hood, "In Pursuit of Privilege."

48. Burrows and Wallace, *Gotham,* 886; Edward K. Spann, *Gotham at War: New York City, 1860–1865* (Wilmington, DE, 2002), 89–91, 167; Iver Bernstein, *The New York City Draft Riots: Their Significance for American Society and Politics in the Age of the Civil War* (New York, 1990), 286.

49. *JM,* 8 May 1863, 24 June 1864; *New York Times,* 1 May 1863; for Purim balls, see ch. 8.

50. Burrows and Wallace, *Gotham,* 887–901; Korn, *American Jewry,* 162–163; Wolf, *The American Jew,* 284; Bernstein, *The New York City Draft Riots,* 34.

51. *JM,* 26 July 1863, 28 August 1863, 4 September 1863. After the first day of the riots, most Germans abandoned violence and some joined the authorities. Burrows and Wallace, *Gotham,* 894. In *The Great Riots of New York* (New York, 1873), Joel Headley argues that the German population "had no sympathy with the rioters" (246).

52. Burrows and Wallace, *Gotham,* 903; *JM,* 26 October 1864, 4 November 1864; Bertram J. Korn, "The Jews of the Union," *AJAJ* 13 (1961): 221–224; McKay, *The Civil War and New York City,* 148.

53.; Beckert, *The Monied Metropolis,* 135, 137; Muir and White, *Over the Long Term,* 46; Lee, *Discontent in New York,* 175–177, 180–181, 204–205. McKay, *The Civil War and New York City,* 116, 140, 216–224, 285–286. Tailors' wages dropped from sixty-seven and a half cents per day to thirty-seven and a half cents per day in 1861. A number of trades staged wartime strikes. On the plight of women workers, working sixteen hour days and ravaged by inflation, see *New York Times,* 2 April 1864.

54. Bertram Korn, the prominent historian of American Jewry in the Civil War, wrote that "New York Jewry was solidly behind Lincoln." Korn was almost certainly too optimistic. Korn, "The Jews of the Union," 222; Cohen, *Encounter with Emancipation,* 58; Spann, *Gotham at War,* 109–112, 172; Kamphoefner and Helbich, *Germans in the Civil War,* 64 (Emilie Weslau, 10 November 1862), 65–66 (Karl, Marie, and Emilie Weslau,

28 July 1863); Stanley Nadel, "Jewish Race and German Soul in Nineteenth-Century America," *AJH* 77 (1987): 8; Bernstein, *The New York City Draft Riots*, 223–224, 286. For ward-by-ward election results, see *New York Times*, 9 November 1864. After the election, a Republican analyst, bemoaning the loss of the German vote, blamed it on the Republican failure to have any lasting organization in the German wards. Unlike the Democrats, Republicans only showed interest there during the elections and did not cultivate Republican supporters afterward. The Germans felt "much more the instinctive hatred of slavery" and were "more intelligent" than the Irish, but they were also "simple minded" and "suspicious" and, as they never heard anything from the Republicans, drew apart from them. *New York Times*, 20 November 1864.

55. *JM*, 21 April 1865, 9 June 1865; Brav, "The Jewish Woman," 64.

56. Korn, "The Jews of the Union," 239–243; *JM*, 28 April 1865.

57. Kamphoefner and Helbich, *Germans in the Civil War*, 71 (Karl and Marie Weslau, 13 June 1865); *New York Times*, 14 September 1863.

58. *New York Times*, 28 November 1862, 1 May 1863, 27 November 1864.

59. Isaacs, "A Jewish Army Chaplain," 137.

60. Fuchs, *The Political Behavior of American Jews*, 42, 49–50; Emmanuel Hertz, ed., *Abraham Lincoln: The Tribute of the Synagogue* (New York, 1927), collects a number of the addresses by New York (and other American) rabbis. Few discuss slavery in the short excerpts, but there is a sense of common identity with Lincoln and the nation. Unfortunately, the strongest antislavery speaker, Samuel Adler, is represented with only a few passages. Rabbi Raphall, while expressing shock and sadness, again demonstrated that he had not been a Lincoln supporter, including in his remarks the wrongs Lincoln committed by imprisoning people who should not have been incarcerated, his early military failures, and his carelessness in being seen in the open so readily. The most passionate spokesman for Lincoln as a great emancipator was Max Lilienthal, who lived in New York for years but had left in 1855. In 1865, some rabbis were more willing to represent a common identity with bondage than others; that changed in the years to come. The book includes many later addresses in which the speakers are not reluctant to make these comparisons. The book also includes rabbis' remarks on Lincoln in the early twentieth century, two generations later, allowing a good understanding of the immense change that the war brought to the Jewish community.

■ NOTES TO VISUAL ESSAY

I thank Deborah Dash Moore for graciously inviting me to be part of this project, for her support of my work, and for her deep appreciation of objects and images. Jennifer Hammer of New York University Press has worked magic with my writing. It has been a delight to work with all four coauthors: Jeffrey S. Gurock, Annie Polland, Howard Rock, and Daniel Soyer. Danny earns a special thank-you for driving me around New York City to see murals and architecture. I also thank the anonymous readers for their helpful suggestions and advice. Numerous archivists, curators, librarians, collectors, and subscribers to the American Art listserv and the American Jewish History listserv offered valuable information. I appreciate all the living artists who granted me permission to reproduce their work.

Laura Holzman, Nina Liss-Schultz, and Shoshana Olidort were terrific research assistants, and Alexandra Maron was of great help with the illustrations and permissions. Sonja Assouline, Kate Breiger, and Amanda Koire were loving, responsible, and very fun babysitters to Alex and Emily, allowing me to work.

Friends, family, and colleagues have all generously given support, citations, personal stories and photographs, criticism, and beds on which to crash while in New York City. I thank Susanne Hunt for morning walks and for two years of hearing me go on about this book. She makes Claremont, California, home. David Brody finesses the perfect balance between his "amazings" to his "oy gevalts," and I love him for that. Tom Burke, Sarah Cash, Kate Fermoile, George Gorse and Susan Thalmann (both of Pomona College), Martha Grier, Carol Hamoy, Camara Dia Holloway, Russet Lederman, Dr. Erica Rosenfeld, Kerri Steinberg, Craig S. Wilder, and Karen Zukowski—I thank you all. And Carolyn Halpin-Healy is just golden in all regards.

My mom and dad, Joan and David Linden, put a subway map and a subway token in my hands at an early age with the mandate to go learn and love New York City. They are also the world's greatest grandparents. My husband, Peter Ross, offers an unlimited supply of love, humor, understanding, and appreciation; he also holds everything together when I am off to New York on research trips. As my twins, Alex and Emily Linden-Ross, are New York Jews by heritage rather than birth, I am proud that they recognize the Flatiron Building at a distance, love Junior's cheesecake, and hold on tight when the subway sways. I hope that they too will discover the magic of the City of Promises.

1. Jules D. Prown, "Mind in Matter: An Introduction to Material Culture Theory and Method," in Robert Blair St. George, ed., *Material Life in America, 1600–1860* (Boston, 1988), 18.

2. John R. Hebert, "The 1562 Map of America by Diego Gutierrez," Library of Congress, http://lcweb2.loc.gov.ammem/gmdhtml/gutierrz.html (accessed February 1, 2010); and James A. Delle, "The Control of Space: Maps, Images and Patterns," in Mark P. Leone and Neil Asher Silberman, ed., *Invisible America: Unearthing Our Hidden History* (New York, 1995), 106–107.

3. Delle, "The Control of Space," 106.

4. I would like to thank Professor Susan V. Webster, College of William and Mary, for helping me locate images of the Inquisition and the Expulsion.

5. Richard I. Cohen, *Jewish Icons: Art and Society in Modern Europe* (Berkeley, CA, 1998), 10–67.

6. Steven Nadler, *Rembrandt's Jews* (Chicago, 2003), 61–62.

7. Cohen, *Jewish Icons*, 33–34, concerns the controversy over identifying the figure represented by Rembrandt as Menasseh ben Israel, comparing textual and visual description of the rabbi. For decades, the Rembrandt Research Project, based in Holland, has been authenticating works by the Dutch master.

8. Art historian Michael Zell's *Reframing Rembrandt: Jews and the Christian Image in Seventeenth-Century Amsterdam* (Berkeley, CA, 2002) is, to my knowledge, the first work to posit the idea of "philosemitism" and its shaping influence on Rembrandt (quotation on p. 3). I thank Michael for his guiding me through the vast literature on Rembrandt.

9. One of the three versions de Witte painted of the Esnoga might possibly have been commissioned by a well-established Dutch Jew. See Yosef Kaplan, "For Whom Did Emanuel de Witte Paint His Three Pictures of the Sephardic Synagogue in Amsterdam?," *Studia Rosenthalia* 32 (1998): 133–154.

10. Helen Rosenau, "The Synagogue and Protestant Church Architecture," *Journal of the Warburg and Court auld Institute* 4, nos. 1–2 (October 1940–January 1941): 80–84; Angela Vanhaelen, "Iconoclasm and the Creation of Images in Emanuel de Witte's *Old Church in Amsterdam*," *Art Bulletin* 87, no. 2 (June 2005): 249–264; Matthew Scribner, "Illusion and Iconoclasm in Emmanuel de Witte's *A Sermon in the Old Church in Delft*," *SHIFT: Queen's Journal of Visual & Material Culture* 2 (2009): 1–12.

11. Jill Lepore, "The Tightening Vise: Slavery and Freedom in British New York," in Ira Berlin and Leslie M. Harris, ed., *Slavery in New York* (New York, 2005), 58–60.

12. Ibid., 59–60.

13. Ibid., 353n. 1. David Grim, "Notes on the City of New York," New-Historical Society.

14. Paul Needham, *The Celebrated Franks Family Portraits* (New York, 2008), 20.

15. Erica E. Hirshler, "The Levy-Franks Family Portraits," *Antiques*, November 1990, 1021.

16. Jonathan D. Krasner and Jonathan D. Sarna, *The History of the Jewish People: A Story of Tradition and Change*, vol. 1, *Ancient Israel to 1880's America* (Springfield, NJ, 2006), 162.

17. For a brief and persuasive discussion of the art of embroidery in relation to the creation of separate male (public) and female (domestic) spheres and, therefore, the differences between their arts, see Amy Elizabeth Grey, "A Journey Embroidered: Gender Redefined," in Mark P. Leone and Neil Asher Silberman, *Invisible America: Unearthing Our Hidden Heritage* (New York, 1995), 140–141.

18. Ellen Smith, "Portraits of a Community: The Image and Experience of Early American Jews," in Pamela S. Nadell, ed., *American Jewish Women's History: A Reader* (New York, 2003), 19.

19. For an informative discussion of the role of Jewish women in colonial America, see Holly Snyder, "Queens of the Household: The Jewish Women of British America, 1700–1800," in Pamela S. Nadell and Jonathan D. Sarna, eds., *Women in American Judaism: Historical Perspectives*, 15–45 (Hanover, NH, 2001); and Hasia R. Diner and Beryl Lieff Benderly, *Her Works Praise Her: A History of Jewish Women in American from Colonial Times to the Present* (New York, 2002).

20. Artist's statement, September 2009. See also Amy Stone, "Feminist Funerals: Art Opens the Conversation," *Lilith*, Summer 2009, 3; susan c. dessel, interview with author, 1 October 2009, New York City.

21. Joanne Reitano, *The Restless City* (New York, 2006), 11.

22. Ellen Smith, "Portraits of a Community in America at the Time of the Revolutionary War," in *Facing a New World: Jewish Portraits in Colonial and Federal America*, exhibition catalog, Jewish Museum (New York, 1997), 13–14.

23. Ibid., 14.

24. David Barquist, *Myer Myers: Jewish Silversmith in Colonial New York* (New Haven, CT, 2001).

25. This is now the busy thoroughfare of South William Street in New York City's financial district.

26. David de Sola Pool, *The Mill Street Synagogue: 1730–1817* (New York, 1930).

27. Jonathan D. Sarna, "Colonial Judaism," in Barquist, *Myer Myers*, 13.

28. Jane Frances Amler, *Haym Salomon: Patriot Banker of the American Revolution* (New York, 2004), 45.

29. Norman L. Kleeblatt, *The Jewish Heritage in American Folk Art* (New York, 1987), 35.

30. Erin E. Eisenbarth, *Baubles, Bangles, and Beads: American Jewelry from Yale University, 1700 to 2005* (New Haven, CT, 2005), 17.

31. Robin Jaffee Frank, *Love and Loss: American Portrait and Mourning Miniatures* (New Haven, CT, 2000), 130–132.

32. Ibid., 132.

33. Ira Berlin and Leslie M. Harris, introduction to Berlin and Harris, *Slavery in New York*, 4–5.

34. "Register of the Manumission of Slaves, New York City, 1816–1818," 2:51–52, now housed at the New-York Historical Society; Morris U. Schappes, ed., "Four Documents Concerning Jews and Slavery," in Maurianne Adams and John Bracey, eds., *Strangers and Neighbors: Relations between Blacks and Jews in the United States* (Amherst, MA, 1999), 137–146.

35. Michael W. Grunberger, introduction to Michael W. Grunberger, ed., *From Haven to Home: 350 Years of Jewish Life in America* (New York, 2004), 16–17.

36. Joshua Brown, "Reconstructing Representation: Social Types, Readers and the Pictorial Press, 1865–1877," *Radical History Review* 38 (Fall 1996): 5–38.

37. Library of Congress, "Confronting Challenges," *From Haven to Home*, exhibition companion website, http://www.loc.gov/exhibits/haventohome/haven-challenges.html (accessed November 12, 2009).

38. Robert Marcus, the owner of the photograph, shared the following with Shoshana Olidort, research assistant, in an email dated 11 March 2010: "The photographer's imprint at the bottom reads, 'Art Gallery, No. 411, Broadway.' The men are unidentified. The uniformed man is a naval engineer." According to Simon Wolf's 1895 rosters published in *The American Jew as Patriot, Soldier and Citizen*, the following Jews were naval engineers, and the man in the photo could well be one of them: Jonathan Manly Emanuel of Philadelphia, Frederic D. Henriques, and Charles H. Levy.

39. Joan Sturhahn, *Carvalho: Artist-Photographer-Adventurer-Patriot: Portrait of a Forgotten American* (Merrick, NY, 1976), 150–151.

SELECT BIBLIOGRAPHY

▣ PUBLISHED PRIMARY SOURCES

Abraham, Lewis, "Correspondence between Washington and Jewish Citizens," *PAJHS* 3 (1895): 87–97

Blau, Joseph L., and Salo W. Baron, ed., *The Jews of the United States 1790–1840: A Documentary History*, 2 vols. (New York, 1963)

"The Earliest Extant Minutes of the Spanish and Portuguese Congregation Shearith Israel in New York, 1728–1786," *PAJHS* 21 (1913): 1–81

"From the 2nd Volume of Minute Books of Congn: Shearith Israel in New York," *PAJHS* 21 (1913): 83–172

Gottesman, Rita Susswein, *The Arts and Crafts in New York, 1800–1804* (New York, 1965)

Hershkowitz, Leo, "Another Abigaill Franks Letter and a Genealogical Note," *AJHSQ* 59 (1969–1970): 223–226

Hershkowitz, Leo, ed., *Wills of Early New York Jews, 1704–1799* (New York, 1967)

Hershkowitz Leo, and Isidore S. Meyer, eds., *The Lee Max Friedman Collection of American Jewish Correspondence: Letters of the Franks Family* (Waltham, MA, 1968)

"Items Relating to Gershom M. Seixas," *PAJHS* 27 (1920): 126–143

Lyons, Jacques J., *The Lyons Collection*, 2 vols. (Baltimore, 1913–1920)

"Manuscripts: Items Relating to Congregation Shearith Israel, New York," *PAJHS* 27 (1920): 1–126

Marcus, Jacob R., ed., *The American Jewish Woman: A Documentary History*, 2 vols. (New York, 1981)

Marcus, Jacob R., ed., *American Jewry: Documents, Eighteenth Century* (Cincinnati, 1959)

Marcus, Jacob R., ed., "Jews and the American Revolution: A Bicentennial Documentary," *American Jewish Archives* 27 (November 1975): 103–275

Marcus, Jacob R., *Memoirs of American Jews, 1775–1865*, 2 vols. (Philadelphia, 1955)

Noah, Mordecai M., *Discourse on the Restoration of the Jews* (New York, 1845)

Pinto, Joseph Jeshurun, *The Form of Prayer Which Was Performed at the Jews Synagogue in the City of New York on Thursday October 23, 1760* (New York, 1760)

Prayers for Shabbath, Rosh-Hashanah and Kippur, trans. Isaac Pinto (New York, 1766)

Schappes, Morris, ed., *A Documentary History of the Jews of the United States, 1654–1875* (New York, 1971)

Schuldiner, Michael, and Daniel J. Kleinfeld, eds., *The Selected Writings of Mordecai Noah* (Westport, CT, 1999)

Seixas, Gershom, *A Discourse Delivered . . . the Ninth of May, 1798* (New York, 1798)

Seixas, Gershom, *A Religious Discourse Delivered . . . November 26, 1789* (New York, 1789)

Wise, Isaac Mayer W., *Reminiscences* (New York, 1901)

■ SECONDARY SOURCES

Angel, Marc D., *Remnant of Israel: A Portrait of America's First Jewish Congregation* (New York, 2004)

Barquist, David, *Myer Myers: Jewish Silversmith in Colonial New York* (New Haven, CT, 2001)

Beckert, Sven, *The Monied Metropolis: New York City and the Consolidation of the American Bourgeoisie, 1850–1896* (New York, 2001)

Bien, Julius, "History of the Independent Order of B'nai B'rith," *Menorah* (1886–1889)

Birmingham, Stephen, *"Our Crowd": The Great Jewish Families of New York* (New York, 1967)

Bloch, Ruth, *Visionary Republic: Millennial Themes in American Thought, 1756–1800* (New York, 1985)

Bodian, Miriam, *Hebrews of the Portuguese Nation: Conversos and Community in Early Modern Amsterdam* (Bloomington, IN, 1997)

Bortman, Mark, "Paul Revere and Son and Their Jewish Correspondents," *PAJHS* 43 (1953): 198–234

Brumberg, Stephen F., "The Education of Jewish, Protestant and Catholic Children in Mid-Nineteenth-Century New York City," *AJAJ* 61 (2009): 11–41

Burrows, Edwin G., and Michael Wallace, *Gotham: A History of New York City to 1898* (New York, 1999)

Cohen, Naomi W., *Encounter with Emancipation: The German Jews in the United States, 1830–1914* (Philadelphia, 1984)

Cohen, Naomi W., *What the Rabbis Said: The Public Discourse of Nineteenth-Century Rabbis* (New York, 2008)

Cohen, Robert, "Jewish Demography in the Eighteenth Century: A Study of London, the West Indies and Early America" (Ph.D. diss., Brandeis University, 1976)

Daniels, Doris Groshen, "Colonial Jewry: Religion, Domestic and Social Relations," *AJHSQ* 66 (1976–1977): 375–401

Diner, Hasia, *A Time for Gathering: The Second Migration* (Baltimore, 1992)

Eisenstein, J. D., "The History of the First Russian-American Jewish Congregation," *PAJHS* 9 (1901): 63–72

Endelman, Todd M., *The Jews of Britain, 1656 to 2000* (Berkeley, CA, 2002)

Ernst, Robert, *Immigrant Life in New York City, 1825–1863* (New York, 1979)

Faber, Eli, *Jews, Slaves, and the Slave Trade: Setting the Record Straight* (New York, 1999)

Faber, Eli, *A Time for Planting: The First Migration, 1654–1820* (Baltimore, 1992)

Feldman, Egal, "Jews in the Early Growth of the New York City Men's Clothing Trade," *AJAJ* 13 (1960): 3–14

Finkelman, Paul, " 'A Land That Needs People for Its Increase': How the Jews Won the Right to Remain in New Netherland," in Pamela S. Nadell, Jonathan D. Sarna, and Lance J. Sussman, eds., *New Essays in American Jewish History* (Cincinnati, 2010)

Fuchs, Lawrence H., *The Political Behavior of American Jews* (Glencoe, IL, 1956)

Gappelberg, Leonard I., "M. M. Noah and the Evening Star: Whig Journalism, 1833–1840" (Ph.D. diss., Yeshiva University, 1970)

Gelfand, Noah L. "A Transatlantic Approach to Understanding the Formation of Jewish Community in New Netherland and New York," *New York History* 89 (Fall 2008): 375–396

Gilchrist, James T., ed., *The Growth of the Seaport Cities, 1790–1825* (Charlottesville, VA, 1967)

Glanz, Rudolph, "German Jews in New York City in the 19th Century," in *Studies in Judaica Americana* (New York, 1970)

Goldman, Karla, *Beyond the Synagogue Gallery: Finding a Place for Women in American Judaism* (Cambridge, MA, 2000)

Goldstein, Israel, *A Century of Judaism in New York: B'nai Jeshurun, 1825–1925* (New York, 1930)

Goodman Philip, "The Purim Association of the City of New York, 1862–1902," *PAJHS* 40 (1950–1951): 134–173

Greenbaum, Alfred A., "The Early 'Russian' Congregation in America in Its Ethnic and Religious Setting," *AJHS* 62 (1972–1973): 162–171

Greenberg, Gershom, "The Dimensions of Samuel Adler's Religious View of the World," *Hebrew Union College Annual* (1975)

Greenberg, Gershom, "A German-Jewish Immigrant's Perception of America, 1853–54," *AJHSQ* 67 (1977): 307–342

Grinstein, Hyman B., "The American Synagogue and the Laxity of Observance, 1750–1850" (M.A. thesis, Columbia University, 1936)

Grinstein, Hyman B., "The 'Asmonean': The First Jewish Weekly in New York," *Journal of Jewish Bibliography* 1 (1939): 67–71

Grinstein, Hyman B., *The Rise of the Jewish Community of New York, 1654–1860* (Philadelphia, 1945)

Grusd, Edward E., *B'nai B'rith: The Story of a Covenant* (New York, 1966)

Hellman, George S., "Joseph Seligman, American Jew," *PAJHS* 41 (1951–1951): 27–40

Hershkowitz, Leo, "By Chance or Choice: Jews in New Amsterdam 1654," *AJAJ* 57 (2005): 1–13

Hershkowitz, Leo, "New Amsterdam's Twenty-Three Jews—Myth or Reality?," in Shalom Goldman, ed., *Hebrew and the Bible in America: The First Two Centuries* (Hanover, NH, 1993)

Hershkowitz, Leo, "Some Aspects of the New York Merchant Jewish Community, 1654–1820," *AJHSQ* 66 (1976–1977): 10–35

Hershkowitz, Leo, "Those 'Ignorant Immigrants' and the B'nai Jeshurun Schism," *AJS* 70 (1980): 168–179

Hirsh, Joseph, and Beka Doherty, *The Mount Sinai Hospital of New York, 1852–1952* (New York, 1952)

Huhner, Leon, "Daniel Gomez, a Pioneer Merchant of Early New York," *PAJHS* 41 (1951–1952): 107–127

Huhner, Leon, "Naturalization of Jews of New York under the Act of 1740," *PAJHS* 13 (1905): 1–6

Israel, Jonathan, *European Jewry in the Age of Mercantilism, 1550–1750*, 2nd ed. (Oxford, UK, 1989)

Jaher, Frederic Cople, *A Scapegoat in the Wilderness: The Origins and Rise of Anti-Semitism in America* (Cambridge, MA, 1994)

Jick, Leon A., *The Americanization of the Synagogue, 1820–1870* (Hanover, NH, 1976)

Karp, Abraham J., *The Jewish Experience in America*, 5 vols. (New York, 1969)

Kessner, Thomas, "Gershom Mendes Seixas: His Religious 'Calling,' Outlook and Competence," *AJHSQ* 58 (1968–1969): 444–471

Kirsch, Guido, "*Israel's Herold*: The First Jewish Weekly in New York," *Historia Judaica* 2 (1940): 65–84

Kohler, Max J., "Civil Status of the Jew in Colonial New York," *PAJHS* 6 (1898): 81–106

Kohler, Max J., "The Jews and the American Anti-Slavery Movement," *PAJHS* 5 (1897): 137–155

Kohler, Max J., "Phases of Jewish Life in New York before 1800," *PAJHS* 2 (1894): 77–100; *PAJHS* 3 (1895): 73–87

Kolmerton, Carol A., *The American Life of Ernestine A. Rose* (Syracuse, NY, 1997)

Korn, Bertram W., *American Jewry and the Civil War* (New York, 1951)

Korn, Bertram W., *Eventful Years and Experiences: Studies in Nineteenth-Century American Jewish History* (Cincinnati, 1954)

Korn, Bertram W., "The Jews of the Union," *AJAJ* 13 (1961): 131–230

Marcus, Jacob R. *The Colonial American Jew, 1492–1776*, 3 vols. (Detroit, 1970)

Marcus, Jacob R., *The Handsome Young Priest in the Black Gown: The Personal World of Gershom Seixas* (Cincinnati, 1970)

Marcus, Jacob R., *United States Jewry, 1776–1985*, 4 vols. (Detroit, 1989)

Meyer, Michael A., *Response to Modernity: A History of the Reform Movement in Judaism* (New York, 1988)

Moore, Deborah Dash, *B'nai B'rith and the Challenge of Ethnic Leadership* (Albany, NY, 1981)

Nadel, Stanley, *Little Germany: Ethnicity, Religion, and Class in New York City, 1845–80* (Urbana, IL, 1990)

Noll, Mark A., *America's God: From Jonathan Edwards to Abraham Lincoln* (New York, 2001)

Oppenheim, Samuel, "Benjamin Franks, Merchant, and Captain Kidd, Pirate," *PAJHS* 31 (1928): 229–234

Oppenheim, Samuel, "The Early History of the Jews in New York, 1654–1664: Some New Matter on the Subject," *PAJHS* 18 (1909): 1–91

Oppenheim, Samuel, "The Jews and Masonry in the United States before 1810," *PAJHS* 19 (1910): 1–94

Philipson, David, *Max Lilienthal, American Rabbi: Life and Writings* (New York, 1915)

Pool, David de Sola, "Gershom Mendes Seixas' Letters, 1813–1815, to His Daughter Sarah (Seixas) Kursheedt and Son-in-Law Israel Baer Kursheedt," *PAJHS* 35 (1939): 189–206

Pool, David de Sola, *Portraits Etched in Stone: Early Jewish Settlers, 1682–1831* (New York, 1952)

Pool, David de Sola, and Tamar de Sola Pool, *An Old Faith in a New World: Portrait of Shearith Israel, 1654–1954* (New York, 1955)

Rezneck, Samuel, *Unrecognized Patriots: The Jews in the American Revolution* (Westport, CT, 1975)

Rosenwaike, Ira, *On the Edge of Greatness: A Portrait of the American Jew in the Early National Period* (Cincinnati, 1985)

Roth, Cecil, "A Jewish Voice of Peace in the War of American Independence: The Life and Writings of Abraham Wagg, 1719–1803," *PAJHS* 31 (1928): 33–75

Ruben, Bruce L., "Max Lilienthal and Isaac M. Wise: Architects of American Reform Judaism," *AJAJ* 55 (2003): 1–29

Salomon, Herman P. "Joseph Jeshurun Pinto (1729–1782): A Dutch Hazan in Colonial New York," *Studia Rosenthalia* 13 (1979): 18–29

Sarna, Jonathan D., "American Christian Opposition to the Jews, 1816–1900," *Journal of Ecumenical Studies* 23 (1986): 225–238

Sarna, Jonathan D., "The American Jewish Response to Nineteenth-Century Christian Missionaries," *Journal of American History* 68 (1981): 35–51

Sarna, Jonathan D., *American Judaism: A History* (New Haven, CT, 2004)

Sarna, Jonathan D., "The Debate over Mixed Seating in America," in Jack Wertheimer, ed., *The American Synagogue: A Sanctuary Transformed*, 363–371 (New York, 1987)

Sarna, Jonathan D., *Jacksonian Jew: The Two Worlds of Mordecai Noah* (New York, 1981)

Sarna, Jonathan D., and Adam Mendelsohn, *Jews and the Civil War: A Reader* (New York, 2010)

Schappes, Morris U., "Anti-Semitism and Reaction, 1795–1800," *PAJHS* 38 (1948–1949): 109–137

Snyder, Holly, "Queens of the Household: The Jewish Women of British America, 1700–1800," in Pamela S. Nadell and Jonathan D. Sarna, eds., *Women and American Judaism: Historical Perspectives* (Hanover, NH, 2001)

Snyder, Holly, "'A Sense of Place': Jews, Identity and Social Status in Colonial British America, 1654–1831" (Ph.D. diss., Brandeis University, 2000)

Sndyer, Holly, "'Under the Shado of Your Wings': Religiosity in the Mental World of an Eighteenth-Century Jewish Merchant," *Early American Studies* 8 (2010): 581–622

Sokolow, Jayme, "Revolution and Reform: The Antebellum Jewish Abolitionists," in Jonathan D. Sarna and Adam Mendelsohn, eds., *Jews and the Civil War* (New York, 2010)

Stern, Malcolm H., "Jewish Marriage and Intermarriage in the Federal Period (1776–1840)," *AJAJ* 19 (1967): 142–144

Stern, Myer, *The Rise and Progress of Reform Judaism: Temple Emanu-El of New York* (New York, 1895)

Swetschinski, Daniel M., *Reluctant Cosmopolitans: The Portuguese Jews of Seventeenth-Century Amsterdam* (London, 2000)

Swierenga, Robert T., "Samuel Myers Isaacs: The Dutch Rabbi of New York," *AJAJ* 54 (1992): 607–621

Temkin, Sefton D., *Isaac Mayer Wise: Shaping American Judaism* (New York, 1992)

Wischnitzer, Rachel, *Synagogue Architecture in the United States: History and Interpretation* (Philadelphia, 1955)

Wolf, Simon, *The American Jew as Patriot, Soldier and Citizen* (Philadelphia, 1895)

INDEX

Page numbers in italics refer to a figure or a caption on the page.

ABOUT THE AUTHOR

Howard B. Rock is Professor of History, Emeritus, at Florida International University, where he has taught since 1973. His books include *Artisans of the New Republic: The Tradesmen of New York City in the Age of Jefferson*; *The New York City Artisan, 1790–1825: A Documentary History*; *Keepers of the Revolution: New Yorkers at Work in the Early Republic* (with Paul A. Gilje); *American Artisans: Crafting Social Identity, 1750–1850* (with Paul A. Gilje); and *Cityscapes: A History of New York in Images* (with Deborah Dash Moore).